History of
American Congregationalism

HISTORY OF
American Congregationalism

By

GAIUS GLENN ATKINS

AND

FREDERICK L. FAGLEY

The Pilgrim Press

BOSTON AND CHICAGO

PRINTED IN THE UNITED STATES OF AMERICA

BY R. R. DONNELLEY & SONS COMPANY

CHICAGO, ILLINOIS, AND CRAWFORDSVILLE, INDIANA

Foreword

TOWARD the end of the last century Williston Walker, then Professor of Church History in Hartford Theological Seminary, wrote *A History of the Congregational Churches in America* for the *American Church History* series. Dr. Walker has put all American church historians deeply in his debt for his profound scholarship and his books have been standard. But great chapters in all history have been written in the last fifty years and there have been highly important developments in Congregationalism which now merit record and recognition. It has seemed to representatives of the Congregational fellowship, therefore, that the time had come for another history of their beginnings and subsequent fortunes and achievements. This book is the result.

It has been written in collaboration, and the division of labor between the two authors is evident in its structure and organization. But some of the later chapters are of composite authorship and throughout the whole really demanding enterprise there has been, between the writers, a constant interchange of suggestion and mutual criticism. There is in the book some measure of repetition; this both the reader and the critic will note. That was inevitable, though the authors have sought to reduce it to a minimum.

There are differences of opinion between all authoritative students as to the confused beginnings of English Separatism and Independency. The statements herein contained are supported by dependable documentation, but the specialist may find occasion for disagreement. All possible pains have been taken to achieve accuracy in names, dates, and facts. If there are still errors they should not, the authors trust, affect the general accuracy of the narrative.

The authors confess their affection for the Fellowship of Churches to which they belong, their pride in its achievements, and their confidence in its principles. So much the critic will soon discern for himself. But they have not, they hope, permitted their loyalties to cloud their critical faculties. They have not minimized the more unhappy phases of early American Puritanism, nor failed to recognize the significant contribution of other communions to American religious life through any sectarian concern.

They trust that the appendices and bibliography may be of service to students not only of Congregationalism, but of American religious history generally. They have sought to acknowledge their many indebtednesses for subject matter and are grateful to patient and cooperative librarians of many libraries.

Much of such a history as this lies in past and present controversial regions. The Congregational historian can do no more than offer, as best he can, the records of three hundred years of Congregationalism— and rest from his labors.

Table of Contents

History of
American Congregationalism

CHAPTER I

The Religious Situation in England
at the End of the Tudor Period

JAMES STUART, King of Scotland, became James the First, King
of England in March, 1603. His ill-fated mother, Mary Queen of
Scots, was the daughter of Margaret Tudor, sister to Henry the
Eighth. Margaret's daughter, Mary, was therefore Elizabeth's cousin; and
Mary's son, Elizabeth's cousin once removed. He inherited the crown of
England from the Virgin Queen and consummated, among other less
happy things, the union under one sovereign of England and Scotland.
The tragedies of the Scotch court and the pity and folly of his mother's
life had early left their mark upon him.

James was awkward in carriage, spoke with a slobbering gravity, and
inherited the Tudor passion for absolute power without the wisdom to
adjust it to changed times. "Do I mak the judges?" he asked. "Do I mak
the Bishops? Then, God's wouns, I mak what likes me, law and gospel."
He had been more humble in Scotland, where he once praised God before the General Assembly of the Scotch Church "that he was born in
the time of the light of the Gospel" and "to be King of such a Church,
the sincerest Kirk in the world. . . . As for our neighbor Kirk of England, their service is an evil-said Mass in English," and he told his Scotch
Parliament "that he minded not to bring in papistical or Anglican
Bishops."[1] His Presbyterianism fell away as he went south to take another
crown and become the head of another Church.

The Tudor period, much of which a very old man could remember,
had been epochal. It had seen the end of medieval and, perhaps, merry
England, and the effective assertion of the power of the throne over the
remnants of feudalism and the religion of the state. The sovereign had
ousted the Pope; no Papal Bull ran in England. Sea captains had claimed
for England the North American seaboard and its unmapped hinterland.
The gentleman adventurers of Elizabeth had singed the beard of the
King of Spain. Drake and a tempest had broken his Armada against all
the coasts of the North Sea and made her realm secure:

> "A Sceptered isle, a precious stone set in the silver sea
> Which serves it in the office of a wall."

[1] This in general from Neal's *History of the Puritans*, part II, chap. 1.

I

A great literature had been evoked; an efflorescence of genius made a single reign as nearly immortal as the temporal can be timeless. Milton, a little later, would see England as an eagle flying proudly into the sun, a puissant people superbly self-confident. But the nation was not inwardly at peace. It had still to carry an unfinished religious and ecclesiastical reformation to some accepted issue within the framework of the English love of liberty, respect for authority, concern for established order, reverence for precedent, and militant tenacity of individual convictions and opinion. In a spacious way, the action and interaction of these essentially English qualities had made English history since Magna Charta and determined its splendid and stormy course, politically, socially, and religiously.

They were and are always the same qualities in action, though they may contest different fields, and there might be a loose way of organizing British history according to the fields contested. During the first half of the Seventeenth Century religion furnished the field,[2] and the representatives of three contestant religious forces did not even wait for James to get housed in Whitehall before they came into action. They went, or sent, to meet him with protestations of loyalty, with petitions and remonstrances. The bishops of the Anglican Church were first in the field. Directly the queen was dead, Whitgift, Archbishop of Canterbury, had sent his Dean express to Scotland to assure His Majesty of the unfeigned loyalty of all the bishops and clergy of England and "to recommend the Church of England to his countenance and favor—." The King assured them.

I

THE PURITAN POSITION

While the King was on his way south, the Puritans presented their "Millenary Petition," so called because they had hoped to have it subscribed to by one thousand petitioners (actually there were about eight hundred). They called it, having a liking for a good phrase well capitalized, "The Humble Petition of the Ministers of the Church of England, desiring Reformations of Certain Ceremonies and Abuses of the Church." The signers were, they said, neither factious nor schismatics, but faithful ministers of Christ and loyal subjects to His Majesty. In substance they asked that the cap and surplice be not urged; that the rites of baptism be modified; that the ring be dispensed with in marriage; that the church service be shortened; that church songs and music be moderated to better edification; that none but canonical scriptures be read in church.

----

[2] This, of course, is to oversimplify. Contestant convictions about church, creed, and religious faith involved social and political forces equally opposed.

They sought also more able ministers and better preachers; that the bishops should, in substance, consider the need of the Church in their disposal of its funds; and much else which aimed at the correction of actual abuses not "agreeable to the word of God" and equally not agreeable to a most considerable number of Englishmen.

There is no need here to follow the entirety of what was involved in this petition to its momentous conclusions. Among other things it would eventually provoke civil war, mobilize Oliver Cromwell and his Ironsides, create a brief, strange, splendid Puritan Commonwealth in England and new Commonwealths in a new world—nothing of which could then be foreseen.

The immediate issue was the Hampton Court Conference held in January, 1604, where the King heard the controversialists and contributed his own wisdom. To begin with he had nominated the disputants and so predetermined the result. The Anglican side carried much the heavier weight of metal: batteries of bishops, and the favor of the King. The Puritans had only four disputants, whom the King sought to abash with majestic frowns, says Neal. Dale[3] believes the deference of the bishops to have delighted and influenced the King, since his Scotch clergy had shown him no such deference. "One had told him that all Kings were the devil's bairns." How could he doubt the apostolic succession of a bishop in lawn sleeves "kneeling on the floor and declaring that there had been no such King since Christ's days," or the authority of an archbishop who assured him "that he had spoken with the special assistance of the Holy Ghost."

Neal laments the result of the Hampton Court Conference. There, he says, was "lost one of the fairest opportunities . . . ever offered to heal the divisions of the Church."[4] Two of the religious factions in England had thus presented their prayers and complaints to the King. Between them they represented the religious majority of his subjects in numbers, influence and stations.[5] They would be the main actors in the drama whose momentous action was beginning to develop.

There were also His Majesty's Roman Catholic subjects, then commonly called "papists." They were an entirely subject group and in no position to ask for anything save tolerance. Their petition for open

[3] Dale, *History of English Congregationalism*, book III.
[4] The Conference did determine upon an authorized translation of the Bible. We owe the King James Version to its initiative.
[5] "Religious majority" is a cautious phrase. Actually religion in England at the beginning of the Seventeenth Century was in a sad way. The discipline of Catholicism was gone and no compensating discipline had been developed. "To the great mass of people, then, religion meant little." "The people without discipline, utterly devoid of religion, come to divine service as to a May-game; the Ministers for disability and greediness be had in contempt." *Essays Congregational and Catholic*, edited by Albert Peel, pp. 242–243.

toleration was phrased to evoke from the King responses both of recollection and affection. He was asked to remember that he was born of Roman Catholic parents and had been baptized according to the rites of the Church of Rome; that his mother was a martyr for that Church; that he had called the Church of Rome his Mother Church, and therefore they presumed to welcome His Majesty into England.

II

THE SUPPLICATION OF THE SEPARATISTS

His Majesty had other subjects, neither Anglican, Puritan, nor Papist, who hoped much from his accession. They were behind the rest in seeking access to the royal person, for they were relatively few in number, of an humble sort, not well organized or else not organized at all. The only groups which could speak for them in any representative way, moreover, were in Holland, mostly in Amsterdam. Dale thinks there might have been about three hundred of them, organized after their conception of what they believed a true church should be.[6] They would also have been drawn and held together by their English speech, their love of England, their lonelinesses and homesicknesses. They had, as yet, no name for themselves save "True Christians" but they were reasonably agreed as to what a Christian church should be and in their "supplication" they were joined by their brethren still under grievous persecution at home.

These "True Christians" asked only to be permitted to live unharried in England nor be compelled "to the use or approbation of any remnants of papery and human tradition." They enclosed in their supplication a copy of their Latin confession, possibly to prove that there were scholars among them who could carry on a controversy in the accepted language of the scholarship of the age; certainly to prove that they "were neither Anabaptist, Familists, nor heretics of any sort."[7]

[6] The choice of a starting point in the history of a religious movement or body is more or less arbitrary; in any history of Congregationalism it is much debated. We have begun this history with the reign of James I to get a reasonably definite dating for the beginnings of Congregationalism as it afterwards essentially continued to be both in England and America. Having established the movement, its past may then be examined with a definite control.

[7] This "confession" was first drawn up in 1596 after conference and correspondence between George Johnson, still a prisoner of England, and the home group and Henry Ainsworth, "teacher" of the Amsterdam group. It was a twenty-two page quarto, sufficiently named and described "and published for the clearing of ourselves" (spelling modernized) "from these unchristian slanders of heresy, schism, pride, obstinacy, disloyalty, seditions, etc., which by our adversaries are in all places given out against us." Three years later (late December 1598, or January 1599) a second edition of the Confession was translated into Latin to command the respect of the Universities and men of learning and influence in England and Holland and elsewhere. Dexter believes Ainsworth, an entirely competent scholar, to have been the translator. This note in substance from *Congregationalism as Seen in Its Literature*, Henry Martyn Dexter, pp. 269 ff.

The suppliants, though not doubting the King's Latinity, thought it wise to send along with the Confession a statement in English, exhaustive and well phrased, though spelled and capitalized after the manner of the time, setting forth "the Heads of differences between them and the Church of England as they understood it." These fifteen "Heads of differences" may be taken in substance as an adequate statement of that way of conceiving a Christian church and the right relation between church and state, which, as yet unnamed, would become historic English and American Congregationalism. Substantially they expressed the position of the group who, sixteen years later, would migrate to America for the precise purpose of enjoying, unpersecuted therefor, a Christian fellowship so conceived in churches so organized.

The document itself is so compactly drawn as to make condensation difficult, so significant that generalization is unfair. They believed, they said, that Christ the Lord, by his last testament, left clear and sufficient instructions in all necessary things for the guidance and service of his Church to the end of the world, and that every particular church has full interest and power by all ordinances of Christ so given. "That"— and this single sentence is of crucial significance—"every true and visible church is a company of people called and separated from the world by the word of God, and joined together by voluntary profession of the faith of Christ in the fellowship of the gospel." Only those thus called and separated from the world can "be received and retained a member in the Church of Christ, which is his body."

A church so gathered possesses, they held, a sovereign power in the control and direction of its own affairs, both temporal and spiritual. It may appoint discreet, faithful, and able men (though not yet in the office of ministry) to preach the gospel and the whole truth of God. A fellowship of believers thus joined together in holy communion with Christ and one another have power to choose their pastors, teachers, elders, deacons, and helpers and should not be subjected to any anti-Christian hierarchy.

Ministers thus lawfully called by the church should take no civil office nor be burdened with the execution of civil affairs. Here there is a curious limitation of the ministerial office. They "should not celebrate marriages nor bury the dead," which things belong as well to those without as within the church. Church officers should be maintained by the free and voluntary offerings of the church. State support is abjured. In addition, the suppliants prayed the King to convert the endowments and revenues of the prelates and clergy to a better use (a request sure to array the whole Establishment against them).

Each particular church possesses the right of discipline over its own members. The church should be governed only by the laws and rules appointed by Christ in his testament. Worship should be in spirit and in truth without liturgies or prayer books. There are but two sacraments, which are to be administered according to the simplicity of the gospel. The Lord's Day alone is to be observed; all monuments of idolatry (a most sweeping phrase) are to be abolished; schools and "academies" should be thoroughly reformed in the interest of true learning and godliness. Finally, all churches and people are bound in religion to only one rule—that which Christ as Lord and King had appointed, "and not to any other devised by man whatsoever."

This or any other history of Congregationalism, as it follows the movement through, must take account of the modifications to which this fundamental document will be subject. Much of it was projected against backgrounds now greatly changed. In detail it lacked balance and made too much of what has since proved inconsequential. There is in it an excess of separatism and independency which time would correct, and yet behind its dated phrasing and spelling there is a conception of the Church, its fellowship and its office, which goes to the root of all Christian organization and communion. It opposed itself simply and superbly to all then existing hierarchies and establishments. One reads it blindly who does not feel its prophetic quality. One reads it superficially who does not see that a millennium and a half of Church history are needed to explain it.

III

PETITIONS AND SUPPLICATIONS DENIED

The king took little account of the Puritan protest, nor did the "Vice-Chancellor, the Doctors, both the Proctors and others, the Heads of Houses in the University of Oxford." These awesomely denominated churchmen and scholars made and published their answers to the "humble" petition of the "Ministers of the Church of England desiring Reformation of certain ceremonies and abuses of the Church." They refused to allow any changes in the processes or liturgies of the Established Church or to acknowledge any validity in complaint or criticism.

Having thus confounded the Puritan to their own satisfaction, they paid their compliments to the Amsterdam suppliants: These were "absurd Browneists" abounding in a "selfe conceited confidence," holding "pestilent and blasphemous conclusions." The exiles tried once more. They issued in 1604 "an Apolojie or Defense of such true Christians as are commonly (but unjustly) called Browneists," in which they published their three petitions, reviewed their case, answered the doctors and dedicated their effort "to the high and mighty Prince, King James, our sovereigne Lord." Their sovereign Lord was still unmoved and nothing was done to mitigate their sad estate. They thereupon gave up any hope of going home to England and faced an indefinite residence in Holland.

They had gone to Holland to escape persecution: so much from any school history. But persecution is what the sociologist now calls an "end effect," a quick and often tragic attempt to resolve tensions for which no really sane resolution has as yet been found. Persecution is, therefore, a proper subject of study for the moralist, the sociologist, the psychologist, and the historian. The historian's task would seem to be to furnish the data. The explanations belong, strictly speaking, to other specialists, though such a clear-cut division of labor is practically impossible. History is written with something else besides ink, the overtones of its heroisms and tragedies are part of the still, sad music of humanity. One cannot write of them unmoved.

There was once a proper technique of kindling a fire around a person tied to a stake. (They did it awkwardly around Joan of Arc, and pity still sees her through the smoke.) But the passions which kindled such fires had always been engendered by long and complicated processes and the fire itself was only a final flaming out of the conflict of irreconcilable forces, as though the martyr's constancy were the flint, and the pride and power or fear and stupidity of those who thus sought to vindicate and defend their authority were the steel. These between them kindled the fire, and the historian has few more difficult tasks than to trace the genesis of the forces which finally engaged with so devastating a concreteness. It needs the whole course of Christian history to explain Ainsworth, John Smyth and John Robinson in Holland, or Barrow and Greenwood hanged in London of an April morning. And it needs also some examination of the whole course of the English Reformation up to James Stuart's accession. For these Separatist suppliants who petitioned the King for mercy were, among so many other things, one of the as yet unresolved issues of the English Reformation bequeathed as incorporeal hereditaments by Elizabeth to James. Few royal inheritances have caused a ruling house more trouble.

IV

FORMATIVE FORCES IN THE ENGLISH REFORMATION

The English Reformation had taken its own line, a line by no means simple. England had a tradition of Christian beginnings older than Augustine, and had never been a docile daughter of Mother Church. It is possible for the Anglican to make his case for an historically national Church in whose administrations the pretensions of Papal power were an intrusion, to whose real life they were extraneous. There might have been a distinctively English Reformation of an entirely different character; a scholar's reformation, such as Erasmus sought; a purging of abuses; a reassertion of the spirit of the New Testament; a slow leavening of inherited ignorance by the new learning; the reformation the "humanists" sought.

There was always, Dean Inge maintains,[8] a tradition of "idealism in English religious thought, neither Catholic nor Protestant," Platonic in its sources, manifest in English poetry, discoverable in the positions of the more free-minded theologians and even churchmen. It was sheltered and continued in Cambridge, which may explain the sympathy of Cambridge with Puritanism. These forces between them might have written an entirely different chapter in English history, creatively transforming the English Church.

There had also been since Wycliffe a scriptural and non-ecclesiastical strain in English religious life, which anticipated and broke ground for the Reformation. In a quiet, transforming way this might have inaugurated a less dramatic Reformation and did actually reinforce the Reformation once initiated. But an amorous King's caprice became the point of departure for the whole movement. Henry the Eighth, for all his Tudor absolutism and gusty passion for Anne Boleyn, would not have dared the course he took without, at least, the inarticulate consent of a strong minority of the English people and the cooperation, willing or forced, of Parliament. But he did inaugurate the Reformation by a *tour de force*. He broke with Rome for his own ends. He released not so much a reform as a "Church Revolution by Royal Prerogative and Acts of Parliament."[9]

V

THE BREAK WITH ROME

The long story of the King's quest for annulment of his marriage to Catherine of Aragon needs no retelling here. Its issue was subjection of the English clergy to the throne and a clean break with Rome. He had been excommunicated and naturally had no mind to take that lying down. The complete severance of his realm from the authority of the "Bishop of Rome" was carried through by three acts of Parliament. The first subjected the clergy to the crown absolutely. The second forbade the payment of annates to the so-called Bishop of Rome or the presentation to him for ordination of any candidate for the office of bishop or archbishop. Finally, no contributions of any sort should go to Rome from England. Henceforth "the King's Realm was to be subject only to laws made within it."

[8] Inge, *The Platonic Tradition in English Religious Thought.*
[9] Taylor, *Thought and Expression in the Sixteenth Century*, vol. 2, chap. 23 ff.

But it was not the intention, it was added, "to decline or vary from the congregation of Christ's Church in any things concerning the very articles of the Catholic faith in Christendom or in any other things disclosed by the Holy Scriptures and the word of God necessary for . . . salvation, but only to make an ordinance, by policies necessary and convenient, to repress vice and for the preservation of this realm in peace, unity, and tranquility."[10] Within this spacious frame the actual drama of the English Reformation was to be played out. The issue was neither peace, unity, nor tranquility.

This complete severance of the realm of England from Papal authority, administration, tribute, or contribution left the religious situation within the realm apparently unchanged save for one strategic fact. Thereafter all reorganization and reform, doctrinal or ecclesiastical, was the affair of the English people themselves, uncontrolled save by their recognized political and church authorities, "any usage, foreign law . . . to the contrary notwithstanding." A required oath of allegiance made it treason to "utter speech or writing derogatory to the King or Queen, their titles, dignities, and orthodoxy." For refusing this oath Sir Thomas Moore, so tolerant in Utopia and so rigid in England, and Fisher were executed.

The course of reformation under Henry the Eighth need not be followed here in detail. He suppressed the monasteries and seized their lands and plate; he gave about half the monastery lands to his friends, who were thereafter sure to be more friendly than ever. He established Biblical studies at the universities and ended Duns Scotus' scholasticism and the Canon Law. He made Cromwell his vicar-general and proceeded to a reformation of doctrine—dogma, if you please. Ten Articles were drawn (1536) "to stablyshe Christen Quietnes and Unitie amongst us." They were cautious articles, and a good Catholic with some accommodation of his conscience might have subscribed to most of them. They suited neither the Right (largely Catholics) nor the Left, those zealous for more reform.

The Right won and the Six Articles of 1539, called the "Six Bloodys" were as Anti-Lutheran as they were Catholically orthodox. A final epistle from the King to all his faithful and loving subjects softened a little the rigidities of the Ten and Six Articles with such spacious phrases as theologians, pressed a little, know how to use. The King finally died, already much consumed by decay, and was gathered, one may trust, to his fathers. They would have received him with mixed emotions.

His son, Edward the Sixth, ruled under rival Protectors and a Council, all favorable to the New Learning. They repealed the worst of

[10] Taylor, *Thought and Expression in the Sixteenth Century*, vol. 2, p. 79.

Henry's highly penal statutes enforcing conformity and thereby loosed a confusion of tongues. There was sore need, it appeared, of uniformity in worship and the administration of the sacraments. This Cranmer and certain discreet bishops accomplished "with the aid of the Holy Ghost" and delivered to His Majesty "The Book of Common Prayer and Administration of the Sacrament." Of the Book of Common Prayer, its sources, contents, sense of liturgical order, the harmony of its prose, the exquisite music of its prayers, the cameo quality of its collects (Cranmer was a master at collects) and its influence upon the worship of English-speaking people, enough has been written to make a library. It articulated the Reformation in England. Newman has rightly held that the Prayer Book, and not the Articles, is the norm of the faith of the Church of England. Under Cranmer, Henry's Ten Articles became Forty-two, strongly tinctured with Lutheranism. For all this, under Mary, he paid with his life, but his mind "with its gift of cadenced utterance" and passion for English religious autonomy, lived on.

The five-year reaction under Philip and Mary was bitter and costly, with three hundred made martyrs to their faith. When Mary died in 1558 "all the churches in London did ring and at night [men] did make bonfires in the streets and did eat and make merry for the new Queen." Thereafter, for forty-five years Elizabeth had two cares and one purpose: the cares were to save her crown and her realm and these cares, continued, became her purpose. In the contention of Spain and Rome she was born out of wedlock and no lawful queen, and her realm might therefore be taken by Spain for Rome. Hers was a parlous position, and all that she did must be understood primarily in the light of her position and her dominant purpose. How she maintained her throne and defended her realm is an epic of English history. The telling of it fascinates and baffles the historian.

VI

THE ELIZABETHAN SETTLEMENT

Elizabeth worked by strategies and indirections, by compromises and inconsistencies, with a woman's wiles, a statesman's grasp, and a soldier's courage. She loved power as she loved jewels, and wore her power as she wore her pearls. She knew how to choose her advisors and, without consenting, to be guided by them when it pleased her. She had the erudition of a scholar and the tongue, if needed, of a fishwife. She evoked passionate loyalties which she repaid with royal caprice. She used her virginity as a counter in a game where her life and her realm were the stake, but she considered her coronation ring the pledge of her wedlock and marriage with her Kingdom and said it would be to her a full satisfaction if there were engraved upon her tomb: "Here lieth Elizabeth which reigned a virgin and died a virgin." She loved royal progresses which bankrupted her hosts. She was jealous of the marriage of men whom she could not and would not marry herself. She grew old and faded under her red wig, her jewels and her pearl-bordered silks, and bequeathed to England the beginnings of its empire, the sea-girt safety of the state, the glory of its literature and religious contentions still unresolved.

She inherited two main religious orders not to be reconciled: the old Catholics, of which there were still a great number, and the new Anglicanism which had not yet found itself. There would be in her time the emergence of Puritanism and some restless promise of religious separatism and ecclesiastical independency. Her main concern, naturally, was with Catholic and Anglican. Puritanism she probably never understood and for Separatists she had no use at all, only a relentless enforcement of conformity. Her Catholic subjects needed careful handling. Froude believed three-fourths of the nation, say 3,600,000, to have been Catholic before the defeat of the armada.[11] Her Protestant government was, therefore, administered by a vigorous minority group. The Queen's own secret sympathy was probably with her Catholic subjects. She had an altar with candles in her own chapel. She told a protesting Spanish ambassador that no Catholic subject of hers who acknowledged her as lawful sovereign had suffered anything and that in spiritual matters she believed as they did. It was a question of authority: "She would permit no authority in England which did not center in herself."

England, threatened without, could not afford a civil war within. The Queen saw, as she looked abroad, the Low Countries split up religiously; France torn by religious and factional fighting; the German states hopelessly at odds. This must not happen to England, and there were divisive elements enough in her imperiled realm.[12] England would

[11] This estimate is open to question. Hallam thought the Protestants two-thirds the population; Lingard thought they were about equal. The Spanish ambassador (1559) reported the nobility heretical, London and the seaports very heretical, the rest of the country sound and Catholic: in the aggregate Catholics were in the majority. The Papal Nuncio at Brussels (1607–1610) thought four-fifths of the people would become Catholics if the old religion were established. Macaulay thought those ready to run any risk for religion relatively few. The undetermined majority would go with the government. These various estimates do not invalidate the statement that the Protestant government was administered by a minority.

For a most carefully documented study of the Elizabethan settlement of religion in her realm, see Albert Peel's chapter 12 in *Essays Congregational and Catholic*.

[12] One may, in a paragraph, understand Elizabeth's attitude toward religious divisionists from the present attitude (1941) of American public opinion toward radical economic groups. These religious groups which now seem to us to have been so harmless, asking only very simple freedoms in religion, were for Elizabeth the equivalent of Communists, Fifth Columnists, "borers from within," and other various groups under investigation by the "Dies Committee." (1941).

not in the end escape civil war, but it would be postponed until the
realm was secure from invasion, and Oliver Cromwell would face
Catholic Europe masterfully unafraid. Many English religious leaders
favoring reform fled to the Continent to escape persecution during
Mary's brief reign. There they came under Luther's influence in a
measure, still more under Zwingli's, and most of all under Calvin's at
Geneva. They seem to have been impressed by the simplicity of Calvinistic worship, the austerity of Calvinistic morals, the Biblical character of Presbyterian polity, and, in general, by the logical completeness
with which Calvin had made an end of the old systems. Geneva was not
then a city either of religious reaction or religious compromise. It was
instead the foyer, as Michelet says, of the Reformed faith. If there was
need anywhere in Europe of a martyr to be broken on the wheel or
burned at the stake, he was there in Geneva ready to keep his rendezvous
with death, singing his psalms and praising God.

VII

The Case for the Puritan

The English, who had savored the Genevan ardor, naturally found
Elizabeth's Anglican Church with its haltings, compromises, survivals of
vestment and liturgy, and general "Mr. Facing-Two-Ways" character, a
poor thing and not even their own. Even some bishops wanted a more
thorough-going reform, and a considerable number of the clergy wanted
no bishops at all. The New Testament, they believed, did not contemplate Anglican bishops. They would have "elders" instead and make
the administration of the Church the business of the clerical group
rather than an Episcopal autocracy.

The bishops themselves for the most part could hardly be offered
as exhibits, unspotted by the world, of a divinely instituted Episcopacy.
They were rich beyond proportion in a poor society and at the sore cost
of the lower clergy. They were given to assertions of power—and in cruel
ways—for which they had no legal support. Their vestigial vestments
were irritating because they clothed hard hearts. The hungry sheep
looked up and were not fed.

All this ferment was beginning to be Puritanism, would presently
become quite completely Puritanism, and would write its own chapters
in English and other history. The threat of the Armada had unified
England and won for Elizabeth the deepened loyalty of her Roman
Catholic subjects. Since they had to go to church, it was politic to make
church as homelike to them as possible, especially in liturgy and symbolism. This naturally increased the dissatisfactions of the Puritan wing;
the "right" and "left" grew further apart.

All these slow, uneven, and hotly disputed modifications of the medieval religious order in England were carried by a minority in state and church officialdom. The laity were to do as they were told and were for the most part content to do it. No such dramatic moments ever attended the English Reformation as Luther's burning of the Papal Bull or any such pastoral idylls as that of the folk of a German parish who left their parish church one Sunday morning and went out to worship, as Luther would have them, under the trees. But no one was left at all in the church, and so they went back as a congregation. There was little of the idyllic in the English Reformation and few discoverable enthusiasms. Its procedures were, as Taylor and Sibelius hold, typically English, and it was in a profound way representative of the English temper and temperament. The Tudors, autocratic as they were, knew their England and in what and how far they could carry their realm with them. The Stuarts never did, and so lost their realm. The long contested action of the Elizabethan settlement had begun in 1558, when "the Lorde began to shew mercy unto Englande by removinge Queene Mary by death." It was ended as far as legislation could end it in 1571, when Parliament by statute compelled the clergy to subscribe to the English version of the Articles of Religion. The result was the Anglican Church, in substance, as it has since continued. But the Anglican Church was far more than the Thirty-nine Articles. These seem then to have been almost marginal to the real controversies. There is no way of stating the issues involved either clearly or concisely.

If one says that a strong minority of the clergy wanted more of Geneva and less of Roman Catholic compromises and accommodations, he would be right and vague enough. Actually it was a kind of fourth dimension warfare, an engagement carried on between contestant conceptions of religion itself, of worship, of piety, and the very drama of the soul; between symbolism and literalisms; between ethics and aesthetics; between the Bible and tradition; between high-handed authority and an embattled instinct for at least a modicum of liberty for the Church in the conduct of her own affairs. There was the grand strategy.

Minor matters, and not so minor either, were involved. The relative stipends of the clergy were unbelievably unfair. The clergy themselves were too largely incompetent. The religious needs of the realm were not being competently met—and so on and on. The ejection of non-conforming clergymen made all these conditions worse, since Elizabeth and her Archbishop Parker seemed set to harry out of the Establishment the most spiritually sensitive, intelligent, and religiously earnest clergymen, with consequences which had a long repercussion both in Old England and New England.

For our purposes here three things are significant. First, the Queen had her way; second, the action so far had been between the two wings of the Establishment, carried on within the Establishment. Finally, no sufficient account was taken of an obscure, formless stir of protest and quest in the realm, arresting in its possibilities and destined to write a noble history of its own. It was not strong enough to register in high places or secure any support; only disquieting enough to irritate authority and occasion cruel suppressions. Officialdom seems to have sensed the portent of it by instinct rather than foresight. It brought with it to begin with only flotsam and jetsam; little movements, nominally religious, of obscure folk, strangely and variously named, with no agreement among themselves but only disagreements over the apparently inconsequential, signs of a rising and potent tide behind them. They, too, had their own long and significant genesis which it is the task of the next chapter to trace.

CHAPTER II

Historic Backgrounds of
Congregational-Separatism

NO CHRISTIAN communion has ever been quite content until it has claimed for its doctrines, polities, and practices the authority of the New Testament, and usually to the exclusion of any other communion's right to advance such claims. An earlier school of Congregational historians claimed New Testament authority and priority for Congregationalism and supported their claims both with zeal and documentation. Most competent historians would now agree that they made their case too strong. No competent scholar would deny that there have been throughout the entire course of church history marginal movements tending to assume group forms of organization and asserting some independence from outside ecclesiastical authority. These movements were fluid as water, appearing and disappearing without apparent organic connection and yet with arresting persistence.

This has made it possible for so sound a historian as Dale to find true Congregationalism in Corinth and Ephesus, and prophetic intimations of Carr's Lane Church throughout the whole course of church history. Waddington[1] traces what he calls "the development of the principles denominated Congregational" from the zenith of the papacy under Innocent, the Third, to the commitment of the poor folk of Richard Fitz's group—the first church of the Congregational order in the English Reformation, he says, of which we have information—to Bridewell Jail in 1567. His learned and voluminous survey includes many movements whose leaders would be much surprised to find themselves nominated the forerunners of English Congregationalism and whom most Congregationalists would not, without some urging, accept as their spiritual forebears.

And yet there is through these hundreds of now yellow pages a principle of historic control and an approach to Fitz and the Plumbers' Hall group, which any historian of the genesis of Congregationalism must at least broadly take into account. In substance it comes to this: there has never been since apostolic times an entirely unified Christian Church. The task of completely satisfying the incalculable variety of

[1] Waddington, *Congregational History, 1200–1567.*

15

minds, temperaments, regions, and races included for at least twelve hundred years in the administration of western Christianity, was beyond the power of any ecclesiastical organization. The "Great Church" succeeded in that impossible task to a degree which the most critical historian must recognize with respect and even admiration, though he might question both method and results as not always being of the essence of Christianity. The non-conformities, refusals, adventures, escapes—no one word is enough—took various forms. The Church simplified the whole affair by calling all those who refused her obedience heretics and dealt with them accordingly. But this was far too easy, begged too many questions, and finally resulted in the dissolution, beyond repair, of the order the "Great Church" sought to maintain.

I

THE "GREAT CHURCH" NEVER GREAT ENOUGH FOR THE
WHOLE OF CHRISTIANITY

There were, to begin with, theological and doctrinal divergencies, militant antagonisms of belief. These evoked passions and partisanships, created contentious literatures, were debated in stormy councils. Some of them died out through the sifting years. Some of them were silenced by the sheer assertion of ecclesiastical authority, others were left unresolved, being not crucial enough to arrest the slow formulation of orthodoxy. Still others were, with a strange audacity, set face to face in the historical creeds and left there.

Then there were survivals of earlier and simpler faiths; old, old provinces, so to speak, of fellowship and worship which the "Great Church" never completely subdued, but against which she maintained a kind of guerilla warfare. It is difficult to maintain, as has been done, their uninterrupted derivations from the primitive church, but one may safely assume another succession besides the Papal or apostolic; a succession of those for whom religion was never an order of priests and prelates, nor worship the adoration of a jewelled altar, nor faith submission to a many-articled creed. These believed that they continued the simplicities and intimacies and sanctities which the Acts of the Apostles record. Dale thinks there is evidence for such survival of apostolic teaching and fellowship among the shepherds living in the secluded valleys of the Alps. Milton had voiced this belief in one of the noblest of his sonnets:

"Avenge, O Lord, Thy slaughtered saints, whose bones
    Lie scattered on the Alpine Mountains cold;
    Even them who kept thy truth so pure of old."

When one considers the tenacity of folk-lore and folk-custom, the persistence of beliefs and habits near to field and hearthstone, the survival of a primitive Christian faith and practice under favoring circumstances does not seem unlikely. The Waldensian Church claimed such a succession.

There are certainly curious parallelisms of both faith and worship under similar conditions in widely separated regions. Simple and lonely folk without much resource for liturgy and ceremonial fall back naturally upon simple forms of praise and prayer. They develop also a strong "group" consciousness and, having or seeking none to direct them, take control of their own affairs. (This was essentially the situation "of the true Christians falsely called Browneists" in Amsterdam beneath the high towers of old churches or in Plymouth between the sea and the pines.) Or else, seeking a norm for their own Christian lives and a correction of costly departure from the Christian way there has always been the New Testament for the questing to turn to if only they could find or read it.

So the whole Waldensian movement, whose heroisms and sufferings constitute a noble though shadowed chapter in medieval church history, grew out of Peter Waldo's having the gospel translated by a scholar, the translation written down by a practical writer, and copies given to the common people. Waldo and his Waldensians had no thought of breaking with the church. They were seeking something the church did not supply and there was an implication of revolt in their professed obediences. Zealous historians of Separatist movements have even claimed that monasticism was Separatist because the monasteries were in theory self-governing, at least in their election of abbots and abbesses, and do represent a classic example of withdrawal from the distractions of the world and complete commitment to the interests and services of religion. But for all that, monasticism cannot be accurately exhibited as a branch of the Congregational family tree.

There was, however, as it began to degenerate behind monastic walls, a renaissance of its quest and finer spirit, first in the Netherlands and then in Germany, whose bearing not only upon Protestantism but upon Separatists themselves cannot be ignored.[2]

---

[2] These movements—it is hard to find a better name—produced two classics of Christian devotion: the *Imitation of Christ* and the *Theologia Germanica*. The *Theologia Germanica*, later in date than the Imitation, was and remains anonymous. The Imitation is so associated with Thomas à Kempis that his authorship of it, though questioned, is a tradition it is best to accept. Michelet *(Histoire de France,* vol. 6, book X) thinks the Imitation to have been the voice of the profound hopelessness of Fifteenth Century Europe; the old order was dying, the new in slow and agonizing travail. The devout, being already dead to so much of the world through misery and hopelessness, chose to die to the rest of it and find their peace in the crucifixion of themselves and escape the world through the "Royal Way of the Holy Cross." The *Theologia Germanica* owes much more to mysticism generally and German mysticism specifically than the Imitation.

II

PRE-REFORMATION GROUPS

In the Netherlands, groups of Christian women seem to have been formed almost spontaneously. The distress of their economic condition, the anarchy of society, and the spiritual sterility of a disintegrating Catholicism moved them to create their own sanctuaries of fellowship and peace. Monastic societies supplied a form which they adapted to their own needs. They took no vows binding for life, but they did vow to live unmarried and under the authority of a superior while in the communities. They wore a designated costume, ate at a common table, and had stated hours for prayer and mutual encouragement.

They supported themselves by their own labor (mostly weaving), cared for the poor and sick, and naturally the common people, to whom they themselves belonged, loved them. They called themselves Beguines, or praying women. Michelet, who thinks they also sang, has a nobly imaginative passage describing them singing at their looms in the low rooms of Flemish houses facing narrow streets, and so finding a peace neither the Church nor the world could give them. Men imitated them and their communities were called Beghards. They, too, were unmarried, lived under a master, ate at a common table, wore a distinctive garb, worked at their handicraft, also mostly weaving,[3] and helped the poor and suffering. These communities later fell into grave disorders, but they were links in a long human chain leading to free and democratic religious organizations.

There were also groups more loosely organized who sought to live laboriously, simply, devoutly, and charitably. They took for themselves lovely names: "Friends of God" and "Brethren of the Common Life." The Brethren called their houses Brother-Houses. They took no life-binding vows, but they usually surrendered their property to a common fund. They copied books, preached to the people, and conducted schools. Such as these had no quarrel with the Church and lived in obedience to and communion with it. They were simply trying to be Christians as they believed the Gospels wanted them to be and found their spiritual peace in their labor, their charity, their own humble souls, and their group fellowship.

All these movements, escapes, supposed returns to a true Christianity,

[3] The significance of the weaver's trade in the complicated mediation of religious influence, particularly between Holland and England, is more than economically significant. It was the one international handicraft. A Dutch weaver could support himself in London, an English weaver in Amsterdam. Persecuted groups could thus maintain themselves in exile. These paragraphs should be either qualified or amplified. Actually the beginnings of these orders seem as old as the last crusades.

had for their background an extremely distressed economic order. Following the discovery of America and the Spanish exploitation of the gold of Central and South America, there had been a long process of rising prices which bore hard on the already poor. The tentative beginnings of the capitalistic system were slowly displacing the Medieval guild system, which was overshadowed by merchant-companies needing relatively enormous capital. There began to be "rich" and "poor" in new senses of those old words; a "proletariat" class within the cities, which was liable to be swollen by the influx of discontented and ruined peasants from the country districts. All the lands were war-ravaged. The ancient liberties of free cities were beginning to be lost and their hopeless rebellions put down with fire and blood. Little was left of feudalism save the pride and rapacity of the barons, and these were gradually being brought to heel by a new type of king. Nationalisms, splendid and portentous in promise, were taking shape. The Reformation of the Church herself, long overdue, was profoundly and on the whole disastrously affected by all of these conditions.[4]

All this, in the line we are following, culminated in distinctly separatist groups in which there was the promise and potency of Protestantism—the nebulae of Protestantism. Most of these were still communicants of the Catholic Church, but their nominal attachments were loose, their real allegiances were to their own groups and what they believed to be the true way of Jesus Christ. They dissolved in the vast upheavals of the Reformation but they left, on the Continent, an unpurposed and undesignated bequest: the quest for a simple, fraternal, non-ecclesiastical form of religious life. That went underground; it did not disappear.

III

THE CRUCIAL PROBLEM OF THE REFORMATION

For the purposes of this study, then, almost one thousand years of European history had so unified Church, state, and society that any disentangling of their interwoven fabric would be unbelievably difficult; and yet the unification was never complete. The Church had a theory, which it tenaciously maintained, of its own sovereign apartness. The state, whatever its form, was only its instrument. The ultimate loyalty of the citizen being thus to the Church, the Church was able to impose its own unified will upon society and so secure, in theory at least, a spiritually unified order.

Much is to be said for such a unity, and the ideal is now strongly

---

[4]There is now most extensive literature to document these general statements. Later historians have specialized in the social and economic causes of the Reformation. Lindsay's *History of the Reformation* is sound and accessible.

urged not only by the Roman Catholic Church, which has never surrendered it, but by Protestants who would like to regain it. But it
furnished Reformers and the Reformation their most difficult problem:
how to adjust their conceptions of a Church and a Christian order to
their massive and tenacious inheritance. Any simple statement of the
problem is too simple, but this might do: Was the new order to be simply
a purged, reformed continuance of the old order; or must there be a
new gathering together out of the debris of the old order—a new order
of individuals, reborn in loyalties, confession, and religious experience?
An almost literal beginning of Christianity all over again? One position
would conserve historical unities, though greatly modifying them. The
other position challenged them, disregarded them, sought at any cost to
get clear of them.

The history of the Reformation may, spaciously, be written in terms
of the travail and confusion of these two contestant conceptions, and
always with the Papal Church in the background contesting both positions and winning back much lost ground through the division of its
opponents. The German Reformation was finally compelled to adjust
itself to the conception of the continuing Christian order. It divided
Germany into blocks whose orientation was determined by the attitudes
of the heads of the picture-puzzle of curiously named little states which
made up Martin Luther's Germany. Something, of course, beside the
caprice of Margraves, Electors and the rest was in action: the religious
tempers and reactions of the German people; but the result was a kind
of anomalous, sectional state-church or churches, which might explain the
strength and weakness of Lutheranism in Germany.

John Calvin's Church, if it had been confined entirely to France,
might have been a "gathered" Church. It was in theory. But his residence
in Geneva made his Presbyterianism a state-church as completely served
by the magistrates as the Roman Church had ever been. There was then
even in Calvin's Church, and at the same time, a "gathered" and a continuing Church—a contradiction which eventually perplexed a Puritanism deeply in debt to Calvin and the Reformed Church leaders. How
they wrestled with it in New England we shall presently see. Old England under the Stuarts was nearly torn apart by these embattled conceptions. The North-Netherlands and Scotland adopted *in toto* the Genevan
system. It came to be called the "Reformed Church," the purified continuity of a going Christian society which had ceased by crucial tests to
be Roman Catholic, but sought still to maintain the organic unity of
the Church and society. At the same time, the "Reformed" Church had
either surrendered or denied the theory of the saving power of the sacraments, which was really the umbilical cord which had attached the new-

born of almost thirty generations congenitally to Mother Church. This type of Protestantism was thus entangled in contradictions it has never been able to escape.

IV
OLD MOVEMENTS WITH NEW NAMES

Such pre-Reformation movements of a semi-Independent and Separatist character as we have so far considered were submerged and their distinctive forms lost in the vast upheaval of the Protestant Reformation. Then they began to reappear with new names and in response to new occasions. They had been essentially withdrawals from the travail of an anarchical world. They reappeared as distinct assertions of religious and ecclesiastical independence, and in defiance of all the established ecclesiastical orders which issued out of the Reformation. As one sees them now detachedly and as a whole, they were in their formless movements the ground swell of a new social order. They did not know the word democracy, nor had they, to begin with, any theory of a democratic church or a democratic state; but they presaged a democracy both in church and state, and as their scattered tides gathered confluent power they would presently wash the bases of the thrones, both of kings and prelates, overturn immemorial inheritances and usher in a new order.

This is possibly a too-grandiose generalization, but the course of events from the middle of the Sixteenth Century validates it. For all that, it oversimplifies a movement which cannot possibly be simplified. In its earliest continental forms it was certainly a protest, amongst other things, of the common-folk of central Europe against their unendurable economic conditions already noted. Very likely the tragic issue of the Peasants' War contributed to the lawless aspect of these obscure movements of the socially and spiritually submerged. On the Continent there was one general, if unsavory, name for all these groups. They were Anabaptists. The whole Anabaptist movement has for thirty years now been most carefully examined by most competent historians. They do not agree in their conclusions as to its causes and its character; they do agree as to its significance. Actually their attitude toward infant baptism, for which they were named, was always only a detail. They represented the revolt of the dispossessed against society and the turning of Demos in his sleep. There were moral excesses in the movement, mostly marginal, which gave thoroughly immoral authorities the advantage of spurious moral indignation. Churches and states which could unite in nothing else united in persecuting them. The fiendish instruments of torture in Nuremburg Museum are still rusted red with their blood.

It is not easy to put into words the essentially revolutionary character of the whole movement. It was driving at the very heart of sacerdotal authority, the mystic and imponderable creation of a thousand years which had held Western Europe in fee, and which by its approvals and consecrations had supported all secular authority. More than that, the whole movement was the logical and inevitable result of the dissolutions of the Protestant Reformation. The reformers themselves had refused to accept the implications of their own attitude. Luther went so far and hesitated. Calvin masked the revolutionary character of his reform with a rigid theology and a stern discipline, but here was the revolution itself, bare-boned and irreverently crude.

It was quite impossible, as we have seen, to confine other and more acceptable consequences of the Continental Reformation to the Continent itself. A Shakespeare's sceptered isle set in a silver sea which served it in the office of a wall, might maintain itself against armadas, but there were other invasions against which the channel was no defense. Confessedly it is quite impossible to understand the English Reformation without some examination of the action and interaction of Continental influences upon the English religious estate. This is a commonplace as far as the genesis of Puritanism is concerned, and yet there has been a tendency on the part of historians generally to limit Continental influence to these more respectable and recognized forms. That contention on the face of it seems indefensible, but no conclusion which does not more or less beg the question is possible. The question of the influence of Continental Anabaptists upon English Separatism has been long and carefully considered and most competent authorities hold that there was no such influence, or else that it is negligible or untraceable.

Burrage[5] finds a tendency toward Separatism making its first appearance in England about 1550. It was a process of evolution, and there may have been roots of it in old England herself in Lollardism, in other obscure movements, and in very human tendencies. A few isolated Anabaptists had been found in England before 1550 "chiefly or only foreigners" and had been banished or burned. The term is loosely used to designate ". . . any persons of irregular or fanatical religious opinion," a spacious phrase whose incidence depended a good deal upon the station of those who used it to indict others. Apparently these early conventiclers who engaged the unfavorable attention of the authorities were only marginally heretical. One of them held that predestination was "meater for devils rather than Christian men." Another claimed "that learned men were the cause of great errors, the children were not born in original sin."

They debated "whether to stand or kneel at prayer and whether

---

[5] Burrage, *The Early English Dissenters in the Light of Recent Research*, vol. 1, pp. 41 ff.

with their hats on or off." They did refuse communion in the Church of England and for this eventually two of their leaders were burned. But these were not technically Anabaptists, and if historians should recognize that Anabaptism is an entirely inadequate name for all these related movements it would clear the air. It was not so much against pestilent opinions that the authority was defending the realm as against profoundly revolutionary attitudes whose implications they seemed to have felt. The precautionary measures which the authorities took and the books published as wholesome antidotes against the heresies and sects of the Anabaptists would seem to indicate an obscure sectarian ferment in England by the middle of the Sixteenth Century. An unusually tolerant opponent of such movements did not advocate using "Material fyre and faggot" against them. The heresies themselves he thought were no "materiall thynge" but ghostly, that is, "a woode spirite," and they would be best exorcised "with the sworde of Goddes word and with a spiritual fyre."

Turner was wiser than perhaps he knew. There was a movement in the air as real as it was intangible and pervasive. Apostolic Christianity once went along with caravans and galleons, with the sailor, the trader, the traveller. All religion has always moved with human contacts; dominant movements of the human spirit can never be kept in mind-tied and spirit-tied compartments. No censor can black out a "woode spirite."

V

THE RELIGIOUS INFLUENCE OF HOLLAND UPON ENGLAND

The ghostly invasion of England is more likely to have been by way of Holland than any other Continental source. The Dutch seem to have been the only people who learned toleration from their own sufferings. Early Anabaptists had been persecuted in Holland (1522), but time corrected their excesses. They changed their name to Mennonites and became exemplary Christians, almost too exemplary.[6] There was a constant commerce between England and Holland. English and Dutch sailors could understand each other's language. England became an asylum for the Dutch persecuted under Spain; Holland an asylum for persecuted English. A good deal of all this is later of course than, say, 1550. One can only hold that it implies an exchange of influence through a considerable period, an influence which cannot be traced through any

---

[6]Campbell, *The Puritan in Holland, England and America*, vol. 1, pp. 245, ff. Campbell possibly overstresses his thesis: the debt of Puritanism to Holland—but his position could probably now be accepted less critically than in 1892. Erasmus wrote from Basle in 1535 "The Anabaptists are crowding in here from Holland. . . These Anabaptists are no joke. They go to work, sword in hand, drive their creed down people's throats" etc., Froude, p. 419.

literature. Its carriers were illiterate persons and not the written word. Bunyan's old women sitting in the sun and talking of God are far more significant for the hidden ways of religion than documents and theologies. It is surely not a mere coincidence that eastern England, commercial and trading England, nourished the Puritan and the Separatist.[7]

One may assume, therefore, a contagious religious quest and restlessness, marginal it is true, but with a power of penetration. The radical social and economic groups in the present period are like that. Their patterns would be the same: Always a mutually sympathetic group, generally a leader around whom they coalesced, an excess of argument with consequent disagreements and petty lesions, unstable as water and yet registering like a tidal river the pressure of the sea behind them, the compulsion of celestial forces. No authority could understand them, no authority has ever understood such movements; and since authority could not understand, it would not tolerate them.

The positions, contentions, convictions for which and around which these groups organized themselves were impossibly various in detail, but sought one thing: the recovery of New Testament Christianity in one form or another, in doctrine, worship, simplicity or austerity of life; also liberty, Luther's liberty of a Christian man. That was for them the condition precedent of everything else. They might not be fit for it, might abuse it, might not understand it; and they really did not seek a great deal of liberty, only to pray as they pleased, argue as they pleased matters too high for them, and meet in low rooms undisturbed. The early Christians asked only the same. Their supplications for such liberties are pathetic with the tears of things, and their supplications being denied, they were deported or burned. Those who were burned are reported to have met death joyfully. What they were dying for seemed worth the cost to them. On the whole archbishops and bishops do not show well against these backgrounds of fire. One of them said of a troublesome heretic that if he persisted in his errors "The Lawe will . . . frie him at a stake." Doubtless for the honor of the "Godhead of Christe and of the Holie Ghoste" which he was reported to have denied.[8]

VI

A NEW TYPE OF CHURCH INEVITABLE

Naturally the prelates would be *persona non grata* to those whom they persecuted. It is against human nature to be grateful for being

[7] But the Scrooby District, as we shall see, was truly rural.

[8] These pages are in debt to Burrage. He maintains, however, that the case against the Bishops should not be made too strong.

"fried at a stake" or seeing one's friends burned. The association of clerical vestments with such vindications of the Church and her faith may also have prejudiced the Puritan and Separatist against such garmenture. The more extreme would be led to question the Christian necessity of bishops, and specifically such bishops. That would lead to consideration of the nature and constitution of a Church more truly apostolic and more essentially Christian. This was in the main the line which English Separatism, eventually to become Congregationalism, took.[9]

A new type of church was therefore inevitable. It was the predestined conclusion in Protestantism of the long, long line of quests, escapes, experiments and separatism in all their variety and confusions already noted. It would be only a conventicle to begin with, a meeting together of the like-minded if enough like-minded could be found to meet together with reasonable agreement. There would be no church buildings for them, not for a long time. The establishment had taken over the old Catholic churches and such of their endowments as kings and nobles had left unplundered. These sectaries inherited nothing save the scaffold, the stake, and the rack. They were beginning as St. Paul's churches had begun; and if they claimed for themselves scriptural authority and believed themselves to be returning to apostolic simplicities and purities, they had a case.

Sooner or later questions about church government and organization, about the ministry, were sure to emerge. These Separatists, unless they had an already ordained clergyman for a leader, were without ordained ministers and had nowhere to look for them. How then should they call and ordain their ministers and what should be their offices? All such questions were equally inevitable; so, for that matter, was their form of organization.

Given any group sufficiently isolated, sufficiently sympathetic, sufficiently argumentative, and at the same time sufficiently committed to any cause, religious or secular, the general form of their organization is already determined for them. It will be a unitary group organization, conducting its own affairs through some expression of its common will. Unless it is organized and assembled from without by a missioner, it

[9] Just here in writing this history a principle of selection becomes imperative. English Anabaptism eventually became the English Baptist Church. We shall meet Baptists later in Boston and Providence Plantations. For the purpose of this book they belong to Baptist historians. Puritanism, as yet only a promise, would eventually become a major force. But though non-conformity tended to be puritanical, Puritanism was not Separatist. It wanted to be the English Church. Separatism, eventually to become Congregationalism, took its own line till 1648 in Cambridge, Massachusetts. That line must necessarily be rather exclusively followed in the next chapters. One of the best compact examinations of the development of group technique in the Reformation is chapter 8, *Tudor Puritanism*, M. M. Knappen.

will choose its own group officials, call them what it pleases, and honor them as the group pleases. These "officials" will be substantially a chairman and an assisting committee.

Once chosen they may become permanent or be changed as often as medieval Florence changed her municipal officers. They may be distinguished by title or garmenture or not. Something like this must have begun in the old Stone Age and been renewed after the last Ice Age, and an immense deal of human business, important or unimportant, has been, is still, and will continue thus to be conducted.[10] It is the first resource of the questing, the visionary, or the prophetic. Whatever breaks off from an established pattern, under whatever impulse, repeats this primitive and inevitable technique.

As group-sects multiply and coalesce, some "at the top" organization naturally develops and presently the whole going affair becomes pretty complicated and quite imposing. Then the ingenious in church or state would invest their own order with some form of "divine right," call any protest against or separation from it rebellion, heresy, or schism and, having the power, make it extremely uncomfortable, dangerous, or even fatal thereafter to doubt, deny, or secede. Also authority would date its own beginnings back as far as it could go by the records, then further by tradition, and then clear back by gratuitous and deftly argued assumption, and discover schism where there was as yet nothing really to be schismatic from, save the anachronistic ideology of the reconstructors of vanished pasts.[11]

VII

It Will Begin to Become Congregational in England and America

This process of group fission and fusion is abundantly illustrated throughout the whole history of the Christian Church. Where secession from or protest against the "Great Church" has taken formidable forms, through numbers or the influence of a popular leader, such movements constitute the historic heresies, and the historian deals with them, so to speak, in the mass. Where the Separatists have been few in number, isolated, widely spread in time and geography, they have taken, inevitably, some form of group expression. This is what makes it possible for even a trained historian, with strong "Congregational" predilections,

[10] H. G. Wells in his *Shape of Things to Come* anticipates a group of survivors forming themselves into a cell of a new civilization after about one hundred years of the fighting now going on (1942).

[11] This is a perfectly unpatterned digest of Church—and much other—history. Those who would disagree with it, and there are enough, would call it fanciful and irreverent and even those who would agree in substance would call it naïve, or trivial, or wanting in dignity of documentation. For all that, it is about what happened in the development of Christian organization. It had to. See Guingnebert's *Christianity*, to make it respectable.

to find "latent Congregationalism" in early protest movements[12] or to make "Congregationalists" of Lollards and Waldensians, not to speak of the churches in Corinth, Ephesus, and Philadelphia, all of which has a measure of truth, but tends to overprove the case.

Finally, the members of any more or less experimental group cannot escape the influence of their inner and outer inheritances. It is impossible for any cause in any extremity to break all the filaments which hold society together. The social or religious experimentalist must always tie into his new fabric some thread of the pattern he seeks to escape; some habit older than he knows will control his more radical departures, and the disciplines of the past subdue him in spite of himself.

A group of English men and women, therefore, in dissent and religious adventure, will still be English and weave the texture of their race into their new fabric. English Congregationalism, using the word in its simplest meanings, will not be Dutch or German. It will still express the English love of liberty in some precedent of law. Its disorders will be orderly. It will have due regard for use and wont. Moral excess will be the exception. It will not be theologically speculative; it will be a way of faith and worship within the frame that is England, and if it should cross the seas, it will name its new home New England—and become American Congregationalism.

[12] Dale, *History of English Congregationalism.* chaps. 2 and 3.

CHAPTER III

The First Adventures in
English Congregationalism

SINCE, as has been said, some form of group organization is almost inevitable in any pioneer movement, one must be cautious in reading back the later meanings of Congregationalism as a denominational name into the appearing and disappearing perilous little fellowships of humble English folk toward the end of the Sixteenth Century.[1] They were always in danger, compelled to secrecy, always being broken up only to get together again. There could be no organized association of groups. That would come later. The remarkable thing is that we know as much about them as we do. We owe what knowledge we have more largely to the records of those who harried and tried them than to their own "remains." They were in no position to elect a clerk or keep "minutes." Such papers would be perilous.

There was, under Mary, at least one "congregation" composed of members of the Church of England.[2] They used the Second Prayer Book

[1] They did not name or particularize themselves save to think that they sought to be "true Christians." They were mostly named by those who harried them, and beside being characterized as pestilent and unreasonable, they were named for their leaders, Brownists or Barrowists and the like. They would come out of the established Church, but it would be very difficult to document their own use of "Separatists" as a confessional word—and the same with "Independents." The word "congregation" does not appear in Browne's 185 Questions and Answers "Concerning the Life and Manners of all True Christians." It is always "the Churche." So in the London Confession of 1589, though in its third printing (1641) "congregation" is substituted for church. In the Second Confession of the London-Amsterdam Church (1596) "Church" and "Christian Congregation" seem interchangeable, and congregational autonomy is plainly set forth, but even so, "congregation" is a synonym rather than a label. The congregation are the faithful who constitute the church, and the implicit "Congregationalism" of the Confession is a means to an end and not an end in itself.

An introductory word may be said about the names "Independent" and "Congregational." Some prefer the former as being the older, but the oldest name is "Separatist." Next came "Congregational," which occurs in the writings of Henry Jacob (1563–1624?), whereas "Independent" was still a novelty in 1643—a novelty to which the "Dissenting Brethren" vehemently objected. The historical circumstances explain why "Independent" and "Free Church" became the designated terms during the next 150 years or more in Great Britain, while in the United States "Congregational" became the universally accepted denominational designation. (F. J. Powicke: *Third International Congregational Council*, p. 260.)

[2] Burrage, *The Early English Dissenters in the Light of Recent Research*, vol. 1, p. 70. John Smith, so-called minister of Plumbers' Hall, said under examination: "We bethought us what were best to doe, and we remembered that there was a congregation of us in this citie in Queene Maries dayes."

28

of Edward the VI. They were not in any sense of the word "Separatists." Their number varied and they did not often meet in the same place; in Alice Warner's house, in shoemaker Frogg's house, in a dyer's house. Their ministers were Church of England or "a Scotchman." They did not pray for Mary or Philip, nor did they apparently celebrate the sacrament of communion. Their alms were given to prisoners and to the poor. They met at seven in the morning or eight or nine. They dined together, "tarried after dinner till two of the clock" (p.m.) and, among other things, "they talked and made officers."

There were foreigners among them, "Frenchmen, Dutchmen, and other strangers," who called each other brothers. The Englishmen "seemed young merchants." They lived a hunted life; one can see them fleeing through the alley-streets of old London, or taking to a ship. Once, when the house in Thames Street where they were meeting was beset with enemies, they were saved by a mariner, who rowed them over the river "using his shoes instead of oars." There was a similar congregation at Stoke who covenanted "by giving their hands together" that they would not receive the mass at all. Such congregations sought to separate not from the Church of England, but from Queen Mary's return to Catholicism. Their organization was necessarily fluid, but Burrage thinks reformers like Browne might have known of them through Foxe's Book of Martyrs, then in its first (Latin) edition. Quite as likely Browne could have heard them talked about by sympathizers.

Churchmen who had fled to Geneva to escape Mary came back to Elizabeth indoctrinated with Calvinism and strongly inclined to the Reformed policy, as well as to a much more thorough reform in worship. They found manners and morals in England in sad contrast to godly Geneva, and they hoped to be humble instruments in the further purification of the Church. They were not immediately silenced; they were heard for a season, but in 1565 all licenses of preachers were called in and new licenses were granted only "to such as proved conformable and agreeable." This naturally left a considerable number of unlicensed ministers without occupation and aggrieved. About this time (1566?) the name Puritan appears (Burrage) in English literature.

The Bishop of London was deeply grieved over the prevalent controversies about things of no importance, as vestments and the like. The more learned clergy seemed on the point of forsaking their ministry. The pained Bishop does not note that their licenses had probably been revoked. Many of the people also contemplated forsaking "us" and setting up private meetings. "However . . . through the mercy of the Lord [and the Act of Uniformity] most of them have now returned to better mind."

I

THE PLUMBERS' HALL SOCIETY AND RICHARD FITZ

Not all. Bishop Grindal wrote (1568) that controversy broke out again. London citizens "of the lowest order with a few ministers remarkable neither for their judgment nor learning" openly separated, met in fields, private houses, or ships, administered their sacraments, ordained ministers, elders, and deacons. Also they were beginning to follow a hallowed pattern in excommunicating those who separated from them. There were about two hundred of them, more women than men. The Privy Council, implementing the "mercy of the Lord," imprisoned their leaders and sought to put a "timely stop to this secte." This was the Plumbers' Hall Society. They do not seem to have been Separatists, accurately so called. They were "retired" members of the Church in protest against corruption.[3] One "congregation" like Plumbers' Hall, meeting in different places, might easily be mistaken for many congregations and, since the authorities acted upon information received, the informers themselves would so differ in what they reported as to make the groups seem more numerous than they really were.

There was as yet no uniformity of procedure. One newly-invented sect called themselves "the pure or stainless religion." Their preacher used half a tub for a pulpit and was girded with a white cloth. They brought their own food and divided money amongst those who were poorer, seeking to imitate the life of the Apostles. So far, save for the half-tub and the white cloth, they might have been the Church at Corinth. Because they would not enter the churches nor partake of the Lord's Supper, the Queen's Council arrested the preacher and the leaders and appointed persons to convert the rest.[4] So the Spanish Ambassador reported to the Escurial.

There were seceders from Plumbers' Hall, on Bishop Grindal's authority, and also the excommunicated. These, Burrage holds, did not return to the state Church but moved still further to the left, a phrase

[3] Whether they were or were not Separatists has been much debated. Burrage thinks not and documents his position. They were independent Puritans, using the German order of worship, etc. (See Burrage, *The Early English Dissenters in the Light of Recent Research*, pp. 82 ff.) Peel thinks them to have been Separatist but not "specifically Congregational." They desired to be like "the best Reformed Churches." The congregation in the house of "James Tynne, goold smythe" may have been another group. They are as likely to have been the same general group meeting in another place with variations in personnel. The experiences, disciplines, and feuds of the congregation of English exiles at Frankfort in the main belong to this general period and have a bearing not here considered upon English Independency.

[4] There were, according to the estimate of a well-informed Catholic, about 5000 followers of the "pure or apostolic" religion in London in 1568. They also called themselves Puritans or "Unspotted Lambs of the Lord." Carlyle also held that if a preacher could find a tub he had a pulpit. (*Sartor Resartus*.)

the bishops would not have recognized. There had been a congregation in 1567 with Richard Fitz for their minister. A careful comparison of names leads Burrage to believe that the seceders from Plumbers' Hall united with the "Privy Church" of Fitz. This group suffered various and ill fortunes. Fitz eventually died in prison; the members were in sad repute with the bishops. Twenty-seven of them appealed to the Queen. There is also still extant a paper signed with Fitz's name, in which he defined the object of the "Privy Church," and a third paper in black-letter which seems to be the covenant of the group.

On the basis of these documents, Dr. Robert Dale in his monumental *History of English Congregationalism* concluded: "The first regularly constituted English Congregational church of which any record or tradition remains was the church of which Richard Fitz [he signed his name Fitze] was pastor; and he died in prison for his loyalty to Congregationalism." This conclusion is challenged also on the basis of the documents. The group were Separatist and Congregational enough, but Congregationalist by accident, and it could not have been a regularly constituted English Congregational church.[5] It was not concerned at all with being "Congregational," which some may hold the most significantly Congregational thing about it. It simply wanted the Queen and her ministers "to bring home the people of God to the purity and truthe of the Apostolyck Churche." For that blameless desire they had, they told the Queen, been so persecuted that the very walls of the prisons "about this city would testify God's anger against this land for such injustice and subtle persecution." Burrage is probably cautiously right. English Congregational policy was an evolution; here was an early stage, and its tradition survived. Ainsworth and Robinson refer to it: "A Separatist Church in the beginning of Queen Elizabeth's days."

Meanwhile the national Church was having troubles of its own. The Queen and Parliament did not agree over Church legislation; a relatively strong party wanted a Presbyterian and not an Episcopalian Church, "thereby bringing the bishops into incredible disfavor." Thomas Cartwright, Lady Margaret professor of divinity at Cambridge, contended for the Presbyterian Puritans; Whitgift, Master of Trinity, Chancellor of Cambridge, and afterwards Archbishop of Canterbury, championed the Establishment. Personal rancors embittered a discussion by no means academic. Whitgift had helped depose Cartwright of his professorship and drive him into exile. Theological and ecclesiastical controversy has rarely been overly courteous and Elizabeth's age was used to strong

---

[5] So Peel concludes: "Richard Fitz's church was simply the earliest Separatist congregation of which any considerable historical record has been preserved." *The First Congregational Churches.*

language. Cartwright lost, but the question had still to be settled. Something more, Dale says, than a dispute about the New Testament standing of bishops and elders, or the Geneva gown and surplice, was involved. For one thing, the people wanted preaching and the majority of the Established clergy could not preach. Some of them lived in "notorious vice" or else they were sluggish and inefficient. The Puritan wanted better ministers with more religious zeal. These were the real matters in issue behind a murk of words. The essential and incidental were hopelessly involved.[6]

II

"WITHOUT TARRYING FOR ANY"

Cartwright and his party put their hope in the Queen and the bishops. Robert Browne would not "tarry for any" and put his hope, as he believed, in the Great Head of the Church. Browne alive was a storm-center of and for controversy, and has so continued dead. He was long misrepresented by those who loved neither him nor his system and equally a source of pride and embarrassment for his friends and the friends of his system. Since the turn of the century, say from 1905, the more critical use of available documentary material and a calmer temper has made a more just estimate of him possible. He was born a gentleman; his ancestors can be traced back to the Fourteenth Century: prosperous merchants, aldermen, a sheriff, a coat of arms. Robert's grandfather, Francis, had a charter from Henry the Eighth to remain covered in the presence of the King and all his Lords. Robert himself, born about 1550, was the third of seven children. He went to Cambridge University (1570), matriculated at Corpus Christi, and probably took his degree in regular form. He became domestic chaplain to the Duke of Norfolk, disseminated doctrines the authorities thought seditious, and was cited to appear before the Ecclesiastical Commission, but by the Duke's protection and advice refused to appear.[7]

He next taught "schollers"[8] for three years and lectured to whomsoever would come to a gravel pit on Sundays, to the distaste of the rector. Then came the plague and he went home (1578). When it was safe he returned to Cambridge, studied theology, and began preaching "without leave and special word from the Bishop." He was gladly heard, having

---

[6]For a detailed and documented account of the complaints against and criticisms of the Established order and its "amazing state of disorder" see Peel's chapter in *Essays Congregational and Catholic.*

[7]Burrage, *The Early English Dissenters in the Light of Recent Research*, chap. 3 Burrage's chapter is compact, judicious, well documented. Dale's study is the kindest. Dexter's long chapter the most analytical. Peel does not believe that Robert was ever chaplain to the Duke of Norfolk. That was John.

[8]His own declaration.

power, unction, and a genius for irritating authority. There was in him, the Master of Trinity felt, "something extraordinary . . . which would prove the disturbance of the Church if not seasonably prevented." He declined the offer of a Cambridge pulpit and sent back the money they would have given him, being convinced that they were not yet rightly grounded in Church government. He was especially concerned about the bondage of the parishes to the bishops. He fell "sore sick," doubtless through inner conflict, and while ill was inhibited by the Bishop from further preaching. It is difficult to condense his own account of his seeking, but in the end it led him entirely out of the Established Church, and in 1581 (possibly 1580) he began to gather a "company" in Norwich, which became "the first *regularly constituted* Congregational church on English soil."[9] (Italics author's.)

III

The Norwich Church Examined

First of all this was a "gathered church." Browne had been led to conclude that "the Kingdom of God was not to begin by whole parishes, but rather of the worthiest, were they never so fewe." This was epoch-making, fundamentally divisive, and creative. It challenged, at its source, the entire conception of what one may loosely call the organic continuity of the Christian order, and found the joints in the armor of the established Anglican Church.

Latin Catholicism had developed a consistent system bound together by living filaments. Every child was born into her order and spiritually incorporated therein by baptism. He was thereafter nurtured and instructed, confirmed, confessed, absolved, and continued in his Christian life and hope of salvation by sacramental grace. The sacraments, faithfully received and administered by those who had the power to make them effective, carried him beyond any power of his to carry himself. The Church asked only obedience and assured salvation. She dismissed the dying as she had received the new born; and if there was some painful waiting in Purgatory, even that could be expedited. No words are quite equal to evaluating this system. Even the most Protestant imagination must acknowledge its spell. It was the soul of Western culture for almost a thousand years.

The Reformers groped for ways of preserving this organic continuity, but none of them succeeded. Something was gone. (Incidentally, no ecumenical Church can hope to recover it either.) The Anglican reformation sought institutional continuity within the political frame of the realm of England, but had then, and even in its most extreme Anglo-

[9] Peel supports this conclusion.

Catholic forms has now, no equivalent for sacramental grace. Its liturgies, disciplines, and instructions sought to foster "a godly, righteous, and sober life." There were dimensions below this level into which a communicant might and did fall, and above it into which he might ascend, and did; but it was admirably adapted to the felt needs of the English soul.

There was always an alternative. The condition precedent of a Church might be a fellowship who had become, as they believed, Christians through their own considered choice and confession; or else being already Christians by nurture and baptism, as were Browne's flock, should accentuate their Christian life by such qualities of devotion and earnestness as would set them apart both from the Church and the world. It was impossible, then, of course, for any body of confessed Christians to set out as if there had been no true Christianity or any right Church since St. Paul was carried off to Rome. The Separatist was bound to society by countless and unbreakable ties and was thus from the first involved in a contradiction between his profession and his estate. Browne's company brought into their meeting place in Norwich more of their religious inheritances than they left outside. Nonetheless, they had ceased to be a "parish" and had become a "congregation."[10] (This distinction will reappear in the American Unitarian Departure.)

In the second place it was a definitely organized congregation in accordance with clearly expressed principles: the principles of covenant,[11] agreement, and mutual consent. "So a covenant was made and their mutual consent was given to hold together." The covenant idea was not new. Anabaptists had used it. Given such situations as those in which helpless groups found themselves, some sort of covenant was almost

[10] If the distinctions between those two familiar and now somewhat interchangeable words were traced to their historic sources and analyzed as to their two "ideologies," they would illuminate the whole controversy between the continuing and the gathered.

[11] The New England churches made the "covenant" specifically the basis of their existence. The collection of "visible saints," said Richard Mather, is the "matter" of a church: the covenant which unites or knits the saints into one visible body is the "form." "Some union or band there must be amongst these whereby they come to stand in a new relation to God, and one towards another, other than they were before; or else they are not yet a church, though they be fit materialls for a church, even as soul and body are not a man, unless they be united; nor stones and timber an house, till they be compacted and conjoyned." Mather further defined the covenant quite precisely: "a solemne and publick promise before the Lord, whereby a company of Christians, called by the power and mercy of God to fellowship with Christ, and His providence to live together,... do in confidence of His gracious acceptance in Christ, binde themselves to the Lord, and one to another, to walke together by the assistance of His spirit, in all such ways of holy worship in Him, and of edification one towards another, as the Gospel of Christ requireth of every Christian Church and the members thereof." This is essentially very lovely, true and adequate. Quoted in *The New England Mind*, pp. 435–438, Perry Miller, an exhaustive, rather tough-fibred, indispensable study of the backgrounds of all New England thinking, writing, and preaching in the Seventeenth Century.

automatic, either expressed or implied. They must "hould" together. The Norwich covenant is included in the sections of Browne's "True and Short Declaration" which describes the organization of his congregation, not as an official document but as an almost artless narration of what and how they did. Like so many old and artless narratives, it achieves a very perfect art. Dexter believes the covenant proper to have been incorporated in the first three sentences of Browne's narrative.

The basis of the covenant was Scriptural, as they understood the Scriptures. "There were certain chief points [spelling modernized] proved into them by Scriptures, all which being particularly rehearsed into them, with exhortation, they agreed upon them . . . saying to this we give our consent."

"First, therefore, they gave their consent, to join themselves unto the Lord, in one covenant and fellowship together and to keep and seek agreement under his laws and government; and therefore utterly flee and avoide such-like disorders and wickedness as were mentioned before."

"Further they agreed of those which should teach them and watch for the salvation of their souls, whom they allowed and did choose as able and mete for that charge. For they had sufficient trial and testimony thereof by that which they heard and saw by them, and had received of others. So they prayed for their watchfulness and diligence, and promised their obedience."

"Likewise an order was agreed on for their meetings, prayer, thanksgiving, reading of the Scriptures, exhortation and edifying by all men which had the gift or by those which had a special charge therefor, and for the carefulness of putting forth questions, to learn the truth. . . ."[12] A long paragraph on discipline and good conduct follows and what would now be the by-laws of such a Church. There is a significant sentence on "seeking to other Churches to have their help." "Thus," Browne concludes, "all things were handled, set in order, and agreed on to the comfort of all, and so the matter wrought and prospered by the good hand of God." Certain words, later to become familiar, are wanting. There were no pastors, teachers, elders and deacons; only "teachers, guards and releavers."[13]

IV

BROWNEISTS' TRIBULATIONS

The last sentence of Browne's was prematurely optimistic. Since Browne was vehement against bishops, they reported him "to have

[12] Burrage, *The Early English Dissenters in the Light of Recent Research,* p. 98.
[13] What a "releaver" (reliever) might be, the account does not say. He would still be useful in most churches.

greatly troubled the whole country and brought many to great disobedience of all laws and magistrates." Browne himself was at least
twice imprisoned and the congregation so harried that in 1582 they removed to Holland (Middelburg in Zeeland) where the magistrates
granted them freedom of faith and worship.[14] There was already an
English Church in Middelburg (Cartwright's). Historians unfavorable
to Browne maintain that Browne, Harrison, and their company joined
that congregation and then withdrew. Dexter finds no evidence for that.
The fortunes of that self-exiled little company remain obscure. There was
only loneliness for them abroad, persecution at home. They seem never
to have been numerous (thirty or forty persons), and they found agreement difficult. Also Mrs. Browne enters into the rather sad, drab picture.
Browne apparently held that under certain conditions "the covenant
between husband and wife might be dissolved."

Browne's own two years in Middelburg were his book-writing period.
The books were sent "in sheets" to England, there bound and circulated.
The authorities found them incendiary documents, two men were hanged
for dispersing them, and the Queen issued a proclamation against them,
naming specifically "Robert Browne and Richard Harrison." The proclamation was long and verbose, but pointed for all that. Having anything at all to do with Browne's books was sedition and so punishable.[15]

In 1584 Browne went to Scotland to reform the Scotch Kirk. This we
take to have been his most valiant folly. That Kirk had no mind to be
reformed nor to be told that "the whole discipline of Scotland was
amisse." He travelled Scotland extensively and concluded from his own
observations that there was more wickedness in the best of Scotland
than the worst of England, which should have won him Samuel Johnson's approval. He went back to England, to contentions and imprisonments, and finally to conform to the doctrine of the Church of England,
and through Burleigh's influence to be received again into the ministry.
Thereafter for forty years he was the rector of a little rural parish. His
conformation could not have exorcised the revolution in his restless soul,
for he died in Northampton jail. He had been in jail so much that he
might have thought a prison his true home.

For a long time after his death he was a storm center of controversy.
Later Separatists, as we have seen, protested against being called "Browne-

[14] There was then a large Dutch population in Norwich. They had been brought
over to revive a decayed weaving industry. They had a church of their own, under
Elizabeth's protection. This has led many authorities to conclude that Browne began
by preaching to the Dutch, who had Anabaptist leanings, and so leavened his own
countrymen. Dexter thinks this at least exaggerated.

[15] Browne's third book, *A Book which Shewth*, develops his idea of church polity.
Burrage thinks it was his idea of an ideal polity for England, along completely democratic lines, magistrates included. No wonder they did not like it.

ists." Bradford defended Plymouth men against such a charge. An Anglican said that he left to the Church of England the ample legacy of his shame. Dexter thinks him to have been broken in mind as well as body, living in that strange borderland between far-sighted wisdom and immediate folly in which creative dissenters have so often lived. At the same time there was in his extravagant, controversial, over-written writing and preaching, insights, contentions and convictions which the future would purge, continue, and even adopt. It is impossible to trace the channels through which what he released reached a more ordered issue, but his spirit marched on.[16]

V

The Martin Mar-prelate Affair

Satire is a very old weapon and supposedly effective. It is at least eminently satisfactory to the satirist, though there have always been two edges to it. It usually attends an order already for one reason or another fallen into some kind of decay; and when it seems to have given the *coup de grace* to classes or institutions, it is usually because they have been otherwise weakened. But literature would have been less bright without it, and contemplating its employment against what one already dislikes is one of the respectably reprehensible pleasures of life. The priest and the prelate in all religions have been since most primitive times, vulnerable to satire. The reasons therefore belong to the psychologists and moralists; the results belong to the historian. English literature had for long been thus brightened. Chaucer had a genial gift along these lines and there had been Piers Plowman for whom

> "The frere with his phisike, this folk hath enchanged
> And plastered them so easily, they dread no synn."

Earlier anti-Church satire had been discreetly done in Latin—a scholar's game. Erasmus had published his "Praise of Folly" about the same time as his "Edition of the New Testament." It is difficult to say which publication was the more popular or strategic.[17] Erasmus' technique was sure to be borrowed by men with less scholarship and far less wit and used against English prelates. For the purposes of this study, the "Martin Mar-prelate" little, black-letter brochures are the most important. They were in the main an answer to one John Bridges, Dean

---

[16] Burrage is kinder to Browne than Dexter who, he thinks, shared (say) Bradford's feeling and later Congregational prejudice against Browne as not being on the whole an ancestor one would boast of. At his best he was a literary and religious leader not unworthy of a place beside Hooker and Cartwright.

[17] See for example the Dialogue between Julius II, a familiar spirit, and St. Peter. *Life and Letters of Erasmus*, James Anthony Froude, p. 149. Erasmus' authorship of it is not established. He denied it mockingly. The general opinion was: "Either Erasmus or the Devil."

of Sarum, who had published 1400 pages in "Defence of the Government Established in the Church of England for Ecclesiastical Matters," with a half page of verbose and curiously capitalized subtitles. These old authors wanted their readers to know definitely what their books were about.[18]

Fourteen hundred highly controversial pages present a long and vulnerable front, and Martin found his openings, presented his compliments to the Dean of Sarum, and proceeded to irritate him as with porcupine quills (the simile is Dexter's). The cause of sincerity, he affirmed, was wonderfully graced by John's writing against it. "For I have heard some say," (spelling modernized) "that whosoever will read his book shall as evidently see the goodness of the cause of reformation and the poor, poor nakedness of your government, as almost in reading all Master Cartwright's books." Martin sadly lacks reverence for the hierarchy. The Archbishop of Canterbury is "paltripolitan" and "his gracelessness" John of London has "a notable brazen face." Brother Bridges was very likely hatched in a "goose nest." The devil, he thinks, is not better practiced in bowling and swearing than the Bishop of London.

There are anecdotes of no credit to the clergy and plainspeaking of their faults, and so on and on. It is dull reading now; anything but dull then. The humor is no coarser than contemporary Elizabethan humor, and seemed to suit the time. Oxford and Cambridge students read the tracts. One was shown to Queen Elizabeth, who may have enjoyed it, for Her Majesty could use much the same language if she were moved to it. Altogether there were seven little books. They called out answers in Latin and bad verse. There was never such a tempest in a tea pot. Not a tea pot either, for there was in the Tracts the challenge of another ecclesiastic order, carefully considered and searching judgments of the Church and churchmen hard to confute. The realm was disturbed and all its agents mobilized to hunt down the writer and printer.

The poor presses and the types were moved from place to place; if one set was destroyed another was hidden somewhere to be used. The authorities were baffled and the question of authorship still plagues the historians. Dexter thinks two men managed it all: John Penry, printer and publisher, and "Martin" himself. It was generally believed that Penry was also the author, though it was never proved definitely against him. Dexter argues at length that Barrowe was the author (Dale does not) and that the two—Penry and Barrowe—took the close secret to heaven with them within sixty days of each other in 1593. "Small wonder," Dexter adds, "that it has been well kept since."

[18] Sixteenth Century equivalent of the publishers' "blurb."

VI

The First Separatist Martyrs

The bearing of the Martin Mar-prelate brochures (which have evoked a most considerable literature) upon Congregational history is, first, to illustrate the bitterly controversial temper into which Christians had then fallen, and, second, to demonstrate tragically the then helpless estate of humble folk who met in little scattered groups always in peril of their lives and watered the future with the blood of their martyrs. For through a course of events directly related to the Tracts, Greenwood, Barrowe, and Penry (or Ap-Henry) are chronicled as the first Congregational martyrs. That designation is probably too precise. They were Separatists, militant against the Establishment and seekers of another way. They would, for all that, have found it difficult to say themselves for what they died, save that the authorities did not know what else to do with them but to hang them. Neither did the authorities ever make clear to themselves or their victims what case they had against them.

Greenwood and Barrowe were more conspicuous in the whole affair than Penry. John Greenwood matriculated in Corpus Christi, Cambridge, where Browne and Harrison had been in 1577-8. He was in due course ordained deacon and priest. He had no peace of conscience in Episcopal orders, withdrew from the Establishment, and was arrested in 1586 while holding a "private conventicle" and sent to Clink Prison. There was little then to choose between being publicly executed and dying in prison, except that hanging was kinder. The prisons were too foul for words and their dark and verminous dungeons enforced a living death upon those who finally died and were obscurely buried and forgotten.[19]

In Clink,[20] of a November (1586) morning whose probable gloom must have deepened the darkness of Greenwood's dungeon, Greenwood was visited by Henry Barrowe whom His Grace the Archbishop had been seeking to apprehend. The occasion was too convenient. Barrow was taken by the keeper of the prison and shipped by boat the same afternoon to Lambeth. Barrowe was ten years older than Greenwood, well born and a barrister. He had led a disorderly life, but passing a church one day with a friend he was halted by a sermon loud enough to be

[19] A footnote of Dexter's records the fate of twenty-five "falsely called Browneists"; Robert Aweburne died in Newgate; Scipio Bellot died in Newgate; Robert Bowle died in Newgate; Margaret Farrar discharged from Newgate sick unto death, dying in a day or two—and so on and on—"died in Newgate," "died in Newgate," till the list is finished.

[20] That name seems to have persisted and became a convenient general name for a night's lodging for (say) driving through a red light.

heard in the street. He went in and there was wrought in him such a reformation of life that the libertine became a Puritan of the strictest sort, and the barrister turned to theology. The suddenness of his conversion explains its radical completeness.

He was attracted to Greenwood, and together they agreed upon the need of a complete reorganization of the Church and its affairs. They may have been influenced by Browne, whose books had for four years been accessible in England. Barrowe protested to no purpose the illegality of his arrest. (The Anglican authorities show very badly in the long procedure against him.) The examinations and his replies range along the whole front of embattled religious conceptions and church systems. He was virtually asked to incriminate himself, and the clarity of his legally trained mind in his answers gave to the records a revealing precision. The questions of right and truths are incidental. Barrowe stood for something the Anglican prelates meant to break and they had the power. The structural qualities of two positions can be seen through all the verbosities.[21] There was no reconciling them. Between Barrowe and his prosecutors a great gulf was fixed.

The prosecutors did not find it easy to make a case which would satisfy the forms of the law. The processes against Greenwood were associated with the processes against Barrowe, and the pitiful affair dragged on for six years. Their condemnation was predetermined. The ropes were finally "tyed" around their necks and they were in the act of praying for the Queen when they were for the last time reprieved. There had been a supplication to the Lord Treasurer that "in a land where no Papist was put to death for religion, theirs should not be the first blood shed, who concurred about faith with what was professed in the country. . . ."

Nothing was gained but six days. They were hanged of an April morning by the contrivance of the Prelates "as early and secretly as well they could in such a case." (Their friends believed the Queen did not know of it.) "Two aged widows were permitted to carry their winding sheets to the gallows."[22] The case against Penry was still more difficult to establish, but they got him hanged also. None of these men denied their faith or proved unchristian in their death.

Meanwhile, for the safety of the realm and the convenience of the Lords Spiritual and Temporal, "An Act To Retain the Queen's Subjects in Obedience" (act Eliz. 35 CI) was passed. In the verbose substance of it any person or persons over sixteen years old, who refused for a month

---

[21] If one would dissect out the essentials on either side—a weary task—one would have a clear understanding of the radical religious mind of the period.
[22] Dexter, *Congregationalism as Seen in Its Literature*, p. 245.

to attend Divine Service as established by Her Majesty's Laws, or influenced others in any way so to do, or denied Her Majesty's power in causes ecclesiastical and so on and on, being lawfully convicted, should be committed to prison, without bail, until they conformed. If convicted offenders did conform within three months, they should abjure the realm (get out of England)! If they refused to flee—or having fled should return —they should die as "Deemed" felons without benefit of clergy.[23] (Eliz. 35 CII).

There was a terrible finality in this act. It made any kind of nonconformity almost fatally dangerous and group meetings impossible. It left the little questing congregations no choice. They must conform or flee; so two congregations, one of them destined to become historic, fled to Holland.

[23] Arber, *The Story of the Pilgrim Fathers.* Introduction. This is an invaluable collection of original documents to which this history, for a chapter or so, is deeply in debt.

Note—This chapter has been written and in parts rewritten as the writer has sought new authorities, precised his facts, and corrected conclusions. There are necessary qualifications to any conclusions in the general field here covered. It is extremely difficult to nominate the first Congregational church by later tests of the polity. It was to begin with and has since continued an always developing and changing order. Robert Browne's church seems to meet more of the tests for the honor of Congregational primacy than any other candidate. We shall see in later chapters that it is extremely difficult to date the first user of "Congregational" and "Congregationalism" as now understood.

If any reader should desire to explore the backgrounds of these and later chapters there are three rather massive works of outstanding value. The first is *Tudor Puritanism, A Chapter in the History of Idealism* by M. M. Knappen. The second, *The New England Mind: The Seventeenth Century,* by Perry Miller. The third, *The Rise of Puritanism,* William Haller. To these for brilliant interpretation might be added the second volume of Henry Osborn Taylor's *Thought and Expression in the Sixteenth Century.* These books are treasure houses for the understanding of the deep rooting of an order now (1942) embattled.

CHAPTER IV

Sifted Seed Corn

THE congregations already considered by no means complete the lists of Non-Conformists, Seekers, and Separatists in England. East Anglia and London nurtured most of them, but they penetrated England, "sparsed of their companies into several parts of the realm, and namely into the West, almost to the uttermost borders thereof."[1] These congregations were widely separated. They broke out sporadically, were broken up, appeared again, had a power to outstay relentless persecution. They must, therefore, have had a tenacious rooting in one racial characteristic of the English people. Any movement so tenacious, so spontaneous, so epidemic, and for all its petty variations, so definitely patterned, cannot be dismissed, as Anglican historians and others dismiss it, as an irritating species of contrary-mindedness, fanatical about the inconsequential, sadly unappreciative of the blessings of bishops and the established order.

The only possible conclusion is that the Anglican Church was not, and never has been, a completely national Church. There was something in England it could not and would not contain. The Wesleys were to prove that in another way 200 years later. Henry Osborn Taylor in his admirable study of Sixteenth Century thought and expression concludes that the "Middle Way" of the Anglican Reformation was "the only path religion could have trod." England could not be Puritan. Otherwise it would have gone against the very grain of the "vigorous love of life, the expansion of its daring, the vaunt and happiness of its poetry, and withal to its love of seemly form and fitting social conventions,"[2] which were the very essence of Elizabethan England.

All that is true enough, though finally the best of Puritanism—English Puritanism—would temper the spirit of England and give it a splendid and militant force. Still less was Presbyterianism native to the English spirit. But Independency was and is native to the English spirit, and to a degree the secular English historian has been far more ready to recognize and glory in than the religious historian. It was and is an expression of the English love of liberty which the poets have sung and the orator

[1] Burrage (*The Early English Dissenters in the Light of Recent Research*, p. 185), traces these obscure congregations with an investigator's patience and a scholar's documentation.
[2] Taylor, *Thought and Expression in the Sixteenth Century*, vol. 1.

praised, and to which in her seasons of extremity those whose stupidity, bishops included, has more than once imperiled British liberty, have appealed—and never in vain—to save them. An instinct for free group-management of their own affairs by those whom those same affairs most intimately concerned is as old as the Saxon occupation of English soil.

I

THE DIFFICULT ESTATE OF ENGLISH NON-CONFORMITY

Naturally it would seek to express and realize itself in their religious life. These experimental religious groups appearing and disappearing, stamped out and down and presently in evidence again, had deep-down, interlacing and far-reaching roots, unconquerably vital. In some ways the treatment of English religious Independency by Anglican authority is one of the most unworthy and arrogant chapters in English history.[3] For one thing, it reveals, as all similar repressive movements reveal, the Established Church's sheer lack of confidence in its own cause. When a Church for centuries uses every device in its power to compel people to come to it and fails, it would better look to its own assumed catholicity. The whole pressure of English power and advantage has been from the first, and in subtle ways still is, against the Free Churches.

When these groups ceased to be harried with exile and imprisonment, they were denied office unless they conformed by taking the sacrament, the strangest use of it ever devised. The national universities were shut in their faces, and Matthew Arnold called them Philistines for their lack of culture. Their worship was ridiculed and their meeting places, when at last they had them, denied the name of a church. Always social prestige was against them and eager to make their more successful children conform. And yet, they have persisted, shared with the Establishment almost half the population of England,[4] created their own schools and colleges, written Milton's *Paradise Lost* and Browning's *Ring and the Book,* sent Bright and his like to Parliament, and furnished England some of the greatest of her preachers, the wisest of her statesmen and the more humane and sensitive elements of her national conscience. It is presumptious, therefore, for the Anglican churchmen to claim that, save in its official status, theirs is unqualifiedly the national Church, and a judicious historian, like Taylor, generalizes too broadly in finding in the Elizabethan settlements a *via media* entirely representative of the English temper, religious or otherwise.

[3] And it now begins to be paralleled from rather unexpected sources in American church history writing.

[4] A loose statement, though in the peak period of the Free Churches twenty-five years ago it was probably so. The "Free Churches" of course include the Methodist (several branches) and the Baptists.

What one really traces through a tangle of documents and detail, which only a specialized scholar can cite and an extremely specialized historian digest, is the superficial disorder of a great tide charged with destiny, gradually finding its true channels. It was all bound to be a process of trial and error, of costly experimentation. There were excesses, crudities, and also a long-suffering patience and courage; an anvil-like power to wear the hammer out. If, as the devout have always believed, there is a Power beyond ourselves, slowly realizing great purposes and reaching toward ends which at last reveal the meanings of the process, it needs a dogmatic astigmatism to deny that Power in action in the emergence of Free Churches.[5]

The long, costly, and heroic history of English Congregationalism and the Free Churches does not lie within the scope of this volume, though we shall see presently how the English and American movements found each other. A combination of conditions, circumstances, and inner and outer pressures made American Congregationalism and something vaster: the Pilgrim adventure and the Pilgrim contribution to religion and statecraft. The pioneers of the movement held that they were seed corn, sifted and tested for the harvests of the future, and certainly they were sifted. Any teller of a great tale has to take care not to read too much back into beginnings. But the issue we are following needed for its really creative inception an unusual group. They must be tenacious, they must have a faculty of coherence, they must have a wise common sense, and above all they must have capable leaders of a practical genius. They must have a sense of order, power of adaptation, and unusual courage. Their enthusiasms must not mislead them, but they must at the same time be obedient to the vision they believed heavenly. The choice was finally between two exiled congregations: one in Amsterdam, the other in Leyden, Holland.

II

REFUGE IN HOLLAND

The martyrdom of Greenwood, Barrowe, and Penry troubled the English authorities. After all, a magistrate should have some concern for justice and a bishop for Christianity. The state, as has been said, could imprison, banish, or hang sectaries under the Act of Elizabeth 35. chapter 1; or hang them without benefit of clergy under chapter 2. They were reasonably content, therefore, to let the nonconformists exile themselves, though, on the general principle of harrying them as much as possible. they made even that cruelly difficult. The unusually forward position of Holland as to religious tolerance has already been noted, and

[5] For example, Charles Clayton Morrison in *What Is Christianity*.

an ease of movement between the Dutch states and England was facilitated by transportation, a working, mutual linguistic understanding and
opportunity for livelihood. (Weaving again.)

Francis Johnson was well born, master of arts and fellow of Christ's
College Cambridge. He had not been preaching long before his Presbyterian leanings were complained of.[6] The want of elders in the Establishment was, he doubted not, the cause of ignorance, atheism, idolatry,
profanation of the Sabbath and, in general, the failure of Anglicans to
live godly, righteous, and sober lives. For this more or less hypothetical
opinion, he was for long imprisoned and then expelled from the university. He finally went to Holland and became pastor of English wool
and cloth merchants at two hundred pounds a year, which proves the
prosperity of the merchants. He discovered in a printing shop copies of
a book of Barrow and Greenwood. These he reported to the magistrates
who instructed him to burn them, and he himself fed the flames. But he
kept out two, "that he might see their errors." Instead they converted
him. He gave up his charge, returned to London and inherited, as near
as may be, the leadership of the Greenwood and Barrowe group. Meanwhile members of the group found their way to Amsterdam.

There for four years they were without pastors or teachers and very
poor, "miserably rent, divided, and scattered." Henry Ainsworth joined
them presently and with his aid they published a True Confession of the
Faith, protested their loyalty to Elizabeth and complained of the unchristian slanders which their adversaries had given out against them.
Those still in London, having pastors and elders, continued and functioned as a Church. They must have found it difficult, because Francis
Johnson and later his brother George were in prison. For Francis there
were mitigations; while still in prison he found opportunity to woo and
wed a well-to-do widow of desirable person and undesirable, so George
thought, pride.

Francis disregarded his brother's advice and "being inveigled and
over-carried" with the lady, married her secretly. The marriage irritated
the Archbishop of Canterbury and he put the groom into closer confine-
ment. The lady showed an unscriptural fondness for whale-bone stays,
"golde rings," an "excessive deal of lace" and a preposterous hat, all of
which grieved the saints, led George to unfraternal expressions and promised no excess of brotherly love in Amsterdam, where about April, 1597,
the brothers and many of their flock after diverse hindrances and some
perils, managed to get themselves. With those who had preceded them,
they became the "Ancient Church" in Amsterdam.

The Ancient Church did not prosper. The leaders could not or did

[6] Dexter, *Congregationalism as Seen in Its Literature,* chap. 5.

not agree as to polity, the laity were undisciplined, George was jealous of Francis, Mrs. Francis could not be reformed in her love of dress. On the contrary, her whale-bones went from bad to worse, though Francis said his wife paid for her own clothes and had the right to wear them. Mrs. Johnson was reported to have expressed regret for her marriage, and so on and on. Evidently this congregation was not the destined seed corn.

III

LEADERS AND SOURCES OF THE PILGRIMS

Other seed beds were in preparation, this time outside London. All these groups were of necessity fluid. Any attempt to trace all their half-hidden filaments is almost hopeless, and there was not, could not have been, much overt cooperation between them. Travel was difficult, and they were always under suspicion by the authorities. Yet there must have been some movement of the faithful from one group or region to another group or region.[7] There is also in a period of great intellectual ferment a contagion of impulses and ideas as difficult to trace as the course of wind-borne seeds. But now, having got the Johnsons with their followers and Mrs. Johnson's whale-bone "busks" unhappily in Amsterdam, Lincolnshire in England comes next, and the Pilgrim's Progress of the Rev. John Smyth. Whether or no "fate sought to conceal him by calling him Smith" it has made his biography most difficult to write, since the most careful investigators do not agree as to which John he was, at least to begin with, for there were three contemporaneous John Smiths, all clergymen, two of whom wrote and published upon prayer. It was perhaps to distinguish him from the others that he changed Smith to Smyth or Smythe.

Arber identifies him as the John of Christ's College, Cambridge, who took his M.A. in 1593, and concludes that he was born about 1572, entered the university about 1586 and was forty years old when he died in 1612. So much for dates. He was for two years, then, preacher or lecturer in Lincoln and a conforming clergyman, though he had earlier been cited before Cambridge authorities for an Ash-Wednesday sermon, in which he advocated a disturbingly strict observance of the Sabbath.[8] After the fashion of preachers then and since, he published four of his sermons on "The Bright Morning Star"; later still, a long and imposingly titled book on prayer. He entitled himself, "John Smith, Minister and Preacher of the Word of God." John Cotton thought his Lincoln ministry exemplary. His later career Cotton chose "rather to tremble at than discourse of."

---

[7] Their names can be traced through records and legal processes. The lists of names in the last chapters of St. Paul's letters show similar movements of individuals.

[8] Arber, *The Story of the Pilgrim Fathers.*

But he was a born "seeker" (Francis Johnson had been his tutor), and after a period of "doubting" he renounced the Church of England and became pastor (1606) of a congregation in Gainsborough, which had covenanted together "as the Lord's free people." Smyth organized this group on his own lines; only one kind of elder he held to be truly Scriptural. Two years later this congregation also went to Amsterdam. Arber thinks the Pilgrim (Scrooby) church migrated about the same time because, in October 1608, Bishop Hall published a volume of controversial letters, the first of which he addressed to Master Smith and Master Robinson, ringleaders of the late separation at Amsterdam. The Scrooby church thus enters the picture for the first time and by way of Gainsborough, since the Scrooby group met with Smyth's congregation at Gainsborough for a short time. (Gainsborough is George Eliot's St. Oggs in the *Mill on the Floss*.)

IV

SCROOBY MANOR

What Arber calls the Pilgrim District in England lies in the broad valley of the lower Trent, a pastoral region still, and in 1600 apparently so retired, Arber thinks, as to have been inaccessible to religious unrest coming from without. Scrooby itself lies toward the north of the region. There was once an Archepiscopal palace of which little remains save the memory of Cardinal Wolsey. There he sought to escape King Henry's wrath when he had swum too far in his sea of glory, and remained for a season (1530), ministering many deeds of charity. The farm house which Brewster occupied and from which his company set out remains. The land belonged—perhaps still does—to the Archbishop of York.[9]

[9] Queen Elizabeth in 1582 requested by letter Edwin Sandys, then Archbishop of York, to lease to Her Majesty two manors: Southwell and Scrooby, upon what seemed to the grieved Archbishop very hard terms. The Queen would pay forty pounds a year for the manor of Scrooby which had been paying the Archbishop one hundred seventy pounds a year; also His Grace was compelled by law to keep in repair the two manor houses. "Whither I resort for my lodgings . . . as I come thither for your Majesty's service. By this lease . . . if it should pass: I am excluded out of both."

There follows a careful inventory of the resources, tenantry, timber, privileges and possible revenues of the manors. The Archbishop concludes that if he should execute the leases, the See of York would lose 70,000 pounds (multiply now by 5). "Too much, Most Gracious Sovereign! too much—." Two or three sentences hid under legal verbiage are unexpectedly significant. The one thousand tenants of the manors, "poor copyholders for the most part" (no guarantee of permanence) "had enjoyed great liberties and customs." All these by this lease may be "racked" (rent raised to the uttermost) and as the Prophet saith "the skin pulled off their backs." *The cry whereof would sound in your Majesty's ears to your great discontent.*" (Italics author's.)

This should not be overpressed, but one does not wonder that poor "copy holders" likely to be rack-rented by a greedy Queen and spiritually nourished by an Archbishop who could lose 70,000 pounds in the rewriting of two leases, may have felt doubly that their souls could be less expensively saved and that they might, by the temporal head of the Church, be more justly ruled. I [Atkins] have seen no examination of this possibility in the sources, but there is most likely to have been an economic unrest behind English Separatism as behind Continental Anabaptism.

The Separatist movements we have so far considered were distinctly urban, mostly London, or else their leaders had disturbed the universities. Traceable also amongst them is the influence of trade and travel, especially with Holland. The Scrooby region, on the contrary, was remote, sparsely populated, truly rural, passing slowly from Roman Catholicism to Protestantism.[10] The peasantry were illiterate. (Shakespeare's Nick Bottom, Peter Quince, Tom Snout.) They were far from the outside world, the Great North Road only an unfenced horse track. How could the religious ferment of the time have reached them? (Here the author follows Arber's documentation.)

In the main Nottinghamshire men founded the Pilgrim Church under the influence of Richard Clyfton, William Brewster, and, for two years, Richard Bernard. Bernard stayed in the Establishment, and Clyfton was pastor of the church at Scrooby from 1606 to 1608, John Robinson being his assistant. Robinson afterwards reproached Bernard sharply for dissolving his covenant. Clyfton, Brewster, and Robinson were Cambridge University men. Arber's conclusion, therefore, is that these three leavened the Pilgrim region with Separatism and that without them there would have been no Pilgrim Fathers.

Bradford confirms this substantially. It was, he wrote, "by the travail and diligence of some godly and zealous preachers and *God's* blessing on their labours . . . in the north parts, many became enlightened by the *Word* of God and had their ignorances and sins discovered unto them. . . ." This has been so far a chronicle of clergymen who had been moved to protest against and separation from the Established Church of England. They were various in temper and capacity. They have left us, voluminously written, their arguments, controversies and confessions. There is, besides, a moving record of their imprisonments, banishments, or executions. They have, in addition, one thing in common: their minds and speech are Elizabethan; they belong, in spite of all their struggle to get free from it, to the order which nourished them. Now suddenly a layman emerges of wisdom and force enough to carry through an essentially great enterprise with limited means and against almost unbelievable difficulties, and a minister whose mind did not belong to Elizabeth and her time at all. The layman is William Brewster; the minister, John Robinson.

V

WILLIAM BREWSTER—POST-MASTER

Brewster had been a Cambridge undergraduate, which argues a reasonably well-to-do father and a family love of learning, who became post-

[10] Arber thinks it likely that of the three men who were in succession postmasters at Scrooby, the grandfather was a Catholic, the father a Protestant, the grandson a Separatist. Other authorities do not accept Arber's estimate of the Scrooby region. They think it to have been relatively well populated with an intelligent folk.

master at Scrooby upon his father's death. That was a position whose importance then is not indicated by rural postmasterships now. It was actually a position demanding marked executive ability and substantial capital.[11] The office must have been unexpectedly lucrative. No wonder Stanhope wanted it for his cousin. One takes it also that in 1590 Brewster was in good standing with the authorities.

Brewster, not yet an elder, would have been then the first lay "pillar" of a Congregational church of whom we have record.[12] Of Brewster's conversion to non-conformity there seems no record. "He did much good in the country where he lived," Bradford wrote, "in promoting and furthering religion." He practiced what he professed, encouraged others to his example, procured good preachers, and bore most of the charges. (A most admirable "pillar"!) For three or four years the general fellowship met (as has been said) at Gainsborough. But the distance was long for Brewster's neighbors; they could not conceal their comings and goings—always at peril. They therefore formed a separate church with Clyfton for pastor, Robinson for leader, and Brewster for elder. (So Dale, but Brewster became elder only later in Leyden.) If Brewster was the executive force in the Scrooby church, John Robinson went far toward shaping all its subsequent history and much other history besides.

[11] Arber's chapter 6 is as fascinating as it is illuminating. There is, to begin with, a letter from John Stanhope, Master of the Posts (1590) to William Davison, sometime a secretary of State to Queen Elizabeth. When "Old Brewster died," Stanhope had apparently promised to use his influence to have his own cousin appointed, on the ground that "Young Brewster" had not used the office during his father's lifetime and had besides been too independent about the whole affair, never went to see Stanhope, "made his way according to his own liking," (apparently always William Brewster's way), and so on. To this Davison replied that Brewster had administered the post, by record, before his father's death and had been postmaster himself about a year and a half. (Since this correspondence is dated 1590, "Olde Brewster" must have died early in 1589.)

Next: There was her Majesty's accounting with the Post of Scrooby. Beginning April 1, 1590, William Brewster's "ordinary wages" ran about thirty pounds a year (multiply now by 5). Brewster's wage ceased the last of September, 1607. (Therefore the Pilgrims could not have started to leave England before late autumn, 1607.)

Next: A list of the posts between London and Berwick-upon-Tweed. (One of the four "post roads" in England.) Twenty-nine stations across 337½ miles. (Scrooby almost halfway—152 miles north of London.)

Finally, the orders of Her Majesty's Privy Council for the posts between London and Scotland (with additional instructions from Stanhope.) Each postmaster must have in his stable (for Her Majesty's service) three good horses, with saddles and furnishings, three stout leather bags, three horns to blow by the way. Only fifteen minutes will be allowed for change of horses, etc. Each post must have in addition four good horses, and two horns for contingencies or commissions. The posts shall ride, from March to September, seven miles an hour (London to Berwick forty-two hours). In winter five miles an hour (sixty hours each way). In such a way Her Majesty expedited her mails and documents, through every weather and some peril. Finally the postmaster has general control of the traffic. He would forward unofficial travelers and perhaps lodge them. He would have (beside his wage) from one-and-a-half pence to two pence per mile for the use of his horses and gear.

[12] Dale (*History of English Congregationalism*, p. 195), says that Brewster had been private secretary to Davison, "who esteemed him as a son." There is no mention of this in Davison's reply to Stanhope but it may explain Davison's attitude.

VI

JOHN ROBINSON

Robinson matriculated at Corpus Christi, Cambridge, a nursery of Independents and Puritans, in 1592, at about seventeen years of age. The Elizabethan Age was then at its peak, a summit in English history, luminous with fadeless lights or else a sky studded with stars. The universities would have acknowledged and reflected all this. There were then in Cambridge about three thousand collegians. Corpus Christi had one master, twelve fellows, fourteen scholars and one hundred and thirteen students. There seems to have been a severe discipline, a long listening to prayers, exercises in Latin, Greek, Hebrew, logic, public disputations, beer and beef and a possible "birching" for attending a bear-baiting or a cock fight. But in Robinson's time these regulations were relaxed. There were Puritan irregularities in worship.[13]

Robinson seems to have been at Cambridge for seven years and to have won a fellowship. His studies were controlled by Elizabethan statutes: Rhetoric, Logic, Philosophy, for a Bachelor of Arts degree; Philosophy, Astronomy, Perspective, Greek, and Divinity for a Mastership in Arts. Any graduate entitled to a Master's hood would have a sound grounding in the classics, Hebrew, and such philosophy as was then recognized. Also he would be a logical disputant though withal somewhat dry. The time and the place lent themselves to religious controversy. The consciences of the Puritans were uneasy over bishops and prayer books. A newly appointed Lady Margaret Professor of Divinity

[13] Dexter thus fills the gaps, which a then rather scanty knowledge of Robinson's early life occasioned, with an extended and possibly idealized account of undergraduate life at Corpus Christi, Cambridge in 1592. Burgess' *John Robinson*, undertakes with new documentation to fill Dexter's gaps with more pertinent facts than 'trundle beds.' The result is a work of about 400 pages, but the net gain in added significant knowledge (of Robinson's youth) is not especially pertinent.

He was a Robinson of Sturton—son to John Senior, and grandson to Christopher. The Robinsons seem to have stood well with their neighbors, the Essex gentry, to the extent of witnessing a will or even executing it. Their own wills show them a careful and thrifty stock who did not mean that a "lyninge sheet" or a "silver spoone" should be left unbequeathed. Also they remembered the poor and commended their own souls to God and their bodies to the earth. As in most family trees of comparable men their women-folk command respect.

John Jr., Burgess thinks, was born about 1576, one of four children. Nothing is known of his boyhood, save that at some school or other he gave enough promise to continue his education at Cambridge, which his father could then afford. Burgess then gives Dexter's description of undergraduate life at Corpus Christi with slightly more detail and so eventually gets John, Fellow of Corpus Christi, to Norwich. In a prematurely placed chapter Burgess deals with the White (or Whyte) family, one of whose young women, Bridget, Robinson married, and for whom possibly he gave up his Fellowship. She made him a good wife; she connected him with the Carvers. Some of the White family money bought the famous house in Leyden which housed not only John and Bridget but the Pilgrim Church.

For the rest Burgess' book goes into details not too useful here.

seems to have doubted predestination. There would have been no dearth of argumentation for Robinson to hear and share. He was a good enough scholar to be elected Fellow after a rigid examination (one of twelve of his college).

This has always been a most desirable academic honor, carrying with it dignities, emoluments, good dining, and a secure and sheltered station in which a Fellow may grow old and, if he pleases, picturesquely peculiar and sterilely learned. There seems to have been no condition against tenure till death, save getting married.[14] Robinson might have lived and died in lovely Cambridge, untroubled and forgotten.

A Fellow could serve a parish and hold his Fellowship. Robinson took orders in the Anglican Church, went north and took a cure of souls near or in Norwich. But he felt the cure of his own soul uncertain and not to be accomplished in the Established Church. He inclined more and more toward the principles of Separatism. Now "Separatism" was then and still is an elastic word, ranging from inner withdrawal to bitter, militant antagonisms. Robinson began gently. Suspended but not excommunicated, he sought permission to preach in a "leased chapel" or to be master of the hospital at Norwich.[15] These were refused him. They could hardly have been more than way stations in his Pilgrim's Progress. He was under an inner compulsion "as a burning fyre shut up in my bones." It is not easy to explain a "burning fyre" in cold words.

And this Robinson never quite succeeded in doing, nor any of his fellowseekers. When he sought to justify his separation from the Church of England (1610) a single sentence in which he examines his own state of mind and soul runs to nearly three hundred words, wanting in order and clarity. Dexter is naturally a sympathetic interpreter. Robinson, he thinks, loved the Church into which he was born and baptized, left it reluctantly, and only when he gave up hope of its becoming a true New Testament Church, as he understood the New Testament. There was no hope of that under James and his bishops. He knew in some way of the Gainsborough group and determined to join it, resigned his Fellow-ship, and presented himself at Gainsborough (1604). When a little later it seemed wise for the group to divide into two bodies for safety and a company under Smyth went to Amsterdam there to "bury themselves and

[14] Newman, who had a genius for dramatizing himself, made an epic of his gaining a Fellowship, and had no desire at the time save to live and die in it.

[15] This seems to indicate a desire to continue religious work (he was still a Fellow with its stipend) quietly and semi-independently. He would have been a kind of chaplain in the hospital, or else a preacher in his own hired church. Bishop Hall said (1610) and acidly, that he did not doubt to say that if Robinson had been granted either the "Hospitall or a lease from that Citie," "this Separation from the Communion, Government, and worshippe of the Church of England would not have been made by John Robinson," which is pure and unlikely conjecture.

their names," Robinson went with the Scrooby group. They had peace of spirit in the old manor house, but no safety. So they resolved to go to the Low Countries where, they had heard, was "freedome of Religion for all men."

VII

From Scrooby to Leyden

That was more easily proposed than done. Bradford's narration of their fortunes and misfortunes is an epic in miniature. They were to begin with an humble farming folk, not acquainted with trades nor traffic and used to a plain, country life. They must, in a country they knew naught of, learn a new language and make a living they knew not how. They had heard also that Holland was a dear place and subject to the miseries of war. Many thought it an adventure almost "desperate." "But these things did not dismay them . . . they rested on [God's] Providence: and knew whom they had believed." The English authorities, having given them no choice but conformity, exile or death, would not suffer them to go. "Ports and harbors were shut against them." The mariners whom they paid to take them, charged them exorbitantly and betrayed them to searchers and officers, who plundered them to their shirts. They were imprisoned in Old Boston, families were separated, women left behind without a "cloth to shift them." One boat encountered such a storm as St. Paul suffered and was driven almost to Norway. But, says Bradford, they reached their desired haven. The troubles of those left behind made their cause famous for courage and constancy. All got over at length, some in one place, some in another, and they met together again, according to their desires and with no small rejoicing.[16]

Robinson and Brewster were the last to get over. Everything was so different "as it seemed they were come into a new world," though the poverty they faced belonged then as since to the immigrants' world. They were not at home in Amsterdam nor in the "Ancient Church," torn by scandal and opposing counsels. Therefore, in 1609, by the records of Leyden, "with due submission and respect: Jan Robarthse (John Robinson), minister of the Divine Word, and some of the Members of the Christian Reformed Religion, born in the Kingdom of Great Britain, to the number of one hundred persons or thereabouts, men and women, represent they are desirous of coming to live in this city by the first of May next (1609): and to have the freedom thereof in carrying on their trades, without being a burden in the least to anyone."

[16] Arber (*The Story of the Pilgrim Fathers*, p. 93), precises all this with geographical detail. Any comment on the courage of this little group is an impertinence. Comfortable theologians and churchmen who have not better names for all this than "schism" and "unimaginative biblicism" make themselves verbosely ridiculous. St. Paul would have understood them better in A.D. 60.

In response the Court of the City of Leyden declared: "that they refuse no honest persons free ingress to come and have their residence in this city; provided that such persons behave themselves and submit to the laws and ordinances: and therefore the coming of the Memorialists will be agreeable and welcome" which against the background of King James of England must have convinced them that they were in a "New World"; also Leyden in the cleanness and breadth of its streets, its Lindens and canals, the charm and elegance of its buildings—all as compared with London would have confirmed that conviction.

Thereafter they had twelve reasonably peaceful years "enjoying much sweet and delightful society and spiritual comfort together." Their numbers grew from England. They were adaptable, thrifty, laborious. They learned weaving or else they were hat makers, twine spinners, masons, carpenters, cabinet makers, tailors, brewers and bakers, even tobacco pipe makers.[17] They married, as the registries in Leyden Stadhuis record with detail of dates, witnesses, and their estate in pleasant detail. Familiar names appear: White, Carpenter, Fuller. Some of them even matriculated in Leyden University.

Nothing anywhere, say from 1609 to 1620, could have been so peaceful as Bradford twenty years after remembered the Christian Fellowship of Master Robinson's Church to have been. But as far as in them lay they did live at peace with all men. If they could not, they purged the church of the incurable and incorrigible "when no other means would serve; which seldom came to pass." (The discreetest of sentences.) There were at this time daily and hot disputes in the university, apparently between two members of the theological faculty.[18] Naturally Robinson could not stay away and being himself well grounded in the controversy, began to be "terrible to the Arminians" and finally put the Arminian professor, so Bradford held, to inglorious rout in a public disputation. (The opinion of said professor not on record.) Also in May, 1611, Robinson, his brother-in-law Tickens (a looking-glass maker), and two others bought a house of which transaction there is a detailed record in the Leyden equivalent of the Registry of Deeds, price about fourteen hundred English pounds; three hundred fifty pounds down and eighty-seven pounds, ten shillings annually thereafter "to the last penny." "And all this in good faith and without fraud."

---

[17] Dexter, *Congregationalism as Seen in Its Literature*, p. 386. An admirable training for living in a really new world.

[18] Calvinism vs. Arminianism. A classic controversy involving the Grace of God, human freedom, sin, etc., to be continued later in New England.

VIII

The Leyden Church become Pilgrims

For all that they were still exiles of poor estate and English. Leyden could not be final. There is pathos and a little humor in Bradford's analysis of the motives which led Robinson and Brewster to consider another migration: that Holland was a hard country to live in; that many, having spent their estate, were forced to return to England; that it was "grevious to live from under the protection of the State of England"—a strangely proud, pathetic, homesick reason. The only protection England had ever given them was the Clink, or Newgate or the shadow of the hangman's noose. Also they were likely to lose the name and language of Englishmen and very unlikely ever to influence the Dutch to keep the Sabbath properly, nor could they properly educate their own children.

Then follows a statesmanlike paragraph too long to quote, impossible to condense. In substance, if God would discover a place for them, "though in America," and the King and state permit them, they would there demonstrate the blessings of liberty, enlarge the dominions of the state and the Church and therefore the more "glorify God, do more good to our country,[19] better provide for our posterity . . . than ever in Holland." So much Governor Winslow wrote in 1646. Bradford says the same things, perhaps more intimately. They were getting old and tired. Leyden was not a good place for their children, who were becoming soldiers or sailors. There was also, though not mentioned, the unhappy example of the Ancient Church in Amsterdam. In Holland they would be lost. In some remote part of the world, they might become at least stepping stones for others to use to propagate and advance the "Kingdom of Christ."

There is behind and through this loose account of the twelve Leyden years an amount of detail, impossible to reduce to the scale of this volume. Three lines deserve a much more extended attention. First, the development of Robinson's views and convictions. Burrage, pp. 290 ff, thinks Henry Jacob to have strongly influenced Robinson in Leyden. He defines Jacob "as a Congregational, Non-Separatist Puritan."[20] He believed that within the framework of the Church of England each congregation was sufficient to manage its own affairs, without help from Archbishops and Bishops, apparently on a "covenant" basis. Jacob and

[19] Which is, perhaps, why "There'll always be an England."

[20] Jacob gathered a church of his own. It later followed the Pilgrims, almost as a body, to New England, settled in Scituate where part of it has maintained an unbroken existence (now Unitarian). Another part now in Barnstable claims to be the original Jacob church.

others were in Leyden (1610–1616) and modified Robinson's rigid Separatist attitude. Robinson ceased to be a "Close-Communionist"—if he ever had been one.

He received into his congregation members of the Church of England "without any renunciation of the Church of England, without any repentance for their idolatries" which pained the more strict. Not long before his death, Robinson stated his own attitude toward the Anglican Church in sympathetic but discriminating terms. He esteemed many in that Church, he said, as true partakers of the faith and fellow members of "that one mistical body of Christ scattered far and wide through the world." And that he had always, in spirit and affection, Christian fellowship and communion with them. But he could not, he stated, submit unto their church order and ordinances without being condemned of his own heart. In all this, and much else, Robinson was about two hundred years ahead of his time. He did give to the Leyden group a leaven of true catholicity which Congregationalism has conserved and exercised to a degree far beyond later, and now contemporaneous, groups which specialize in Church Unity.

A second line deserving attention is the publishing activity of Brewer and Brewster, who founded the first "Pilgrim Press." They published nothing but Pilgrim books, and their press was suppressed for it. The Pilgrim publications pained King James, a sensitive monarch. He moved Whitehall to action. Sir Dudley Carleton (apparently Ambassador at the Hague) was instructed to trace their authorship and ask the States General to apprehend him "as they tender His Majesty's friendship." The States General passed the task on to the authorities of the University of Leyden. They got Brewster (and his type) and "laid him fast" in the University's prison, a significant item for a University, which led sympathetic scholars to plead "Privilege." The University refused to surrender Brewster and after any amount of heated correspondence, Master Brewster's types were kept in jail and Brewster dismissed, which also pained King James, who rebuked his Lord Ambassador. Brewster was sought unsuccessfully for a year. His friends sheltered him and it is doubtful if the Dutch authorities really wanted to find him. But could the Mayflower have sailed without him?[21]

[21] Arber has thirty-five pages of letters *re* Brewster and his press. They are most intriguing. Their substance is that Brewster "being *incerti laris,* he is not yet to be lighted upon."

CHAPTER V

Pilgrim and Puritan in a New World

THE Pilgrim has made the historian his debtor by furnishing a detailed account of the conditions and difficulties of English migration in the seventeenth century. His was the second group to gain and maintain a foothold upon the Atlantic seaboard of what was to become the United States of America, and this has subordinated his religious quests to his social adventure. Many things combined to make the Pilgrim an ideal colonist. He was a born adventurer, else he would not have been a nonconformist. He was a nationalist (the word had not yet acquired its sinister significance) by all his racial inheritances, made proudly self-conscious by the Elizabethan Age. Lost in Leyden, he felt himself called to enlarge the dominions of his realm and the realm of Christ, a dual motivation whose combined force cannot easily be exaggerated. He had won strength from the disciplines he had undergone, the self-reliance they had engendered. He was the survival of the fittest for the task to which he half-unconsciously had been called.[1]

He drew the courage and capacity to endure, without which New Plymouth would be only a memory, from the high sources of his religious faith and devotion, though for a time the magnitude of their secular adventure naturally turned the minds of the Leyden group away from religious and ecclesiastical controversies. Having none to gainsay them, their free and simple worship became only a part of the routine of their always-endangered and laborious lives. The drum which called them to worship might at any time call them to the same "meeting house" to stand off the Indians and there must have been times when the Separatism for which they had so long contended became an almost unbearable loneliness. With a great price they obtained their freedom. Their story then must now be continued in terms of negotiations, decisions, and the details of getting to Plymouth Bay.

They began it all with a clear knowledge of perils and difficulties. They would be, they knew, "liable to famine and nakedness and the want (in a manner) of all things. . . . Then there would be the continual danger of the savage people, the very hearing of whose cannibalistic cruelties could not but move the very bowels of men to grate

[1]The saga of the selection of wheat fit for high Northern latitudes or corn to ripen in a short summer is the best analogy.

within them." They would need more money than their combined estates would amount to; neither did the issue of such other adventures in migration as they knew about assure them. On the other hand the Spaniard in Holland "might prove as cruel as the savages in America" (actually these savages were amateurs in cruelty as compared with the then Spaniard), "the famine and pestilence as sore, and their liberty less to look out for remedy."[2] So it was concluded to put their design into execution "by the best means they could."

Some of them were earnest for Guinea, where, they had heard, little labor was needed to live and less clothing. Others were for some parts of Virginia. But a sound instinct warned them against Guinea, and their concern for their cause of religion made them cautious of the Virginians. They were willing to live under the general government of Virginia, but at a protective distance. They began, also, negotiations with the Dutch, looking toward settlement in that indefinite region then known as the New Netherlands. The States General did not favor this, since they feared that English colonists in Dutch territory might dispose "His Majesty of Great Britain to people the aforesaid lands with the English Nation," a well-grounded fear. There was then (1620) actually no colony on the Island of Manhattan, only fur traders. But these negotiations, though fruitless, did leave them with a favorable impression of the Dutch territories in America and they later sought to get the Mayflower nearer the Hudson River before they left her.

I

THE LEYDEN CHURCH SEEKS SUPPORT AND A DESTINATION

In the late winter or early spring of 1620 Thomas Weston came to Leyden representing certain "Gentlemen Adventurers" in London who were willing to underwrite (so to speak) a colonial enterprise for the sake of the profit to be gained thereby in trade. The King was about to make a grant, to "sundry honorable Lords," of the more northerly regions of the Virginia Patent, to be quite secluded from the Jamestown government, and called New England.[3] Fishing off these coasts was said to be good and promised a return on investments. So Master Weston argued. The negotiations with the Dutch were broken off, and John Carver and Robert Cushman were sent to London to conclude an agreement with the Adventurers. (This in early spring, 1620.)

It had been a tedious and tricky business on the part of the London gentlemen, a vital affair for the Pilgrims. As early as 1617 the Leyden

---

[2] All this Bradford's narration.

[3] This grant was not signed till November, 1620. Arber thinks they could not have heard of it before they left the Continent (*The Story of the Pilgrim Fathers*, p. 304). But they might have heard.

group had sought to conciliate the King, with migration to Virginia in view. In seven articles signed by Robinson and Brewster, they professed their assent to the Thirty-nine Articles of 1562. They sought, they said, to keep spiritual communion in peace with "Conformists and Reformists." They acknowledged the King's majesty and authority to be supreme. He had the moral right to appoint bishops and civil overseers throughout his realm. They acknowledged the authority of the English bishops as derived from the King. (There must have been some mental reservation in this.) They desired to give all superiors due honor, to be in fellowship "with all that fear God, to have peace with all men and wherein they erred to be instructed."

The King's Secretary of State advised His Majesty favorably about this petition. The petitioners, he said, were troublesome in England but they might in America advance His Majesty's dominions and enlarge the gospel. The King thought it a good and honest notion and, being Scotch, asked about possible profits. Fishing, he was told, promised gain. "So *God* have my soul!" he exclaimed, " 'tis an honest trade! It was the apostles' own calling." Thereupon the agents of the "pilgrims" went to the First Virginia Company (this must have been still 1618) from whom they received a patent (February 1619), a loan of three hundred pounds, which they later paid back, and a definite agreement. Now there were, for the confusion of the historian, two Virginia Companies, both chartered in 1606: (a) The London Virginia Company with a grant of territory between 34° and 41° North Latitude; (b) The Second or Plymouth Virginia Company with a grant between 38° and 45° North latitude.

This apparent inability of the King's proper bureau either to add or subtract resulted in confusions and counter-claims and, as far as the Pilgrims were eventually concerned, uncertainty first as to where they wanted to go and, second, once on the high seas as to where they really were going. The London Company went bankrupt, the Plymouth Company surrendered its charter, and the New England Company, as noted, took over the Northern coasts. The Pilgrims seem to have held under the Plymouth Company to begin with and finally to have landed on territory to which they had no patent.

The "Adventurers" who financed the Pilgrim's migration were a voluntary association of about seventy persons of various station and possession. "They aimed," so Captain John Smith said, "to do good and plant religion." They entertained also, mistakenly as it turned out, some hope of worldly gain. They helped plant religion and so did great good, but made no profit. They must have known the religious and church convictions of the Leyden group, their history and the disfavor in which they were held by English authorities, since these things had not been done in a corner. One may assume amongst them, therefore, a sympathetic attitude toward Independency, though their later attitudes should qualify that assumption.

It is difficult to brief the agreement finally concluded, after much negotiation and amendment, between the Leyden group and the Company. It was a joint-stock enterprise. The shares seem to have been rated at ten pounds each. The Company paid in money and the migrants contributed themselves, each person over sixteen years of age being rated at ten pounds. All profits and benefits were, for seven years, to remain undivided in the common stock. In substance there would be no private property. At the end of seven years there would be an equal division between the Adventurers and the Planters. These conditions were sufficiently modified in the course of the negotiations to permit the Pilgrims two free days a week to work for themselves and to receive their houses and improved lands at the end of the seven years. Actually the right of private property and individual initiative was permitted long before the seven years were up, and the Colony bought out the Company.

All this fascinating detail is complicated enough, but there is in all the documents which deal with the enterprise—and there are more than one would think—a showing of good sense and practical wisdom on the part of Robinson and Brewster. They seem to have been men who would hold their own in any directors' meeting. They were shrewd and far-sighted and as little like Sixteenth Century religious enthusiasts as could be. After about three years of planning, exploring, bargaining, much letter writing, journeys from Leyden to London and back, and Elder Brewster's being sought by the English authorities, they were ready. The Gentlemen Adventurers would furnish them ship and gear and they hoped to land somewhere on the North Atlantic Seaboard, God willing.

"They sought the Lord by a public and solemn fast for his guidance." The guidance so secured seems to have been soundly practical. They would not all go at once. The youngest and strongest should go first and they that went should freely offer themselves. If the majority went, the pastor would go with them; "if not, the Elder only." Finally, "if the Lord should frown" upon their proceedings, those that went would return, those who remained helping them. "If God should be pleased to favor them," those who went and stayed would "help over such as were poor and ancient and willing to come." The major part stayed.

II

THE DEPARTURE FROM LEYDEN

The partings were like those of St. Paul with his friends at Miletus, or like all partings across which lies the shadow of finality, tender with the tears of things. Winslow's and Bradford's descriptions (here combined) are classic: "They that stayed at Leyden feasted us (this was after the Fast) at our Pastor's house, being large, where we refreshed ourselves after our tears with the singing of Psalms . . . there being many of the congregation very expert in music: and indeed it was the sweetest melody that ever mine ears heard." "The time being come that they must depart, they were accompanied by most of their brethren . . . into a town . . . called Delftshaven where the ship, the Speedwell, lay ready to receive them. So they left that goodly and pleasant city, which had been their resting place near twelve years, but they knew that they were pilgrims and looked not much on these things, but lifted up their eyes to the heavens, their dearest country, and quieted their spirits."

Winslow gives a summary of the "wholesome counsel Master Robinson gave them." It was wise as Robinson was always wise and for openness of mind and spirit could not then, or too often now, easily be matched. A sentence or two has become memorable. They were to follow him no further than he had followed Christ; "and if God should reveal anything to us by any other instrument of his, to be as ready to receive it, as ever we were to receive any truth by his ministry. For he was very confident that the Lord had more truth and light to break forth out of his holy word." He urged also—and this bore strongly on the whole future of American Congregationalism—that they should study union with English Puritanism.[4]

They came with a prosperous wind to Southampton where they found the "bigger ship" come from London with all the rest of their company. (The name of the "bigger ship" does not occur in the Bradford manuscript. Her name, The Mayflower, first appears in the Official Records of the "Old Colony" in 1623.) It was not safe for Brewster and others against whom the bishops had acted to go to London. Hence, they went to Southampton. The company managed in the end to get away without official hindrance, but the Speedwell was something else. Her unseaworthiness may have changed the pattern of New England colonial history.[5] She was "leaky as a sieve" under full sail because she was overmasted. She had been refitted in Holland and pressed with too much sail (the fault, Arber thinks, of the Pilgrims themselves). The master of the ship, Reynolds, had no stomach for the enterprise at best and welcomed an excuse first to put in for repairs at Dartmouth and,

[4] The magistrates of the city of Leyden gave them a good recommendation. "These English," they said, "have lived amongst us now these twelve years; and yet we never had any suit or accusation come against any of them." Arber, *The Story of the Pilgrim Fathers*, p. 152.

[5] Normally the ships should have left Southampton early in August and made the Hudson River in early autumn. What then? No New Plymouth; maybe no American Congregationalism—so Arber.

finally, a hundred leagues beyond Lands-End to go back to Plymouth and put everything in the "bigger ship." These delays disheartened some, who themselves went back, and finally put the rest to sea in an over-crowded vessel in September to face the autumnal North Atlantic and disembark in winter on a desolate shore. (The tradition is that Master Reynolds was a tricky rascal, which may be. He had only to crowd sail to make the Speedwell a sieve.)

III

The Epics of the Mayflower

One hundred and two persons finally left Plymouth on the May-flower. William Butten died on the way across and Oceanus Hopkins was born. So there were one hundred and two of them when the "com-pact" was signed. In December Peregrine White, the first born in New England, made one hundred and three.[6] They were at sea over two months, storm-tossed, imperiled, uncomfortable beyond description. One tradition is that their captain deliberately kept them away from Vir-ginia, but what they seem actually to have desired was a landing near the Hudson. The New World welcomed them with shoals and breakers and Cape Cod's Pollock-rip. It was perilous navigation in the unchar-tered waters. They had the sea behind them and an empty region before them out of which to choose, and which they had not purposefully sought. The charter of the Adventurers may not have covered that par-ticular territory, but that was a detail which could be remedied.

For all that the region was not superficially unexplored or unmapped. It was already known (Captain John Smith takes credit for that) as a marvelous fishing ground. Thirty to fifty sail went yearly, says Captain John, to the New England coast to trade and to fish, which does not fit in with the isolation of the Plymouth Colony. Smith later (1630) claimed that if the group had taken his advice and used his maps, they would have saved themselves much misery. Instead, to avoid charges, they "would try their own conclusions though with great loss" being "con-trarious" people who would learn only through costly experience. For all that he thought well of the Pilgrims, though they refused his help and made too little, he held, of his advice.[7]

It is a shame to condense their great little epic. They deemed the first land they saw to be Cape Cod, "goodly land wooded to the brink of

[6] There are full and detailed lists of families, individuals, and their economic station, but these should be the specialty of the genealogist.

[7] The most vivid and detailed account of their first experience is found in a "Relation or Journal of the Beginnings and Proceedings of the English Plantation settled at Ply-mouth in New England" etc., London, printed for John Bellamie, 1622. It is anonymous (signed G. Mourt, possibly George Morton). It would seem of composite authorship "writ by the various actors."

the sea." The harbor at Provincetown was commodious. Whales were playing in its waters, but there were no cod. They tried the "mussels" with distressful results. The beach being shallow, they were forced to wade ashore (result: coughs and colds). All this did not conduce to harmony and, there being some appearance of faction, they drew up the "Association and Agreement" famous in history as the Mayflower Compact. (Spelling modernized. See Appendix for original form.)

"In the name of God, Amen. We whose names are underwritten, the loyal subjects of our dread Sovereign Lord King James; by the grace of God, of Great Britain, France and Ireland King; Defender of the Faith; etc."

"Having undertaken for the glory of God, and advancement of the Christian faith, and honour of our King and Country, a voyage to plant the first colony in the northern parts of Virginia; [we] do by these presents, solemnly and mutually, in the presence of God and one of another, covenant and combine ourselves together into a Civil Body Politic, for our better ordering and preservation; and furtherance of the ends aforesaid; and, by virtue hereof, to enact, constitute and frame such just and equal laws, ordinances, acts, constitutions, offices, from time to time, as shall be thought most meet and convenient for the general good of the Colony; unto which we promise all due submission and obedience.

"In witness whereof, we have hereunder subscribed our names.[8] Cape Cod, 11th of November, in year of the reign of our Sovereign Lord King James of England, France and Ireland 18: and of Scotland 54, Anno Domini 1620."

This needs no comment. The compact was as simple as it was inevitable. It was natural for men whose corporate religious life was supported by a covenant so to constitute their "Civil Body Politic." The genesis of it was in the essential fibre of their being, the inevitability of it in their situation, the direct simplicity of it in their souls and their speech. Not until Gettysburg battlefield was dedicated would so epochally much be said in an equal space of words, or the words themselves carry so grave a weight.[9] And the Gettysburg classic did no more than continue the Covenant. King James was still their "dread sovereign" but they were their own men. If a partisan cared to press it, it was and is a Congregational covenant drawn by a great social and religious philosophy, articulating a timeless passion, meeting a great occasion with the directness of freedom and the wisdom of discipline. Alongside it a "State

---

[8] This compact was signed by 41 out of the 65 adult male passengers then on board.

[9] I (Atkins) have not counted, but I should think that from "Having" to "Obedience" Lincoln's address and the Covenant are almost the same length.

Church" is an artificial ingenuity; here religion and society for a brief but shining time were one "in the Name of God. Amen."

The Covenant was part of the day's work, but where should they settle? Autumns on Cape Cod are often late and soft and kind—and misleading. There should have been some bronze of oak leaves in the forests against the green of the pines and whiteness of birch. The ground they found, under the sand, to be excellent black earth. "The wood for the most part open and without underwood; fit either to go, or ride in." They used juniper for firewood while they lay at Provincetown. It smelled strong and sweet. Their first enterprise of discovery covered a good deal of the shank and hook of Cape Cod, brought them minor alarums with Indians, tantalizing sights of game and birds and thirty-six goodly ears of corn which they brought away with them. Also there was much wading in the shallow sea, and coughs and colds.

Their second enterprise of discovery led them through regions further west to a vacant Indian village and netted them still more corn. "It was God's good Providence that we found this corn: for else we know not how we should have done." Neither of these "discoveries" quite satisfied them. There was, their pilot had heard, another promising harbor twenty-four miles across from their then anchorage. Thither they made shift to go in their shallop; and, being landed, were for the first time under arrow fire from the Indians. (Enter Captain Miles Standish —no casualties.) They found Plymouth Bay at last, thought it right for their needs, and returned to the Mayflower. The master sailed that much-enduring boat into Plymouth Bay. A party explored still further, so far as Kingston, but now the need to disembark the whole group was urgent and the season had turned vile. So finally they brought, not without peril, the people ashore at Plymouth.

IV

ASHORE AT PLYMOUTH

Now they had been on and off the Mayflower for a month, any day of which might have been Forefather's Day. Romance has chosen Monday, December 11, O. S., for on that day, says the narration, "we sounded the harbour and found it a very good harbour for our shipping: we marched also into the land: and found divers cornfields and little running brooks, a place very good for situation." The Mayflower was then still at Provincetown with the majority of the company.[10] She weighed anchor on the fifteenth to make for Plymouth Harbour, which, after

[10] It seems, therefore, that the delightful picture of the Pilgrims, men, women, and children, disembarking in a body and going ashore with "Plymouth Rock" as a stepping stone can hardly be documented.

bearing off to sea because of a northwest wind, they managed on Saturday, December 16, "so it pleased God . . . [that] we came safely into a safe harbour."

What follows in this narration is both trivial and epic, pitiful and splendid. They built shelters for themselves and a fort. They had a sense of Indians moving about them in the shadowed forests. They strove through sleet and rain and wind. They were grateful for food and safety and made little of their miseries—and they died, almost half of them. In 1621 they laid out "meersteads" and "garden plots" which must have been of a communal character. This got them too little corn and too much misery so that in the spring of 1623 they resolved to "set corn, every man for his own particular: and in that regard trust to themselves." This had very good success, for it made all hands very industrious. "Even the women now went willingly into the field." And they kept learning. There was for a time a little peace amongst the Indians themselves . . . and "we for our part walk as peaceably and safely in the wood as in the highways of England."

Something must be allowed for Winslow's roseate descriptions, as though the guile of the real estate promoter touched his usually sober goose quill. For the temper of the air he finds as agreeable as England. There is an abundance of fish and fowl; "our Bay is full of lobsters;" "here are grapes . . . strawberries [there still are], plums [still highly esteemed for jelly], and roses." "The country wanted only industrious men to employ it." Also the Pilgrims, pilgrims no longer, had learned out of bitter experience how future expeditions should be fitted.[11] By 1623 the colony was small, fairly well rooted, very slowly growing, but a going concern.

V

CONCERNING THEIR RELIGIOUS AND FINANCIAL ESTATE

Now for men and women whose master motive for almost twenty years had been free worship in their own way, the paucity of reference in letters home to their great joy in free worship is arresting. The explanation would seem to be simple. The sheer struggle for existence took everything they had. They were in a new world which had captured their imagination. They were beginning, inside of three years, to become Yankees, a shrewd type which, except on rare occasions, does not allow its religion to get out of hand. Also they had no longer anyone to argue religion with until they had developed their own contentious factions, and Plymouth Colony could not as yet afford the luxury of faction. The neighboring Indians, on the contrary, had an oversupply of factions and

---

[11] The detail is fascinating: paper and linseed oil for windows, cotton yarn for lamps. Butter they wanted very much (no cows yet), etc.

sought to entangle the colonists therein at considerable and tedious length, the accounts whereof gain interest from the attempts of the early chronicler, who spelled his own English inconsistently, to Anglicize Indian names.

Since the Pilgrims, in setting out, had advanced hopes of doing missionary work among the Indians as one of their lawful reasons for emigrating, they did their best as opportunity offered. The Indians hearkened with grave attention and "liked well to hear of God's work of creation and preservation; of his laws and ordinances, especially the Ten Commandments." They excepted against "only the Seventh," thinking there were many inconveniences in it, that a man should be tied to one woman. The Pilgrims also sought to teach the Indians to say grace before meals.

In theory the new Plymouth church and the Leyden church were one church under John Robinson, pastor. He had expected himself to follow the Mayflower, but the Pilgrims were poor and the merchant adventurers, rather inconsistently, were willing to finance the congregation's passage but not that of the minister, who was still held a Browneist. But a pastor three thousand miles away is little comfort, and the church suffered. Critics complained that there was "wante of both the Sacraments." The reply of the colonists is just and sad. "The more is our greife that our pastor is kept from us, by whom we might Injoye them, for we used to have the Lords Supper every Sabbath, and baptisme as often as there was occasion of children to baptize."

The poor little colony was everybody's fair game. Puritans made them as much trouble as the Establishment.[12] They kept Robinson in Leyden and sent over one John Lyford or Lyforde, an unctious rogue whose unmasking brightens a sombre narrative. They would impose "the French Discipline" upon Fort Hill. Their concern for Presbyterianism did not prevent them from charging outrageous interest on small loans to keep starving women and children alive.[13] The factors to whom the Pilgrims entrusted the trade goods cheated them going and coming. One of their shiploads was captured by a courteous French pirate. The letters which passed between New Plymouth and Leyden are sad and tender. Robinson died on March 1, 1625. Roger White of Leyden wrote

[12] The final liquidation of the commercial aspect of the enterprise is a long and complicated story. The colonists finally bought themselves out for nine annual payments of 200 pounds a year. Their leaders became their trustees (with the equivalent of a lien on the colony). They traded in beaver furs and Indian corn, bought up a bankrupt trading post (at Monhegan Island), salvaged a wrecked French ship, and in nine years paid out. They were embryonic Yankees, shrewd, laborious, honest to the last penny.

[13] The Lyforde episode is told at length in John Brown's *Pilgrim Fathers*. Plot and counterplot, opened letters, espionage and counter-espionage, Seventeenth Century "Fifth Column" business.

a moving account of his death to Bradford: "if either prayers, tears, or means would have saved his life, he had not gone hence." He was buried in St. Peters Church and "the University and ministers of the city accompanied him to his grave with all their accustomed solemnities, bewailing the great loss . . . some of them sadly affirmed, that all the Churches of Christ sustained. . . ."[14] It was a year before they knew it at Plymouth. (Miles Standish brought back the news after a business trip to London, where the plague made negotiations difficult.)

The Pilgrims were equal to the adjustment of a pastorless state. There is a classic description often quoted of the settlement written in 1627 by one De Rasièrés, a Dutch envoy sent over to further trade between the colony and the States General. Their houses were hewn plank with gardens behind, enclosed in a stockade. They had a corporate meeting place with cannon atop (one 1200 pounds in weight). They assembled for worship to the sound of drums and marched up and in military form, cloaked and armed. The Governor brought up the procession with the minister at his right and Miles Standish marshalling it all. Then they did celebrate the sacrament of the Lord's Supper, heard the word and prayed, listened to "prophecying" (Roger Williams was there that Sunday), and went afterwards gravely home. There would have been in 1627 an abundance of other processions in the great churches of Christendom, vested and ordered according to historic liturgies, but one may gravely wonder where there was anywhere any processional so significant in its simplicity, so hallowed by faith and courage and sacrifice as that silent procession up Fort Hill. If all those who had hoped and suffered and died to make it possible could have become there and then reincorporate, they would have matched the innumerable company of the Book of Revelation.

For eight years and seven months the Leyden-Plymouth church was the only church in what is now New England. The colony grew slowly. Its possible constituency was always a minority and limited in resource. One may measure its territorial extensions along the pleasant coast by the dates of the founding of new churches, always coincident with the setting out of a new town ("township" outside New England). By 1632 there were folk enough to plant Duxbury (say eight miles from Plymouth) and Marshfield (say fifteen miles).[15] They prospered modestly, but they lacked ships for trade and fishing. The beaver would soon be used up and out, there was water power only for little neighborhood mills. The soil could be coaxed into productiveness but was not encouragingly

14 Burgess, *The Pastor of the Pilgrim Fathers, a Biography of John Robinson*, pp. 302 ff. This is an admirable book and sets forth much new knowledge about Robinson.
15 The town of Marshfield dates its incorporation from 1641.

fertile.[16] The later history of Plymouth church will presently be touched upon; the general history of the "Old Colony" belongs to Massachusetts history. The general bequest of the Pilgrims, their faith, their courage, their wisdom and their ways of worship, was peace and kindliness. The shadows of intolerance and fanaticism which darken the early history of Massachusetts Bay do not reach to Plymouth. They dealt more fairly with the Indian than any other colony save William Penn's or Roger Williams'. Their descendants have good reason to be proud of them.

Though they could not of themselves have populated Massachusetts nor framed New England Congregationalism, they did when the times were ripe influence it in ways far beyond their numbers and their status. In many ways the currents of population and power which set toward Boston Bay were far more full and strong, but the true genesis of American Congregationalism is from Scrooby to Leyden and from Leyden to Fort Hill in New Plymouth, where for one bleak winter the living did not dare to mark the graves of their dead lest the Indians lurking in winter woods should know how few they were.

VI

ENTER THE PURITAN

The same letter (April 28, 1625) in which Roger White wrote "his loving friend, Mr. William Bradford, Governor of Plymouth in New England," the news of John Robinson's death, reported another death. ". . . we have lost our old King James, who departed this life about a month ago . . . and we have a new King Charles of whom there is great hope of good. . . ." That hope was premature. For as White wrote to his "very loving friend" the first of December, 1625, the King had already in a proclamation dated the 13th of May (1625) expressed his full resolution: "to the end that there may be one uniform course of government in and through all his whole monarchy," Virginia included, "so that some conceive he will have both the same civil and ecclesiastic government that is in England, which occasioneth their fear."

This resolution of the King, with the conception of his own divine right to be both state and church which lay beneath and behind it, began an epochal chapter in England and New England. His headless body would finally write "finished" at the end of it, and unfinished as well.

[16] It must have been well timbered. No first growth pine are likely left. There were oak certainly for so late as 1840 (and later) the North River was famous for its ship-yards and sailing craft. And there were stones. It is hard to see how the Pilgrims could have escaped landing on one. Old stone walls, mute witnesses of an incredible toil now loose themselves in old fields retaken by second or third wood growth. And the amateur gardener still finds the supply unexhausted. But it is a lovely region in which the old is treasured and restored and the quiet roads wind through three hundred years of memory.

For beginning with Charles' taking the throne, the tension of forces which had been in action in England since Elizabeth's death would finally issue in civil war, and what no conference had been able to resolve would be fought out on the fields of Marston Moor and Naseby, and not there resolved. The throne and the Church were finally to be called to account by embattled Puritanism and the auditing would be at once tragic and nobly creative.

This study began with a reference to the "Millenary Petition" addressed to King James on his way to Whitehall, in which almost a thousand ministers of the English Church prayed him for a much more thorough-going reformation of Queen Elizabeth's Church. They would have more preaching and less liturgy, fewer vestments and more well-educated clergy. They would restrain the bishops, purge English worship of any vestige of Roman Catholicism and enforce upon both the clergy and the laity of the Church a far more godly, righteous, and sober life than was then in evidence. How far the King could have carried England with him had he enabled the Millenary Petition with his full royal power is beyond knowing. Very likely he could not have so carried it.

But there must have been possibilities of adjustment which might have altered the future course of English political and religious history. Whether or no it was in the King's power to have made them, he had no mind to try. The Hampton Court Conference, as we have seen, settled nothing, save that the King meant to have his way and having savored the quality of Presbyterianism in Scotland, meant to have none of it in England.[17] The first result of the King's policy was the alienation of the pulpit, at a time and in a situation when the power of the pulpit cannot easily be exaggerated.[18] The realm was seamed with discontents, rivalries and ambitions, and the Stuarts had an infallible gift for alienating in turn every recalcitrant group, every protesting interest. The harm, in the long last, they did others was not comparable with the harm they did themselves.

It is impossible to understand the course of Puritanism during this period of English and American history without a recognition of the strategic part played by the Puritan preachers. Puritanism itself was a preachers' movement, the prophet challenging the priest. This has always been a risky business, especially when the magistrate is on the priest's side; but until the outbreak of the Revolution it was possible for the

---

[17] This is a loose statement, for Puritanism should not be too closely identified with Presbyterianism. But Cartwright and his associates certainly looked to Geneva for the Scriptural model of Church government.

[18] For an entirely competent study of Puritan preaching see *The Rise of Puritanism,* William Haller. Parts of this chapter are deeply in debt to Haller.

preacher campaigning, so to speak, upon a purely religious and theological terrain to supply the magistrates no case against him, and at the same time to create political and social attitudes which would in, time become an affair not only for magistrates but for armies.

"The Puritan imagination," Haller says, "saw the life of the spirit as pilgrimage and battle." As a pilgrim, a Christian should not and would not entangle himself in the things of this world, and yet the labor and austerities with which he carried through his pilgrimage conduced to a most comfortable accumulation of the things of this world. Vanity Fair was only a way station, but he proved himself a shrewd trader in its booths. Any pilgrim must, however, contemplate some issue of his pilgrimage in a better country or else his heart would fail him. He might naturally therefore sometimes wonder, confusing the temporal and the eternal, whether his own present realm might not become that better country and, like Blake, let not his sword sleep in his hand till he had

> ". . . built Jerusalem
> In England's green and pleasant land."

Since life is a battle, he might also find it difficult to distinguish between material and purely spiritual weapons.

The Old Testament and not a little of St. Paul supplied the preacher with enough "images of wayfaring and warfaring"[19] to kindle his imagination and adorn his rhetoric. The result was an ornate pulpit style and a kind of nebulous splendor in Puritan preaching which confuses and fascinates. There is an astounding excess and ingenuity of imagery along with keen insight and the forthright use of strong words. Satan is always on the alert, and though a man may "take twelve of the thirteen steps to heaven, yet except he stride the thirteenth, he shall misse Heaven-Gate, and fall into the fire of Hell forever."[20]

The Anglicans were not behind in preaching either, and yielded to none in ingenuity of image and device (for example, John Donne). They prided themselves on their finer culture and continued the "Elizabethan love of witty phrase and poetic image." The Puritan thought himself more spiritual, if less witty, and opposed the "Word of Wisdom" to the wisdom of words. In the end the Puritan preacher and not the Anglican, in the battle of the pulpits, won the popular mind. (Haller again.)

Now, to repeat, all this was done in a region where the writs of the magistrates did not run, nor as yet involved the preacher in any pronounced opposition to the authorities. It did stir up and maintain highly emotional attitudes, and there were implications in it of a revo-

---

[19] The fine phrase is Haller's.
[20] Out of all this John Bunyan would presently make Everyman's *Pilgrim Progress*; after which all the rest could be forgotten.

lutionary character. Such preaching habituated the popular mind to the ideal of warfare and made it easy, when the times were ripe, to exchange the sword of the spirit for the weapons of Cromwell's Ironsides. Somewhere in and through it was the conception of a state ordered and controlled in the Puritan way, the realm of God on earth.

All this was in action during the whole reign of King James. He dealt with it as he could, but so much was beyond his reach. The Independents and Separatists who wanted Reformation without tarrying for any could be reached and were reached and dealt with as we have seen, but this slow shaping of a public opinion, militant, discontented, seeking partly what it knew and more it did not know, could not be reached and controlled. It could be threatened, irritated, and mishandled, all of which intensified the force with which it finally came into action. What it did in England is a great chapter in English history.[21] Our concern is what it did to and in New England.

VII

MASSACHUSETTS BAY IS CHARTERED .

The Puritans, Independents, and Separatists had trouble enough under James. Their estate became much worse under Charles and theological rancors grew. The Puritan had always been and continued Calvinist, but to a considerable degree so were and are the Thirty-nine Articles. They offered little ground for theological disputes. But around 1630 the Church theologians began to repudiate election and reprobation. One of them wrote that he considered predestination the "root of all rebellion and disobedient intractableness, and schism and sauciness in the country." The Puritans did not take this lying down and accused the bishops of "Heretical and Grace-destroying Arminian novelties which have of late invaded, affronted and almost shouldered out of doors the ancient, established, and resolved doctrines of our Church."[22] "Our Church" is significant. They, the Puritans thought, were the true Church; the bishops were usurpers.

The high churchmen not only provoked the laity by new doctrines; they so affirmed the Divine Right of Kings in general and Charles in particular, that to resist any ordinance of the King was to resist the ordinance of God and receive damnation; which would make any Parliament either an assembly of rubber stamps or candidates for damnation. This would involve the power of the purse in any disputed question of money sought or granted, and on this, the question of taxation,

[21] Carlyle, *Oliver Cromwell Introduction*, called it the "last of all our heroisms." But there have been new English heroisms since Carlyle's time.
[22] Miller, *Orthodoxy in Massachusetts*, pp. 41 ff.

the King and Parliament finally came to fatal odds. The accounts of the last days of the Parliament of 1629 are stirring enough. His majesty dissolved it by Proclamation, calling some of its members "vipers." For about eleven years thereafter he reigned without a Parliament. During these eleven years the Massachusetts Bay Colony was founded.

It was in its inception purely a trading company.[23] The chartered companies of the period were not corporations in the present legal sense. They were a participation by the members in a common line of enterprise. They secured travelers in foreign lands the favor and protection of the crown and avoided the dangers of competition between fellow countrymen, being, therefore, in theory monopolistic. Their charters, therefore, gave them (the trading companies) unusual rights. The "governors" and "assistants" had a power not only to supervise and direct the business venture, but they could also "oversee the conduct of the members in many ways," and regulate the details of their social and private activities. They were in fact or possibility "bodies politic" and thus had in them the germs of self-directing political communities. But the Massachusetts Bay Company was the only trading company which became a political commonwealth. (Hart as cited)

This the Company owed to provisions peculiar to its own charter and the careless generosity, which he must have regretted, of Charles the First.[24] The genesis and development of the Massachusetts Bay Company is a history in itself, compact with factual detail, complicated in action and indispensable to any understanding of American Congregationalism.[25] The Pilgrims planted the first permanent settlement in New England, but the Bay Colony became the Province and the Province became the Commonwealth. For all its religious content Massachusetts Bay was in structure and legal form a trading company and it so remained until the charter was annulled in 1684. It all began, specifically, with the "Dorchester Adventure."[26] Dorchester (England) merchants had been sending ships to fish for cod off the New England coast. It would be well, they thought, to have a base on the New England mainland. They would not then need to send so many fishermen across, which was slow and costly.

[23] Hart, *Commonwealth History of Massachusetts*, vol. 1, p. 64. "British Colonial expansion from the days of John Cabot to the days of Cecil Rhodes has proceeded almost always in its first stages through the medium of private business enterprise."

[24] This complicated business of "Charters" in New England colonial history must have given generations of school boys and girls headaches.

[25] This account is taken from two authorities: *Commonwealth History of Massachusetts*, edited by Albert Bushnell Hart, and *Orthodoxy in Massachusetts*, Perry Miller. This general acknowledgment makes it unnecessary to be always citing authorities and pages. Miller's contribution will be indicated as needed. John Dickinson contributed the chapter (5) in Hart which is here most drawn upon.

[26] A schoolboy's headaches would also be aggravated by the fact that the companies were sometimes named from the English City in which the merchants seeking trade lived, and sometimes from the region they sought to colonize.

They would get help from the settlement and between seasons the settlers could turn farmers and so provision the ships for their return voyages, or sell to other fishers using the waters. Also the fishermen, being nine or ten months from home, suffered from a want of religious instruction. This seems to have been the suggestion of John White, local Dorchester minister.

It is likely also that the somewhat roseate account of the semi-paradisaical character of unpopulated Massachusetts, which the Pilgrims about this time were getting published in London, may have captured the imagination of the Dorchester adventurers. So a little religion, the hope of gain and the allure of a new world led them to contribute needed capital and try for a new world settlement. They put Roger Conant, who had left the Plymouth Pilgrims because of religious difference, in charge and naturally named the new settlement Dorchester. The Dorchester venture was a failure, eventually came under the direction of John Endicott, took on a definite religious character, and lost its nominal distinction. Meanwhile a new accession of strength came from England.

VIII

Winthrop's Fleet is Launched

The Earl of Warwick (Puritan) secured from the Council for New England and for Endicott and five associates a spacious grant between the Merrimac and the Charles Rivers, reaching indefinitely west.[27] The religious motif now enters strongly. The project attracted Puritans of rank and resource who would plant their gospel in New England. These associated themselves with Endicott and secured another Charter from the crown, this time as the Massachusetts Bay Company. The King was off guard when he granted it, being much occupied with a recalcitrant Parliament. The Charter was granted March 4, 1629.[28] Six days later the King dissolved Parliament and announced that thereafter he would give no account of his actions save to God alone. Evidently he did not secure divine approval, for he was subsequently compelled to reconvene Parliament.

The last eight years had been hot with controversy in England and confusion amongst Puritans. They were concerned with larger things (so they thought) than trade in Massachusetts. The crisis of 1629 brought matters to a head—significant and far-reaching matters on both sides of the Atlantic. Oliver Cromwell went home to stock a grazing farm and Winthrop began to assemble his fleet. Eleven ships bearing Winthrop,

[27] Some of this territory had already been granted to Robert Gorges. Result: future complications. The same territory was later granted to Massachusetts Bay. The council was ungeographically generous.

[28] The "1621" in Hart must certainly be a misprint.

the Charter, between nine hundred and one thousand immigrants, the future Commonwealth of Massachusetts, a history beyond the dream of the most daring, and the enabling force of American Congregationalism, sailed from Cowes and Southampton in the spring of 1630. Oliver Cromwell was then being named Justice of the Peace for the Borough of Huntington. They reached the New England coast in June and the loveliest month in the somewhat capricious climate of that coast welcomed them.

All the freight of these eleven ships was historic and prophetic. But why was the Charter aboard? And by what right? There is no denying the significance of its being there. That meant self-government for the colony, the beginnings of American democracy, and other things much less praiseworthy. Historians and lawyers are never done debating the legality of the transfer. There was no express language in the instrument itself requiring "the company to reside and exercise its power in England," but the docket under which it passed the Seals states in as plain language as possible that it provided for "the election of governors here in England" which doubtless was the official mind and intention.

The provisions of the Charter were simple. The stockholders or "freemen" should meet every three months in a "General Court." The "General Court" elected the officers—twenty of them—governors, deputy governors, eighteen directors. The Governor governed, the assistants (directors) managed. The General Court could admit freemen (new stockholders) and "make laws and ordinances for the good and welfare of said company, provided such laws and ordinances were not contrary or repugnant to the laws and statues of the realm of England." The criminal jurisdiction could go no further than lawful fines, imprisonments or such and other corrections as were permitted similar corporations in this "our realm of England." In general by precedent and judicial decisions an appeal lay, in criminal jurisdiction, from the courts of the corporations to the courts of the realm.

In plain words the General Court of Massachusetts Bay could not impose or execute the death penalty save after an appeal had been heard by an English court. When, therefore, the four Quakers were executed in 1659, the authorities exceeded their lawful power, but this made no difference to their victims. In substance, self-government went to New England with the Charter. Competent historians maintain that the adventurers meant from the first to remove the company to New England. All this affected the religious conduct of the colony so directly as to have become an important phase of Congregational development.

So much for the Charter. The seven hundred-odd emigrants aboard Winthrop's fleet were assembled by Winthrop and a small group on Cannon Street in London. White had found supporters for the "Dor-

chester Adventure" in the west country. Winthrop's company came from
London City and the eastern English counties. This region—old East
Anglia—was the nursery of Independents and Separatists and was in general strongly opposed to the established Church. Names are always significant, being carried across seas and continents by the homesickness of
the migrant. The names of towns and cities in eastern England are repeated in America along the eastern division of the Boston and Maine
railway, like, as Uriah Heep said, "the ringing of old belles;" the names
on the smoke-darkened headstones in Bunhill Fields burying ground have
been continued on headstones in uncounted New England burying
grounds. The motives of Winthrop's migrants were not wholly religious.
The hard-pressed tenantry of the nobility and landed gentry responded,
as the "homesteader" has always responded, to the promise of a hundred
acres of land in a new world. And there were always born adventurers.

The leaders of the movement were in sympathy with the Puritan
elements in the Establishment but apparently that was not pressed.
Many of Winthrop's passengers were still loyal to the English Church,
and they meant still to be Englishmen. So Higginson said in an often
quoted passage. "We will not say as the Separatists were wont to say at
their leaving of England, 'Farewell Babylon! Farewell Rome!' But we
will say, 'Farewell Dear England! Farewell the Church of God in England and all the Christian friends there! We do not go to New England as
Separatists from the Church of England; though we cannot but separate
from the corruptions in it; but we go to practise the Positive Part of
Church Reformation and propagate the Gospel in America." A little of
this may have been meant for the King and all those in authority, and
the substance of it sincere.[29]

IX

THE PURITAN IDEAL OF THE CHURCH

The Winthrop Company scattered themselves through the Boston
Bay region and their settlements eventually became what is now the
Boston "Metropolitan Area." Other ships followed and by the end of
1630 there were an estimated two thousand persons in the colony. The
religious or at least the ecclesiastical picture changed almost immediately.
Three thousand miles of "unplumbed, salt, estranging sea" changed every
perspective. The Puritan would naturally have set up the ecclesiastical
system of Scotland and Geneva in New England, but you cannot have
Synods and General Assemblies with only two thousand people.

[29] For a most detailed account of Winthrop, his fleet and his company see Banks,
The Winthrop Fleet of 1630.

Perry Miller, in an excellent study of orthodoxy in New England maintains, in a well argued and documented chapter, that there was a strong element amongst the protestors against the Establishment who might be called "Non-Separatist Congregationalists," though the name is anticipatory. These had as little love for Presbyterianism as for bishops. "What a terrible Popedome and Primacie these rigid Presbyters desire." It is not easy to put what they wanted in plain words. They could not do it themselves. They apparently wanted the solidity of an established Church and the free action of independent churches—a pretty impossible combination. If such a system could be managed, it would still be a part of the Church of England, but would have at the same time a measure of self-government impossible under Episcopacy. It could still be a "gathered" Church with a covenant basis. The way of calling and ordaining of pastors seems to have been their greatest concern. In their theory, pastors ought to be chosen by their flock; in Anglican theory and practice, they were usually nominated by someone who owned the "living" and installed by a bishop.[30]

The more moderate sought a compromise. The people could "consent" to the pastoral candidate and thereby make the nomination good because a "believing congregation consenteth to have him." Such consent might be merely mental with mental reservations but it would save the face of everybody concerned, and you have a Congregational pastor under a bishop. There might even be a kind of under-cover spiritual reordination by the congregation which would suit their theory and add as it were Congregational sanction to Episcopal validity.[31] Parish churches would thus, in theory, be Congregational. The Bishops would be "general visitors and overseers of the churches to see that the pastors doe their duties" —on the whole an engaging idea—and maybe an approximation to what might have been one stage in post-apostolic development of Church polity.

Neither the King nor his bishops cared for any of these things. They meant to break Puritanism and all its branches, though Charles, according to Cotton, was more tolerant of Separatists than of Puritans, probably because he thought them relatively harmless. For Puritanism carried a double threat, political as well as religious. The King may have been,

[30] One does not find in the voluminous literature of the period—or later—a due recognition of the "patron" situation. It is pretty complicated but the great land-owners owned also the right to nominate incumbents for their parish churches, a privilege often sadly abused and used to provide a respectable station and an assured livelihood for a younger son or somebody else's younger son. The parishioners had nothing to say, and the Bishop was usually cooperative. An underground rebellion against this confessedly curious system must be taken into account.

[31] This procedure, vaguely felt for in this line of argument, has since been definitely proposed as a bridge between Presbyterianism or Congregationalism and Episcopacy. It might work.

from the first, more fearful of the political implications of Puritanism than its threat to the Establishment. At any rate the political and the religious were tied up in one bundle. The Puritan was naturally on the side of Parliament by every inheritance and came into his own, so he believed, for one tragic and heroic period, through political upheaval become rebellion.

For Parliament was the citadel of English liberty. A King without a Parliament was a despot, and a Parliament without the power of the purse was an empty form. Charles' blind determination to reign without a Parliament drove him straight toward civil war. The Puritan had been told by his preachers for a long generation that life is a warfare. He not only identified himself with the Parliamentary cause; he was the cause incarnate. Laud, to make the King's case more hopeless, harried the realm with religious persecution. The issue was thus predetermined—"To your tents, O Israel" or else to Massachusetts Bay. For all this combined not only to launch Winthrop's fleet, but within eleven years to bring the population of the colony up to twenty thousand. New England became for the Puritan a wide "door of liberty." There he might set up a form of church government impossible in Old England. His magistrates would still enforce religion (that he clung to), but the magistrates would be of his own choosing, the religion they enforced would be his kind of religion, and his dream of a divine order of society be realized.[32]

X

Dr. Samuel Fuller Is Called to Salem

Details of this conception suffered, almost immediately upon the Puritans' landing, a most significant sea-change. They brought two ministers with them, Francis Higginson and Samuel Skelton. The Company had given them also a wide door of liberty in the future exercise of their ministry "in teaching both our owne people and the Indians," expressing only the pious hope that they would make God's word the rule of their actions. Both these men, Miller thinks, had Congregational leanings. They were therefore predisposed to conversion. Now Endicott, with a group which had out-sailed the rest, settled at Salem—or, better, named their settlement because there they would find peace. Endicott fell ill with scurvy, then and long afterwards the plague of slow-sailing ships. Dr. Samuel Fuller, deacon and doctor at Plymouth, was the only physician on the lonely coast. He would have been skilled in the treatment of scurvy, for his colony in the first winter had almost perished of

---

[32] This is the crux of Miller's argument. It explains the long course of religion, and many other things, in the colony and clears them of inconsistency. They had as yet no theory of tolerance at Massachusetts Bay.

it. So he went to Salem and, as Endicott writes Bradford, was of great service to them. Fuller had been a deacon in the Pilgrim church at Leyden and was competent for spiritual as well as bodily ailments. He not only defended Plymouth against the evil reports "that hath been spread of you touching their particular," but, according to a tradition Congregational historians cherish, converted doubting Endicott to Congregationalism. (So Dexter)

Miller has less confidence in sudden conversion, and in this case with reason. Two Stuart Kings and the Bench of Bishops had been trying vainly to get Puritans to change their minds and mend their ways for thirty years, and they had powerful instruments of persuasion. And here was Fuller doing it almost overnight. One may allow something for the amenable mind of a sick man and more to Fuller's evangelical power. But, Miller holds, Endicott was already half-converted, or else Deacon Fuller could not so suddenly "persuade a headstrong man like Endicott" or lead ministers like Skelton and Higginson so easily to see the Separatist light. They were all predisposed to the Congregational way.[33]

Consequently, on the sixth of August, 1629, the Salem Company united to form a church by covenant. They elected and ordained their "pastor" and "teacher," though both had received established ordination in England.[34] The Salem Church, seeking peace, sent their first "letter missive" to the Plymouth church that they might have their approbation and even guidance. The Plymouth delegates, headed by Bradford, went by sea and were hindered by cross winds, "but they came into the Assembly afterwards and gave them the "right hand of fellowship." Salem was living up to its name. Winthrop and his company, therefore, found Salem church a going concern and followed the pattern in founding new churches. This, says Walker, was the real inception of American Congregationalism.

The number of churches could grow but slowly. They could not outrun the slow increase and dispersion of population. There were but five

[33] There were all sorts of cross lines here too numerous to disentangle. John Robinson had urged the Pilgrims to recognize their Puritan brethren. Jacobs (who influenced strongly Congregationally-inclined Puritans) had himself been influenced by Robinson or else vice versa. There was a prepared liaison between Plymouth and Salem. When, later, the news of what was happening in their colony reached the Company in London—as it did through the brothers Browne, who brought their Prayer Books with them and for the public use of them were shipped back home (first case of deportation)—the London Company rebuked Endicott most mildly, and mostly for his lack of tact. (Miller in part.) Dexter thought differently. He reads in the letter displeasure and rebuke.

[34] Which was true of the early Massachusetts Bay ministry. If there is any virtue in Episcopal ordination, though much attenuated, there are more vestiges of its virtue in Congregationalism than any other American communion save the Episcopalian—which a Presbyterian would deny. Walker dates the organization of the Salem Church a few months earlier.

Congregational churches on the continent ten years after the Mayflower discharged her Pilgrims. Twenty years after, there were but thirty-five. But the sifted seed-corn was planted. The problem was to save the Congregational way from the reproach of disorder and prevent the Presbyterian way from becoming too magisterial. The next chapter considers their solution of that problem.

CHAPTER VI

The New England Way
Becomes Congregational

MASSACHUSETTS Bay Colony prospered economically from the first; there was no starvation there. There was apparently ample capital behind it; its executives were capable, its people competent and inventive. They had fish, fur, and wood to export and within ten years had begun to build their own ships, make their own bricks, glass, and textiles. They printed an Almanac for 1639 upon their own press (imported) and next year the Bay Psalm Book. Agriculture was basal; the whole family delved and span from dawn to dark. Religion was their only avocation and that they took with a seriousness beyond exaggeration. Indeed their concern for their souls made it their real vocation. Were they not wayfarers seeking Heaven Gate and always in peril of missing it?

The church, therefore, was fundamental in their social and even political organization. Their slowly widening circles of settlements were churches before they were towns. Being essentially a religious and not a political commonwealth, the ministers, not the magistrate, were masters. For if Plymouth suffered from want of ministers, having none but absentee John Robinson for almost ten years and then a parson suspected of the Puritans, Massachusetts Bay had too many from the beginning. They were masterful, well educated, had been in danger or without parishes in England, and so were eager to share the Puritan Land of Pure Delight. They were welcomed and honored beyond their desert. Winthrop was hard-headed enough, but he wrote: "I honoured a faithful minister in my heart and could have kissed his feet."[1] When the Governor is like that, the magistrates are clay and the minister the potter.

In 1631 the colony took momentous and far-reaching action. It was enacted: "that for time to come noe man shall be admitted to the freedom of this body politicke, but such as are members of some of the Churches . . . within the same." No one, therefore, could vote who was not a church communicant, and no one could become a church member save on a minister's allowing. This was destined to make both church

[1] Adams, *The Emancipation of Massachusetts*, p. 32. This is a careful study of the New England way.

79

and commonwealth all kinds of trouble. The actual issue was not a state church but a church-state which John Calvin in Geneva would have envied. The town meeting was the church meeting, a little secularized; the church meeting was the town meeting, supposedly spiritualized. The system would in time become democratic; it was in its inception entirely the contrary. It "was a speaking aristocracy in the face of a silent Democracy." And the clerical aristocracy was the more autocratic because it supposed itself to be doing the will of God.

The people went to church too much, so the Court of Assistants thought,[2] since their daily services left them too little time to work. Legislation was helpless before this avidity for sermonic delights. The devout sat for hours in frigid "meeting houses" emotionally swayed by fear and longing. No wonder the minister was master. Historians cannot escape calling all this "Congregational" and "Congregationalism," but it was not so named to begin with. It was the "New England Way" (Dexter), distrusted in England, worked out by processes of trial and error in New England. The name Congregational, like Topsy, "just growed." John Cotton uses it definitely in *The Way of the Congregational Churches Cleared* (1648) and that assumes an earlier controversial use of it. It would not become more definite until set against the backgrounds of later denominationalism.[3]

I

"Clearing the Way"

It was not easy to clear "the way of the Congregational churches." The final, historic adjustment was a working resolution of three forces: first, a Separatist-Independency which crossed in the Mayflower and had behind it in England and then in America two long generations of trial and error, persecution, exile, courage, and adventure; and above and behind all that an increasingly consistent conception of how a church should be gathered and administered. Second, a complete or Puritanical semi-Presbyterianism whose emulation was Scotland and whose ideal was Geneva. Third, the inherited and still continued conception of the right of the magistrate to order religion. Doctrine was not so much involved as yet; they were all in substance Calvinists. The migrations from England became increasingly Puritan in personnel after 1629–30. The King and Laud were for the time supreme, but the Puritan and Parliamentary rebellion was gathering head. Naturally immigrants so tinctured were critical of Independency. It still for them smelled of Browneism.

---

[2] Adams, *The Emancipation of Massachusetts*, pp. 34 ff.
[3] Very likely it formulated itself in opposition to Presbyterianism, but one cannot document that guess.

There were always dangers to be guarded against: heresies, evildoers, dangerous leaders, etc. (Cotton names them at highly rhetorical length.) If then a church were trusted with complete autonomy, the cause of religion and the safety of the commonwealth would be imperiled in three possible ways: "Blasphemers" might covenant together in a congregation; an established church fall from grace, or an unsound minister let black sheep into his flock. Against these perils a system of defenses was built. Since the church generally preceded township organization, the General Court must not and would not, it enacted in 1635, approve any new church save as the company proposing to establish it "first acquaint [spelling modernized] the magistrates and the elders of the great part of the churches in this jurisdiction with their intentions and have their approbation therein." Further, no person, being a member of a church not thus approved by magistrates and the majority of the churches, "shall be admitted to the freedom of this Commonwealth."

The Cambridge Platform of Church Discipline gave the magistrate coercive power over corrupt or schismatical churches "as the matter shall require." Since it was the duty of Christian magistrates to take care that the people be fed with sound doctrine, no person would be allowed to preach to "any company of people or be ordained against the veto of two churches, the Council of State, or the General Court." In case of proposed ordination the approbation of neighboring churches was required. Finally, no meeting house could be built without leave from the freemen of the town or the General Court, all of which is in substance a curious combination of some of the later statutes of Queen Elizabeth and what became and has continued good Congregational usage. The "New England Way" was complete in theory as far as legislation could define and support it.

Within this general frame, for almost two generations, details of worship, administration, authority, and belief were worked out. The forms of worship were almost inevitable, following Geneva's pattern: prayer, a psalm, the Word, God there and then present and speaking through the Old and New Testaments; the sermon to give the sense and apply the use of the Word. The minister in his wooden pulpit, the elders on both sides, the people listening with "Reverence and Attention."[4] If there were "prophets," men with a gift for exhortation, present they might, if time and the elders permitted, speak as they were moved. Questions were allowed, save from women. Baptism and the Lord's Supper administered, a psalm again, an offering and the final word of blessing.[5]

[4] Dexter, *Congregationalism as Seen in Its Literature*, p. 423.
[5] Dexter (from Cotton), *Congregationalism as Seen in Its Literature*, p. 423.

What was actually happening during this period was an attempted fusion of Congregational and Presbyterian theory and practice. The status and authority of the elder had been in debate in England from the very rise of Puritanism. The attempt to impose the "ruling elder" upon New England congregations created reams of disputatious writing, long vanished and long-winded arguments and in general a now excessively dusty detail. Two conceptions were in opposition which could not finally be reconciled in one church body: government from the top by the clergy and assisting authorities—the elders—or Congregational control. Each has its virtues when singly and consistently followed. They could not be tied up in one bundle; then nor practically since.

II

THE CAMBRIDGE SYNOD

The immediate result of this situation was the famous Cambridge Synod, usually and rightly considered a most significant milestone on the New England Way. The position of the Bay Colony was perilous. The Puritan in England was beginning to control Parliament. Migrants to New England were, therefore, increasingly of a Presbyterian persuasion and it pained them deeply to be denied the right to vote. They therefore petitioned the General Court for relief. If relief were denied they would, they lamented, be "necessitated to apply our humble desires to the honorable house of Parliament, who, we hope, will take our sad conditions into their serious consideration." Oliver Cromwell was then very soon to take the sad condition of Parliament into his serious consideration and, through Colonel Pride, purge it to his liking.

Massachusetts then as afterwards prepared to legislate for herself. The General Court, therefore, "desired" that the churches "sit in Synod (in September, 1646) to discuss, dispute and cleare up, by the word of God" questions of church government and discipline. Also they invited delegates from Plymouth, Connecticut and New Haven. Most of the Massachusetts churches and a few from the other colonies responded—cautiously. They got so far as appointing a committee (a hallowed Congregational procedure) to draw up a scriptural mode of church government. They were dispersed by an epidemic and met again in August, 1648. Result: the Cambridge Platform—seventeen chapters—covering about everything. It has since furnished Congregational church historians an ample and fascinating material.[6] The situation was the thing. Here was a society destined to democracy in both administration and religion, and at the same time afraid of it. Their little commonwealth was im-

---

[6] The Platform will be considered at length and with documentation in the second part of this history.

periled by a distant but unsympathetic Parliament and Quakers and Baptists at home. There was as yet no social tradition, no long habitude to steady and support them.

The local setting of the Synod was across the Charles River from Boston but the backgrounds and necessities of it were as much in old as in New England. There also the religious situation was complicated enough. The Civil Wars had been fought by Cromwell and his Ironsides under the supposed control of Puritan parliaments of a strong Presbyterian persuasion. To Puritan parliamentary action British and American Calvinism owes the Westminster Confession which "for substance of doctrine" the New England church accepted and long professed. There was therefore on both sides of the Atlantic a brotherly unanimity of belief. But Cromwell himself was more sympathetic with the Independent than with the Presbyterian, finding him probably less obstructive, and the Independent wing of the New England leaders could count for the time upon his far-reaching support in the contentions about church government which were the real matter in debate at Cambridge. A few years before this Council was called, a group of English divines had sent over a list of nine "positions" on which they asked the advice of the Colonial ministers. Another group of Puritan ministers in England drafted a set of thirty-two questions which they sent to America.

The Colonial churches had two champions, Reverend Thomas Hooker and Reverend John Cotton, two men who had been friendly rivals in England where each had reached a position of eminence. They came to America in the same ship after persecution in England. Both were considered by the First Church of Boston where John Cotton was called. Thomas Hooker took the church at Newtowne (Cambridge), and as has often been told, Hooker very soon gathered up his followers and removed to "Hartford-on-Connecticut."

When the "questions" and "positions" of the English leaders demanded attention, Cotton and Hooker not only spoke on these matters, but both took up their pens in defense of the freedom of the American churches. Cotton's *The Keyes to the Kingdom of Heaven,* published in England in 1644, had been widely read. The English had also read his *Way of the Churches* which was published in England without Cotton's consent. The manuscript of Hooker's great work on church doctrine was lost at sea, but other of his writings were circulated. Later on *The Summe of Doctrine* was published from his notes after his death in 1648. Although these books were either published or in process, the church leaders felt that a more definite reply than individual witness was needed to the questions from England. These, then, were the "agenda" of the Synod—these and the future of the New England Way.

For the problem was to save the Congregational Way from the reproach of disorder and prevent the Presbyterian Way from getting the control of the congregation. The issue was a system of checks and balances.[7] Authority, according to the Cambridge Gospel of John Cotton, is reserved wholly to the elders; the elders are prevented from tyranny and oligarchy by the liberty of the brethren, and the Platform was quite confident that the power of the elders and the privileges of the brethren "may agree sweetly together." Somewhere behind it all was the perennial question of the hen and the egg or vice versa—which came first? For there would be no elders without the call of the congregation, and no congregation without the approbation of the elders. After that, though, the pious hope was expressed that the final authority would be from Christ and not from men, and the elders held the whip hand, which they meant to keep.

Miller, to whose interpretations this section is in debt, calls this theory of dual authorities cooperating a "triumph of ingenuity." Dexter saw in it a Congregationalized Presbyterianism or a Presbyterianized Congregationalism which was Genevan outside the local congregation and Pilgrim inside the local congregation. The Cambridge Conference has another distinction: it was a laborious and sincere effort on a small scale to reach a working accommodation between the non- (or anti-) Anglican groups of the more moderate sort, to break down the walls of partition between Puritan and Pilgrim and of the twain to make one new man. Seen now in retrospect it was an early experiment in ecumenicity; or in plain words, the attempt to unite what English Calvinistic Protestantism there was then on the American continent.

Had it held creatively and widely for the next one hundred years, American Congregationalism and Presbyterianism would have continued one fellowship, become one denomination.[8] Actually forces beyond the control of Cottons and Hookers were against it. There was a tenacious independence, a tough-grained individualism in the common folk of the colonies which the stony soil nourished and the perils of the frontier, then so near to Boston, tended to harden. They meant in half-unconscious and inarticulate ways to manage their own affairs. The New England way socially, temperamentally, politically, was more spacious and potent than the new England Church Way, and in an inelegant phrase, soaked it up. The elders fade out of the picture; synod became in time an alien word. The shrewd New England faculty kept what it felt it

[7] No one as far as we know has yet found in the Cambridge Platform the germinal rudiments of the United States Constitution. Both sought the same ends.

[8] A most alluring supposition. Perhaps if all immigration from the British Isles had come for the next hundred years through the Port of Boston it might have come true. But when the Scotch Irish began to crowd in through Philadelphia and Baltimore—!

needed; the fellowship of the churches, their mutual responsibility for the common well being, and quite literally, a neighborly oversight, sharing, and submission. This would in time become a habit, a tradition, a self-imposed and self-accepted discipline, native to the soil and the soul of the region then; native, since, not so much to soils as to souls who found and still find it a good way for them.[9]

III

THE CHURCHES GROW IN NUMBERS AND COMMUNITY

Between forty and fifty churches adopted the Cambridge Platform for "substance of doctrine." (Dexter.) This indicates a relatively rapid growth in New England population and a corresponding increase in churches. Since New Haven was asked to Cambridge (an interchange of visits is now a habit, though not for purely religious ends), there must have been followers of the way in New Haven. The relation of the colonists to the Indian is no part of this history, though it has important bearings upon it. Plymouth got on kindly with them, with qualifications, but in general the colonists with intervals of trying to convert them, fought them to extermination.

The Pequots were strong and hostile. As long as they held the interior lines of communication, travel was unsafe between Massachusetts, Rhode Island, and Connecticut and interior colonization perilous. The situation was complicated by feuds between the Narragansetts and Pequots. Urged by Roger Williams, the Narragansetts made a treaty with Boston. The Pequots ravaged the little interior settlements, especially in Connecticut, whose colonists called for help. The first joint action of all New England colonies seems to have been in the campaign which followed and wiped out the Pequot nation (1637). It was a cruel but effective business. The Connecticut coast could now be colonized and travel was safe.

The last wave of Puritan migration, therefore, chose New Haven harbor and settled New Haven in the spring of 1638. The noble old church on the "Green" inherits the tradition of the First Church of Christ in New Haven. Its first pastor, John Davenport, Oxford graduate, eloquent and forceful, was conservative, theocratic. The power of the clergy was extreme, only church members could vote, and though the "blue laws" were an impudent and unveracious invention of the Rev. Samuel Peters, ecclesiastical control of manners and morals was rigid in New Haven. Hartford was another story. Adventurous John Oldham explored the Connecticut Valley in 1633 and brought back glowing reports. Attempts

---

[9] It should be added—and the ministers, elders, and magistrates would be shocked to find it in a footnote—that the Synod safeguarded orthodoxy by agreeing upon a list of eighty-two errors condemned by the word of God.

at settlement followed; one of them tragic in experience and heroic. Meanwhile Thomas Hooker, pastor of the Newtowne church, was at odds with the Boston heirarchy, politically and ecclesiastically. He was on the side of the sturdy "freemen" who wanted to be freemen and had no love for a self-perpetuating closed corporation of either magistrates or ministers. Winthrop favored restriction of the suffrage: "The best part," he said, "is always the least and of that best part the wiser part is always the lesser."[10]

"In matters which concern the common good," Hooker maintained, "a general council chosen by all, to transact businesses which concern all, I conceive most suitable to rule and most safe for relief of the whole." Hooker and his Newtowne congregation sought a terrain more favorable to this noble philosophy than a Boston suburb. In June 1636 a hundred of them, Hooker at their head, went through the woods to Hartford, taking along one hundred and sixty head of cattle. That pilgrimage was one of the idylls of New England colonization. There would be laurel in the pine woods, the thrush and the veery singing at sunset, clear brooks to follow across the height of land, and at last the bright waters of the beautiful river. Immigration from England was at its peak and the settlements along the river grew. The Dorchester and Waterbury congregations followed in a body. Here at last freedom was on the march, the dreams of a thousand years come true. For a year Massachusetts Bay governed the towns through commissioners, but next year Windsor, Hartford, and Wethersfield set up a General Court of their own. At its opening session Hooker proclaimed that "the foundation of authority is laid in the free consent of the people"; "that the choice of public magistrates belongs unto the people by God's own allowance"; "that they who have power to appoint officers and magistrates have the right to set the bounds and limitations of the power and place unto which they call them." Afterwards the freemen of the three towns wrote a freeman's constitution. "The first written constitution," says Fiske, "known to history, that created a government."

IV

Intolerances and Hysteria

Meanwhile in Boston the preachers and magistrates proceeded to write a chapter of provincial history which went far to disprove Winthrop's assurance that the few are always the wise "and the fewer the wiser." The Puritan treatment in New England of the witches, Quakers, and Baptists has created a most considerable literature, emotive or critical. It was shameful and, from what only yesterday was a modern point

[10] All this from John Fiske's *The Beginnings of New England*, p. 151ff. Cotton and Hooker, Fiske comments, anticipate Hamilton and Jefferson.

of view, impossible,[11] and apparently terribly inconsistent. No proper understanding of it is possible save against the backgrounds of its own actors and its own time. The smallness of the stage itself magnified the drama, but it was an aspect of the general mind of the period. Witchcraft is an immemorial superstition. Anabaptists had rusted instruments of torture with their blood since the beginning of the Reformation. The Quakers were hunted people in England as well as America.

The Puritan was ruled by an iron creed. Otherwise he would himself have been broken. But an iron creed may become too strong for weak hands. "So," says a possibly prejudiced writer, "Augustine's predestination was safe with him, comprehensible in Calvin, tiresome in the English Puritans."[12] He was a hard man, otherwise he also would have been broken, and he was consumed by his own intensities. The people were on edge emotionally. Their excess of churchgoing and what they heard in church obsessed them with hopes and fears. They were lonely, a handful on the fringe of a continent. They had no releases but religion. The frame of Puritanism was never large enough for the whole of life anywhere, and least of all in a frontier settlement pathetically bare of cultural resources. The passions of the frontier are always violent since there are so few channels to carry them off; and finally, when religion goes cruel, it is cruelly cruel.

It is impossible here to separate the social from the religious, or know whether one is writing a secular or church history because in and about Boston then nothing was purely secular. There were two intolerances and one hysteria, the first intolerance against the Baptists or the Anabaptist, so-called. Puritan Congregationalism was going to have troubles enough of its own over infant baptism, but it would suffer none to deny it. So with much verbiage and archaic spelling, the General Court (1644) ordered and agreed that anyone condemning or opposing infant baptism or seducing others to do so, should, if they could not be brought to change their minds, be banished. There were protests against the act from divers merchants and others, and Parliament asked questions about it. Edward Winslow quieted Parliament with the assurance that it would be gently executed, which they proceeded to do by whipping "one Painter, for refusing to let his child be baptized." Painter bore it without flinching and boasted that "God had assisted him." For Baptist leanings Henry Dunster was removed from the presidency of Harvard and driven out of the colony with a sick wife and child in March, his salary unpaid. He found sanctuary in Plymouth.

[11] Its vast and tragic parallels in European anti-Semitism, concentration camps, etc., qualify that statement.
[12] Williams, *The Descent of the Dove*.

The case of Roger Williams is classic. No doubt Williams was argumentative, difficult, a born nonconformist. He tried Massachusetts Bay sorely and in about every possible way. He advocated complete separation of church and state; equal protection for all forms of religious faith; no compulsory church attendance; no tithes or taxes for the support of religion; and perhaps worst of all, he denied the right of the colonists to their lands. The soil belonged to the Indians; it would be held rightfully only by purchase from them. The King's Patent was invalid and the acceptance of it a sin needing to be publicly reported.[13] There was no place about Massachusetts Bay for such a man as that (he had been minister at Salem), so the General Court sought to deport him. He escaped through the wintry woods, found shelter with Massasoit whose language he could speak and of whom he sought to make a Christian—or something like it. In the Spring he went on to Narragansett Bay and so began Providence Plantation (1636), whose name is beautifully significant and whose street names perpetuate the spirit of its settlers. Islands in the Bay were named after Williams' daughters. There he sought to make operative his doctrine of "soul liberty."[14]

The colony's dealing with the Quakers was far more tragic. This again must be understood from that time and not ours. The wisdom and grace of the "Friends," won through many tribulations and now exercised for the healing of the nations, invests the very name with the finest of Christian qualities. But their beginnings were erratic and their early peacefulness has been vigorously denied by such apologists as Dexter and others. They maintain that Williams and the Quakers were the aggressors, had no business in or about Boston anyway, asked for persecution and drove the authorities to frenzy. (So Ellis, quoted by Adams.) There is no doubt about the frenzy. It was contagious, and magistrates and Quakers were possessed by it.

The action against Baptists and Quakers covered thirty-odd years and began in 1642. The first period ended by royal decree when Charles II interfered and ordered those under arrest sent to England. A year later the King confirmed the Massachusetts charter, excluding by a royal letter the Quakers from general toleration. Thereupon the General Court passed the Vagabond Act (since in substance found useful in various states for dealing with undesirables). Under this Act anyone deemed a vagabond could be whipped without limit after a second conviction, and the whips were no toys. During these twenty-one years three men and

---

[13] In substance from Fiske, *The Beginnings of New England*, pp. 140–141.

[14] For a carefully documented and detailed account of the actions against the Baptists see Adams, *The Emancipation of Massachusetts*, chap. 4. He does not soften the story but the documents speak for themselves. "Bridewell" and "Clink" were duplicated in Boston.

one woman were hanged, others branded, many otherwise cruelly dealt with. These pioneer Quakers, possessed by a sense of mission, met persecution with fanaticism, even to the unclothing of their bodies, and sadly disturbed the decorum of the meeting house. But for all that only a counter-fanaticism gone sadistic would have whipped three women on their bare backs from Dover to Durham, ten stripes in each town.

Anne Hutchinson, who proved a unique insurgent, was a "movement" all by herself. She was an early feminist, gave lectures which drew their hearers away from the churches, and founded a woman's club (a pioneer Margaret Fuller) which criticized sermons. Her theology was highly objectionable to the orthodox. She claimed the spirit of prophecy and proclaimed "the inner light." Here, perhaps, was the head and front of the Quakers' offending, though Anne was not a Quaker. The Puritan light was God's word, there on the preacher's pulpit; final, authoritative, inerrant, and the preacher was its instrument. There could be no compromise between the "word" and the "inner light." This may explain the Puritan dislike and distrust of "enthusiasm" and his consequent treatment of the Quaker and other self-nominated prophets or prophetesses. So Mrs. Hutchinson and her friends were ordered out of the colony, possibly with some unconfessed regret on Cotton's part; he seems rather to have liked the lady, who had been his parishioner, follower, and quite sympathetic friend in Boston, England. She was thereafter a pilgrim herself, she and her group. Followers founded Exeter and Hampton in now New Hampshire. She herself with others settled at the mouth of Narragansett Bay, eventually Rhode Island Plantation, and with nearly all her children was at last murdered by the Indians near Stamford (Connecticut). Thomas Hutchinson, last royal governor of Massachusetts, was one of her descendants. So much for Anne Hutchinson and for the Quakers. (These datings need precision. The persecution of Baptists began in 1642. The Quakers began to come in 1656.)

V

SALEM WITCHCRAFT

Salem witchcraft was the last hysteria. This also needs to be understood from the time, the setting, and the temper of the actors. The colony was under political and social strain. Its charter had been revoked and the set-up was being reorganized under William and Mary. The new charter changed many things, especially the relation of the colony to the crown (no part of this history) and overthrew "the temporal power of the Church," though by no means the influence of the clergy. It is possible that their passion to keep their sorely-threatened dominance over the people started the whole foolish and tragic business. Everybody believed in witches; England was as bad as New England. Perhaps only a sincere regard for the safety of their flocks led to a proposal to collect stories of sorceries and such.

Increase Mather made the book (1683–84) and soon suggestion began to act. Four years later some children showed, it was thought, signs of possession. (Compare the Wesleys at Epworth.) Their symptoms would now be familiar to any alienist, but they hanged an Irish washerwoman with whom one of the daughters had quarrelled. The Mathers, Increase and Cotton, blew up the fire. The governor created a court to try witches. The devil and his servants rode abroad and unseen devils as well. The only defense was accusation. No one was safe. None were burned, but more than enough were hanged. There was confiscation of property, doubtless a good many satisfied envies and grudges, and apparently a general scaring of people back to church. "In the whole," concluded Cotton Mather,[15] ". . . the devil got nothing, but God got praises, Christ got subjects, the Holy Writ got temples, the Church got additions, and the souls of men got everlasting benefits." And the Mathers would eventually get a most unsavoury reputation. Then it all ended.

But there was a power of correction in the commonwealth for all these follies.[16] The people themselves. No dispassionate student can read democracy back into the first sixty-odd years of New England church history, nor political history either. It was not there. The situation was always anomalous: a trading company exercising sovereign powers, the mother country in revolution, and beneath or above it all the dream of God's own state, and they (magistrates and ministers) his vice-regents. Hart, surely an impartial historian, held the power of the clergy in the Massachusetts system to have been undemocratic and unfortunate.

But a deeper current ran against all this. If one calls it ecclesiastically the bequest of Plymouth and John Robinson, he will be right enough. If he called it the destined issue of the society itself, men and women being slowly disciplined into free obediences and self-obedient freedoms, he will be more right still. If he maintains that it was, both ecclesiastically and politically, Congregationalism getting itself disentangled from an alien system and finding itself at last, he may seem a special pleader, but he will be hard to confute.

[15] Adams, *The Emancipation of Massachusetts.* "Wonders of the Invisible World" quoted.

[16] There has been on the part of historians an unfair discrimination against New England in studies of religious intolerance. New England had no monopoly of it. Virginia, for example, had its share. There was a decade (1760–1770) of violent persecution of Baptists in that colony—a period of complete toleration in Massachusetts. "Baptist preachers were stoned out of Culpepper County in 1765 and jailed in Spotsylvania County in 1768." *James Madison, The Virginia Revolutionist, 1751–1780,* by Irving Brant. This fascinating biography also stresses the influence of a growing hostility to Virginia Anglicanism upon the whole movement toward colonial independence.

CHAPTER VII

Entanglements and Disentanglements

I T IS impossible to do anything with the history of American Congregationalism without recognizing its organic relation to and entanglement in the very structure of New England colonial society to begin with; in past and contemporaneous English history, in a strategic phase of the Reformation and, finally, in the stern, heroic, and impossible Puritan ideology. It cannot possibly be dissected out of its age and its environment until it disentangled itself. The limitations of the stage complicated the whole situation. It was always crowded with actors believing their seacoast fringed the cosmos. There was and is a superabundance of documentation. How so much of so little consequence said and written was saved is a marvel and a snare to the specialists. It is difficult to see the wood for the trees.

Standing far enough off one can trace the continuing forces. First of all was the attempt to make the colonies God-ruled societies through legislation and legal enforcement, and if need be by the two-handed whip and the gallows. Second, the effort to continue the autocracy of ministers and elders in the face of a tenacious instinct for freedom and social and economic interests; third, the determination of the colonies not to be governed without representation by Kings or Parliaments or bishops three thousand miles away; fourth, and most significant for American Congregationalism, the effort of the Presbyterian-minded to make New England Presbyterian, an ecclesiastical frame to which the real genius of the province was not native.[1] Finally, though Massachusetts by no means dominated the Connecticut and New Haven churches, it did supply the larger outlines of the New England way.

For these reasons the acts and actors of Massachusetts Bay almost unescapably get an apparently disproportionate attention in all studies of American Congregationalism. Once one gets clear of that period, the going is easier. If one stands far enough back from the relatively short period from 1630 to 1689, he sees among many other things significant changes in the small populations themselves. After 1640 many of the best men in the colony went back to England to reinforce the Puritan

[1] Any Presbyterian would want that statement qualified and in the light of what American Presbyterianism became it should be. But colonial Massachusetts was three hundred years nearer Geneva.

91

and Parliamentary forces there. There was consequently less competent and broadminded leadership and a lowered morale. The immigrants who later followed Winthrop's fleet did not all come for religious reasons. They came to trade or to better their conditions or to get on in the New World.

If the first phase, then, of American Congregationalism was a struggle between Independency and Presbyterianism, the next phase is one more chapter in the long story of the Church and the world. Very soon the ministers began to lament the sad estate of manners and morals. They sound a familiar note, and after 1660 are dark with despair. Their real trouble is as easy now to see as it is hard to condense into a brief statement. The earliest Congregationalists, projecting the name backward, were all for a "gathered Church." Real Christians should leave the Established Church, find each other out, covenant together and so become a true Church on their own initiative. That needed, then, both burning conviction and courage, and in this first phase there was little need for recruiting. When the Pilgrim came to Plymouth, his little group was entirely unified, religiously and socially. Town meeting and church meeting were the same folk. But presently there would be children and children's children and, maybe, the "ungodly." What then?

When the Puritan came to Massachusetts Bay or New Haven, the company of church communicants and the entire society were also very nearly identical. The restriction of suffrage to communicants was almost automatic and created no tensions. And there was the pious and almost pathetically unconsidered expectation that this quite ideal—to the Puritan—condition would continue. He meant to have no intruders. The continent was spacious; let them go, if need be with his vigorous assistance, somewhere else. His children and children's children would be, he also assumed, as godly as he was himself. That was what his ministers and elders were for. These hopes were, naturally, disappointed and in their defeat his troubles began.

I

The Half-Way Covenant

Within thirty years the bases of citizenship had to be broadened. The state could not be limited to the church; there was too much pressure of all kinds against it. By the King's Mandate (1664) all freeholders "not vicious in conversation and orthodox" (though of different persuasions concerning church government) "must have the vote." This took away from the churches a powerful, though indefensible, argument for church membership. Also the first religious impulses had spent themselves and for all the preaching of all the preachers there was nothing entirely to take its place. There began to be an increasing number of noncommunicants, the always expanding margin of secularized society. Morale was lowered; children were not as pious as their parents.

The whole religious system met its most unexpected challenge and problem in a little child, the child of a nonchurch member. It must be baptized. The saints had dealt harshly with those who denied that; but on what grounds beside an immemorial custom, and with what safeguards? Catholicism had a coherent position. Besides his mother's arms, the child was born into the arms of Mother Church. Baptism was a saving sacrament, the first of the sacraments which assured his salvation, as Extreme Unction was the last. He spent his years between the two, a corporate member of an indivisible order. The Anglican Church had a device: godparents. Communicants could always be found who would sponsor the infant and for him or her renounce the world, the flesh, and the devil. After that he would be taught, confirmed, admitted to communion and, so assisted, lead a godly, righteous, and sober life.

The Baptist had a logical position: do not baptize any infant. Let baptism and conscious confession of faith go together. The Puritan-Congregationalist could not accept Catholic sacramentarianism, he would have nothing to do with godparents, and he was not a Baptist. A profound instinct with all its implications of affection and faith was met by a rigid system which had not foreseen the situation. The church leaders were in a dilemma. They could neither deny the child of a noncommunicant baptism nor consistently administer it. For in the second and third generations family discipline had become more relaxed and not all the children of the members "owned the covenant" and, hence, were not "of the church." According to the rules of the day,[2] the children of nonmembers could not be baptized, but only children of church members. To remedy this situation, the famous Half-Way Covenant came into use, whereby children whose grandparents were members of the church, but whose parents were not, could be baptized, although such persons were not received into full membership. They did not have the right to communion, but males so received, when they came of age, had the right to vote in town elections. Even so the Covenant was not easy to subscribe to. In the archives of the Old North Church in Boston, there is the record of a covenant to which these "half-way" members assented:

You now from your Heart professing a serious Belief of the Christian Religion, as it has been generally declared and embraced by the Faithful in this Place, do here give up yourself to God in Christ; promising with his Help to endeavor to Walk according to the Rules of that Holy Religion all your Days; Choosing of God as your best Good, and your last End, and Christ as the Prophet and Priest, and King of your Soul for ever. You do, therefore, submit unto the Laws of his Kingdom, as they are administered in this Church of His; and you will

[2] Walker, *The Creeds and Platforms of Congregationalism*, p. 238.

also carefully and sincerely labour after those more positive and increased Evidences of Regeneration, which may further encourage you to seek an Admission unto the Table of the Lord.[3]

This pledge would now admit to full membership in Congregational or most other churches—with a generous margin. The covenant engendered divisions and controversies of an extent which does not now seem believable.

Those early church members lived in close relationship to God, who was concerned with their thoughts and deeds and, according to the theology of the day, sometimes punished wrong-doing through sickness and misfortune. Calamities and accidents were frequently taken as expressing God's displeasure of wrong-doing. This belief was the foundation of the practice of public and private fasts and days of repentance. When, therefore, there came a series of sorrows, from droughts to sicknesses, hard times, and King Philip's War, it was no wonder that the General Court ordered a synod to find out the evils that had provoked the Lord to bring his judgments upon New England and, more important, what could be done in the way of reformation. The synod reported thirteen prevalent sins and suggested twelve ways of amendment.[4] Some of the sins seem quite modern; many of the recommendations for reform might be the report of the "resolutions committee" at the annual meeting of almost any denomination. Also many held the Half-Way Covenant itself was the chief occasion for Jehovah's wrath.

The peculiar tribulations and tensions of such groups and movements as we have been considering from almost the first page were direct or indirect results of their ideals and intensities. Life was wayfaring and warfaring, and there were many adversaries. But they had from the first an unformulated instinct for the salvation of society as well as their souls. "Social Salvation" was not in their vocabulary, but they sought to achieve it by outer and inner instrumentalities. Their relative failures and positive excesses were due to their programs of legal prohibitions and enforcements. Their enduring achievements were down or up another road. All these beginnings, dreams, darings, possible and impossible ideals, need to be seen against the vaster backgrounds of England and even Europe. So seen they gain by every test. "Despite [their] errors . . . it may fairly be questioned whether any public in the early stages of any frontier settlement showed higher qualities. . . . Proof of this is the influence which they left behind them in this country and the ideals which they have set before other lands."[5]

[3] C. Mather, Magnalia Christi Americana, v:84 (Quoted by Dexter, p. 476.)
[4] Dexter, Congregationalism as Seen in Its Literature, pp. 478–479.
[5] Hart, Commonwealth History of Massachusetts, p. 391.

II
EXTENSION OF CHURCHES AND POPULATION

All the colonial churches being, in a way difficult now to understand, the religious expression and organization of their entire corporate life, the number of churches grew organically with the needs of a growing population. There were not and would not be until almost the Nineteenth Century any societies organized for home missions and no entirely unchurched frontiers in northeast America until after the Revolutionary War. The migratory movements in Massachusetts were northeast along the coast (Maine was then part of Massachusetts), and slowly west. Frontier settlements like Deerfield and Northfield were long in peril of the French and Indians, but tenaciously they held lonely outposts on the edge of the northern wilderness. Little colonization was possible in what is now Vermont until the power of New France was broken on the plains of Abraham.[6]

The result was a century of digging in rather than spreading out. Colonial New England society was unified and particularized. It was purely an English stock. Class distinctions, though definite, were not extreme and never rigid. Colonial New England never overdid democracy. No more than one-third the adult male population could vote in Boston as late as 1775.[7] There were from the beginning the elements of a provincial aristocracy: lesser English gentry, "university men," the clergy, merchants whose sons' sons would freight their ships for the seven seas, the governors, deputies to the colonial legislatures, and magistrates. These would in the course of time with a proper admixture of pride of ancestry and the climate, combine to create a type which history and literature have delighted to characterize, not always kindly. But the type did not dominate the social pattern.

The root-hold of the society, and therefore of its churches, was in a stony and inhospitable soil. It functioned, for all intimate and really vital ends, as we repeat, through the town meeting and the church. The town meeting for all its early limitations of suffrage came as near being democracy in direct action as is humanly possible. In a single sentence, demanding much enlargement, the whole interrelated order functioned from the ground up. This made it tough-fibered and coherent. The

---

[6] The growth of American Protestant denominationalism is therefore tightly tied up with the irregular expansion of the whole seaboard frontier. New England was contained by an indefinite Canada and New York. The small Middle Atlantic colonies more or less contained each other. Southern and eastern New York was contained toward its own interior by the Five Nations—until Sullivan broke them. And the whole English terrain was contained by strategic French forts at the headwaters of the Ohio and in the Mississippi Valley.

[7] Hart, *Commonwealth History of Massachusetts*, chap. 7.

menace of the French and the Indians, a growing opposition to royal administration, and the strange undefined sense of destiny which directed the whole enterprise from and before the sailing of the Mayflower, drew the New England colonies together. Their first confederacy was prophetic. Socially and religiously they became an organism whose members were at once independent and interdependent. One moved without any sense of strangeness from colony to colony. As the adventurous pushed against the always yielding wilderness, the filaments of the body, social, religious, and political were lengthened but never broken. When there were enough of them the central administration set off a town and such as desired became a church. Thereafter, the town was part of a commonwealth, the church part of a fellowship.

We should not make it too simple nor too idyllic, but the situation would be difficult to match for unity, coherence, and organic development in the long records of colonization. The contemporaneous confusions of English history sheltered the growth of New England autonomy. Presbyterian-Puritanism as a force to be reckoned with faded out of the English picture. Cromwell himself sympathized with the religious Independents. The second Charles was occupied with his mistresses, and with the second James the curtain fell for the Stuarts. The colonies were heckled and irritated; but their social, political, and religious structures were intensified rather than weakened. There was as yet no real equivalent of modern denominational competition. The Anglican came and for a season got, in plain words, a dose of his own medicine which he took with a wry face. He found himself the dissenter. One cannot say that it did his soul any good or moved him to suggest a more Christian attitude toward the so-called dissenter in England; his disabilities were removed in New England long before the disabilities of the non-Anglican, Protestant, or Catholic were removed in Old England. Methodism was still far below the horizon. When the alarums and excursions against Baptists and Quakers were over, the apprehensive found that nothing happened, though there were forty-eight Baptist churches in Massachusetts by 1780.

III

THE STATE OF THE CHURCHES GENERALLY: TWO CASE STUDIES

Congregationalism was for the time, the region, and the folk a "natural." One may doubt if since the Reformation anywhere, save in Scotland, society, a religion, and a church-way were so one and indivisible. Statistically, to repeat, the churches grew with the increase and extension of population; in theory, one to a town. Getting to church or anywhere else was difficult. There were no roads in any modern sense anywhere on the fringes. Settlers used Indian trails for years and the early highway commissions planned only for "horse and foot."[8] And there would have been more "foot" than "horse." Therefore the churches must not be too far apart. The magistrates could veto the establishment of a church or the "town" vote one. There were very likely always enough.

The churches were usually named after the towns and the towns got their names from Old England, the Bible, the Indians, an important first settler or some natural feature. Level terrain was always noteworthy; so Wethersfield, Springfield, Deerfield. Once the town was named, a characteristic economy in nomenclature designated its minor localities by the quarters of the compass: north, east, south, west, and center. So the churches were locally known: the South Deerfield or North Hadley or else "The Center Church." In the growing centers of population simple arithmetic sufficed: First, Second, Third, or Fourth. Streets were useful to name a church after—if there were streets; so Brattle or Park. Saints were not thus commemorated until the fellowship got some saints of its own. The total result was a rather standardized and unimaginative nomenclature. A case study of any old Congregational church would clothe such bare bones as these with flesh.

We may use as example the Marshfield, Massachusetts, church, which disputes with Duxbury the high honor of being the first-born of Plymouth. (As a matter of fact, it is a kind of Jacob and Esau affair.) The little church was the germ of the settlement. All meetings were held in the church building; all the freemen were church members—ideal but not permanent. There were individual gifts to establish the church. Winslow gave land, and William Thomas, draper, gave a nine-foot linen cloth for the communion table. When a pastor was finally found he was moved at the expense of the town. His "passing rich at forty pounds a year" salary—not then so bad—was to be paid by the town; by 1661 it was two years in arrears (how he made out is not on the record). Two years later the town voted thirty-five of the forty pounds to be raised by taxation; the church should pay the other five in cattle, butter, or English goods. Arnold was under suspicion for heresy, and the church had its own dissenters. A citizen was imprisoned for saying of the Marshfield Church that "they were all liars."

Concise church records date from 1696. The old building was repaired, another built, sites were changed, ministers came and went. (The Great Awakening, still to be studied, changed the picture.) Doctrines were disputed, a slave was baptized, a fourth church was built, etc. In due time Daniel Webster discovered Marshfield and went to the First

[8] James Ford in a fascinating chapter on Colonial Social Life (Hart, *Commonwealth History of Massachusetts,* chap. 10) touches on about everything which could be put in thirty pages but says nothing of roads and transportation, which are the first condition of any social life at all.

Church. He is said to have been regular in attendance and the pew he used is now marked with a brass plate. (All this from Joseph Hagar's delightful history of Marshfield.)

The First Congregational Church in Milford, Massachusetts, is another interesting case study. It was founded in 1743, through extension of population and the thorny matter of tax-supported religion. A group of younger men had moved away from the "Center," and when it was proposed to build a new church on the old central site they protested. If they were to be taxed to support a church, they wanted it nearer their homes. After four years of dispute and fifteen town meetings, the voters decided on the old site, whereupon the protestants organized themselves into the "aggrieved" party and a church, not without much difficulty. The basis of their fellowship was a covenant. By belligerent persistence the aggrieved party got not only a church of its own but an independent taxation "precinct" and a "learned and orthodox minister" who shepherded it for forty-nine years. After his death it took ten years to find a successor and the church is said to have heard forty candidates. A Mr. David Long was finally chosen (1801) whereupon the church requested the "selectmen" to concur, since his salary ($450) was raised by taxation. But after 1780 Baptists, Methodists, and Universalists had settled in the precinct (now become the Town of Milford) and formed their own societies. They naturally objected to being taxed to support Mr. Long and made their own case. The town meeting voted to exempt all other denominations from taxation for the cost of settlement and salary of Long; whereupon the town voted to concur with the church in calling him.

This did not bring peace to Milford. Fifteen years later (1815) the Congregational church organized itself into a separate parish and renounced town support. And still there was no peace in Milford. For when the church decided to move and sell the old church building, a party in the town claimed that the building belonged to it and, therefore, could neither be moved nor sold without the consent of the town. In the end the church did what it meant to do; dismantled the old building, moved it—the records do not say where—and built anew. Prayer each day began and ended the labor. The work was crowned with a noble spire, the pews sold for $7000, and a balance of $3000 was left in the treasury.

We have followed these two "case studies" in detail because they are the history of Congregationalism for 150 years. The variation in detail would be endless.[9] Marshfield is typical of the organic growth which churched the whole of New England till the "Great Awakening." Milford

[9] A precise study of case histories would show too many churches built by factions, family quarrels, rivalries, and jealousies. (So Professor Hilda Ives.)

is useful to illustrate the complications which grew out of the town-church theory and tax-supported public worship, and the slow and wrangling disentanglement of the whole inconsistent system. Also for one thing more: the pews were sold. Literally, since by the definition of the common law being fixtures fastened to the floor, they could be held, transferred, or bequeathed by deed and taxed as real estate to support public worship. The corporate church officials were, therefore, in some cases called assessors. This was true of the Second Church in Greenfield, Massachusetts at the beginning of this century. Owned pews, not peculiar to Congregationalism, could naturally be rented or, if transferred, as they eventually were in the churches generally, to the society (the holding corporation), they could still be rented by the society.[10]

The final result of these godly integrations of real estate and worship was the pew-rental system by which, with no longer an actual basis in title deeds for pews, the privilege of worshipping God in a designated pew under the ministrations, say, of the Reverend Henry Ward Beecher (this highly ingenious variant of the system seems to have originated in his Brooklyn church) was auctioned off. The most desirable pews went to the highest bidder and a holy competition (not wholly spiritual) augmented the revenues of the society. The total sum so received tended to become a test of the minister's popularity and a register of the local state of religion. When the pews ceased to rent well, a foresighted minister would better begin to pray for a call. Congregationalism had by no means a monopoly on this procedure. It was widespread in the late eighteen hundreds. The more defensible side was the "family pew," whose dear associations need only to be suggested.

IV

CONCERNING MANNERS AND MORALS

Many of the points involved in any account of the development of first-period Congregationalism, which ended with the "Great Awakening," deserve a monograph instead of a paragraph. To begin chronologically everybody was a church member, but if the churches were to go on they must have new members. In that ideal time prospective members seem to have sought the church rather than to have been sought by it. They made their desire known and were examined, in the semi-Presbyterian era, by the elders, who inquired "as to the work of grace upon their souls, or how God hath been dealing with them about their conversion." The banns, as it were, were then published and opportunity

---

[10] Or by the owners. The pew-holders of the First Church in Burlington, Vermont, surrendered their pews—all save one thrifty family, nonresident, who rented it on their own and used the rentals to pay their own subscription to another church.

for objection offered. If none objected, the candidate in the presence of the church at a proper time made profession of his religious faith and experience. Men were searchingly dealt with and must speak out. A woman, as the weaker vessel, might have her confession read by the pastor or received on the testimony of the elders "without anymore adoe." Thereupon the church members voted by the "usual signe"—uplifted right hand—the candidate assented to a covenant, the church through the elder promised to guard and guide the new member, and after a final prayer "they departed away with a blessing." And this technique, much softened but substantially unchanged even to the "usual signe," still continues.

The churches took the responsibility of discipline seriously and there were sufficient occasions. The procedure was much like joining the church, only in reverse. The case was taken to the elders and by them to the church, whereupon the erring brother or sister was admonished, urged to repentance and if unrepentant, excommunicated. In cases of excommunication the people were not asked for the "usual signe"; silence gave consent. The records of the elder churches well into the nineteenth century are sadly shadowed by the frequency and detail of discipline. Few pleasures were allowed the Christian. Was not life wayfaring and warfaring? The *élan vital* therefore of a physically vigorous people made its own far more blameworthy channels. There is abundant evidence for the potency of New England rum and sexual irregularities.

James Ford (Hart, *Commonwealth History of Massachusetts*) thinks the extent of such immorality to have been overstressed. And it received then, as the records of it have received since, an unusual degree of public and particularized attention. Actually American society everywhere was then mostly a frontier society and the cruder immoralities follow the frontier. Ford also thinks the general repressive system to have accentuated the cruelty of a generally cruel epoch. It was a hard time for children. They were plentifully engendered, for their labor was needed. They were worked hard for long hours, and infant mortality was high.[11] They were baptized on the very first Sabbath after birth, though the ice in a fireless church had to be broken to do it. Thereafter they were told that they were by nature utterly depraved and in peril of hell. And the rod was not spared. Even John Robinson, naturally kind, urged a stern discipline. Such records of their fears and pieties as they have left us are pathetic documents.

Their elders found their religion none too easy. They spent long Sabbath hours in bare meeting houses (Sabbath began at six o'clock p.m., Saturday), a sermon might be four hours long, and the cruel in-

[11] See the pathetic little gravestones in any old burying ground.

tensity of it may have been a substitute for fire in the meeting house. Also if a preacher is to keep it up for four hours, he will need to warm himself up with shoutings and warnings. The form of worship did not greatly change, or else changed but slowly. Their elements were always simple: prayer, praise, the Word, and the sermon. The only possible variations were in the arrangement of the elements. There had been to begin with apparently only one prayer—the long prayer—and it was long; an opening and closing prayer could be added. There were no hymns, only metrical versions of the Psalms, some of them nobly done. Since most of the congregation did not even possess a Psalm-book, the Psalms were "lined" out. The leader, the elder, when there were elders, read two lines, the congregation sang them, and so on. Organs were taboo, but stringed instruments were permitted and the church choir began its services and its eccentricities.[12]

The sacrament of the Lord's Supper was administered more often than in a later usage, and the chalice (not then so called); the plates and the cups were the first treasured possessions of poor churches. They were pewter in the first period, afterwards silver, much cherished and often very beautiful. There was a semi-closed communion. The church buildings were "meeting houses" from the first. In the Eighteenth Century, as wealth increased, taste was disciplined and architectural plans were brought over from England. They achieved an unmatched distinction of dignity, simplicity, and proportion, built of noble timbers by master craftsmen. The minister or ministers, with the officials, faced the congregation. There they saw their flock, men on one side, women on the other, in order of their dignity and social status. The children seem to have been placed by themselves under the care of a tithing man. Though "public worship" was tax-supported, offerings were taken. All this, one must add, was not peculiar to the New England way. Presbyterians in New Jersey were worshipping in much the same fashion.

V

The "Way" and Its Changing Ways

The significant thing as one follows all this through is not the detail but the structure. The "way," as patterned and stabilized at the Cambridge Synod, kept on. The elder, to repeat, faded out of the picture; the deacon emerged. He inherited many of the elder's duties without the elder's authority and became a type too often caricatured.[13] Actually he was devout and faithful, loving and serving his church, distributing

---

[12] There will be toward the end of this history a brief resumé of the development of Congregational worship.
[13] So still in the David Harum radio broadcast (1941).

charity as a Christian and distributing the elements of the Lord's Supper
with reverential hands. The synod faded out of the picture, too; the last
noted by Dexter in 1708. The method of conference and association continued. Distinctions between pastor and teacher also faded out of the
picture, though the phrase persisted. The churches could not afford a
clerical staff and were fortunate to have one man both pastor and teacher.
The ministers naturally had their own meetings. Sixteen hundred and
thirty-three dates definitely the beginning of such conferences or associations. They felt themselves charged with responsibility for the well-
being of the churches and the body politic and took their responsibility
seriously; also they were responsible for the status and conduct of their
fellow ministers.

These responsibilities also presently became a pattern: permanent
organization, subject to call by a moderator; mutual consideration of
important matters; supervision of clerical manners and morals; examination of candidates for the ministry; recommendation of ministers to
"bereaved" (pastorless) churches, etc. Gradually such associations validated the "ministerial standing" of their members and kept the first lists
of ministers in good standing. They would have the power of trial and
in extreme cases of unfrocking the unworthy. If these associations should,
for the general business of the churches, add to the ministers the lay delegates chosen decently and in order by the churches, you would have a
representative ecclesiastical body. A sound, self-protective instinct kept
these associations within neighborly, local bounds. In rural regions the
county supported a convenient geographical unit; as the cities grew in
population they became units.

This particular line of development was in its inception protested as
savoring of Presbyterianism. Both sides won in that controversy. The
associationists got their associations, but the association could only advise, resolve, suggest. Its power was moral and not legal, but most good
churches did what they were asked to do, if they could.[14] Otherwise they
could be mourned over but not coerced. This one may hold to be far
more significant than the distinction, without much difference between
names. Congregationalism has since developed a most considerable cen-
tralization and state- and nation-wide meetings with delegates and all
the rest; but the vital relations of a Congregational church are with its
neighbors, and a Congregational minister can be reached upon any
charge only through those who presumably know him best. There is
discipline in the background—we are not a lawless folk—but there is de-

[14] The authority of any ecclesiastical body over church property is—back of behind—
the fulcrum for the leverage of any church authority. If the property can legally be
taken over, the congregation is pretty helpless; otherwise it can keep on, though alone.

fense in the foreground. There have been heresy hunts in the Congregational field, but where a minister's own local association refuses to join,
he is secure. That imponderable but tenacious barrier has been, as we
shall see later, the secret of the free movement of Congregational religious and doctrinal thought. By 1740 this general structure had taken
the form and begun to project the lines it would hold to in all its future
extension. Before it ceased to be almost entirely localized in New England, two momentous things would happen. The religious life of New
England would be changed by the "Great Awakening"; Wesleyan Evangelism would become a force in all the colonies; and the coherence of
the old Puritan order, though not destroyed, would be sadly strained.

CHAPTER VIII

The Evangelical Revival and the Revolutionary War

JOSEPH TRACY called his famous history of the revival of religion in the time of Edwards and Whitefield "The Great Awakening," which seems from his preface to have been a current phrase, though he does not indicate the source. Edwards called his account of the movement "Thoughts on the Revival of Religion in New England in 1740." His title, though precise, is provincial. What happened in Northampton cannot be dated to a year and was only one highly dramatic episode in the evangelical movement which, during the Eighteenth Century, in one form or another and under the leadership of men whose names are historic, so profoundly affected English-speaking Christianity as to date an epoch.

Any adequate account of the evangelical revival belongs to large-scale histories, secular as well as religious, of either England or America. By the middle of the Eighteenth Century the forces of the Reformation were entirely spent and the patterns of Protestantism apparently fixed. Persecution was over, but "disabilities" answered the same purpose. The American colonial religious picture was drawn with broad strokes: Congregationalism, and one may here use the designation with reasonable accuracy, from what would now be Maine to the Hudson River; Dutch Reformed, from Manhattan Island up the Hudson to the Mohawk River; Presbyterianism of a strong Scotch-Irish flavor in the Middle Atlantic colonies; the Anglican church dominant in the South; Baptists and Quakers in Rhode Island; Quakers in Pennsylvania, and also Anglicans, some of them quite vociferously unhappy about being themselves "disabled" wherever there were prosperous merchants and English officials.

There were no Methodists yet—only John Wesley with his troubled soul, and Sally Kirkland in Georgia. The interminable processes of European wars first menaced and then involved our northern colonial frontiers. The times were hard but the epochal religious controversies seemed over. It is not easy to say in a sentence or so what this implied or else to say it directly. Irreverently said, all good Christians everywhere had, for two hundred years, been fighting each other with tongue, pen, and sword—Catholic and Protestant to begin with; next Protestants amongst themselves, and specifically in England. But toward the middle of the Eighteenth Century religion seemed to have outlived its militancies and its crusades. One must not say that it had anywhere become consistently noncombatant; but compared with the great campaigns this was guerrilla warfare. And now that the causes were won, lost, or compromised, the Christian occupations of the protagonists seemed gone. Consequently, religion in both England and the colonies lost fervor and direction, became increasingly an aspect of respectable social life, anything but demanding. In addition thought at last was taking its own free and inquiring lines without ecclesiastical let or hindrance, though by no means inclined to let religion alone.

Utilitarian ethics, deistic faith, and a psychology—not quite so named yet, which made of us only tablets to be written upon by our sensations —began to challenge both inherited ethics and religious faith. One may call it, if he pleases, the beginning of the secularization of society. New England church life reflected all this acutely. The intense and demanding practice of religion had been in its social catechism the chief end of man. For that it had waged its battles and organized its society. Its religious leaders would therefore be very sensitive to any falling off in church membership or any lapse in morality, and the rigidity of the Puritan ethic made lapses in morality out of relatively inconsequential things. We have considered already the distress of the ministry over the third New England generation, their endeavor to find a formula for the baptism of the children of noncommunicants in the Half-Way Covenant and the controversies thus occasioned. All such things as these conditioned the "Great Awakening."

I

JONATHAN EDWARDS IS CALLED TO NORTHAMPTON

The town of Northampton, Massachusetts, as Ebenezer Pomeroy, moderator, attests, voted by a very great majority on November 21, 1726, that a proper committee "should invite the Reverend Mr. Jonathan Edwards to settle amongst them in the work of the ministry and in convenient time to take office amongst them, . . . to assist our Reverend Pastor Mr. Stoddard in the work of the ministry." Stoddard had been minister in Northampton for fifty-five years, and the assistant chosen by the town committee was his grandson. It seemed the happiest of arrangements. Stoddard was eighty-four; Edwards, twenty-three. Stoddard had shared almost the entire growth and perils of a prosperous frontier settlement. He had been of a moderate but liberal temper, had defended the

Half-Way Covenant and baptized all his middle-aged parishioners. He understood their virtues and their faults and doubtless thought Northampton more in peril of an Indian raid than hellfire.

His grandson, who for two years would sit with his grandfather on the settee behind the pulpit, preach at one Sabbath service and so ease his grandfather into an honored tomb, was already known for brilliancy of mind and deep spirituality. The unusual distinction in American life of the descendants of Jonathan Edwards and Sarah Pierpont has furnished students of heredity fascinating data, perhaps over-stressed. His biographers have therefore naturally sought to account for Jonathan himself. Their research shows no more than that he came of good English stock.

His immediate forebears were either coopers or clergymen; but, save that all pioneers have force and courage, nothing in them explain him. John Robinson has as good a family tree. One can make a better case for the distaff side than the male. He was born at East Windsor, Connecticut, October 5, 1703, the fifth child and only boy in a family of eleven children. His parents were in their early prime. His father Timothy was clergyman of a recent and growing settlement where churchgoers carried muskets to church during his infancy. Eunice Williams of Deerfield, half-sister of Esther Edwards, had been killed by one blow of the tomahawk by a "cruel and bloodthirsty savage" along Green River when Jonathan was four months old. Travel was hazardous. The people lived and died within the limits of their townships. All rural ministers were also farmers and young Jonathan was habituated to farm chores. His dawning sense of God was inseparably associated with the sights and sounds of the countryside in which he grew up.

He had accurate powers of observation and he wrote an essay on spiders of which his biographers make what they can. He thought them, however, "the corrupting nauseousness of the air" and in time found them a fit symbol for sinners whom an angry God would at his pleasure drop into hell. He was early taught Latin and to remember that he was born to die. When he was thirteen years old he rode away on horseback to Yale College. His austere and lonely boyhood was over, if he ever had a boyhood. Yale and Jonathan were about the same age then and both troubled with growing pains. Actually, Edwards was better orientated than the College, since it had so far belonged to the peripatetic school, its students scattered, its location still undecided. The trustees finally decided on New Haven in November 1716. Ten Freshmen matriculated and, disliking their tutors, presently went as a body to Wethersfield and the tutorship of Elisha Williams. There they stayed for two years. Aided and abetted by the Hartford factions they even put on a rival commencement in 1718. All these episodes brighten the early history of Yale, but they were not conducive to sound learning.

They doubtless also confirmed Edwards in that inner detachment from outer turmoil which became the habit and resource of his life. Locke's essay on the human understanding stimulated his precocious mind and revealed to him the serene domain of abstract speculation that would thereafter be his homeland, though not always serene. The significant thing about these youthful speculations is their philosophic idealism, arrestingly parallel to Berkeley. Debate exists therefore among his biographers as to whether he could have read Berkeley or did. There is no decisive proof either way. His kind of mind was equal to reaching, independently, such conclusions. Indeed the nucleus of all his future speculations and conclusions were in the nine foolscap pages of his undergraduate composition on the mind.

Meanwhile Yale undergraduate manners and even morals tried him sorely. He lamented "monstrous impieties and acts of immorality lately committed." It reads now like a combination of John Bunyan and St. Augustine recounting the sins of their youth. Only for Edwards these were the sins of other youths. After graduation he was pastor for eight months of a Presbyterian church in New York. He was next called to Bolton, Connecticut, but never settled, for Yale wanted him for a tutor and Sarah Pierpont was in New Haven. His tutorship there was as trying as his engagement to Miss Pierpont was beatific, so after two years he accepted the Northampton call. He began at once by marrying Sarah, distinguished by lineage, beauty, mystic devotion, practical wisdom. It was a marriage made in heaven, and her renown matched her husband's.

Whitefield thought the Edwards household an example of Christian simplicity. In Mrs. Edwards he saw, figuratively, "a daughter of Abraham" and was moved to renew the prayers he had been putting up to God for a similar "daughter of Abraham." He felt it, on many accounts, his duty to marry, but humbly left the choice and bestowal of the longed-for daughter of Abraham to the Lord, having, he said, no choice of his own. Edwards, who himself walked humbly enough before God, had more initiative. He had indirectly had Sarah in mind for four years and what he has written of her is classic. She was seventeen and bore him many children. Also she was a force to be reckoned with in any account of the "Great Awakening."

Edwards was one of William Janes' "Twice Born Men," and his account of his own illumination is classic. He was soul-kin to the great mystics, though with a sense of the presence of God in nature not always found in the literature of mysticism. His experience of what might be called "crisis" conversion—though in his own case very gently modulated and with deep emotional content—colored his evangelical appeal. It would not be accurate to say that "conversion" thereafter took on new meanings and became focal. The "new birth" was old as the gospels or older, and there had been St. Paul on his way to Damascus and a great succeeding company. Also the Puritan had expected those who joined his churches to have had a religious experience and to tell it to the elders. But since then a different emotional emphasis was in gestation in colonial Protestantism, and in England as well; it broke through first in Northampton under Jonathan Edwards' ministry. Enter the revival and revivalist, in a sense little changed in the last two hundred years.

Edwards apparently did not consciously initiate just that. His revival was a by-product of his theology and the whole matter is extremely complicated. A theologian like A. V. G. Allen[1] needed nearly four hundred pages for Edwards; Elizabeth Winslow[2] as much. The Great Awakening and the Wesleys distinguish the religious history of the Eighteenth Century. Condensation therefore is impossible, especially as the examination of a profound and subtle theology is also involved. In a misleadingly spacious sentence or two, the frigidities of Calvinism were challenged by a rival system and religion had grown cold and formal. In consequence the Puritan ethic was giving way and church life was suffering. For Edwards a pure Calvinism, though he did not call it that, was the keystone of the breaking arch, and he became its New England champion. One might call his theology against its contemporaneous backgrounds a "neo-orthodoxy." He had by every testimony a power in preaching which defies analysis.

II

The 1740 Revival

For long he read his sermons from closely written, crossed out, written in and blotted manuscript. Any scrap of paper was precious. He even used the margins of newspapers, though not in the pulpit. He was intensely quiet, like a dynamo. He had the most vivid of imaginations, a power of description both poetic and terrible, an entirely untactful courage and a desperate earnestness. Above all he was not only "God-intoxicated"; he was consumed by the sovereignty of God, the fateful brevity of life, and its eternal issues in a heaven more real than the guardian mountains of his valley and of indescribable felicity and a hell, if anything more real, of indescribable torment.

Also there were wooing notes and an equally indescribable setting out of the sweetness of communion with God born of his own beatific vision

---

[1] Allen, *Jonathan Edwards.*
[2] Winslow, *Jonathan Edwards, 1703–1758.* This chapter is deeply in debt to this excellent book.

in his father's rocky pasture field years before. In time something is bound to give way under the cumulative force of preaching like that, if one adds a cumulative emphasis upon the sinfulness of sin and a definite cataloging, with the pointed and accusing finger, of the sins of Northampton town—sins of so deadly a sort that only the mercy of God, long now overtried, saved that still stockaded settlement from the fate of Sodom and Gomorrah.[3] The break came in 1734. An excessively pleasure-loving young woman came to her pastor, a repentant seeker. This seems to have astonished Edwards himself. Young people renounced their gaieties. Their elders began to ask "what must I do to be saved?" Edwards was wise in council and direction, enemies were reconciled, there were "showers of blessings." The town was reborn, the old church could not hold the people and grew to more than six hundred members, which in a settlement of about two hundred families meant the entire population from (say) ten years of age up.

A movement which began with emotionalism would in the end either break under emotional tension, or, more normally, when everybody had been gathered in the harvest would be over. Both these things happened. Thomas Stebbins tried suicide and failed; Joseph Hanley, uncle to Jonathan, tried and succeeded. There was an epidemic of similar attempts. Reaction set in, ecstasy was over, Northampton must go about its business again and channel religious zeal into the building of a new church. And for several years no one joined that church.

The fires were banked but not out. The Northampton awakening naturally moved other churches to desire and pray for a similar quickening. Five years later there were similar revivals, and not only in New England. The Presbyterians of the middle colonies began to be stirred deeply. Then came Whitefield, an Anglican clergyman, zealous for souls, impatient of Episcopal authority, with a voice like all the pipes of a great organ, a preacher of inexplicable power—literally the first great footloose Protestant evangelist. He ranged the colonies from Savannah to northern New England, was attended by throngs, preached indoors, outdoors, anywhere. And those who heard him were like reeds shaken in the wind. He is a study in himself and until a generation ago amazingly modern. He raised money for his orphanage and railed at the godless and unregenerate ministers who did no more than stay in one parish and do the best they could. They took that with surprising meekness, then as later.

During this period there were such physical manifestations of spiritual struggle as would follow the frontier until almost the middle of the last

[3] Sodom and Gomorrah not quoted from Edwards' sermons: simply the author's rhetoric.

century. Whitefield rejoiced in them, saw in them a manifestation of the power of the Holy Ghost and possibly his own power. He thanked God when the sinners went down as before a cannonball. Edwards was not quite so sure. All this was in so many plain words a fear-motivated, hell-fire-threatened revival within the frame of a Calvinistic theology. Naturally John Wesley and George Whitefield did not see eye to eye. For Wesley knew with a sure insight that an enduring religion of religious experience must be built on another foundation. Both the grace of God and the response of the penitent soul must be more free. So Whitefield was an episode, and John Wesley released a vast, creative, and enduring religious force.

This second stage of the Great Awakening grew to almost a colonial hysteria. Gilbert Tennant of New Jersey became the leader of all that was worst in it. He was hellfire and damnation, shouting and stamping.[4] The preaching for which Edwards is popularly remembered, as far as he is, belongs to this period; for example, the Enfield sermon, July 8, 1741. He was really trying to rekindle fires of which only ashes were left. He took the thunderbolts of the divine wrath in his own hands and hurled them at his congregation. "A most terrible sermon," said Isaac Watts who later read it; needing, he thought, "a word of Gospell at ye end it."[5] So the Awakening ran its course. Yale and Harvard stood out against it, and some ministers (notably Charles Chauncy, Boston First Church).

It certainly brought multitudes into the churches and inflamed religious zeal. One hundred and fifty new Congregational churches (Tracy) were formed from 1740 to 1760, though the increase of population might account for some of them. They were, in a sense the first Separatists never contemplated, "gathered churches," without roots in any old order. That was gone. There was a considerable increase of Baptist churches, and Methodism was coming. The "evangelical" spirit was released and a concern for the salvation of all men everywhere, which would presently become foreign missions. Also in direct and indirect ways a philanthropic spirit was engendered which would first challenge slavery and later other social injustices. There was an increased need for ministers who must be educated. That meant or would mean more theological seminaries. Whitefield would find many successors. The revival became a technique of church life not to be challenged until Horace Bushnell, and D. L. Moody would, in the memory of some who may read this chapter, do for England and America what Whitefield had done, with a greatness of grace and wisdom Whitefield never possessed. Finally the Awakening occasioned, if it did not create, the first American theology.

[4] Winslow, *Jonathan Edwards, 1703–1758*, p. 189.
[5] Winslow, *Jonathan Edwards, 1703–1758*, p. 192.

III

AN EPOCH-MAKING EXILE

Jonathan Edwards' long and epochal pastorate came to an end in Northampton most unhappily. There were divisions and antagonisms which the brotherly love of the first revival had not ended. The young people were getting out of hand again and reading improper books with distressing consequences. The books, Leslie Stephen thought, might have been such then popular novels as *Pamela* which Richardson himself said he published in order to cultivate the principles of virtue and religion in the minds of the youth of both sexes. Eighteenth Century English fiction lacked Victorian delicacy, but would not now be censured. At any rate when the church officers and their pastor began to consider discipline, they found Northampton's "best people" involved, and the investigation was dropped. The old question of qualification for full communion got involved, the estrangement could not be healed, an ecclesiastical council dissolved Edwards' pastoral relationship, the church ratified the findings of the council by an overwhelming majority, and at the last he was forbidden by a town-meeting vote to enter the pulpit. So he was turned adrift.

The only thing which illumines the whole unhappy passage, save the light it let in on human nature, is the spirit in which Edwards bore it. His only recorded impatience was with the Congregational system. A Scotch friend inquired if he would consider a church in Scotland, sign the Westminster confession, and submit to Presbyterian church government. He would subscribe, he answered, to the confession in substance and, being out of conceit with independent church government—as he well might be—had long thought the Presbyterian way "most agreeable to the word of God and the reason and nature of things."[6] He did not go to Scotland, but his Scotch friends sent him generous contributions. He went instead to Stockbridge, Massachusetts, as missionary to the Indians, a mission supported by a proper Board in Boston—one of the first of many—and a society in England.

His was an epoch-making exile. The Indians could not have profited greatly by his preaching; they did by his friendship. Some of the white settlers, he discovered, were misusing the funds meant for their wards— an early chapter in a shameful story. There was a gritty practical strain in Edwards and a hatred of any evil. He set out to expose both the abuses and the abusers. The main offender's family were prominent and related to his Northampton enemies. It was a two-year fight which he won, but his peace was a solitude which he made historic. The curious desk

6 Allen, *Jonathan Edwards*, p. 271.

upon which he wrote is still in the vestry of the Stockbridge church—a kind of little wooden pyramid turning on a central standard. He made that table a "Maginot Line" in defense of his inherited and rigorous Calvinism. He would have said himself that he was defending something vaster: the sovereignty and grace of God, the validity of his moral order, and the reality of religion as he conceived it. The defense of the whole system, he thought—and his age agreed with him—turned on the nature and function of the human will.

Here not only rival systems but God and man were engaged. If the will were free, then God's predestinations were at the mercy of capricious men, and his elections could be counted out. At the same time, how can any moral responsibility be justified without freedom to choose or to reject? If man is God's puppet, then hell arraigns God's justice, and heaven is a divine caprice. These were burning questions then; Milton's fallen angels discussed them in their lurid dark, and the New England farmer in his rocky fields, not to speak of philosophers and theologians. Edwards wrote his treatise on the will in four months, but all the life-long workings of his powerful mind gave it form and life.

Allen calls it the literary sensation of the Eighteenth Century and one of the few great books in English theology. It made Edwards known in the intellectual capitals of Great Britain and became in its own turn a storm-center of controversy. Careful students of Edwards reduce his argument to, perhaps, a too simple paradox: man is free as he is inclined, but his inclinations are determined for him. Therefore for following his inclinations he is free enough to be judged of God. Which answered Edwards' purpose and adjourned the real question: what or who determines the inclinations? His motives, Edwards answered, but his motives lie outside his control. This would seem to the irreverent to save God's sovereignty at the cost of his honor. Actually Edwards seems to have maintained a limited freedom and to have anticipated conclusions upon which science, psychology, and philosophies would later converge: we are shaped by forces beyond our tracing, carried by currents beyond our control, toward destinies beyond our vision. Edwards founded the mystery of it all in God, and left it there.

IV

AN ERA OF THEOLOGICAL SPECULATION

Having finished with the will, Edwards continued to build the vast structure of his speculative thought until the contemplation of it becomes awesome. They said of Durham cathedral that it was half-fortress and half church of God. Edwards' theology was all that, unassailable save as to its foundations, impregnable if assaulted with the war-gear

against which he designed it, and now left there between earth and sky
as thought and interest moved into other regions.[7] But Edwards remains
the first American theologian and metaphysician, the man who broke the
old order in maintaining it; first also in the long line of Congregational
theologians with momentous consequences. They called him from Stockbridge to the presidency of Princeton which his son-in-law, Aaron Burr,
had resigned. There he died prematurely of a crude inoculation for
small-pox, there he was buried, and there in his weathered, above-the-
ground tomb he found the peace life denied him.

Samuel Hopkins and Emmons, the conjoint products of Edwards' influence (Hopkins lived in the Edwards' home), the Great Awakening, a
temper at once humble and arrogant, very plain living and very high
thinking, initiated and continued an era of theological speculation. Hopkins entitled his first treatise: *"Sin, Through Divine Interposition an
Advantage to the Universe: And Yet, This No Excuse for Sin or Encouragement To It."* All this and much more Hopkins labored through to the
comfort of those who believed it and the irritation of those who did not.
Eternal punishment was, he thought, a bright display of the divine
character and an occasion of so much happiness in heaven "that should
it cease and this fire could be extinguished, it would, in a great measure,
obscure the light of heaven."[8] On such strong meat as this the fathers of
our faith were fed. Somewhere behind it all was a consuming passion for
the glory of God, and the utter prostration of all human interests and
inclinations at the foot of his throne hid in darkness and light. This was
preeminently true of Edwards, whose God was sweetness and severity
beyond Edwards' mystic power to say. The result should be so complete
a dedication of self to God that, as Hopkins held, one should be willing
to be damned for his glory.[9]

The Awakening, as already noted, was criticized by the colleges and
by no means blessed by all the clergy. Edwards' treatise on the will was
quite as much a dressing down of another school of theology as an inquiry into truth. The opposing schools were already entitled—always a
sign that controversy has matured and become embittered. The conservatives were called "Old Lights." The advanced were "New Lights,"[10] and
they forgot their Christianity in their contentions. The "Half-Way Cove-

[7] The Maginot Line is not a bad analogy. It is probably still there (July, 1941) but
France is subject.
[8] Walker, *Ten New England Leaders*, p. 349.
[9] This became a famous test question, much asked at ordaining councils. There is, as
it began to be worn thread-bare, a classic anecdote: A much-heckled candidate for the
ministry was finally asked it. He replied that he was not, personally, but he was perfectly willing the council should be.
[10] The use of "New Light" and "Old Light" through this period are confusing. Sometimes the "new lights" are "revivalists"; sometimes they are theological "liberals."

nant" furnished the occasion, but the forces engaged were vast and various—new minds and new times. As far as Congregationalism was concerned, Geneva was beginning to lose its hold on New England. Eastern Massachusetts, specifically, was going "New Light" theologically and developing a revolutionary temper politically. Harvard College was the contributing temper intellectually. Boston ministers and churches—still a minority—were breaking with their Calvinistic inheritance, slowly but significantly. Connecticut was more conservative. The Anglican church was relatively stronger in Connecticut than Massachusetts and the associations with Middle Colony Presbyterians much more intimate and sympathetic. (Newark, New Jersey, had been settled by Connecticut migrants.)

The result was not only a definite cooperation, the consequences of which are still to be considered here, but in Connecticut itself a Congregationalism strongly colored with Presbyterianism.[11] Given the temper of the time, the rigidity of the systems involved, and the looseness of the ecclesiastical system, the unity of the inherited Congregational order, impaired by the Great Awakening and strained by profound theological disagreement, began to face doctrinal disruption. But a more inclusive warfare on other contested fields subordinated all lesser differences to the epic struggle of the colonies against their mother land. The compact in the cabin of the Mayflower became the unseen, not yet comprehended device on the battle flags of a people who began with no flag of their own.

V

THE NEW ENGLAND CLERGY AND THE REVOLUTIONARY WAR

There were, naturally, other issues in the last half of the Eighteenth Century amongst the colonies which fringed our seaboard and other occasions for belligerency than the purely theological. The colonies were involved from the first in the long series of European wars which began with William and Mary. New England was earlier and more deeply involved than other colonial groups because its frontiers marched with the frontiers of New France and there could be no security in lonely outposts as long as Quebec and Montreal were hostile. French naval bases in waters contiguous to New England menaced its shipping. Besides Britain's cause was the colonies' cause and in defending her own Britain protected them.

American historians generally have held that the French and Indian War and the Seven Years War initiated and then accelerated the move-

[11] So late as 1799 the Hartford North Association told the world that the churches of Connecticut at large were not and never had been Congregational churches according to the ideas and forms of the Cambridge platform. They held the independent churches to be Separatists. Walker, *Creeds and Platforms of Congregationalism*, p. 556.

ment for colonial independence, at least from Virginia north, and most definitely in New England. The colonies were drawn together for defense and consultation and became corporately self-conscious. Their young men were trained in arms; the people became habituated to war. The British government, with some show of reason, thought that the colonies should bear their share of the cost of wars which had made them safe and imposed their taxes, therefore, without so much as saying "by your leave." We would now call them "nuisance" taxes. They did not bear overly hard upon the taxed, but the mischief they did was fateful, or else it was fateful but not mischief. When the historians of this school have stressed the added irritations caused by the determination of London merchants to keep the colonies economically dependent,[12] they rest their case.

All this is beyond debate, but these seeds of political discontent—and eventually revolution—fell upon a soil already prepared for exactly such issues. A temper impatient of any kind of arbitrary control had been native to New England from its beginnings. It had crossed the Atlantic in the Mayflower and sailed with Winthrop's fleet. A long century of theological controversy had toughened its fibre and furnished it supports. The debates about ecclesiastical polity and the relative authority of congregations, elders, parsons, associations, and synods, which now seem inconsequential, were far more than a dress-rehearsal for the Declaration of Independence, the Revolutionary War, and constitutional conventions. For these contestants fought their little battles with heavy guns. The principles they invoked were competent for deployment, in the discussion of social and governmental policies. Alice Baldwin maintains that the Congregational-Puritan clergy of New England were the chief agitators for the Revolution, blessed it when it began and supplied much of the morale which carried it through.[13] (Incidentally, her documentation corrects the loose statements of an earlier chapter of this book about the influence of Eighteenth Century thought upon the New England clergy.) Miss Baldwin's facts and conclusions constitute a fascinating chapter in the history of American Congregationalism.

The very large majority of ministers and churches in New England were then Congregational. In 1760 Ezra Stiles estimated that there were 530 Congregational churches in Massachusetts, Connecticut, and New Hampshire—Maine was still in Massachusetts—and 550 ordained min-

---

[12] The Northern colonies were getting flourishing little industries going. The "South" welcomed English imports.

[13] All this and much more is developed by Alice M. Baldwin in *The New England Clergy and the American Revolution*. Her documentation is as rich as her conclusions are convincing. Reading her book has been one of the compensations of working through a deal of dusty authorities.

isters mostly Congregational, which means that the folk of the colonies were, say, eighty per cent Congregational before the Revolution. The clergy had lost the undue and unwholesome respect in which they had been held but they were still the learned men in unlettered communities sharing in a most intimate way community life. They were means of contact between their parishioners and the outside world.

They tutored promising boys for college and so directed their minds. They preached then, as now, on the events of the day. In the larger towns they lectured once a week on whatever they thought their audiences needed to be advised about and they supplied sermons for all important civic occasions. The "Election Sermon" delivered on general Election Day by some distinguished preacher specially chosen for that honor was really the "keynote" address. It was usually printed by order of the Assembly or General Court and widely distributed. Naturally, the preacher brought all his forces into action, quoted impressively, exhorted the magistrates and pled for the well-being of the Commonwealth.[14]

All this is a pattern for ministerial conduct which held for more than a hundred years.

VI

POLITICAL PREACHING

There were, besides, sermons preached on Muster-Days, on the anniversaries of the Ancient and Honorable artillery, on Thanksgiving and Fast Days. No clerical group before or since had more opportunities for influencing public opinion upon the entire conduct of the common life of the colonies. (Sainte-Beuve noted, in *Port Royal,* the significance of the sermon before the era of newspapers.)

They dealt with the fundamentals of government, they sought the sources of authority. Their theology was legalistic, God was sovereign and his laws should be supreme in all affairs, sacred and inviolable. There they were for all to read in the Old and New Testament, unwritten but regnant in the "law of Nature," "twisted into the very Frame and Constitution" of the human soul. God himself, in his divine administration, is bound by the laws of his own nature. God and man are bound together in a "covenant" relationship of mutual rights and duties. The divine government is the pattern for all human government, itself a compact between the governing and the governed, which neither party must violate. This is pure Eighteenth Century political theory.

---

[14] Channing's sermon on Spiritual Freedom is a noble example of an "election sermon" of a later date (May 1830). His passages beginning, "I call that mind free—" are classic and have been often declaimed.

VII

ANALOGIES BETWEEN CHURCH AND STATE

It is easy to see what room there was upon such ample foundations to build the structures of Church and Commonwealth. Churches were enabled by a covenant relationship between the members and God and between the church members themselves. All civil government was of divine origin, founded in common consent for the common good, to maintain good order, liberty, and prosperity. The majority agreed with Elisha Williams that any government which did not originate from the people and in which they did not make their own laws was a tyranny and "absolutely against the Law of God and Nature," and he quoted Locke to prove it. Sturdy Samuel Stoddard held that God deeply resents abuses offered unto rulers by the people or by the people unto their rulers. Liberty, of course, had its dangers and must not be overdone. "The majesty of laws must be revered, where the liberties of a people must be secured." Liberty must not get out of hand.

So early as 1715 it seemed to be getting out of hand. We have noted the dissolution of the old order, the lapses from Puritan ethics and the want of religious zeal which so troubled Jonathan Edwards. It troubled the clergy generally. There were, the more conservative thought, dangerous "leveling" forces in action. Those who should have been godly had grown worldly. There began to be the poor and the prosperous, taxes were heavy, distinctions of rank began to be ignored, the discontented criticised the authorities, there were floating phrases of a sinister sort—"liberty" and "equality."

The clergy, however, did not agree in their apportionment of blame. The conservative blamed the people and reminded them that the powers that be are ordained of God. The liberals blamed the governments for failing in their duties and between them they threshed out over and over again the right principles of administration and citizenship both in Church and state. There could not have been a better training school for what was to come. Both wings seemed to have agreed that government was a compact; they differed simply about which party to the compact had broken it. Rulers, John Hancock of Lexington and grandfather of John Hancock, maintained, must be "Benefactors." If they are not they are "Burdens," "Plagues" and "Punishments." He told the General Court in plain words that they would thus forfeit respect, become obnoxious to the people, and incur divine displeasure.[15]

So the sermons went on, but as one follows them through Miss Bald-

[15] They would, he said actually, "become * * obnoxious * * to the Divine Displeasure"—a subtly puzzling sentence.

win's citations, he sees an emerging philosophy of society and theory of government surprising in range, solidity and penetration. These preachers were advanced and courageous thinkers and quite shrewd politicians.[16] They naturally held an uneven front. Those of a Presbyterian complexion stood up for discipline and authority. The Congregationally-minded stressed the liberty of the believer and the citizen and the obligations and limitations of rulers. Less was said about equality, but they were all agreed about the sanctity of property. Liberty and property were more often associated than liberty and equality. Jared Eliot analyzed (1730) the just powers of government in the province of taxation with an acumen which would do credit to a modern specialist in political science.

There were, also, then as now, middle-of-the-road men who reconciled extremes with spacious phrases. "Liberty must not be overlaid, nor authority trampled under foot;" "That there may be a reconciliation or due concurrence in the balancing of one justly with the other." This balance Urian Oakes thought was a characteristic of the "Congregational Way" whose "sweet temperament" preserved both liberty and authority. Thus they preached on and on. The entire ecclesiastical machinery of Connecticut during the pre-Revolutionary period only missed being Presbyterian by want of a General Assembly (ecclesiastical) at the top. Connecticut was slipping from the "sweet temperament of the Congregational Way." Result: alarums and excursions and certain churches went their own sweet, temperamental independent way. They were called "Separatists" and ill-spoken of. In return they lamented "priest-craft" in the colony and warned the people against "an ambitious and designing clergy."

The Great Awakening led many Connecticut ministers, magistrates and the "chief gentlemen of the colony" to take extreme measures against itinerant preachers and evangelists at large, and the formation of additional Congregational churches. In 1743 the legislature forbade the establishment of new churches without its permission.[17] All this was, Protestants held, a violation of the Connecticut Constitution and William and Mary's Act of Liberation. There is no denying that the authorities were foolishly high-handed. Boys were expelled from Yale for attending "Separatist" meetings, men and women were imprisoned for conscience sake and legally elected representatives opposed to such a policy refused

[16]Lyman Beecher, who should know, said that in his youth all Connecticut parsons were politicians. Actually a Congregational minister had then and still has to be something of a politician in his own parish—also a diplomat.
[17]Yale College took a strong stand. Any student who said "directly or indirectly" that college officials or tutors were "hypocritical, carnal or unconverted" must for his first offense make "publick confession in the Hall" and for a second offense be expelled.

their seats in the Assembly.[18] All this reads now like the Wars of the Kites and the Crows, but the fundamentals of civil and religious liberty were involved. New churches were being organized to meet the needs of the newly-converted, denominationalism was coming into action. Baptists, for example, were taxed to support the ministers of what was, in substance, a state church. The "Separatist" Congregational folk were taxed to support the official churches. "Taxation without representation" was more than a phrase; it became a burning question and a very concrete reality.[19]

VIII

Taxation without Representation

After the middle of the Eighteenth Century, the principles involved in these ecclesiastical and religious controversies were deployed upon a vaster field. The growing tensions between the colonies and the British government slowly solidified the colonies. The more glaring internal injustices were corrected; the disentanglement of the Puritan Commonwealth in governmental action and the church and religious life of the people was getting on, though as yet far from final. Liberty, so the colonists felt, was being endangered by its English authors. The full examination of this belongs to American history generally and involves great chapters in British history.

The bonds of every sort which bound the colonies to Great Britain were strong; they were not easily broken. So late as 1760, said Ezra Stiles, "all the New England sects are loyal, but the principles of loyalty to the illustrious house of Hanover are inculcated on the people by the Congregational clergy with peculiar sincerity, faithfulness and constancy." A dozen years later all this was changed, which argues a fatal ingenuity of irritation on the part of Parliament and the then reigning representative of the "illustrious House of Hanover." The clergy generally were all, and naturally, for the French and Indian War. They contrasted British liberty and French tyranny in heated exhortations which sound, with some significant changes, an arrestingly contemporaneous (1941) note. "Election Sermons" thundered against King Louis and his slaves. Liberty, property, religion, happiness were all at stake. "Better to die than to be enslaved." The churches became recruiting stations and with then unforeseen consequences "liberty" became an issue to live and die

---

[18] Baldwin, *The New England Clergy and the American Revolution*, p. 61.

[19] The complaints of the sufferers may be exaggerated but there is ample evidence of injustice. Cows and household furnishings distrained, oxen taken out of their teams, the heads of households imprisoned. So Solomon Paine of Canterbury in a pamphlet (1752). Baldwin, *The New England Clergy and the American Revolution*, p. 75.

for; a temper hot with fiery zeal was engendered ready to turn against any invasion of liberty.[20]

The Excise Laws, the Stamp Act, and the inept attempts of Parliament to tax the colonies became for the colonists the head and front of an invasion of their so cherished and dearly bought liberties. It was by no means entirely a question of taxation. Presbyterians and Congregationalists had, they thought, a well grounded apprehension that the establishment of Anglican Episcopacy was contemplated by the Crown. At least the activities of the "Society for the Propagation of the Gospel" —a particularly irritating assumption on the part of the Anglican authorities that there was no "Gospel" in the colonies—lent weight to that fear. They were, therefore, suspicious of the British policies and easily moved to utterance. One must not say that the American Revolution began in the colonist pulpits, but he would have a case. Boston ministers worked hand in glove with Otis and Adams. Their technique, now familiar, was then new. They rehearsed past heroisms and sacrifices, evoked a patriotism as yet provincial but potentially national and furnished the emotional appeals which have ever since been so apt in stirring American public opinion.

They did more; they examined the fundamentals of constitutional and representative government, the relation of law to liberty, the province of checks and balances in government. So early as 1738 Jared Eliot, a friend of Franklin, argued for something very much like Dominion Status for British plantations. Parliament and the King might well have studied the sermons of these unconsidered ranters. They might have saved England her greatest colony; they would certainly have saved the British government long and costly processes of trial and error in the evolution of her colonial policies.

IX

"STAND ARMED, O YE AMERICANS"

The "Stamp Act" set the pulpits on fire; its repeal furnished the substance of Thanksgiving sermons. "A deliverance from slavery; nothing less than from vile, ignominious slavery." The fire once kindled could not be put out; complete independence began to be talked of. Brown College students debated it in 1769, and Harvard College, had there been a Dies Committee,[21] would have been investigated for its political radicalism. The spilled blood of the "Boston Massacre" found tongues and spoke from the dust. Rebellion was in the air. "What right," said Isaac Skill-

---

[20] The significance of this can not be exaggerated. These colonial preachers evoked and released a timeless force in American life. Their sermons have for two hundred years been repreached and have become our national passion.

[21] See most American newspapers, 1939–1941.

man, "has the King of England to America?" "Only what the people have by compact invested him with." "Stand armed, O ye Americans."[22]

Naturally the Loyalists did not take all this lying down. The clergy of New England, a gentleman of New York wrote a London friend, were wicked, malicious, and inflammatory; their pulpits were "converted into Gutters of Sedition" and they substituted politics for the Gospel. Chief Justice Oliver was deeply pained; the pulpits, he said, rang their peals of malice against the Courts of Justice.

Directly the Revolution became inevitable, the clergy not only blessed it, but became chaplains, were invaluable in recruiting, maintained the morale of their congregations, served as privates or officers, gave sacrificially to the cause, remitted their salaries to relieve parishioners, and when the war was over began to write its history. Finally after the Declaration of Independence, when new constitutions were in order for the new Commonwealths, the clergy contributed their knowledge and their ideas. There were thirteen clergymen in the Massachusetts Constitutional Convention (1779–1780). We owe to them and their contemporaries more than to any other single source those "Bills of Rights" which in the federal and state constitutions are still the safeguards of the essential liberty of the individual.[23] In such ways as these the colonial ministry made their invaluable contribution to the temper, tradition and political corps of American life. No Congregationalist can justly claim that New England Congregationalism was alone in this service. They did take a part of which those who seek to retell their story may justly be proud.

[22] The growing use of "America" and "Americans" is extremely significant.

[23] This probably claims too much for the New England clergy. In 1776 a convention of delegates "from the counties and corporations of the colony of Virginia" gathered at Williamsburg and made history. The convention anticipated the Declaration of Independence and adopted a Declaration of Rights which could be exhibited as the source of the Bill of Rights in the American Constitution. Actually these things were in the colonial air. The clergy voiced them in New England with others; in Virginia, Mason, Madison, Jefferson, and Patrick Henry.

CHAPTER IX

The Unitarian Departure

THE Revolutionary War supplied the New England clergy an entirely sufficient field for their militant exercises, and a limited moratorium in theological controversy was tacitly declared for the duration. There was, however, no cessation of theological speculation and divisive forces continued in action. That was inevitable. The general lines along which Nineteenth Century thought was to move had their genesis in the Eighteenth Century, though that of course is an arbitrary dating. At least a central line of cleavage had become clearly recognizable.

The consequent division was never either precise or consistent; the central lines were crossed and recrossed by the sheer complexities of human nature. But, as one may trace a great watershed, it was there, and what drained down from it in any region took opposite courses with far-reaching consequences. There are names enough, since no one name is ever enough, for these two opposing orders. We now name them in their Nineteenth Century alignments "Liberal" and "Conservative." They involved two radically opposed ways of approaching the meanings and mysteries of life and conducting the human enterprise. They began, still in the Eighteenth Century, as engaging abstractions suitable to a philosopher's closet or a theologian's study, but they refused to remain abstractions or confine themselves to closets.

They became American and French Revolutions, political processes, laws and constitutions. They wrote liberty, fraternity, and equality across the façades of the palaces of Bourbon kings, and altered the status of religion and ecclesiastical orders. And between them on a somewhat provincial terrain, though the issues involved were by no means provincial, they provoked what is now irenically known as the Unitarian Departure. For New England theology reflected in its own limited geographical field the ferment of the age and was thereby eventually profoundly affected. Puritan-Congregational doctrine had from the first held and been held within the limits of a rigid Calvinism, even though early Separatists had thought predestination an ungodly doctrine. The first phases of the movement had not therefore been doctrinally controversial. The focal interests of nascent Congregationalism were in another region: the true nature and constitution of the Church and the right way to worship God.

When Plymouth Pilgrims had won through suffering and exile the liberty to have their own kind of church and say their prayers without vestments, bell, or candle, they had for a little season nothing to contend against save Indians and an inhospitable soil, and nothing to contend for save a bare and lonely existence. They wanted only peace. Moreover, the first independent churches, being "gathered," were organized on a covenantal and not a creedal basis. Orthodoxy was not yet a burning question and needed no creedal definitions.

Time and militant Puritanism changed all that. "Peace" and "Puritanism" have, historically, had little in common save their initial letters. The Cambridge Platform required "a personall and publick confession and declaring of God's manner of working upon the soul" as "both lawfull, expedient and useful." "This profession of faith and repentance . . . must be made by such at their admission, that were never in church-society before."[1] The seeds of doctrinal controversy were in that requirement from the beginning and they developed, in time, an ample growth. Since a man's salvation depended upon a sufficiency of theology, there was never anywhere else, save in Scotland, a more fertile field for doctrinal controversy.

The effects of such discussions upon the Scotch and American minds have been so often considered as to need no more than reëmphasis here. That so many students of formative forces in American life can leave religion out is simply one more proof of that article in the creed to which most disputants then subscribed: that our minds were hopelessly ruined by the "Fall." The themes which engaged such seekers after salvation were great enough to challenge the most disciplined minds; the arguments they fed upon were as close-reasoned as they were subtly maintained or denied by master metaphysicians. Plain farming folk read by firelight or candlelight books of which we speak awesomely, though never having read them ourselves. Thus trained and being competent for the sacred and eternal, they were more than competent for the secular and the temporal. They came to town-meeting from a consideration of the decrees of the Almighty and went to colonial legislatures with the persuasion of an "election" of which their earthly majorities were only a validation.

I

THE INFLUENCE OF BRITISH THOUGHT UPON NEW ENGLAND THEOLOGY

For all that, the colonies, still under administration of the British crown, were not immune to the influence of British Eighteenth Century

[1] Williston Walker's massive and authoritative *Creeds and Platforms of Congregationalism* is the source book for the creedal history of Congregationalism up to the date of its publication (1893).

thought, which was increasingly skeptical and rationalistic. If one should say that the Eighteenth Century supplied for the first time since the dominance of Christianity a philosophic basis for religious skepticism, he would not be too far wrong. For religion itself the significant thing was the rise of what might be called secular systems of thought. Logically they began, continued, and ended entirely outside the province of religion, but they could not as yet disentangle themselves from their religious inheritances nor ignore them. They would neither accept Christianity nor leave it alone.

The result was that Eighteenth Century thought, as Leslie Stephen interprets it with a wealth of erudition and brilliancy of comment,[2] is seen playing in and out of religion along its entire front and always with a dissolving influence upon inherited orthodoxies. Stephen needed two massive volumes to tell his story, the point of which, for the purposes of this chapter, is that so vast and contagious a body of thought, mobile in literature, was sure to reach and influence New England which was, after all, English and Eighteenth-Century. The question is, how much? One cannot see that classic, conservative New England divines positively reflect much of that influence, though consciously or unconsciously they may have been "shadow-boxing" with it. They were, however, by no means ignorant of it (Edwards had read Locke) but they moved upon a clearly defined theoretical terrain. They were not fighting Hume and his philosophy. They were fighting a holy war for their Calvinism, and carrying it to conclusions which might have surprised Calvin himself. For his doctrine, he knew, was meant to live by in the face of great perils.

There is, on the other hand, adequate proof that the liberal wing was not only familiar with English thought but influenced by it. Chauncy of the First Church in Boston loved Tillotson and Baxter as ardently as he disliked "Great Awakenings" and Edwards' theology. Jonathan Mayhew of the West Church in Boston was steeped in Seventeenth and Eighteenth Century theology and philosophy—anything but Calvinistic sources. The safe conclusion seems to be that British thought penetrated and modified Congregational theology unevenly. The seaboard went liberal; the Berkshires kept the faith.

The influence of Harvard was disturbing, for that college had not, from the first, fulfilled to the letter the pious expectations of the founders. Its methods of free-inquiry favored theological laxity.[3]

---

[2] Stephen, *History of English Thought in the Eighteenth Century*.
[3] The influence of Eighteenth Century British thought upon American theology would be an admirable subject for a thesis. The influence of British literature is apparently negligible—A Boston book store in 1700 had for sale 2,504 titles, *Pilgrim's Progress* the only representation of literature; the rest religion and theology. The majority of these titles must have been British.

It is difficult to follow the engagements of rival theologies and the alignments of faction through the last half of the Eighteenth Century without using "liberal" and "liberalism," either with or without capital letters. Actually they were not then in use as we use them now. The word "liberal" is not in Leslie Stephen's index, which means that there was in the Eighteenth Century no English school, cabal, or party so named. Not that the age lacked labels. It continued the time-honored classifications of heresy such as "Arian" and "Socinian," though "Unitarian" was to displace "Arian." "Calvinism," the hall-mark of sterling orthodoxy, and "Arminian" were in general use. Calvinists were "New-lights" or "Old-lights," only the "New-lights" were the conservatives. Cooke thinks "Arminianism" to have then meant about what "liberalism" or "modernism" has since meant.

It was as much a state of mind and frontage of faith as an articulate creed. Theologically it maintained the freedom of the will as against inexorable decrees and predestinations, and it magnified the Grace of God as the Calvinist magnified his bleak sovereignty. For Edwards and his school it was a particularly irritating form of theological dissent and the head and front of pretty much all the current offenses against religion and morality which plagued Northampton and adjacent regions. In short, they did not like it. At any rate Arminianism meant in New England, say, in 1750 about what liberalism meant in and about Boston in, say, 1900 and later. So the terms are fairly interchangeable.[4]

II

The Lines Begin to Form

To what extent individual churches began to frame their own creeds in conformity with the Cambridge Platform could only be determined by an examination of church records not possible here.[4] But the precedent of authoritative doctrinal tests for church membership had been established. Ten years after the meetings at Cambridge, Massachusetts, English independents, supported by Cromwell, made their own declaration of faith. Their pastors and delegates met (September, 1658) in the old Savoy Palace on the bank of the Thames. Their *"Declaration* of the *Faith* and *Order* Owned and Practiced in the Congregational Churches in

[4]No historian of American Congregationalism during its first 175 years can escape the charge of provincialism. He must write as if Massachusetts and Connecticut were everything on this side of the Atlantic, be always referring to New England, and use all his ingenuity to keep clear of Boston. The defense is simple. American Congregationalism was thus geographically localized. Since English Congregationalism was during the first part of this period dormant, about all the Congregational churches there were anywhere were between the North Atlantic seaboard and the Hudson River. Few religious dramas of equal significance have been played out upon so small a stage. But there are other dimensions beside geography.

England: agreed upon and consented unto by their *Elders* and *Messengers*—" was therefore called the "Savoy Declaration."

It was a most weighty document—a dozen fine-print pages of preface, thirty-two chapters of doctrinal affirmation, and thirty articles dealing with the pure institution and order of churches. It was fundamentally trinitarian and inexorable about predestination for the glory of God. "Some men and angels are predestinated into everlasting life and others fore-ordained to everlasting death"; and nothing can be done about it. "Their number is so certain and definite that it cannot be either increased or diminished."[5]

Cromwell's death, almost on the day of the Savoy meeting, was also apparently a death blow to English Congregationalism. When it revived much later, the "Declaration" had passed out of the picture in England, but it had become authoritative in America. Massachusetts made it official in 1680. Delegates from the Connecticut churches met at Saybrook in 1708 and recommended it in substance[6] to the "Honorable General Assembly of Connecticut for adoption" as the faith of the churches "of this colony"—which seems to have been done with ultimately decisive consequences in Connecticut. So late as 1865 a National Council of Congregational Churches declared it quite satisfactory for "substance of doctrine." Considering its weary, wordy thirty-five pages, one may gravely doubt how many of the 502 delegates gathered in Old South meeting house in Boston had really read it, or with what mental reservations they approved it.[7]

We have already noted the natural reluctance of Baptists and Anglicans when taxed for the support of Congregational worship, and the disinclination of the non-communicant to be taxed for the support of any kind of church; also the rigors of Puritanism were being relaxed, not without protest. Whether or not to "sing by note" became a burning question; so did an organ offered to Brattle Street (refused, but King's Chapel accepted it). Chauncy prayed at Mayhew's funeral, said to be the first prayer ever offered at a Boston funeral, and so on.[8]

[5]It has been maintained that the long, stiff creeds of local Congregational churches date largely from the period after the Unitarian controversy. The orthodox thus meant to consolidate their position. The older churches were certainly organized upon covenants.

[6]Actually Massachusetts had adopted it in 1680.

[7]An insistent minority made their reservations vocal and started a hot debate. Result (this belongs to a later chapter in this history), an irenic declaration was drawn and read first on Burial Hill at Plymouth over the graves of the heroic dead and in sight of the wideness of the sea. It was afterwards adopted by the Council in Boston—a masterpiece of adroit and soothing terminology. At any rate it buried the Savoy Declaration—on Burial Hill.

[8]Also the Bible began to be read as a part of the order of worship, instead of a point of departure for exposition—all this from Cooke, though the engaging studies of Alice Morse Earle supply the facts.

Now all this was inevitable and much of it inconsequential, unless magnified out of all proportion. But there was a select core of divinity at the center of the inherited systems around which finally the really significant controversies would come into action. As one follows the engagement of opposed attitudes and tempers along a wide and very uneven front, he must conclude that the logic of the doctrinaire had carried Calvinism to extremes against which protest was inevitable and which invited extreme reaction. It had come dangerously near being a denial of any fundamental justice, let alone mercy, in God's way with men. By the strangest of paradoxes a passion for the glory of God led to extraordinary conceptions of his administrations. It is difficult calmly to characterize them.

Very likely a perfectly natural human and more or less unreasoned reaction against the dogmatic inhumanities of the current theology indicated the first line of liberal cleavage. After that a supporting theology was worked out for the more humane positions.[9] A dominant theology long worked over and out is like a great building whose strength is in its perfect balance of interlocking supports and strains. Take away any of its key supports and it begins to give way at other points. The liberal Eighteenth Century mind, rejecting an unpalatable Calvinism, began to question the whole of inherited orthodoxy. An Arminian could be a Trinitarian—witness the Wesleys—but once started down that road Unitarianism was reasonably inevitable for many of the liberal clergy and laity.

Actually there were then as now, broadly speaking, two kinds of mind—the seeking and the accepting, the critical and the conforming. These begin their characteristic Pilgrim's Progresses with no great depth or width of difference between them, but like navigators who use divergent great circles the distance between them presently becomes too vast for any reconciliation. "Fellowship" is and always has been one of the focal points of Congregationalism. Thereby Independency is controlled, saved from itself, though despite Cambridge platforms and everything since, it was and remains a free fellowship. A church may be left entirely, like Kipling's cat, to walk by itself, but it cannot be coerced, and the only excommunication without "bell or candle," is to leave its name out of the "Year Book" upon the recommendation of its ecclesiastical neighbors. There is a clerical as well as a church fellowship. Ministers belong to groups and associations, exchange pulpits, give each other right-hands-of-fellowship and the like. These are precious and vital filaments, and when they are broken they bleed.

[9] That is too easy a generalization. The complicated relationships of the ethical and the doctrinal in any religion cannot be so easily summarized.

III

THE CHURCHES CEASE TO "FELLOWSHIP"

New England Congregationalism, divided by theologies and more deeply by attitudes and tempers, began to lose its unities just along these lines of association and exchanges. It was a slow process; the bonds which held these relatively small groups of churches together would stretch before they broke. The first division of a church on doctrinal grounds, outside Boston, was in Worcester in 1785. The First Church there had been "hearing" candidates and could not agree upon any one of them. The majority wanted a Calvinist. "The more intelligent minority"[10] wanted a very pronounced liberal, withdrew, organized another church (a too familiar Congregational procedure) under Mr. Bancroft's ministry, and enjoyed it, one trusts, for many years. Dates now become significant. The American Revolution, as has been said, naturally furnished the religiously militant an ample channel for their belligerencies, and the colonies needed to hang together. Otherwise they faced the alternative that Franklin indicated.

In 1780, however, the "New Divinity," being the old Calvinism whose development under and after Edwards has been traced, had found in Hopkins and others its strongest and most decisive formulations. It possessed a tremendous driving power—has always possessed that power. It generated missionary fervor, sought converts, kindled revivals. In 1790 another period of revivalism began whose history only a specialist could trace. It followed always expanding western frontiers, created evangelists of endless variety, multiplied churches of all evangelical Protestant denominations, founded theological seminaries and colleges, created home and foreign missionary boards, and wrote dramatic chapters in the history of religion in America. The movement, however, was sadly divisive and accentuated theological and temperamental differences and historical regroupings. In addition, the influences of the English Unitarians[11] began to tell.

[10] So George Willis Cooke, the Unitarian historian, naturally. Cooke calls the minority candidates an Arminian and Arian. No wonder the Conservatives jibbed.

[11] Some implications of this too spacious paragraph need correction. Methodism was anything but Calvinistic. It was by its genesis nobly evangelical. It began and has continued its evangelical mission along its own theological lines. American "revivalism" therefore cannot be claimed by any one school of theology. It has been amongst other things, the product of general American social and religious conditions.

It is difficult to locate the very first uses of "Unitarian" and "Trinitarianism." Thomas Evealyn, Cooke says, was the first English preacher "who called himself a Unitarian." He published a "Humble Inquiry Into the Scripture Account of Jesus Christ" in 1702. It was republished in 1756 and appeared in Boston. He had established a Unitarian congregation in England in 1705 (Cooke, *Unitarianism in America*, p. 67). Leslie Stephen uses the terms as current and definitive in England in the last half of the Eighteenth Century. It was "the prevailing creed of the most intelligent of the old

The Revolution had naturally speeded up the independent temper of the population and shifted centers of loyalty. Americanism began to displace provincialism. A new economic era was beginning. There were congressmen and presidents to elect. Politics of a pretty virulent type came into action. The churches and the clergy lost in authority as they were seen in a new perspective. Hell began, very slowly, to be less vividly menacing at the terminals of village streets. Universalism became for a while a kind of theological catch—all for escapists from creeds they had come to hate, perhaps because they still feared them. There was in the new "border states" a movement back to Biblical religion. The "Book" was enough and a Christian was a Christian or a Disciple. The Nineteenth Century was in the making.

What became New England Unitarianism was the most intellectually sophisticated of all these movements, and with one significant difference. Other movements created new churches. "Unitarian" became a new name for a group of very old (for America) churches.

IV

The Tractarian Period

"Chairs" of theology are always strategic positions, since their learned occupants exert a telling influence upon the future through the students they train. Ecclesiastic authorities have always, therefore, taken great care to have them properly and safely filled. In strong centralized communions their appointments must be validated by the supreme denominational courts, and where strong factions are opposed an appointment may precipitate a major engagement. Even where there is no denominational control, a disputed appointment may still become a storm-center of controversy.

They needed a "Hollis Professor of Divinity" at Harvard College in 1805. The appointment lay entirely within the power of the college authorities, but the conservative and liberal parties in an already embattled Congregationalism welcomed it as a cause of war. The conservatives

dissenters" and manifest within the borders of the Establishment. Joseph Priestly is usually credited with being one of the great popularizers of Unitarianism. Stephen gives pages to his brilliant and more or less self-contradictory contentions and positions. He discovered oxygen, was mobbed for his political opinions, wrote 153 publications, and died in the United States. (He began as a Presbyterian minister. English Presbyterianism largely went Unitarian—one of the strangest little chapters in the history of English Protestantism.) In general "Unitarianism" was a convenient covering term for rationalistic and critical religious movements, which still wanted to be religious. In England it was the religious aspect of congenial "circles" and societies devoted to "culture" and intellectual activity, and associated with a rapidly rising industrialism. One might call them the "intellectuals" of their time.

Erasmus Darwin was cynical about their religious zeal. "Unitarianism," he said, "is a feather-bed for a dying Christian," but they included eminent names. American Unitarianism was later quite parallel to the English situation.

claimed that by the conditions of the trust-fund which supported the chair only a Calvinist could legally sit in it. This the liberals denied. Hollis had not only made no such restrictions; he was by nature incapable of making them, then being both liberal and catholic.[12]

The Overseers agreed with the liberals, and elected Henry Ware, who forthwith left Hingham Meeting House (with its bell rope in the middle of the building) and moved Hollis' chair considerably to the "left." This accomplished fact did not end the controversy; it lasted a quarter of a century, and the lines of division between the churches and the clergy were thereby more definitely drawn. The next phase might be called the Tractarian period. The belligerents took to print vigorously. They published pamphlets with awesome titles and provoking contents. John Sherman's *One God in One Person Only* was described as "one of the first acts of direct hostility against the orthodox committed on these western shores!"[13]

The conservatives naturally replied and counter-attacked. Theological magazines were born and died and Andover Theological Seminary was founded (1808) as a bulwark of orthodoxy. The founders, determined that there should be no repetition of the Hollis incident, made subscription to a confession of faith, historically known as the "Andover Creed," a rigid condition of sitting in any of its professional chairs. The "Creed" was the quintessence of New England Calvinism and was so well drawn that it held, heresy tight, for three long generations. Toward the end of the century a certain elasticity of professorial conscience made possible a working accommodation between a living scholarship and its "dead-hand" provisions, and later still after long litigation a Supreme Court of Massachusetts found an entirely legal way of annulling its clearly-drawn provisions. But this is a detour.

It is difficult to condense any account of the gradual estrangement between the two Congregational groups. "Groups" is an entirely accurate term. Their very looseness of ecclesiastical organization kept the movement from coming to a head anywhere. There were no heresy trials—no one could try anyone else—nor any excommunications; simply a slow and costly breaking of filaments more vital than any ecclesiastical bonds. In a sense pathetically more realistic than its patterned uses, "communion" between the liberal and the conservative faded out of the historic picture. The issues involved were geographically and ecclesiastically vaster than the little fields upon which the action took place. Profound readjustments in the doctrinal inheritances not only of Protestantism but of his-

---

[12] Cooke, *Unitarianism in America*, chap. 5.
[13] Much like Emerson's description of the first shot in the Revolutionary War fired by "embattled farmers."

toric Christianity were in their irreconcilable action. The whole of western Christianity would sooner or later face the same challenges, feel the searching currents of the same rising tides drawing in from remote and changing orders of thought, knowledge, and even human disposition. Western Christendom in its various communions would deal with this rising tide of a new age in various and characteristic fashions. Catholicism with pontifical authority shut the gates of Rome against it, and they seemed to hold. Anglicans managed to contain extremes as far apart as any in Boston in its spacious organization. American Presbyterians divided into two "schools." Congregationalism simply fell apart.

Its action, to repeat, was in fields paradoxically vast and provincial —as though one could draw a circle of one hundred miles radius around Boston and contain it all. Even then half the circle would have been in the void of the Atlantic. It is demandingly difficult, moreover, to separate the theological from the cultural on that same limited terrain. The word "Unitarian" is not in the index of Van Wyck Brooks' brilliant *Flowering of New England,* but the spirit and structure of the society which engendered it is set out in his first five chapters far more illuminatingly than in any church history. After Edwards and Hopkins and Emmons one comes almost suddenly upon a spirit which no theological vessel could either contain or retain.

Classic names, not only from a Boston but from a national point of view, begin to appear in Cooke's narrative: Thatchers, Lowells, Emersons, Everetts, Ticknor, Alliston, Chauncey, or Parkman. One must sadly confess that orthodoxy could not supply their peers. The liberals thought themselves misunderstood and misrepresented. Naturally they drew together for mutual aid and comfort. Their first meeting for organization was held in May, 1820. There had long been meetings of the Massachusetts clergy in Boston in May. They began by meeting to see that the "General Court" did no harm to the Commonwealth. They kept on coming because Boston was quite a change after a winter in a country parish.[14]

Channing addressed the gathering. They needed, he thought, "a bond of union, a means of intercourse, and an opportunity of conference not yet enjoyed." It would be well if they joined their prayers and counsels toward such desirable ends. When a Separatist movement begins to be accelerated with "prayers and counsels," the end is in sight. The leaders of the movement seemed to have been reluctant to become a separate denomination; partly, one may hope, through sentiment, partly because,

---

[14] There are delightful stories of the general rehabilitation of country ministers and their wives through the generosity of Boston relatives. A bonnet for the lady, broadcloth for the parson—and paint for the chaise.

being markedly independent, they feared any suggestion of denominational control, and partly (though this is mere surmise) they did not know exactly what to become or how with entire agreement to designate themselves.

V

THE "DEPARTURE" IS ACCOMPLISHED

Unitarian denominational machinery was installed before there was actually a Unitarian denomination. A publishing fund was established, though its promoters denied any sectarian purpose. They sought, they said, only the increase of practical goodness. They would furnish good reading to youth, who certainly deserved consideration, and supply adults with a more devotional literature which "yet did not omit to provide entertainment and instruction." Harvard Divinity School—distinct from Harvard College—was founded in 1819[15] with a most competent and well-balanced faculty. They were of the liberal wing, but the Divinity School was by charter unsectarian, given "to . . . the impartial . . . investigation of Christian truth," and requiring "no assent to the peculiarities of any denomination."

Presently there was a Unitarian Book Society and Tract Society and *The Christian Register,* destined to a long, honorable and, toward the end, stormy career. All this before there was a Unitarian denomination. What a lawyer would call the "enabling act" was the formation of the American Unitarian Association in 1825. Now there was finally something to "join" and 125 churches went over to that "Association"—a hundred in Massachusetts, twenty in the rest of New England, a few west of the Hudson river.[16] There was nothing to prevent their going. For historic American Congregationalism it was a catastrophe. Its oldest churches went—twenty out of the first twenty-five organized—including Plymouth. Ten of the eleven Boston churches—and so on; continuities were broken, long associations shattered, roots cut. All these, precious as they should have been, were imponderables. On the other hand, church properties were real estate. Under the medley of New England laws dealing with the holding and administration of church property one thing was clear: the poor communicants, the actual church members, did not own anything, in the contemplation of the law. The titles to their "meeting houses" were vested either in the "town" or in an ecclesiastical corporation specifically organized to maintain public worship. Such a corporation must have trustees, directors, and voting members. But the voting members need not be communicants and a church

[15] Andover Theological Seminary and Harvard Divinity School were thus pioneers in a method of theological education new not only to the United States but to Protestantism.

[16] All this narration is deeply in debt to Cooke, *Unitarianism in America.*

member might not be a voting member of the ecclesiastical body which, again, was the only body existing in the contemplation of the law.

Unitarian historians touch all this lightly, or else fall back upon the "parish theory"—the whole community the church. There were under either system and authority, a body of laymen, supporting public worship but not church members. These supplied the liberals an extensive and most strategically placed following, since they could—still in contemplation of an extremely myopic law—take the church property with them into the Unitarian association and leave protesting church members homeless, out of doors. And this happened. Properties representing the generosity and sacrifice of generations were lost to the orthodox without compensation, and their losing left wounds which were long in healing.[17]

There should have been enough catholicity and elasticity (they mean surprisingly the same thing) in the Congregational order to have contained both wings. That order now includes theological attitudes relatively as far apart as the liberals and orthodox were 125 years ago. The position theologically of the first generation of Unitarian preachers would now hardly provoke a Congregational examining council to argument. And the genius of historic Independency was hospitable to free and inquiring thought. But the religious mind of the time was given to theological debate, debate engendered bitterness, and bitterness made community of thought and faith increasingly difficult and finally impossible.

Unitarianism continued a Congregational polity and the two denominational mechanisms ran in rather parallel grooves: "causes," education, literature, Associations, Conferences, Boards, and geography. The history of American Unitarianism after 1825 belongs to its own specialists. Its cultural distinction must be universally recognized, the contributions of its teachers, preachers, poets, philanthropists, essayists and philosophers are now our common inheritances. It flowered with liberalism and New England, and in a measure has shared their Indian Summer.[18] It should have been one religious answer to the doubts and quests of the end of the Nineteenth Century, and in a limited way it was and is. But not according to the expectation of its leaders. The reason or reasons why belong to an examination of the nature of religion itself and definitely the

[17] Such questions of church property always became crucial in secession or union. E.g., the "Wee Frees" of Scotland or the problems of the United Church in Canada. There were curious consequences in New England. The "Society" of the First Church in Burlington, Vermont, went Unitarian—and found they had no church members. The "communicants" remained orthodox but had no "Society." So the "First Society" hunted around and got a "Second Church." The First Church went to the legislature and got a "Second Society." In this case the First Church kept the real estate.

[18] Its identification with a now-vanishing Boston is the local historian's delight. It was both geography and a state of mind. "One does not," said a Boston woman not so long ago, admonishing a young minister, "speak of Sin in Boston."

Christian religion. If one should maintain that religion lives by its emotion and its mystery, rather than by its reason and its clarity, he might be on the right line.

Beyond debate "orthodoxy" itself was leavened and emancipated directly and indirectly by the free inquiry and insistence upon human values of the Unitarian movement. Many of our now best-loved hymns are the gift of its poets to worship, and those who are alienated by its name are nevertheless deeply in debt to its spirit. "Orthodox" Congregationalism was itself stimulated to new enterprise by the Unitarian defection. During these twenty-five years of controversy it initiated American foreign missions, grew in denominational self-consciousness, followed the frontier, and tried an interesting experiment with the Presbyterians.

CHAPTER X

Westward Ho!

THE successful issue of the Revolutionary War dated, of course, a new epoch of incalculable significance. Every aspect of colonial life acknowledged the change. North Continental geography took on a frontierless and prophetic significance. Great Britain held Canada, actual and potential, north of an indefinite frontier, later to be bitterly disputed from Maine to Oregon. But in substance Canada was there. The peril of the French and Indians was long over; except for boundary disputes, there was no threat from the North.[1] Sullivan's expedition during the war had broken the power of the Five Tribes from Lake Ontario to the northern Pennsylvania border and destroyed root and branch the most highly developed Indian culture in northeast America. The crown lands in the Province of New York were ceded in the treaty of peace with Great Britain and there was no longer any barrier to settlement in that rich, spacious, beautiful, and strategic region (every adjective justified). A gateway to the West was opened through which the builders of an empire would pass.[2]

The creation of the Northwest Territory under the ordinance of 1788 made the then "West" both national and free, and the allure of its fabled wealth in virgin land began to call from regions which already thought themselves over-populated, the strong, the eager, and the adventurous. American church and religious life was thereby profoundly affected.[3]

[1] The fascinating history of Vermont during the Revolutionary period and its own period of proud independency (ending 1791) is here highly significant. The fine art of equivocation by which the Allens kept Great Britain hoping, Congress expecting, baffled New York and New Hampshire, saved their own necks and maintained an unharried little republic all their own, has rarely been equaled in the annals of diplomacy. But they did prevent Great Britain getting and keeping a territorial wedge which would have driven deep between New England and New York colonial territory.

[2] One could become almost lyric in reviewing the movement and development of transportation through the Mohawk Valley and along the southern shores of the Great Lakes. The southern spurs of the Adirondacks, the northern slopes of the Alleghanies determined its first course. Indian trails first threaded it, the pioneer followed on foot, on horseback, with ox-cart (usually keeping to the hills, the lowlands being undrained and marshy). The Erie Canal furnished a many-locked waterway, disdained the Montezuma swamps, tied Albany and Buffalo together with a fluid ribbon. The Railway followed the Canal (rebuilt to become the Barge Canal) and now the aeroplane flies high above it all, following the same routes and always the roads, by land, water or sky, which carried tides of migration toward setting suns and brought back the wealth of the Continent to the eastern seaboard through regions haunted by immemorial memories.

[3] Professor William Warren Sweet has made an exhaustive and completely authoritative study of all this in *Religion on the American Frontier*.

Our particular concern is what happened to Congregationalism and how it happened.

I

THE EFFECT OF THE AMERICAN REVOLUTION UPON THE CHURCHES

The end of the Revolutionary War found the New England churches materially enfeebled, doctrinally divided, religiously impoverished. The war had taken its toll of ministers by death and sickness, of congregations broken up, of properties damaged by neglect or ruined by the enemy. The burden of rehabilitation bore heavily upon folk themselves impoverished by seven years of fighting. At the same time the devotion of the Congregational clergy, already noted, to the Continental cause left them in a favorable position. (Sweet.) They were able to maintain their highly privileged condition. They were consulted and proved influential in state constitutional conventions. They made strategic contributions to the new political and civil orders. They threw a decisive and favorable weight in the debates over adoption of the Federal Constitution. "It is fortunate," General Lincoln wrote to Washington, "for us, that the clergy are pretty generally with us [in the Massachusetts debates]. They have in this state a very great influence over the people."[4]

Religion had suffered through the preoccupation of the clergy and the churches with war, politics, and constitution making. There were other unfavorable influences. We have followed already (in the rise of Unitarianism) the effect of English philosophy and deism upon inherited orthodoxies. There were also the disturbing influences of the French Revolution, the invasion of whose ideas no frontier could prohibit. They were heady and unsettling ideas. Channing thought they diseased the general imagination. Thomas Paine's *Age of Reason* became the Bible of radical youth. Even Ethan Allen turned his restless and exhuberant mind toward a defense of reason and a general condemnation of the established religious order.

There was a consequent laxity in morals probably exaggerated as against austere Puritan backgrounds. They had been complaining of that since before Jonathan Edwards. Timothy Dwight and others rivaled the Old Testament prophets in denunciation of contemporaneous manners and morals. Connecticut and Massachusetts, were, in his opinion, like Isaiah's Judea "from the sole of the foot to the head there is no health in it." More sober historians acknowledge the situation and charge it up generally to the "unfriendly" influence of war upon religion.

For all that the position of the Congregational churches in New England was still outstanding. New England itself was the most compact, populous, coherent and cultured territorial unit in the infant nation. It

[4]Sweet, *Religion on the American Frontier*, vol. 3, p. 4.

had a population of slightly over a million. Congregationalists were three times as numerous as all other denominations combined.[5] The general region was already conspicuous for education and enterprise. Its stock was still so fertile that Horace Bushnell could, much later, discourse upon the "out-populating power of the Christian stock"; by which he meant his own native Protestant stock. He did not foresee what would happen when that population would itself be out-populated.

The hill farms of New England were competent to breed a vigorous race, but their little rocky reaches could not hold them. Until the Civil War finally ended the process of depletion, New England's migrant population made an unparalleled contribution to the making of the West. Then at last it was bled white of its Protestant stock. "Cellar-holes" guarded by purple lilacs still mark the recession of the tide, and stone walls lost in second and third growth timber are mute witnesses to one-time meadows and the unbelievable labor of generations whose tired hands had found rest in little burying grounds beginning to be forgotten:

> "So fleet the works of men
> , Back to their earth again;
> Ancient and holy things fade like a dream."

Normally the Congregationalists, at the beginning of the Nineteenth Century "the most numerous as well as the most influential religious body in America" (Sweet), should have maintained their primary across the continent (especially due west of the Hudson River and the Great Lakes) and secured for Congregationalism a statistical and institutional priority it does not now possess. What happened?

II

CHANGES IN THE HOME BASE

Changes, to begin with, in the home bases. The inherited alliance between minister and magistrate, always the Puritan ideal of the Kingdom of God on earth, was slowly being dissolved. Sturdily independent laymen, Anglicans, Baptists, Methodists were all against it—and even more potently the trends of the time and the policy to which the new nation was committed, of the complete separation of Church and State. New England orthodoxy was seamed with the doctrinal differences which eventuated in the Unitarian "departure." The inherited system was by no means dissolved, but its ligaments were yielding. All this tended to give Congregationalism preoccupation with its own affairs, prevented a united front in the missionary advancement,[6] and left vulnerable sectors

---

[5] Estimated population of New England at the close of the Revolution: 1,090,000; Congregational Churches, 656.

[6] This section of this history is in debt to Dr. Oliver Wendell Elsbree's *The Rise of the Missionary Spirit in America*. Compact, inclusive, fact-packed.

of which other religious forces were rather quick to take a blameless advantage.

A second great revival period was momentous in consequences. The religious coldness and moral laxity which followed the Revolution invited a religious revival. And it came; the interests and responses of the "Great Awakening" were repeated. This revival movement began in 1797 and continued for five years. Connecticut seems to have been its center, but it spread north into Vermont and "down east" into Maine. The churches were increased in zeal and membership; there was a rebirth of evangelical fervor which turned naturally, inevitably, to missionary enterprises. The newly opened frontiers and the migratory movements across them, soon to attain really vast proportions, sounded a Macedonian call —and the unsaved heathen world was waiting.

By one of those contradictions which have so often saved theologians from the consequences of their own logic, the rigidities of Hopkins' Calvinism, widely accepted—in which there would seem neither room nor need for benevolence of any kind, since all was predetermined—issued in a doctrine of "disinterested benevolence." The Christian who must be willing to be damned for the glory of God could also, at less cost to himself, glorify God by seeking and promoting the highest degree of good (utilitarianism comes in here) to "all beings which exist, capable of good, or that can be in any sense or degree, objects of good will." Hopkins himself grew lyric in anticipation of the results of such benevolence in full action; "it will unite mankind into one happy society, teaching them to love one another as brethren, each one seeking and rejoicing in the public good and in the happiness of individuals; this will form the most happy state of public society that can be enjoyed on earth."[7] Apparently one of the roots of humanitarian liberalism, now under deep condemnation, was in that rocky Calvinistic soil.

III

The Rebirth of the Missionary Spirit

The combined result of reborn evangelical fervor, Calvinistic benevolence and a world then as now desperately in need of disinterested good will was the inception and release of reforms, benevolences, and "causes" which in their full development so finely characterized American church and social life till the first World War. The first result was the organization of propagandizing societies (in the best sense of the word) new to Protestantism and, in many fields, to Christianity. There was no end to them: Bible and Tract Societies; Sunday School and Orphanage Societies; Asylums for Deaf Mutes; for the colonization for Free Negroes; for

[7] Elsbree, *The Rise of the Missionary Spirit in America*, chap. 7.

the Suppression of Vice and Intemperance, and an always fluid list, too long for enumeration, coming and going.[8] The national flair for organization and a general crusading zeal must be included as contributory. Naturally there would be missionary societies, home and foreign. The Connecticut Association (1798) formed the first Congregational state missionary society in New England. Its published purpose was "to extend the blessings of the gospel to the uttermost of their power" and "to be instrumental in diffusing its glad tidings among the inhabitants of the newly settled frontiers of our country, and among the heathen tribes."[9]

The "heathen tribes" had not, before that, been neglected. Both the Pilgrims and the Puritans had justified their new world adventures by the hope of extending the gospel "in these remote parts of the world" and with lamentable lapses they had tried to do it. The story of Protestant missionary work with and for the Indians is long to tell and sad to follow. There were over and over again really promising beginnings but they were always defeated by the greed, inhumanity, and land hunger of the white man, by disease and death, by the inability of the red man to adapt himself to a culture to which all his inheritances made him not only alien but hostile. The whole conduct of their relationships darkens the pages of American history.

The British Society for the Propagation of the Gospel in Foreign Parts (1701) had labored earnestly for the "Propagation of the Gospel" not only among the Indians but amongst followers of the "Congregational Way," who had, the Society must have sadly concluded, no gospel because they had no bishops. There was a suspicion among its ungrateful beneficiaries that its real object was the establishment of Anglicanism in New England, which contributed to their wholehearted support of the American Revolution.

The Puritan in his turn had sought to do something for the Anglican. In the early 1640's Boston reported an appeal from Virginia. A cry "from many well disposed people [there] . . . to the elders here, bewailing their sad condition for want of the means of salvation, and earnestly entreating a supply of faithful ministers, whom, upon experience of their gifts and godliness, they might call to office." There was nothing Boston elders would have liked better than to send their light and truth to Virginia. So they had the letter read on a Lecture Day and set a day apart "to seek God in it." They found guidance and chose for the mission three of their number who "might most likely be spared"—an ambiguous phrase. Among the three was William Tompson of Braintree whose congrega-

[8] Elsbree, *The Rise of the Missionary Spirit in America,* chap. 7.
[9] Sweet, *Religion on the American Frontier,* vol. 2, p. 40. This chapter is also so deeply in debt to Sweet that a general acknowledgement should include all indebtedness. Actually, however, the records of the Association do not contain these quoted phrases.

tion apparently were not at all unwilling to spare him. The chosen went south by water and by slow stages in the late Autumn and at last mid-winter. They suffered many discomforts and dangers, wind bound in Narragansett Bay and shipwrecked in Hell-Gate, where they barely reached shore. Cotton Mather wrote a poem about that, praising Tompson—

> "Upon a ledge of craggy rocks near stav'd
> His Bible in his bosom thrusting sav'd;
> The Bible, the best of cordial of his heart,
> 'Come floods, come flames,' cry'd he,
> We'll never part.' "

These dangers and hindrances continuing they were led to doubt "whether their call were of God or not." Virginia welcomed them with characteristic hospitality and a benign climate. But the authorities would have none of their preaching; in fact, "did in a sense drive them out." They took back much experience and one convert—Daniel Gookins. He made his mark in Boston and Mather summed up Thompson's missionary journey:

> "By Tompson's pains,
> Christ and New England a dear Gookins gains." [10]

The especial and pioneer Connecticut interest in what would now be called home missions was probably due to several causes: less doctrinal divisions among the clergy than in Massachusetts, and more evangelical fervor. Also Connecticut had a stake in the then West, since the state, in the cessions which constituted the Northwest Territory, had reserved for itself a considerable and extremely desirable section in northeastern Ohio. The grounds upon which the state claimed any right in regions so far beyond its own borders should be the concern of specialists in the examination of colonial charters. At any rate, Connecticut got its Reserve (now the "Western Reserve") and named it "New Commecticut." Naturally the churches would be concerned for the religious estate of its citizens in these distant parts.[11]

There was also a considerable migration of Connecticut folk up the noble Connecticut Valley into the then new state of Vermont. There they settled other Hartfords and Windsors, and there the missionaries followed them. Finally there was an unusual migration from Connecticut

---

[10] Adams, *Three Episodes of Massachusetts History*, vol. 2, pp. 596–99.

[11] In June, 1774, the Connecticut General Association voted: "This association taking in consideration the state of settlements now forming in the wilderness to the westward and northwestward of us, who are mostly destitute of a preacher Gospel, many of which are of our Brethren emigrants. . . ." And so on to the familiar effect that missionaries should be sent and money raised to send them, which was done. The missionaries to begin with were settled pastors who would go on four months tours at $4.50 a week and $4.00 to supply their own pulpits. Later new men were sent who would keep at it. Of course the 1774 action antedated the ordinance of 1788. The "northern boundaries of the Province of New York" were then the far Northwest.

into central and western New York. It is said there was a Connecticut regiment under Sullivan and these, seeing how good the land was, returned to settle it and took their neighbors with them. Five hundred loaded sleighs and ox-sleds going west passed through Albany between sunrise and sunset February 28, 1795. (Winter snows furnished the best going.) And, finally, it was easy geographically for Connecticut folk to go across into New York. The Connecticut churches renewed their pre-Revolutionary zeal for home missions and their Association in 1793 had eight workers in its pay. But now the task demanded a special agency. So the Missionary Society of Connecticut was organized and obtained permission of the Connecticut Assembly to solicit funds. The Society was incorporated in 1802 (a representative of the Presbyterian General Assembly was a trustee), and could legally hold property (not in excess of $10,000). It needed an organ and founded the Connecticut Evangelical Magazine, the profits whereof "were turned over to the trustees for the furtherance of missions." [12]

This chapter focuses upon the Connecticut Society for reasons soon to be apparent. Other societies followed, in Western Massachusetts, Boston, Rhode Island, New Hampshire, Maine, Vermont. Women began to form their societies, e.g., the Cent Institution in Boston, a cent a day for Bibles and Tracts; $500 the first year. In one form or another most of these societies still function. Their records are voluminous and fascinating sources; their work has been far flung. They and their like in other denominations are nobly characteristic of American Protestantism.

One could easily get lost here in statistics, reports, and narrations of heroisms and sacrifices which brighten old volumes only the research scholar now consults. And they should be invaluable to the general historian in their vivid portrayal of frontier conditions. These pioneers of the gospel travelled by roads which were only little ribbons of mud, through endless forests or across unploughed prairies. They forded bridgeless rivers, they were pestered by insects, shaken by ague. They preached from pulpits made by setting two posts in the ground and nailing a board across them. They administered the sacrament from glass tumblers and earthenware plates. And they possessed their souls, even when the Connecticut Society was accumulating a surplus. [13]

[12] In 1823 the Society's credit balance was $30,183.38½.
[13] Bascom's *Autobiography*, cited by Sweet, vol. 3, pp. 234 ff., is a little epic of description and vivid narration. But the annual reports of the Connecticut Society from, say, 1812–1827 are invaluable sources. They include Schermerhorn's and Mill's reports of their tours south and west, reports of missionaries and a wealth of detailed though yellow papers which need little help from the imagination to recreate a vanished past. The total receipts of the Society in 1814 were $8000.00½; total expenditures $6,152.16. The thirty-eight missionaries were employed at the highest salary of $358.20 and the lowest $40. The Society received $320 from the sale of Dwight's Psalms and Hymns, and $150 from the Connecticut Evangelical Magazine. The Society distributed rela-

IV

Inception of the Plan of Union

There was, of course, endless duplication and overlapping, for all denominations were doing pretty much the same thing. The foundations of American sectarian excesses and competitions were laid during this period when fields ripe for harvest forbade any anticipation of a time when there should be an excess of harvesters. The practical difficulty of getting missionaries enough for the rapidly expanding work in New York State led to the first effort at coöperation, and naturally between the denominations which were geographically and in temper nearest together, Congregationalists and Presbyterians.[14] This eventuated in the "Plan of Union" which, meant to be coöperative and fraternal, became after it had ceased to be, a subject of rather embittered controversy between church historians and a source of sad regret for representative Congregationalists—not that it ceased to be, but that it had ever been.

Sweet (following Gillett, Walker, and Baird) says the first suggestion of the plan came from John Blair Smith, first president of Union College, Schenectady. Since Union College was a joint enterprise of the Presbyterians and Dutch Reformed, he naturally thought in terms of interdenominational coöperation. He had for a guest for a few days Eliphalet Nott, a young Congregational missionary, then on his way West, and labored with him. Was it either wise or Christian to divide a sparse population holding the same faith, scattered over a vast new territory, into two distinct ecclesiastical organizations and deprive them of the means of grace they might otherwise enjoy?

tively great numbers of tracts and books. The titles are engaging: Dairyman's Daughter, Beecher on Divine Government; Hall's Divine Songs, Hymns for Infant Minds, Guide to Heaven, Porter on Intemperance, Baxter's Saint's Rest, Swear's Prayer (1000 of those in 1815). The Board thanks (1815) the several Female Societies for their liberality, and so on and on. The manners and morals of frontier settlements are vividly pictured. Intemperance is particularly deplored: "health and beauty, wit and genius fall before it." Significantly during its earlier years the statements of receipts and expenditures are made pursuant to resolutions of the General Assembly. That body apparently wanted to know what Connecticut Congregational churches were doing with their home missionary money.

[14] Relations between Connecticut Congregationalists and the Presbyterian General Assembly had been "becoming very friendly." So early as 1790 the General Association voted a "further degree of union with the Presbyterians" desirable and the General Assembly was more than willing. A Joint Committee of the Assembly and Association recommended a plan for "united representation." Recommendation adopted. In 1792 three representatives of the Connecticut churches were sent to the General Assembly. In 1793 three Presbyterian delegates sat with the General Association. In 1794 it was agreed that the "representation of each body should have full right to vote in the meetings of the other" which they did. All this was spade work for the Plan of Union. Walker, op. cit., p. 528. "The question of a permanent adjustment of the relation of the two polities on missionary ground was raised in the Connecticut General Association in 1800." Ibid.

Smith persuaded Eliphalet very much as Dr. Fuller was said to have persuaded Governor Endicott, only, to so speak, in reverse. Nott became pastor of the Albany Presbyterian church, and at the next session (1801) of the General Assembly of the Presbyterian Church proposed the adoption of a "Plan of Union"[15] for the general coöperation of the two churches (Presbyterian and Congregational) in the West. The "Plan of Union" 1801 was relatively simple,[16] and carried few intimations of its actual consequences.[17] Missionaries are enjoined to promote mutual forbearances and a spirit of accommodation between Presbyterians and Congregationalists. If a Congregational church choose a Presbyterian minister, they shall still proceed Congregationally. If congregation and minister fall into difficulties he (the minister) has the right of appeal to his Presbytery, both parties agreed; otherwise to a bi-denominational council.

A Presbyterian church calling a Congregational minister shall proceed according to its own disciplines. In the event of disagreement between pastor and people he has the right of appeal to his Association or else to a bi-denominational council. The paragraph on mixed congregations is more complicated and anticipates the technique of modern federated churches. Such a mixed congregation may settle a minister as they please. A "standing committee" shall call to account every member of the church who shall conduct himself inconsistently with the laws of Christianity.[18] A "condemned" Congregationalist could appeal to "the body of the male communicants of the church" and no further. A condemned Presbyterian could appeal to the Presbytery, and with the consent of the

[15] Professor Robert Hastings Nichols, in an article in *Church History* further to be cited, discredits the Smith-Nott episode.
[16] Walker (*Creeds and Platforms of Congregationalism*, pp. 328 ff.) holds that "there is every reason to believe that the younger Edwards was the originator of the discussions." He was an ideal "liaison" officer, formerly pastor of the Second Church in New Haven, next president of Union College and a delegate from the General Assembly to the Connecticut Association. In addition he was the son of his father who at one time in his career had told the Presbyterians that he not only could sign their creed but thought their polity the more desirable. The younger Edwards grew up in a household which had suffered much from Northampton Congregationalists, which might explain a good deal. To condense: the Connecticut Assembly was hospitable to the suggestion, no matter from whom it came, appointed a committee (two of whom were Presbyterian Delegates,) heard their report, approved their report and appointed their own committee to confer with a similar committee from the General Assembly as to ways and means, "to prevent alienation, promote harmony and to establish as far as possible, *an Uniform System of Church Government* [italics the author's] * * between Presbyterians and Congregationalists in the 'New Settlements.'" The proposition was hospitably received by the Presbyterian General Assembly in May 1801. The Assembly appointed its own committee and approved their report. Result: the historic document. Apparently then the overtures came from Connecticut, the document emanates from the General Assembly. Also, Sweet, *Religion on the American Frontier*, vol. 2, p. 41 ff.
[17] The text is accessible in Presbyterian and Congregational Church histories.
[18] An elusive and suggestive generality; no such provision for unmixed churches. Evidently the fathers anticipated tensions.

church, to the Synod or General Assembly, which opened before a recalcitrant Presbyterian a fascinating vista of appeal.

All this the General Assembly made authoritative for Presbyterianism everywhere. The "Plan" was laid before the Connecticut General Association meeting in Litchfield June 16, 1801, by three Presbyterian delegates and "promptly ratified without alteration" (Walker) for Connecticut. The want of balance between the two contracting systems is here and at once apparent; with no authorization from the whole of American Congregationalism, the Connecticut Association committed with the best of intentions the westward movement of Congregationalism to the control and consequence of the Plan, and for the simplest of reasons: it held the keys by geography and precedence in missionary enterprise to the gateways of the West for New England.

V

How the Plan Worked

Connecticut Congregationalism was, as has been noted more than once, semi-Presbyterian in its theory of polity and in close touch with southeastern New York Presbyterianism and, curiously, with New Jersey. For all that the Plan was generously conceived on both sides, the compromises and adjustments were fair, it proposed a statesmanlike solution of a challenging situation. On the face of the 1801 Plan it was no more than an attempt to furnish Christian ministers enough for the expanding frontier and to meet the more evident situations likely to arise. In 1808 further steps were taken to secure the "uniform system of Church government" which the first Connecticut overture contemplated. This is called the "accommodation plan." (Dr. Robert Hastings Nichols documents this in his illuminating article in the periodical *"Church History,"* volume 5, no. 1, March 1936.) The burning question is: Which polity did the most accommodating?

In the seven years beginning 1801 there had been in Northern, Central, and Western New York a phenomenal growth of churches of all denominations, but Presbyterians and Congregationalists were predominant for many reasons. Congregational churches had their Associations, always a loose organism; the Presbyterians their Presbyteries, very tight organizations. The churches of the two denominations could be and were represented in both organizations by their accredited delegates. The privilege of Congregational representation in the Presbyteries worked to the advantage of the Presbyterians. Beyond debate a Presbytery was a more effective organization than an Association and the Associations took on an increasingly Presbyterial character.[19] Why then should the two

---

[19] There is still in the present redactions of Congregational polity a difference between the function of Association and Presbytery. But it is back of behind.

systems either overlap or run so nearly together in separate channels? The Synod of Albany and the "Middle Association" of Congregational churches (now Onondaga and Cayuga Counties, New York) sought answers to those questions.

The Association made the overture for "some form of Union and Correspondence."[20] The Synod was receptive and "[stood] ready, with the approbation of the General Assembly, to form as intimate a connection with you as the constitutions of our church will admit," whereupon in substance, though with such gravity of language as seems necessary to ecclesiastical pourparlers, the Synod invited the Association to become Presbyterian. The half dozen sentences used here are of a sufficient ambiguity to support either contention—that a plan of union was proposed or that absorption was sought. The case seems to turn upon a single sentence: "unless they shall choose to alter it themselves, the Synod will cheerfully leave them the privilege of transacting their internal concerns in their present mode of Congregational government."

VI

ITS CONSEQUENCES FOR CONGREGATIONALISM

The point is worth laboring, for it is one key to what followed and it defines by implication "Congregational government" as both contracting parties then understood it. It applied only to the "internal concerns" of individual churches, a way of carrying on the business of a local church; congregational voting by the "usual signe," choosing a minister, administering local finance, admitting, dismissing and disciplining members and the like; also through its proper organization the congregation owned and managed its own property. As long, then, as a church possessed these rights unimpaired, it was Congregational. It was possible, therefore, for a Congregational church in respect to the really vast and momentous issues of the corporate life of a fellowship of churches to be Presbyterian and only within its own four walls Congregational, and this was the real issue of the Second Plan of Union, the result of the quest for "some form of Union and Correspondence." Technically such churches were "in affiliation" with a Presbytery. Actually, for all denominational purposes, they were Presbyterian.

It was an unbalanced situation and the stronger pull was toward the Presbyterian side. After two anomalous years the Middle Association became two Presbyteries. It had been overwhelmingly Congregational, "composed," says Nichols, "almost entirely of Congregational ministers."

[20] The French have a proverb, cynically Gallic, that there is always one who kisses and one who turns the cheek. Throughout this whole movement the Congregationalists seem to have been the one who kissed.

Professor Nichols contends valiantly that after the "Association" had become a Presbytery, the Congregational churches still retained their rights and privileges as such, subject to the jurisdiction of the Presbytery. But the jurisdiction of an "Association" was then far less authoritative than the "jurisdiction" of a Presbytery. Essentially it was beside the point that in their internal affairs they were governed by the body of communicants and were represented in the Presbytery by a delegate and not an elder. For American Congregationalism had come to combine the independency of the individual church with the supporting and advising fellowship of other churches. When that fellowship was gone, either a lonely body was left or the substitution of a non-Congregational fellowship, which was what happened in New York.

One by one the "Associations" became Presbyteries. Fourteen years after the second Plan of Union, "there was no Congregational general organization in Central and Western New York." Without regional Associations there could be no State Conference. The organic dissolution was complete. Congregationalism which, if it did not have the priority in "up-state" New York, had at least the most brilliant prospects of eminence along all the always-westward-advancing frontier, had for all organic purposes faded out of the picture. The loss has never since been recovered. Nichols makes his case that all those then concerned were making an anticipatory experiment in a limited ecumenicity; in plain words, they were trying for church union. There was no recorded coercion and a maintenance of Congregational rights as the then fathers and brethren of the two high contracting parties understood Congregationalism.

VII

DEBATED STATISTICS

It may have been that the more authoritative and tough-fibred Presbyterians' order was better suited to loose frontier conditions than the Congregational order and, as Nichols notes, almost naïvely "an obvious preference on the part of Congregationalists for Presbyterian polity runs all through this history." And he seems to be right. It is equally true, as we shall see, that the issues of the differences of statistical opinion about the number of churches actually lost to Congregationalism are beside the mark. Williston Walker accepted the conclusion of Ross that the ultimate result of the plan was the transformation of over two thousand churches which were in origin and usage Congregational into Presbyterian churches. This, Professor Nichols thinks, is a gross exaggeration "based on the heated imagination of a denominational zealot." These are in turn quite heated words and possibly not themselves entirely free from denominational bias. Nichols himself supports Thayer's conclusion that of the 525

"New School" Presbyterian churches in the state of New York, living or dead in 1850, only 145 were originally Congregational.

This leaves out too much, if only the state of New York be considered, and the consequences of the Plan reached far beyond the state. By 1830 or 1835 it was the most populous, prosperous, and strategic commonwealth in the United States, truly the "empire state." The population of what a generation before had been the "New Settlements" was over a million. Excelling in agriculture, it was also becoming a region of cities whose names would literally and figuratively become classic. It was beginning already to abound in large towns, destined to become the most compact and economically adequate small cities in America—ideal for a sound church life. All this Congregationalism lost and never recovered. One can now (1941) count almost on the fingers of one hand Congregational churches in the entire "upstate" region which can be compared with the strong, historic, nobly equipped and vitally maintained "First Presbyterian" churches of a score of cities and any number of prosperous towns. And as a matter of fact, they can't be compared. Half the 145 Congregational churches lost by the most conservative calculation would, if they had run their expected course, have changed the whole picture.

Actually Congregationalism lost the momentum of an always-westerning frontier from the Hudson River to Chicago. It lost that hinterland of rural and village population by whose human contributions strategic city churches are maintained and it lost the thing by which from its inception it had been maintained and through which it had been extended —regional continuity. Any congregational polity, whatever the denomination, is vitally dependent upon regional continuity, upon the living filaments of near neighborliness with other churches of the same order. When that is gone its lines are down.

Beyond much debate the "Plan of Union" facilitated missions in the first period and prevented competitions. It combined with other influences to give the Presbyterianism of the general region a progressive and open-minded quality not shared by that denomination in less favored parts. It has certainly contributed to the concern for reform, anti-slavery temper, and a general flair for causes and movements also characteristic of the region, and for a period it issued in coöperative agencies: e.g. the American Board of Commissioners for Foreign Missions, the American Home Missionary Society, and similar agencies which served the interests of religion and morality at home and abroad with creative wisdom.

For a time the possibilities of united religious action were better illustrated by this movement, centrally and marginally, than by anything else up to the inception of the Federal Council of Churches. There was in it the making, not indeed of an American Church, but of a United Church in New England and the North, which, combining the best qualities of Congregationalism and Presbyterianism, would have had a corporate power and distinction neither communion now alone possesses. But the time was far from ripe for that and the fact remains that by such tests as are usually and justly used to measure and characterize the historical development of any denomination, the Plan of Union was disastrous to Congregationalism. The internal dissentions of the Presbyterians themselves, which resulted in the old school and new school General Assemblies, ended any coöperation between Congregationalism and old school Presbyterianism. The new school was more coöperative. The Congregational churches, as will be hereinafter noted, "denounced" the treaty in 1852.[21]

[21] A paragraph from John Schermerhorn's report to the trustees of the Missionary Society of Connecticut (Dec. 10, 1813) illumines concretely the denominational situation as then conceived. His statistics of ministers then in the service of frontier populations authoritatively tabulated, mention only Presbyterians, Methodists, Baptists, which he thus explains, "The denominations generally noticed in the tables are Presbyterians, Baptists and Methodists. The Congregationalists, Associate Reformed Church, Associate Synod Covenanters, and those churches in connection with the General Assembly of the Presbyterian Church in the United States" are all classed under the title of Presbyterians; for "those minor considerations concerning the externals of religion, which now separate them, and which originated in causes not existing in this country, do not appear of sufficient consequence, in a missionary point of view, to merit separate notice." Which is the Plan of Union in action, unrelieved. Against this set a Presbyterian complaint 129 years later, voiced in a letter to *Monday Morning: A Magazine Exclusively for Pastors* [Presbyterian] Feb. 23, 1942: "The Presbyterian Church in our day is fast losing its distinctive Presbyterianism because we act like churches having a Congregational form of government. The General Assembly hands down recommendations and we all do as we please!" There is no moral.

CHAPTER XI

Congregationalism Carries On

MEANWHILE there were the "home-fires." By a tacit "gentle-men's agreement"[1] under the Plan of Union the Presbyterians sought no further extension in New England and New England, with minor storms and stresses, was entering upon its most distinguished period. There was a truce in theological controversy. Unitarian was completely and perfectly Unitarian. The Calvinism of the Saybrook platform —as we have seen—had been officially validated in Connecticut and Massachusetts, though there was a growing theological dis-ease which would presently and creatively find an epoch-making voice in Horace Bushnell. The rise of competitive denominationalism in America naturally affected the New England situation, but the "orthodox" Church still maintained religious and social priority.

No study of American Congregationalism can easily overstate the significance of its corporate relationship to its social, political, and economic environment. This has been both its strength and its weakness. Outside the nexus of social forces which, speaking historically, combined to create it, it has always been more or less exotic. It requires for its support both socially and religiously more than the sympathetically minded. One begs many questions in saying that Congregationalism has been the religious and ecclesiastical aspect of coherent, democratic populations, trained in self-government, strongly individualistic, capable of highly efficient coöperative action and controlled, in the conduct of their various affairs, by habit and tradition. It has not often found a congenial soil otherwise.

In the early Nineteenth Century the incongruous state-church status which the New England churches inherited from the Seventeenth and Eighteenth Centuries was liquidated by legislation with no great loss save to the unchristian superiority complexes of the clergy and a certain amount of convenience in getting money for the support of public worship (and not always even that). The orthodox churches adjusted themselves to the losses due to Unitarianism. The number of the withdrawing churches was not, proportionately, large. The property losses, especially in eastern Massachusetts, were more serious than the losses in personnel. It required a certain amount of grace for the dispossessed to build them-

[1] Such is the tradition.

selves new and often less distinguished meeting-houses while Unitarian neighbors sat under high mahogany pulpits in churches built by their quite orthodox ancestors. But that, perhaps, had its compensations. The orthodox were at least saved from pious lethargy.

The migrations West had begun to drain the East, but there were folk enough left and the population was still more homogeneous than in any other national area. The rapid growth in manufacturing—especially textiles—had portentous possibilities but these were not yet apparent. The young women in the Lowell and Lawrence weave-sheds were farmers' daughters of native stock, who spent such leisure as their long hours left them in the pursuit of culture. So the churches kept their home-fires burning. Each state had its Home Missionary Society and allied organizations. They established new churches as the growth or extension of the population demanded, aided dependent churches, created and distributed the literature they thought needed—in fact, about what they have been doing ever since.

I

The Era of "Boards" Begins

The structure of Congregationalism made it necessary to create, by acts of legislation, specific corporations for any specific missionary, educational, or philanthropic purpose. These were—and are—managed by boards of directors, variously named and elected. There would be a president and treasurer and salaried secretaries whose business it was to promote their particular organizations and secure needed financial support. The history of these societies is a component part of the history of Congregationalism. They became and have, in one form or another, continued to be the agents of widely coöperative Congregational action,[2] needing a legal basis. The result was a considerable overlapping, since the boundaries of any missionary or philanthropic enterprise cannot be precisely drawn. There was also a pious but nonetheless competitive solicitation for money. The second part of this history will deal with the gradual modification of that system.[3]

The American Home Missionary Society was organized in 1826 with four supporting denominations, though in support and direction mainly carried on by Presbyterians and Congregationalists. There have been

[2] Only a specialist in ecclesiastical organization could authoritatively compare the various ways in which different denominations carry on their corporate affairs. A church must, of course, exist in contemplation of the law and there is a vast body of legislation dealing with ecclesiastical organizations. Highly centralized communions work through a central corporation which includes and directs everything else. In the most centralized the bishop may be the "Corporation Sole" for his diocese. Property titles are, of course, the keystone in any corporate structure, sacred or secular.

[3] Doubtless much has been gained but intelligent intimacies of givers and "causes" have been lost.

natural differences of opinion as to relative preëminence in gifts and devotion. A. E. Dunning thought Congregationalists the more conspicuous in both. Gardiner Spring (Presbyterian) maintained it was predominantly Presbyterian in origin and thereafter in management until 1833. It was the principal agency through which the Plan of Union functioned in the West. It prospered fabulously and the Domestic Missionary Societies in the New England states became one by one subsidiary to it, though not surrendering their own organizations.

The reasons which persuaded them are documented by Sweet in a quoted letter from Absalom Peters, secretary of A.H.M.S. (the era of alphabetical designation had begun), to the Connecticut church authorities, which proves that the fine art of promoting a cause was already perfected. It was certainly effective. The Home Missionary Society of Connecticut became auxiliary to the aforesaid A.H.M.S. for the purpose of "building up the waste places of Connecticut, sending the gospel to the destitute and assisting feeble congregations in other and more destitute portions of the United States."

The Connecticut Society reserved, however, the control of the raising and application of funds, the selection of missionaries and the designation of their field of labor upon mutual agreement between its directors and the executive committee of the American Home Missionary Society. There was as yet no national Congregational Home Missionary Society and it is difficult to see how a state society could operate successfully in the most distant "destitute portions of the United States." But the A.H.M.S. did not confine itself to the West. So late as 1850 and 1851 the Society had 311 missionaries in New England alone.

The ravages of the Revolutionary War had long since been repaired but New England shipping suffered sadly in the War of 1812. The interests of the section were bitterly opposed to "Mr. Madison's War" and even went so far as veiled threats of nullification (to the delight of Calhoun). In these and subsequent tensions between New England finance and commerce and the agricultural West, the clergy were generally on the side of their parishioners and indulged in a deal of intemperate speech. The era of the tall clipper ships had come and the whalers ranged far oceans. The churches shared the prosperity of the merchants.

The significant history of the period should really be written out of the records of all the churches east and the churches going west. That would be a fabric of innumerable strands engagingly various and yet similar in pattern. In New England ecclesiastical architecture, still under Georgian influence, was good, with a flair for Greek pillared porches, and the graceful spires of white churches dominated village greens and elm-shaded streets. There or westward, where there were no white spires or elm-shaded streets, the devout assembled for prayer and praise and preaching. The sermon was still the thing, getting shorter though not alarmingly so. America was still predominantly Protestant, and there seems to have been throughout the nation a general habit of church going, where there were churches to go to.

II

The Westward Expansion of New England

Sweet has made a most suggestive adaptation of maps from Louis Kimball Mathews' *The Expansion of New England,* to graph the westward migration and settlement of the people of New England into lands north of the Ohio from 1820–1850. The St. Lawrence River in New York State, the southern littorals of Lakes Ontario and Erie, and after that almost straight lines across the middle of Michigan and Southern Wisconsin to the Mississippi, furnish the northern boundary line.[4] In a general way the treks out of New England, like all migratory movements, went as directly west as was geographically possible. This map should be supplemented by the map (which prefaces Sweet's volume on the expansion of Presbyterianism) of the "Scotch-Irish settlements in North America at the end of the Colonial period." These settlements dominate the entire Appalachian region from Central Pennsylvania south and west. The two maps between them are the keys to the distribution of the two great British racial strains in the United States.

The Scotch-Irish, with a power to outpopulate the pure English element, stood at the close of the Eighteenth Century at strategic gateways. New England migration used the Mohawk Valley and routes the New York Central now follows. Scotch-Irish migration westward spread fanwise from Philadelphia and Baltimore as ports of entry, using routes the Pennsylvania, Baltimore and Ohio, Chesapeake and Ohio (and more southern) railways now follow. The New England migrations should have carried Congregationalism on their ample tides. That failed largely through the Plan of Union. The Scotch-Irish migrations carried Presbyterianism with them, and did not lose it enroute. Instead they made Congregationalism tributary. There were minor migrations from the border and deep South into southern Ohio, Indiana and Illinois. Congregationalism got no real foothold in those regions. So much for the "geo-politik" (the geographical control) of Presbyterianism (in the North) and Congregationalism. One must, of course, add the infiltration of the entire central sections of both these maps by the Methodists, Baptists, and many other denominations.

[4] This map in a loose way corresponds arrestingly with Professor Arthur Holt's maps of the dominant industrial and financial regions in the United States.

III

CONGREGATIONALISM BEGINS TO BE NATIONAL

Independent Congregationalism began to repair its losses west of New York State by 1829–30. Something was saved in the Western Reserve, though even there Presbyterian influence increased after 1806 and "soon became dominant."[5] The influence of Oberlin College in the agreements and disagreements between Presbyterians and Congregationalists has been much debated. Sweet thinks neither denomination loved Oberlin. It was eccentric in theology, anti-slavery in sentiment and "countenanced coeducation." Presbyteries would not even examine Oberlin candidates for the ministry (a curious refusal of the generally eagerly sought opportunity to heckle heresy). So late as 1842 Plan of Union churches met in convention at Cleveland to find ways of curbing "this fountain of evil and protect the saints from its pestiferous malaria," which proves amongst other things that the "Reserve" suffered from chills and fever.

Indiana was from the first allergic to Congregationalism and has so continued, though New England missionary societies sent missionaries not only into Indiana but also into Kentucky and Tennessee, with the result that more Presbyterian churches were established. In 1829–30 the "Yale-band" made history. Seven graduates of the Divinity School Class of 1829 engaged together to go to Illinois, establish a "Seminary of Learning" suited to the needs of the region, and either teach therein or preach to the surrounding country. They were soon joined by five others, a shining list of brave young names. They founded Illinois College and formed numerous Congregational or Presbyterian churches. Some of them crossed the Mississippi and founded the First Congregational Church in Denmark, Iowa. By 1839–40 the slavery issue had become a burning question, and in Illinois Congregational ministers and people took a more pronounced position against slavery than the Presbyterians. This, says Sweet, hastened and solidified the separation between the two denominations.

Congregationalism had most promising beginnings in Michigan territory. The interest of the Connecticut Missionary Society in Michigan began almost with the creation of the territory. In 1800, while Detroit was still partially stockaded, David Bacon walked over from Connecticut to survey the field and report to the Connecticut Association. He was hospitably received, found Detroit and its noble river most attractive, as so many have since, and so reported when he returned East. A year later he went back with his bride. For several months he taught a school for boys, and his wife, then only seventeen years old, a school for girls. In

[5] All this follows Sweet closely.

due time a son, Leonard, was born to them, who as Dr. Leonard Bacon,[6] wrote

> "O God, beneath Thy guiding hand
> Our exiled fathers crossed the sea";

and was, with his father David, the first of a long, illustrious line.

Bacon's brief sojourn was followed twenty-four years later by Isaac W. Ruggles who had been pastor of one of the few New York State churches which kept the Congregational faith. This argues in Ruggles a stiff denominational backbone, which he needed. He was tireless in serving the rapidly increasing populations in the general Detroit region. He was later joined by John D. Pierce, another "stiff-backed" New York Congregationalist, who went on founding churches of his own order against the warning "that it would not be either wise nor desirable to organize any Congregational church." The agents of the A.H.M.S. seem to have worked against Ruggles and Pierce, and Pierce complained of such discrimination. Nothing apparently came of it. Instead one of the agents complained in turn of Pierce's preference for his own denomination, and lamented that, since Pierce did not belong to a Presbytery, it was impossible to "apply the corrective." Such freedom from Presbyterial discipline probably saved a good deal of Michigan Congregationalism.

The Presbyterians, in addition, were having troubles of their own and in 1837 divided themselves into two "schools" (New and Old) with sufficiently different doctrinal bases to support two of everything necessary to active Presbyterian national organizations. This naturally withdrew their attention from Congregational missionaries and increased the prestige of Congregationalists in the West. In 1839–40 three Congregational associations were formed in Michigan and in 1842 a General Association for the state. These activities in Michigan were unsympathetically viewed from New England.[7] Western Congregationalism, eastern defenders of the faith held, lacked doctrinal stability and should not be "countenanced."[8] In the main, however, the older Congregational churches in Michigan (and this holds of all the older churches clear across to the Pacific coast) were made up of folk of New England stock who went west directly from the New England states, or still further went from New York State. The Erie Canal was opened in 1825, Buffalo became a

---

6 Catlin, *The Story of Detroit*, (The Detroit News) p. 105.

7 Sweet, *Religion on the American Frontier*, vol. 3, p. 29.

8 Congregational Calvinism was modified as it went West, but the matter goes deeper. This study has noted more than once the unusually organic relation between Congregationalism and its social environment. Detached from a naturally Congregational Society, it tends, also, naturally, to become selective and to appeal to the more doctrinally and religiously independent in any locality. This was still true of smaller Congregational churches scattered through Michigan in 1910. A newcomer from New England sensed the difference.

port of entry into the interior, and boats could be taken directly to Detroit. Consequently Michigan in the 1830's and 1840's seems to have captured the New England imagination.[9]

IV

ALWAYS FARTHER WEST

A detailed history of Congregational expansion across the continent is here impossible. The Connecticut and Massachusetts Missionary Societies had been led to take an early interest in the always mobile frontier through reports on religious conditions in the West by Samuel Mills and Schermerhorn (1815). Thereafter the extension of Congregationalism can be dated by the westerning areas of settlement decade by decade: Michigan, 1824; Illinois, 1820; Wisconsin by 1840; Iowa, 1838. These are merely threshold dates. The "Yale Band" had gone to Illinois. Eleven Andover students agreed in 1842 to go as missionaries to Iowa.[10]

Theirs is a bright detail in the whole adventure. Asa Turner, "the agent for Iowa," had been begging for help for a dozen years and had given up hoping. When his prayers began to be answered he advised the

[9] The fortunes of Michigan Congregationalism are a fascinating study, though they do not entirely reflect the romance of Michigan history. Economically the history of the state may be told in four words: furs, lumber, copper, cars. The nefarious but highly profitable business of trading French brandy and English rum for beaver pelts came first, occasioned an epochal enmity between the French and English and entirely ruined the Indians. Detroit Military Post was established by Cadillac on Frontenac's order and under the direction of Louis the Fourteenth's Cabinet, and a little of the romance of King Louis's Court brightened the poor settlement. (All this the murals in the Detroit Public Library nobly picture.)

After the French and Indian Wars, Michigan was for a while part of Canada. The territory was surrendered again to Great Britain in 1812, recovered by the United States in 1813. The immigrants' period followed, and the magnificent stands of pine were exploited with a wastefulness beyond words, though the peak of this came much later. The foundations of the earlier Michigan fortunes were thus laid. Meanwhile the copper of the upper Peninsula made equally fabulous fortunes for absentee stockholders, mostly in and about Boston. Then, as though to mock foresight and reward wastefulness, some of the richest iron ore deposits in America were discovered in stump lands which the lumbermen were willing to default for taxes. And finally, the motor car.

All this gave the state generally an unstable economic history and the fortunes of all denominations reflected it. When the timber was gone, there was nothing to support the Congregational churches which Home Missionaries like Puddefoot got built, but piles of sawdust. The copper veins were worked out and stagnant towns and cities mourned at their shaft-heads. The fabulous expansion of motormaking congested populations and challenged all the denominations to extravagant programs of expansion. And nothing stayed put in cities reaching out blindly. It was always a race between burying dead churches and christening new ones. No state in the Union better illustrates the hectic course of American denominationalism than Michigan, because of the swift, dramatic alternation of its phases.

[10] Their names are on record and their native states, sound English stock family names and for given names Ebeneezer, Benjamin, Ephraim and, curiously, one Erastus. One reads the list very much as one reads the roster of the Apostles whose names were built into the foundations of the New Jerusalem. For such as these, representing the religious force of all American communities, laid the moral and religious foundations of the Republic.

"Band" realistically, "The climate will permit men to live long enough if they do their duty. If they do not, no matter how soon they die. They will not be called the Reverend Mr. Alden or Adams, simply Ebeneezer or Ephraim, and their wives will be Pegg or Polly or whatever her name may be." Above all, they are not to be "ashamed of [their] Mother" as soon as they had crossed the Alleghanies "as many of our good brethren are" (the aforesaid Mother being the Congregational Way).[11] "May the Lord direct your way." Nine of them were ordained in Denmark, Iowa, Sunday, November 5, 1843. The whole region was thereby stirred, and Congregationalism became well established beyond the Mississippi.

The American Home Missionary Society backed both Presbyterian and Congregational churches in Wisconsin. Young men from the Eastern Theological Seminaries were reluctant to go so far and the earlier missionaries were middle-aged men. The quite inadequate salaries may have been a partial explanation.[12] The Plan of Union, although operative in Wisconsin, was considerably modified and came to no more than "harmonious coöperation" between the two denominations, which worked happily till "Old School" Presbyterians became active in Wisconsin.

Home Missionaries then, and since, were men and women of courage, force, and faith. They saw regions of fabulous possibility as they had lain almost unchanged by any human action since the recession of the last Ice Age. One may envy now the adventurers who saw the magnificent hard-wood of Ohio and Indiana still partly holding its own against the axe, the Michigan Pine unviolated, the prairie grass still threaded by buffalo trails, the abundant waters still unpolluted. Like St. Paul, they have left us more vivid accounts of their hardships, though without complaint, than of the beauty of an Iowa early June; but their reports are social documents of the highest value,[13] America in the making. These missionaries were never exploiters, they sought the higher values of a Christian civilization, and they had often a statesman's vision. They naturally reported well of the regions into which they had gone and since their reports were widely circulated, they certainly stimulated migration.

V

The Continent Spanned

Home Missions in the further and far Northwest began as missions to the Indians. (The charter of the American Board of Commissioners for Foreign Missions permitted the Board to send missionaries to the

[11] All this from Sweet, cited from Douglass, *The Pilgrims of Iowa.*
[12] Sweet cites Noah Cook's budget (1840). His expenditures were $458.75, salary $400.00 if he could get it. $125.00 moving expenses, however, are included.
[13] The larger part of Sweet's volume on Congregationalism contains a collection of reports and letters as impossible to condense as they are fascinating to read.

American Indians.) Christianization of the Indians had been one of the professed purposes of both the Pilgrims and the Puritans; but instead they were exterminated or exiled, and thus began the conflict between antagonistic cultures which hunted them across the continent. For all that, the missions of the American churches to the American Indians is the one bright chapter in an otherwise shameful history, and beginning with Jonathan Edwards in Stockbridge the missionaries have been the Indians' best friends and have done their best to safeguard their interests.

Indian missions opened the door for Home Missions in the remote northwest. In 1831 five Oregon Indians came to St. Louis, a center of the fur trade, asking for the "white man's Book of Heaven." The response to such an appeal was immediate. The Methodists responded first, but in 1836 Dr. and Mrs. Marcus Whitman and the Reverend and Mrs. H. H. Spalding were sent out by the American Board. The story of the Whitmans is an epic, bright and tragic. Whitman had a statesman's eye for an imperial domain. He made his way back to Washington, so the epic runs, with almost incredible hardships, reported there the spacious wonder of the Pacific northwest, and so prevented its cession to Great Britain in the strategic and somewhat heated negotiation ending in the Aberdeen-Buchanan Treaty. The bright promise of the Oregon mission was tragically eclipsed. The Indians lost half their number through an epidemic, Whitman was accused of poisoning them for their lands and cattle, and Dr. and Mrs. Whitman and twelve others were massacred and the Oregon Mission was closed. But Congregationalism had reached the Pacific.

VI

SAMUEL J. MILLS—STATESMAN, MISSIONARY-AT-LARGE

American Missions, both home and foreign, owe more to Samuel J. Mills than to any other one person in American religious history. He furnishes an almost unmatched illustration of the far-reaching influence of one entirely devoted life. He was born of a mentally and religiously distinguished ancestry in Litchfield County, Connecticut, that lovely though austere nursery of soldiers, preachers, educators, writers, and theologians.[14] Samuel John Mills, Senior, was a ministerial Connecticut institution, famous as "Father" Mills. He, the father, had been one of the early four-dollar-a-week missionaries in Vermont. His mother was an uncalendared saint, who bore her husband seven children and buried four of them. Her son Samuel she dedicated to the Lord. How otherwise could he have been Samuel?

[14] The list is awe inspiring: Ethan Allen, Seth Warner, Day, Finney, Taylor, Porter, Bushnell, Henry Ward and Harriet Beecher. The principal school for training young men for the ministry in the late Eighteenth Century was in Litchfield County and the first law school in America. Richards, *Samuel J. Mills.*

He also was "twice born," and his second birth was through the "dark night of the soul." So much brighter the light, then, when it broke upon him. He matriculated at Williams College, then "experiencing a revival," in 1806. There his influence paralleled John Wesley's at Christ Church, Oxford. He was older than his classmates and of a most fervent spirit. The most devout formed a prayer group which met Saturday afternoons in a maple grove. An August thunderstorm drove them to the shelter of a hay-stack and there, while the skies played an overture to an epochal enterprise, Mills proposed that they should send the Gospel to Asia. "We can do it, if we will." That meeting was, in event and purpose, the birth-meeting of American Protestant Foreign Missions. Thereafter, these five were the "Brethren" with one shared purpose: to evangelize the world. Mills went from Williams to Yale with the purpose of leavening the college with his own zeal. He found it unresponsive, though he did meet Obookiah, a young Hawaiian who eventually directed missionary interest toward those enchanted isles.

Andover Seminary was more promising. The "Brethren" there renewed their associations and mutually confirmed their purpose. They added others like-minded, graduates of Harvard, Brown, and Union Colleges. Adoniram Judson was co-leader with Mills, easily his equal in zeal, probably his superior in mental brilliance. The group kept the records of their meetings in cipher, which was translated in 1818 and is now an invaluable document.[15] They were ready to go. Who could or would send them? Existing missionary societies contemplated only the United States, though the Massachusetts Society had amended its constitution to include the "more distant regions of the earth, as circumstances shall invite and the ability of the Society shall admit." British Societies, notably the Baptist Foreign Missionary Society and the London Missionary Society, had been in action for about twenty years and had received American support. The Brethren—Judson seems to have taken the initiative in this—asked the London Society whether they would accept "two or three young unmarried men," liberally educated and "susceptible of a passion for missions." The reply was unfavorable and Mills was against the proposal. America, he thought, could and should support her own missionaries.

VII

The Organization of the American Board of Commissioners for Foreign Missions

The "fathers" began to arise, first the Andover Faculty, and then men of influence in the Massachusetts General Association to whom the young

---

[15] These young men had an astonishingly mature understanding of the situations with which they were dealing.

men were advised to submit their hopes and plans. The Association met at Bradford on June 27, 1810. Adoniram Judson, Jr., Samuel Nott, Jr., Samuel J. Mills, and Samuel Newell were introduced and respectfully requested "the attention of their Reverend Fathers" to a momentous statement and inquiries which came to this: Could they expect patronage and support from a Missionary Society in this country or must [they] commit themselves to the direction of a European Society; and what preparatory measure ought they to take previous to actual engagement?[16] So, "feeling their youth and inexperience" they looked up to their fathers in the Church and respectfully solicited "their advice, direction and prayers."

The respectful request was referred to a committee of three who reported the next day in favor of instituting a "Board of Commissioners for Foreign Missions," a power which the amended charter gave to the Massachusetts Association. Hence an historic name. Nine Commissioners were contemplated, five from Massachusetts and four from Connecticut, with power. The Commissioners seem to have appointed a smaller executive committee, called the "Prudential Committee," another historic name.[17] The Prudential Committee lived up to its name. Faced with definite sailing dates and the great responsibility involved directly the young men embarked, only one member of the committee was at first favorable to the venture. Later they had an access of faith and courage, but even so doubted if the funds of the Board warranted them in incurring the expense involved in sending the wives of the "Missionary Brethren." The Brethren themselves had once believed the celibate estate more favorable to missionary efficiency. Human nature and the love of brave young women persuaded them otherwise. The wives went—and to early deaths.

Money was, of course, a practical consideration. A providential legacy of $30,000 (probably to the Massachusetts Association) met that need. Five thousand dollars would cover all expenses for the first year. The three married men were to have a salary of $666.66 a year, the unmarried two $444.44. The five were ordained in Salem Tabernacle Church, Feb. 8, 1812. The day was bitterly cold, but the church was crowded and the dramatic solemnity of the service kindled the imagination of the congregation and moved them to deep emotion; "at times," said William Goodell, later to become himself a distinguished missionary, "the entire assembly seemed moved as the trees are moved by a mighty wind."

There were delays in sailing, which tried the eager missionaries but were thought providential by the Board, which received $6000 in three weeks and was thus able not only completely to outfit the young people,

---

[16] Richards, *Samuel J. Mills.*
[17] An invaluable source is the *Memorial Volume of the First Fifty Years of the American Board of Commissioners for Foreign Missions* published by the Board in 1861.

but advance them a year's salary. They were sent out on two vessels. The *Caravan* sailed from Salem on February 19th with the Judsons and Newells. The *Harmony* cleared Delaware Cape February 24th, carrying Mr. and Mrs. Nott and unmarried Hall and Rice. They had closed their prayer-meeting under the haystack by singing, from Isaac Watts:

> "Let all the heathen writers join
> To form one perfect book;
> Great God if once compared with thine
> How mean their writings look!"

They had now begun to furnish matter for a library of books.

VIII

INCORPORATION OF THE BOARD

Patently here was an enterprise too momentous for a sub-committee of the General Association of Massachusetts. It must be continental in its support and international in its scope. Since it was likely to prove, in addition, an enterprise demanding rare executive specialization, and highly trained oversight, the movers sought incorporation from the Great and General Court of Massachusetts. Therefore, on February 13, 1812 (Abraham Lincoln was then just three years old) Jedidiah Morse and Samuel Worcester recited, in a petition to both bodies of the General Court (suitably denominated and capitalized) the so far brief history of their society and its purposes. They found it very inconvenient, they continued, "to manage and transact their business without an incorporation. Wherefore they pray that they may be incorporated under a suitable name, and invested with the powers and privileges usually granted to similar institutions, and authorized to do and transact business as a body politic and corporate; and as in duty bound will ever pray."[18]

This petition was read in the House of Representatives on February 15 (1812), referred to a committee of three, and read in the Senate the same day; the Senate added two names to the House Committee, and the joint committee of five which drew and asked leave (granted) to bring in a bill. The bill limited the annual income of the proposed Society from real and personal estate to $18,000, which was reduced by amendment to $12,000. These limitations are significant; the money question was the thing. The Amended Bill was first read to the House on February 25 and thereafter had stormy going in both Houses.

The times were difficult; war was about to be declared on Great

[18] Anderson, *Memorial Volume of the First Fifty Years of the American Board of Commissioners for Foreign Missions,* chap. 3. Actually they were petitioning the General Court to make them strangely like what the General Court itself had been in its own beginnings: a chartered corporation to serve religious ends.

Britain, the country thought itself poor, the seas were perilous, the Napoleonic Wars were rocking the western world, trade was stagnant, the proposal was strange and audacious, the home churches were doctrinally embroiled and the state was seamed by political rancors.[19] All these things made passage of the bill, which in kinder times would have met no opposition, highly controversial. Meanwhile the seven young missionaries were on these same perilous high seas. The bill was laid on the table in the winter session of the legislature (1812) by a vote of 139 to 130 in the House of Representatives.

An election was held before the next session of the General Court (May 1812) with resultant changes in the political complexion of the State. The House passed the bill June 6 and sent it to the Senate. Benjamin Crowninshield (Secretary of the Navy under Madison) had opposed the bill in the Chamber of Representatives in the previous session. He was a Salem merchant whose ships went to the far East and he professed to speak with authority of conditions there. The conduct of missionaries, he said, was unworthy and their labors useless (all of which has a familiar sound). Perhaps some unacknowledged sense of the fundamental and unescapable oppositions between the missionary and the trader actuated Crowninshield. Also the enterprise would take money out of the country while Crowninshield's life work was to get it in—at the expense of India or China. The Salem shipmaster had been elected to the Senate and there renewed his opposition.

A classic debate ensued with an often quoted passage. It was objected on the floor of the Senate that the act of incorporation was designed to afford "the means of exporting religion whereas there was none to spare among ourselves." To which it was replied that "religion was a commodity of which the more we exported the more we had remaining." Nevertheless the Senate voted against the bill. But the House still urged it and after joint conferences it was finally passed by the House, June 19 and the Senate, June 20. That was, in more senses than one, Mid-Summer Eve. The Charter of the Board has been acknowledged in every state in the Union and in all lands in which the Board has operated. Its credit has stood unimpaired around the world.

Thereafter the Board wrote its own strategic and distinguished history, which cannot here be followed save as its relation to the history of Congregationalism is involved. It was not an ecclesiastical body. It was meant to be the agent of the churches for foreign missions. It had, apparently and to begin with, "no thought of becoming anything more than a Congregational body." A year before its incorporation, however,

---

[19] The New England clergy and the Massachusetts political party then in power were bitterly opposed to the Federal administration.

the Board suggested to the General Assembly of the Presbyterian Church the formation of a similar body with which they might coöperate. The Assembly replied with a wisdom and grace which should go far to correct any strictures passed heretofore in this history upon the Plan of Union. The business of Foreign Missions, the Assembly said, "may properly be best managed under the direction of a single Board" and its own numerous and extensive engagements, the Assembly thought, forbade its taking part in the business of foreign missions. Also, and this qualified the previous qualification, there were several societies within the bounds of the Presbyterian Church which gave particular attention to foreign missions.

IX

THE BOARD BECOMES INTERDENOMINATIONAL

The American Board, therefore, extended its membership into the Presbyterian Church and added eight commissioners "from among the more prominent members of that Church." In succeeding years commissioners were elected from the Associated Reformed and Reformed Dutch Churches. Until 1837 the Board was recognized by the high Presbyterian courts as a proper agency for the extension of Presbyterian foreign missions, though not the sole agency. In 1837 the "old school" Assembly made the Western Foreign Missionary Society the Church's official board, though "old school" churches continued their support as they desired. No Presbyterian missionaries withdrew and the churches of the "new school" continued their relations and support.

The rise of denominationalism worked against the interdenominational support of the Board. Each denomination wanted its foreign converts to become equally denominational in Asia, Africa, and the islands of the seas. As a result the American Protestant denominational divisions were projected into lands where they had no meaning at all. (Missionary-statesmen finally saw the futility of this and achieved unity in India and China while churches at home talked about it, guardedly.) The American Board in time was, so to speak, returned to the Congregational churches with thanks, but it has never been denominational and within its spacious title there is still a vision unrealized.

This chapter noted, pages back, the stimulating influence of Mills' Western Tours (1813–14) upon the Connecticut Home Missionary Society. He had been equally influential in promoting Foreign Missions. This dual activity indicates his vocation—exploration and promotion. The "Brethren" seem to have recognized that when, in secret session, they decided he would be more useful on the Home Front and sailed without him; but no single continent could contain his evangelical fervor. He followed Jackson to New Orleans, a month after the battle, visited the miserably equipped military hospitals, in which disease took more lives than British bullets had taken, and with incredible hardships traversed the lower Mississippi Valley which had recently been acquired through the Louisiana Purchase.

His and Schermerhorn's report (published at Hartford in 1814) "shed more light on the state of the destitute parts of the country than all other documents then in existence" with far-reaching results. One of them was the American Bible Society. He stimulated city missionary work; he finished his short life, so unbelievably full, in the service of Africa. He had always longed to serve the "poor Africans" and his contacts with southern slavery in the raw increased that longing. He interested home churches in the religious welfare of the Negroes, lent himself wholeheartedly to the project of a free colony in Africa, and volunteered to find a suitable site on the African west coast. His experiences there are a little epic; his reports reveal his acuteness of observation. On June 15, 1818, aged thirty-five, he died of tuberculosis on his voyage home. His body was committed to the deep, but his decade and a half of action and influence transcend time.

CHAPTER XII

Recapitulation and Transition

THE last two chapters have not been well organized chronologically, but the historian can at least enter a plea of "confession and avoidance." The geographical extension of Congregationalism in the United States was a complicated business whose lack of system was fundamentally due to the want of a central directing authority. There was no national Home Missionary Society nor any really supporting denominational consciousness until Congregational churches had crossed the continent. The result was a sporadic and uncoördinated expansion. That so much was accomplished with so little overhead direction is a tribute to the vitality of the Congregational way. It grew according to its own genius.

If one could make a map of it, there would be in its first phase, once it had crossed the Hudson River, a Plan of Union expansion in the State of New York, whose issue was a minimum of Congregationalism and a rich deposit of Presbyterianism. But this was paralleled by a tenacious, though numerically insignificant, extension of churches which began and continued Congregational. Once beyond New York, the Plan of Union became less monopolistic and Congregationalism more self-assertive, but the two movements ran along together with crossing and recrossing lines, though the Plan of Union never got beyond the Mississippi. To add to the confusion, there was a multiplication of agencies. The New England states maintained their own Home Missionary societies. These for the most part delegated their activities, though not their powers, to the American Home Missionary Society which was, in turn, interdenominational in a lopsided kind of way. An analytical touch, practically impossible, is needed to dissect out the purely Congregational factors.

For all that, by about 1850 the frame was achieved within which Congregationalism in America would live and move and have its being. The second section of this history examines with great care what has been done in organic development and growth of denominational self-consciousness within that frame. Chronologically, the inception of foreign missions is an interlude in the history of an expanding Congregationalism (both movements are united in Samuel Mills). Neither interrupts the other; rather they are mutually invigorating and, combined, they represent a dynamic evangelism which, considering the limitations of the home-base, is unmatched in the history of American Protestantism for breadth of vision and essential catholicity. Since the combined enterprises were arrestingly free from denominational self-seeking, they sought only the extension of Christianity in America and the evangelization of the world.

If one takes 1850 for the *terminus ad quem* of the first and really creative phase of Congregationalism, the period covered comes almost exactly to 300 years. Those three centuries are epic. They began with a formless religious ferment in England, feeling along forbidden frontiers for a form of religious fellowship which should reproduce New Testament conditions. Little groups of "seekers" were led and misled. They were always dissolving and reforming, always in danger of their liberty or their lives.

By processes of selection through two generations, one group, disciplined by exile and wisely led, carried themselves and a yet termless future to a New World and survived. Here again are complications. The vaster current of Puritanism sought a new world, too, and claimed a common seacoast with Separatism. In lonely settlements geographically near though by transportation remote, each influenced the other. Ecclesiastically the issue was the "Congregational way" to which Puritanism furnished the doctrinal content, ethical steadfastness, and organic filaments. Plymouth independency had a Congregational core which outlasted all attempts to make the "way" Presbyterian. The ecclesiastical system was, to begin with, only the religious aspect of colonial social and political organization. More accurately the social and political forms were a frame for religion, the secular phases of an essentially religious order. Then followed a long and difficult process of disentanglement, punctuated by religious "awakenings" and revivals, and finally a profoundly devisive doctrinal realignment.

Meanwhile New England's stern and mostly rockbound coast nurtured the most unified, democratic, plain-living and high-thinking population group on the North American continent. They dug into an irresponsive soil, they went down to the sea in ships, they multiplied, prospered, shared their prosperity with the Lord to whom they gratefully attributed it, were aggressively liberty-loving, and cut their eyeteeth on flintlock muskets. They had always lived in peril of something—Indians, French, "Red-Coats," hellfire, what you please—and so became amazingly unafraid. They were colonists by inheritance and instinct, lovers of far and wide horizons. They carried with them toward sunsets always further west ploughs, firearms, schoolbooks, and the Bible. They met the unforeseen with a native ingenuity, coöperated masterfully with the inevitable and left no land they took unchanged for the better. In such ways they wrought for 300 years until they saw the sunset over the Pacific, knowing that it would rise upon their missions in Asia. They had girdled the globe.

I

THE NEW ENGLAND THEOLOGY

There remains then, so far as the first section of this history is concerned, only to fill the frame with such significant items in the life of a Protestant Communion as seem to be needed to complete the picture. All American nonliturgical Protestant denominations have much in common. There are differences, of course, but they are background differences. A quite intelligent person would find in any one of the more representative churches little actual difference in a Sunday morning service. They use pretty much the same hymns, listen to the same lessons from the Bible, hear or share prayers which present to the Throne of Grace the same confessions and petitions, worship in churches which conform architecturally to widely-shared types, meet weekday neighbors who are quite the same on Sunday as on week days though variously denominated, hear sermons of the same general import. This is rather inevitable because all the inheritances and conditions of American life since the colonial period have combined to shape the religious life first of the colonies and then the nation.

Substantially every variant of Protestantism has been transplanted to these shores, not to speak of variants native to the soil. By the Federal Constitution all these were given the freedom of the continent and in consequence a great area of religious action and contention simply ceased to exist. The first and often heroic phase of any denominational history had been a struggle first to exist at all, unpersecuted.[1] Now in the United States any denomination could be what it wanted to be. The only question thereafter was what to do with its freedom. In the main, the activities of American Protestantism followed four lines. First, the organization, operation, and manipulation of its various forms of denominational machinery; second, efforts to maintain and increase the membership of the churches and the faithful administration of all those services which religion renders to life—what St. Paul called the edification of the saints; third, home and foreign missionary extension; and fourth, theological definition, assertion, speculation, discussion, controversy—all or singly.

Congregationalism, being free ever since the Revolutionary War (which ended the threat of an American Established Church) to be as Congregational as it pleased, spent relatively less of its force upon the

[1] This phase began, for Protestantism, with the Reformation itself. Its terminations are not easy to date for any study of it merges with a study of the growth or decline of religious toleration. Intolerance is a tangled growth, has usually outlasted the removal of legal disabilities and has a surprising power of re-emergence.

operation of its denominational machinery than, for example, the Presbyterians. It had less to operate. It delegated home and foreign missions to their proper boards and societies and was, therefore, free in an unusual and almost unexpected way to specialize in theology, which it did with great distinction from 1750 to 1850. The resultant theological systems were not known as specifically Congregational. They are now called, in the histories of American theology, "The New England Theology."[2]

This history has in previous chapters taken account of the concern of the New England churches for the doctrinal bases of their faith and practice. That has been unavoidable: their history has been seamed with that concern. It was implicit in the Cambridge Synod; it became militant with Jonathan Edwards. It occasioned the Unitarian departure. It persisted as a ruling concern, as we shall see, until the formulation of the Kansas City Creed. After the Cambridge Synod, for full two hundred years, the churches were far more concerned with their faith than their polity. We have noted how the Congregational way was the issue here of the confluence of a massive Puritanism and a leavening Independency, which finally leavened the whole lump.

The concern for theology was the contribution of the Puritan stream and took its rise in august conceptions of the mystery of life and human destiny without which Puritanism cannot be understood. Perry Miller, in his examination of the genesis of the Puritan mind, has traced these conceptions to their sources with an insight for which the history of Puritanism had long been waiting. For, he says, the creative impulse of the Puritan was his piety, and his piety was never the rigid and negative asceticism for which he has been maligned and misrepresented. It was Augustine's hunger for God. It was St. Paul's persuasion of life as a warfare with unseen and spiritual enmities. It was Pascal's sense (for strangely enough Pascal is apposite here) of the essential misery of life, as though one always saw a chasm at life's road-edge into which, save for the grace of God, one is sure to fall. Life, therefore, for the Puritan, as Haller also said, was wayfaring and warfaring and, save as the imperilled were undergirded by the sovereign will of God, he was lost and beaten before he started.

Generations of Puritan preachers sounded the same note, though they may not ever have known that Augustine said it, "Thou hast made us for thyself and we are restless until we rest in thee." Puritanism was that restlessness in endless action, and all the Puritan's theology was carried upon his quest for rest in God. His theology (this in Miller) dramatized the needs of his soul. His religious emotion needed a framework of

[2] Any detailed examination of the New England theology seems a life work for a specialist. Reading Edwards, like reading Kant, apparently may become a vocation.

dogma. The New England theology was the drama of the Puritan soul played out here in America for two centuries.

The relation of Congregationalism to this theology is paradoxical. The basal system under examination, interpretation, and "improvement" was Calvinism—the common inheritance of all the Reformed churches. The only contention between Princeton Presbyterianism and the New England theology was: which is the most truly Calvinistic? American Congregationalism accepted the Westminster Confession. It made the Savoy Declaration (considered earlier in this history) official for Connecticut and Massachusetts churches. The National Council of 1865 declared in substance its adherence "to those ancient symbols as being" well and fully grounded upon the Holy Scriptures, "the only sufficient and invariable rule of religion." The whole action of the New England theology was within the frame of historic Calvinism.[3]

But the long succession of distinguished divines, teachers, and preachers who fabricated the New England system were Congregationalists by inheritance and training. The theological schools entirely identified with it were Congregational seminaries and the organization and genius of Congregationalism made the free action of their acute and powerful minds possible. Congregationalism has had a sufficiency of theological controversies, intimations of heresy, much heckling of candidates for ordination or installation and some refusals to do either. But it has never had a heresy trial on the grand scale, for the simplest and most effective of reasons: its teachers and preachers are protected by an encircling group which knows them best and, though not agreeing with them, has refused to cast them out for reasons of opinion. (The whole Unitarian Separation was accomplished without a real heresy trial.) Rigid authoritative imposition of "standards" has therefore been impossible save in the local church, and even then it was most reluctantly exercised. (It has for a long time now been far easier for a Congregational minister to be an economic rather than a theological heretic.)

It is difficult to overestimate the service of this intellectual freedom, not only to Congregational thought but even to American theology. It made possible what Foster calls the "genetic" process, the process of slow, free, gradual, interlinked growth. Moreover, what was most practically effective in Congregationalism was tied up in one bundle with the theology. Foster puts it all in a few arresting sentences: Congregationalism, during the period of the supremacy of the Edwardian theology, took

---

[3] Williston Walker's *The Creeds and Platforms of Congregationalism* is the best source book. It is indispensable. Frank Hugh Foster's *A Genetic History of the New England Theology*, and *A History of New England Theology* by George Nye Boardman, are authoritative and manageable. Foster is more inclusive and easier to read.

an unquestioned lead among American churches in missions, evangelism, education, and denominational coöperation.[4]

An earlier chapter traced, loosely, the succession of the New England theologians from Edwards, Senior, about to the time of Edwards, Junior. Boardman supplies a meticulous chronological table from the birth of Edwards, Senior, to about 1837. These 134 years made and unmade empires, dissolved old and historic orders in social and political revolution, and inaugurated new economic and political orders. But the Boardman table makes little of these things. In the year Wolfe died victoriously on the Plain of Abraham and New France in America ceased to be, Hopkins considered the *Wisdom of God in the Permission of Sin*. In 1765, while the recently-passed Stamp Act agitated Faneuil Hall, he inquired into the *Promises of the Gospel*. In 1770 the Red-Coats fired on Boston citizens and Hopkins replied to Hart. In 1773, they threw tea into Boston Harbor and Hopkins dealt with *The Nature of True Holiness*. While Washington was trying to get his new Federal government going, the younger Edwards was examining *The Salvation of All Men* and concluding that "endless misery" (for some) may, "upon the whole" be good for the universe.

II

THE GREAT SUCCESSION

The men who thus unfolded the ways of God with men are in many ways more interesting than their theologies. The great succession belonged to Connecticut, partly because Yale College nurtured them, partly because of the semi-Presbyterian nature of Connecticut Congregationalism, and partly just because.[5] They were mostly country ministers (though Hopkins had a pastorate in Newport, Rhode Island) with long pastorates and probably patient parishioners. There was, during this period, more "exchanging pulpits" than now[6] which gave to the ministry generally a kind of corporate character.

Thus interest in theology was native to their minds, the region, and the time. It was of the texture and essence of their ministry. They thought it out, preached it out, wrote it out, taught it out, and each one of these four clauses is capable of most ample development. Their finally published systems are, so to speak, the deposit of their whole lifework. Their preaching power naturally varied. Joseph Bellamy, a Bethlehem, Connecticut, pastor for fifty years, was one of the greatest preachers of this period, with every oratorical gift. Hopkins' power was more intellectual.

[4] Foster, *A Genetic History of the New England Theology*, p. 3.

[5] Carlyle says there is no accounting for the leaves on the World-tree Ygdrasil.

[6] A fine old custom which should not have been so completely lost. Long pastorates and congregations which went to church fifty-two Sundays in the year made an "exchange" a relief to everybody concerned.

Channing, who heard him in Newport, said that "his delivery in the pulpit was the worst I ever met with."[7]

The outstanding New England theologians of the last half of the Eighteenth Century taught candidates for the ministry, becoming, as it were, theological seminaries quite on their own. Hopkins, as we have seen, "studied" with Edwards and became in turn the most famous instructor of his time.[8] His house, says Boardman, became "a school of the prophets." Asa Burton, minister in Thetford, Vermont, for more than a half-century, instructed about sixty students for the ministry. Their systems were thus continued and widely preached and awkwardly named "Hopkinsianism" or "Emmonsism." They were recognized and read in Great Britain. The University of Aberdeen made Bellamy a Doctor of Divinity. A succession of New England thinkers influenced English-speaking religious thought.

Their fundamental effort was the reconciliation of the fundamental paradox in Calvinism: the moral responsibility of the individual beneath the complete sovereignty of God which foreordained every soul's eternal destiny. The freedom of the will was the hinge on which the whole divine economy turned. How they argued it and what conclusions they reached and the validity of these conclusions belong to the highly specialized histories of theology. They worked within the framework of an inerrant Bible and found their proof-texts as they pleased. They must have a doctrine for everything. Sin, theologically, was a fatal and universal infection of the human personality dating from the Fall. Sin, practically, was unbelief and not going to church and profanity and licentiousness and intemperances and worldliness. God's responsibility for permitting sin was another burning question.

Virtue was benevolence in motion and expression. Toward the end of their period the more clear-visioned came to see that sin was selfishness and goodness was love. This was preëminently the contribution of Emmons. Nathaniel Emmons (born 1745, died 1840) is perhaps the outstanding transitional theologian in the long process. He was thirteen years old when Jonathan Edwards died. Bushnell was nearing the peak of his power when he (Emmons) died. He was therefore a notable mediator between one age that was ending and a new epoch. He had an unusual mind. He was fitted for college in ten months and was graduated from Yale in 1767, magna cum laude. His own account of "his early religious history" is significant and deeply moving. He had "the awful thought of dying unprepared" and resolved "some time or other" to become truly pious; and he had a peculiar respect for ministers and

[7] Boardman, *A History of New England Theology*, pp. 72–77.
[8] This may be questioned; Emmons actually trained more ministers than Hopkins.

would be, he thought, extremely happy if he could be qualified to become one himself. The death of a sister renewed his "apprehensions of the state of the damned." Then his fears abated for a season. Later he had a renewed sense of the "great importance of being truly religious and began to read the Bible and pray in secret."

But he lacked, he said, any sense of the corruption of his heart and its perfect opposition to God. A thunder storm so terrified him that he lay awake all night "crying for mercy." He continued his theological studies (under Dr. Smalley), studies which served only to deepen his despair. He knew he was a sinner and convinced at the same time that the best desires and prayers of sinners were altogether selfish, criminal, and displeasing to God. (This was the impasse of a rigid Calvinism.) He was delivered by a sudden conversion which filled his mind with joy and serenity; and a "peculiar spirit of benevolence to my fellowmen, whether friends or foes; and I was transported with the thought of the unspeakable blessedness of the day when universal benevolence should prevail among all mankind."[9] It is difficult in view of what followed to overestimate the significance of the rapt vision of Emmons.

His examination for licensure was unsatisfactory to the older clergymen and occasioned controversies which were finally reconciled by a "conciliatory creed." He was finally settled over the historic church in Franklin, Massachusetts. He served a loyal people till he was seized with a fainting fit in the pulpit (May, 1827) and had to be carried home. But he finished that interrupted sermon the next Sunday, resigned, and was thereafter pastor emeritus.

The list of his published sermons, addresses, and works fills almost two pages in Sprague's *Annals*. In addition, Professor Park supplies an acute digest of Emmons' theological positions, with some of which Park said he himself did not "coincide," though he commended his power as a preacher unreservedly and testified to his "vigorous and capacious mind," his matured piety and his indefatigable toil. Park summarizes Emmons' "peculiar positions" under ten heads. He was a consistent Calvinist who believed that all true virtue, all real holiness consists in universal benevolence; hence all sin is selfishness. He allowed man a moral freedom and responsibility under a divine pressure about which he is rather vague. The introduction of sin, according to Emmons, was for the general good, and the sinner must approve of the divine conduct even though God should cast him off forever. He opposed, finally, the sovereignty of God to man's moral responsibility, and left the paradox unresolved. But his emphasis upon benevolence endured; the rapture of

[9] Sprague's *Annals*, vol. 1, p. 693.

his conversion modified the austerity of his creed,[10] and he broke ground for a kinder faith. This long succession of theologians developed their doctrines of the Atonement, predominantly "governmental." God was under bonds by his own nature to maintain the moral order. Sin must be punished, not through divine vindictiveness, but by the impartial and inescapable obligation of a judge to permit no unpunished infraction of the law. The Atonement was therefore such a satisfaction of justice that grace was thereafter possible.

They argued also how that was accomplished through the suffering and death of Jesus Christ with such convincing of themselves and others as they could effect. There were always heaven and hell. Also, the unregenerate must be reborn and they sought to explain how, before regeneration, nothing good a person seemed to do was of any avail; it rather involved him so much the more deeply in condemnation.

The whole system was essentially, though perhaps half unconsciously, meant to supply a basis for evangelical revival preaching—the conversion of sinners and the increase of the church. Edwards so directed it from the first and so it continued to be directed and used. At the last the awe-inspiring edifice they built was strangely interpenetrated by light and shadow and whether those who lived within it saw darkness or light depended upon their position. If through intellectual conviction or the mystical certainty of rebirth they knew themselves the elect, the entire structure was bright with a light the torments of the lost could not darken, but rather enhanced. If they were not sure of election, the whole structure was shadowed by dumb spiritual struggle or dark with despair. Nevertheless as one guided by sound scholars follows the development of the system, one sees it escaping its own limitations, freeing and humanizing its approaches and conclusions, and always seeking more light. This was made possible in part by the elastic and diffusive structure of Congregational polity and the genius of New England Congregationalism.

III
"THE OLD ORDER CHANGETH"; HORACE BUSHNELL

The Nineteenth Century changed the picture, though gradually. Theological education began to be professional, institutional, getting

[10] The bright account of his long life and ministry in the *Annals* humanizes his theology and is far more interesting than the theology. The Rev. Elam Smalley's recollection of what Emmons said (he was, as noted, a famous teacher of preachers) are priceless. He said to one preacher of a sermon just delivered: "It was well arranged, well argued and well delivered. I have but one fault to find with it—it was not true." He inquired of another preacher, his sermon finished, "Do you ever mean to preach another sermon?" "Yes, sir." "What can you say? You have already preached the whole system of theology." Again, commenting upon a preacher famous for fluency, "It is a great blessing to be able to preach a half an hour about nothing. The great body of *extempore* preachers are *pre tempore* preachers."

itself slowly disentangled from general collegiate education of which it had been an aspect rather than a department (there were then no universities in the United States). The first President Timothy Dwight of Yale (1795) was a famous theologian and instructed in divinity students contemplating the ministry, but Yale Divinity School was not opened for service till 1822. The Hollis professorship of divinity was "the chief position of theological influence in Massachusetts" and the oldest in New England. It became the focus of Unitarianism. Andover Seminary was opened in 1808 as a counter influence and quite as specifically to furnish a more highly specialized education for the ministry. The time was passing when a young man could be adequately trained by spending a winter or two with an Asa Burton in Thetford, Vermont. The first faculties were small and composed of ministers who had some special aptitude for the "chair" which fitted them, but the era of specialization had begun in theological education, the theological professor was above the horizon, and the well-trained minister of the future would be the product of a corporate rather than an individual training.

But the individual theology was still dominant even through the media of theological schools. This is still true. Nathanial Taylor, for example, exerted so powerful an influence upon New England theology during its later transitional period that his "powerful and influential" mind overshadowed the detail that he was the first professor of theology in the Yale department of theology. In general, though this is to anticipate a long process of development, each theological school (variously named and successively founded) came to have a distinctive technique, tradition, and theology. One could therefore speak as Boardman does of "New Haven," "Andover," "Oberlin" theology, although in the departments of theology particularly, the institution never eclipsed the teacher.

All Congregational theological schools in America proudly chronicle their long succession of scholars in any department, men of national and of even international distinction, devout in spirit, free and inquiring in mind, arresting in personality, each in his own orbit like Milton's sun a source of light from which, as to a fountain returning, lesser luminaries drew light. Edwards Amasa Park of Andover was, for more than fifty years (1836–1881 and then Emeritus), perhaps the most dominating of this distinguished fellowship. He was an indefatigable student, a mighty teacher, an impressive preacher with the face of a scholar, prophet, and saint. The noble bronze tablet in his memory, now transferred to the Chapel Hall of Andover-Newton Seminary, commemorates one of the most brilliant careers in the long history of American theology and the culminating incarnation of the New England theology.

The man who finally released Congregational theological thought and great regions of American thinking from the confining bonds of a Calvinism which had lost its creative significance, was never in any theological chair at all. Horace Bushnell (1802–1876) was also born in Litchfield of a stock native to the region for eight generations. He was a Yankee by all the implications of the word and yet his true citizenship was in the timeless and the universal. He won his faith through a struggle with much doubting (this does not seem to have been true of the men so far considered) and his strong face, so different from Park's classic profile, was deeply marked by struggling intensities of mind, spirit, and physical limitations.

In station he was pastor of a prosperous and loyal church in Hartford, one of the most delightful of New England cities, and a preacher of spacious and arresting power. In mental action he was the protagonist in a liberation of Christian thought of momentous consequence. Blake's noble verses from "Milton" cannot be forced into this context, but he did not cease from "mental fight," nor did his sword "sleep in his hand." If he did not establish Jerusalem in any green and pleasant land, he did bequeath to succeeding generations of preachers and teachers a creative and rarely abused freedom of Christian inquiry and expression, a freedom which he won for himself at great price. He was accused of new heresies under old names; he was the storm center of controversy in which he gave as much as, or more than, he received. During all that mental warfare he was thrice sheltered: once by his own inner serenity and the stability of his dearly-bought faith; once by his own church, generous and loyal; once by the encircling line of his own ministerial association through which heresy hunters could make no breach. This was Congregational polity at its best.

Foster, in a discriminating appraisal, notes that he approached theology through his preëminent preaching instead of approaching preaching through theology.[11] Foster goes on to say that he did not sufficiently conceive the importance of the historic creeds (at least the Nicene), or the importance either of the New England divines whom he criticized with considerable vigor. This is probably true enough and at the same time shows a faint repercussion in Foster's own mind of the attitude of the professional theologian toward the amateur.

The reach of Bushnell's influence is for this history more important than a precise examination of his positions. Perhaps his greatest service was in the field of Christian nurture. So far in this narrative young people have rarely appeared except in an unfavorable light; "night walking,"

---

[11] Foster, *A Genetic History of the New England Theology*, chap. 14. Every theological faculty should have one theological teacher who has tested and matured and mediated his theology by preaching it. That is about the only way any theology can be vitalized. (Atkins.)

or reading forbidden romances, or disliking two-hour sermons strongly tinctured with terror, or else candidates for a revivalistic regeneration. A child could not be saved unless he were made from birth an alien to the Kingdom of God. Very little children who needed to be baptized had innocently occasioned, in part, the acrimonious controversies of the Half-Way Covenant. All of which comes back to this: that Calvinistic Puritanism had never quite known what to do with a little child.

Possibly his feeling that the "revival" method was being disastrously overworked may have led Bushnell to correct it by calling attention to other forms of entrance into the religious life. The churches, says Foster, "had never entirely forgotten the duty of Christian nurture or denied the possibility of child piety," but their emphasis upon conscious conversion had more than obscured the possibilities of Christian nurture. Against the excesses of revivalism Bushnell advanced a simple but entirely revolutionary idea "that the child is to grow up a Christian and never know himself as being otherwise." Bushnell's mind was far-ranging and always of an exploring quality. Consequently, his development of the possibilities of Christian nurture led him to examine the principles of education generally. His book on Christian nurture was, therefore, epochal and it would be difficult to overestimate its influence or follow in detail what has grown out of it.

Bushnell's essay on language was equally significant. Theology, he saw, had lost itself in words growing more and more impossible of any clear definition, more and more remote from life, as though theologians lived and moved and had their being in a structure of words. "Words," he said, "are the signs of thought to be expressed. They do not literally convey or pass on a thought out of one mind into another." They only, in substance, start another mind thinking along the same line.[12] This contention emancipated theological thought. It did not break historical continuity; it did maintain the right, and even urge the duty, of that creative and critical originality in thinking which became the keystone of later religious intellectual liberalism. Indeed one may date the genesis of that movement more specifically from Bushnell than any other one single source, though that statement is open to challenge.[13]

His own theology now in many quarters would be thought conservative. He developed and, in a limited way, "popularized" the moral

---

[12] Thus Bushnell was also a pioneer in Semantics. His own chief concern was with what would now be called the "emotive" function of language or, at least, the suggestive function of words. The real trouble for theology and philosophy is with the "referential" function of words, what reality supports them and by what objective tests can the other person prove or disprove them. For a philosophy of the function of words, opposed to Bushnell's, see Miller's *The New England Mind.*

[13] From Unitarian historians, but Bushnell did supply theological liberalism, a philosophical basis and a technique. He was an emancipator rather than a revolutionist.

theory of the Atonement, of which there had already been intimations in the New England school. He conceived the Trinity as "modal," a threefold revelation of God in being and action. His systems were less significant than his power as a preacher to touch the dry bones of theology with life. There had been no doctrinal preaching comparable with his for imagination, insight, nearness to life. His most famous sermon, "Everyman's Life a Plan of God," was one of the first attempts ever made in America to discover and illumine the processes of a divine administration in experience. Incidentally, he and the later New England school furnished Princeton Theological Seminary generally, and Dr. Charles Hodge specifically, their main occupation: an unceasing and unqualified condemnation of the aforesaid school and all its works.

IV

INHERITED THEOLOGY MEETS A NEW MIND-ORDER

Meanwhile not only theology but religious faith itself was beginning to be challenged by fundamental changes in science and Biblical criticism. "Evolution" was well above the horizon when Bushnell died (1876), though theology in America had not begun to take much account of it, being still entrenched behind the Genesis narrative. But higher criticism, mostly from German sources, had already begun to question the authorship and datings of the first five books of the Old Testament. That line of defense was becoming vulnerable. These, we know now, were no superficial thought movements. They were destined profoundly to affect both religion and theology and release controversies which would essentially embattle the churches.

The French have an untranslatable word, "fond." Its meanings are fluid, but in the main it designates some fundamental content of thought or body of fact upon which everything else is based, by which developments are controlled. The second half of the Nineteenth Century supplied an almost entirely new "fond" for science and history. It revolutionized the study of sociology and psychology; it compelled philosophers to re-examine their assumptions; it profoundly modified literature. And inherited religious faith had to take account of it all. Theological leaders, to repeat, were slow in recognizing the significance for them of this new order.

Foster, in his final and penetrating pages, stresses this, though his precise theological terminology is like an engineer's description, in terms of strains and structural weaknesses, of a building shaken by an earthquake. No figure of speech is adequate.[14] Here was a majestic structure of

---

[14] Perhaps the noble account of getting new foundations under Winchester Cathedral, England, might do. The wood-piles which had supported it for centuries decayed as the waters around them had drained away. One man gave his heroic life, in darkness and in danger, to replace them with stone and cement.

Christian thought, built through the centuries by many craftsmen, whose very foundations were threatened while the last of a great succession of Christian thinkers still labored at its arches and towers in their studies and their classrooms, believing it still unshakable. For all that one should not for a moment undervalue the significance nor deny the majesty of the body of Christian convictions, laboriously developed and bravely defended, which maintained its august authority over American Congregationalism for almost 150 years.

The procession of theologians from Edwards to Park is an honor to the denomination. Beneath and above all their dogmatisms they maintained an unfailing teachableness, hospitality to new truth, freedom of inquiry, and a passion for intellectual integrity. These made it possible for Congregationalism to pass through the period of theological transition without too much strain, and to lead American religious thought into a new order of thought, faith, and practice.

Bushnell's influence now became clearly evident. A generation of young men was entering the Congregational ministry who were to be denominational leaders till the end of the century. Some of these, like Washington Gladden and Theodore Munger, acknowledged their direct indebtedness to Bushnell and mediated his emancipation through their own ministry. Gladden was strongly influenced by Bushnellism while it was still under the ban of the orthodox and the passages of his autobiography which portray Bushnell are still a little hot to the touch with the fires of now-vanished controversies in whose recollection Gladden's militant spirit relived a martial time. They are also tender with gratitude and marvellously understanding. "I knew," he writes, "that for me there never could be any other doctrine to preach than that which I learned from this great teacher."[15]

V

Religious Liberalism

It is impossible to condense and perilous to generalize the history of the period of theological transition and adjustment which followed the fading out of the "New England System" and the partial dethronement of inherited orthodoxes. The whole vast process can hardly be called theological. It was too many-sided; it moved along a too-spacious front. The issue was the religious liberalism which was at its peak at the turn of the last century. That liberalism (the name is too loose) since about 1935 has been under critical and unfavorable examination by a new generation of theologians to whom the rather ungrateful task of cataloging its sins of omission and commission may be left.

[15] Gladden, *Recollections*, chap. 10. This autobiography is invaluable for any study of the making of the Congregational mind from the end of the Civil War until, certainly, 1908. Gladden's greatly loved hymn, "O Master, Let Me Walk with Thee," was written out of the travail of the controversy which attended Munger's installation.

Such critics should at least recognize that Nineteenth Century liberalism made them possible. They are free born because two heroic generations of teachers and preachers purchased, at a great price, the freedom they bequeathed to their successors.[16] The history of what they did and how they did it is one chapter and by no means the least important of the general history of their time. Every theology had for centuries flowed on and on in its own separate, deeply worn, majestic, or otherwise, channel. For a long period it carried philosophy with it and explained creation.

Now all this was changed. A new mind flooded in and upon an old theology, and theology had no longer any channel of its own. It became an aspect of the thought currents fed from almost numberless sources. One does not mean to say that there was no longer any theology. Actually, there were continuous reinterpretations, restatements of inherited doctrines. But the systematic definiteness of older schemes began to be lost. There began to be instead a religious conservatism and religious liberalisms with variations difficult to follow.

The history of all this has never been adequately written. Perhaps now it never will be, but if it could be rightly done it would be vivid, colorful, in quiet ways dramatic and always multiple in content. *In Memoriam* would furnish the overture. There would be, as in a symphony, a contest of motifs, with reconciliations and stormy developments and intervals of quiet, then action again, always unfinished. Writing more precisely, faith adjusted itself to evolution and found God in the revelation of his eonian processes. Liberal religious faith was able to detach itself from an infallibly inspired Bible and still find a divine and sufficient revelation between its covers. The ethical content of the teachings of Jesus was brought to bear with a new force upon economic and social relationships. Religion was re-related to experience and the conduct of life in fresh and vital ways, and an almost entirely new religious literature began to be created, whole library alcoves of it.[17]

It is too much to claim for Congregationalism an intellectual monopoly of this creative period. It certainly must be conceded an outstanding and far-reaching influence. To this the organic structure of its polity and the free genius of the Congregational mind contributed. There was within the denomination a sufficient and engrossing variety of "tensions," but surprisingly few casualties. The action was confined generally to ordaining or installing councils, some of which have become

[16] In addition, these same critics, recognizing the rise and eclipse of systems, might be a little less dogmatic and confess themselves subject to possible correction.

[17] The careful historian of the period would note, as a demanding detail, the changes in an up-to-date minister's library from (say) 1860 to 1900. An examination of the sequence of titles would really organize his narrative.

historic,[18] not for the magnitude of the forces engaged but for their unexpectedly far-reaching influence. In action they were only a company of ministers and delegates representing the churches of a neighborhood, meeting for an afternoon and evening in the church seeking their advice and approval. Almost uniformly after the candidate had been heard and the Council had sufficiently questioned him 'and heartily agreed or disagreed with one another, they voted to install, or ordain, and drove home under the quieting influence of summer or winter stars, and thereafter, save with their consent, the pastor could not be reached nor dispossessed.

But, in substance, a vast deal more than that happened. Theologies had been debated and precedents established. ("Precedents" have been the common law of Congregationalism just as they were the texture of the common law of England.) The denominational press reported strategic councils and editorialized gravely upon them. In such ways a Congregational public opinion was slowly created, always with freedom of opinion and speech, and a momentous transition was achieved with a minimum of strain, a surprising little persistence of odium theologicum, no schism at all, and no historic heresy trials.[19]

VI

THE ANDOVER CONTROVERSY

The "Andover Controversy" came nearest being a nation-wide issue and that was begun, continued, and ended entirely outside the province of the churches. The controversy grew out of the status of a missionary who held the belief that "heathen" to whom the gospel had never been preached would, after death, have an opportunity to repent during a probationary period. The question involved had long troubled the sensitive. Dante asked it of the Just Kings who conjointly formed the shining, symbolic Eagle of Justice in the heaven of Jupiter.

> ". . . A man will see the light on India's bank where
> there is none to tell of Christ . . . ;
> And all his deeds are good and all his will as far as human
> reason sees, no breath of sin in life or in discourse may dwell;
> He dies all unbaptized and lacking faith;
> Where is the Justice that condemns? . . ."

[18] For example, the Indian Orchard (Mass.) Council which refused installation to James F. Merriam "who was unwilling to assert that all who die impenitent suffer everlasting conscious torment." Also, the North Adams Council for T. S. Munger, who *was* installed.

[19] The significance of all this seems now to have been forgotten. For a long generation the handicaps of the loose organization of Congregationalism have been stressed. The denomination has been asked to take lessons from Communions with highly centralized organization and tighten up its own machinery. It may sometime learn again the really enormous value of its own finest historic inheritances.

The Eagle replied in substance that faith in Christ is the sole means of access to heaven, but qualified his answer with the observation that many heathen are more Christian than Christians.

The conservative members of the American Board of Commissioners for Foreign Missions were less sympathetic than Dante's Eagle. Their missionaries, they held, must believe that the heathen would be lost irrevocably without the gospel, or else the nerve of missions would be cut. The question of the Board's right to become an arbiter of doctrine was also involved. The ensuing controversies lasted seven years (1886–1893) and had wide repercussions. The state of the heathen seems to have been forgotten in factional bitterness and a certain amount of pious politics.[20]

The controversy finally burned itself out, leaving the state of the heathen who had not heard the gospel still undecided. But it established the right of missionaries to the same freedom of theological opinion as the ministers of "home" churches, and it indirectly reaffirmed the general principles of Congregational freedom of religious thought. The issue had actually been a kind of test case between an authoritarian conservatism and the freer movement of the liberal mind. At any rate, it exhausted the zeal of the denomination generally for theological controversy and its leaders turned to other concerns, perhaps as much as anything else to the cultivation of national denominational self-consciousness.

What one may call the period of theological transition ended with the century. Theology, precisely defined, had ceased to be the primary concern of the churches and their leaders. The United States was fabulously prosperous, "at peace with the world," as a presidential message once said, "and in amity with the rest of mankind." The period was kind to generous idealisms; a bright, happy, fraternal world seemed so easily possible, if only the Sermon on the Mount could and would be put into general practice.

Such interpretations of evolution as John Fiske and Henry Drummond popularized supported these idealisms. It was easy for a generation of liberal-minded preachers and religious teachers to fit their warm, theistic faith into these interpretations of evolution. What else was evolution save the eonian method of an immanent God whose design was the King-

[20] Dr. Quint of Connecticut, so Nehemiah Boynton said, once inadvertently entered a room at a Board Meeting in which several members were in consultation. Dr. Plumb, whose accents were always lugubrious and whose orthodoxy was of the stanchest, told Quint that they had met to pray over the sad estate of the Board. Quint sniffed and replied that the meeting looked to him more like a caucus than a prayer meeting.

dom of God here and now. Were there not signs of its immediate realization against all horizons?[21] Was there not

> ". . . . one God, one law, one element,
> and one far-off divine event
> toward which the whole creation moves?"

That quotation and the last sentences of John Fiske's Idea of God furnished glowing conclusions for many sermons.

The then Congregational mind lent itself sympathetically to all this, perhaps more sympathetically than any other denomination save the Unitarian. Washington Gladden shared with Walter Rauschenbusch a widely acknowledged leadership in the development of the "Social Gospel." Congregational writers were outstanding in the field of American religious literature and recognized in Great Britain.[22] In such regions as these then, social, semi-theological and Christian ideology inclusively, the last decades of the Nineteenth Century and the first decade of the Twentieth Century were the golden age of Congregationalism, indeed for American Protestantism. The first world war ended all this with a finality which slowly became apparent, and is now (1942) tragically apparent.

There has been a gradual renaissance of theology precisely defined and strongly influenced by European theologians. Younger men specifically trained have assumed leadership in theological thinking. Some of them postulate a neo-orthodoxy (a term useful through its vagueness); others seek a metaphysical basis—as opposed to a scientific basis—for theistic faith. The majority of them are working again in more speculative regions. The disorders and crises of the last twenty-five years have naturally strongly affected and somberly shadowed their thinking and teaching. There is already (1942) a considerable and growing literature which attempts to interpret and classify the main contemporaneous theological trends and schools. Since all this is still in action, it cannot here be considered. This chapter closes (still 1942) in an unbelievable and indescribable dissolution of inherited orders whose issue cannot now be foreseen.

[21] The darker aspects of struggle were for the time mercifully hidden though there was even then a sinister or pessimistic philosophy which stressed them, fatal as we now see (1942) in its effectiveness. But the idealists of the late Nineteenth Century should be judged by the then order of which they were a part. Nor were they ever either so uncritical as they are now held to have been. It is possible from their sermons and works to quote passages of sad and searching insight to match their more glowing periods. And we ought not now (1942) to grudge them their bright periods. There have been so few bright periods in human history.

[22] This general statement should, of course, be documented, but must here be accepted for substance of accuracy. The American Congregational authors in Scribner's *International Theological Library* might be cited.

CHAPTER XIII

The Growth of National Consciousness

THE council idea is inherent in democracy. The employment of a council as a means to secure the common mind and to plan united action is as old as human society. Through the ages, whenever democracy has flourished, it has come to self-consciousness and carried forward its work by means of councils.

The fifteenth chapter of the Book of the Acts gave the early Congregationalists a pattern for a church council. In the famous Cambridge Platform adopted by the Synod (i.e. council) of 1648, the province of a synod was stated in this way:

It belongeth to synods and councils to debate and determine controversies of faith, and cases of conscience . . . to clear from the Word holy directions for the holy worship of God and good government of the church; to bear witness against mal-administration and corruption in doctrine or manners in any particular church, and to give directions for the reformation thereof; not to exercise church-censures in way of discipline, nor any other act of church authority or jurisdiction. . . . The Synod's directions and determinations, so far as consonant to the word of God, are to be received with reverence and submission, not only for their agreement therewith, Acts 15th, which is the principal ground thereof, and without which they bind not at all; but also, secondarily, for the power, whereby they are made, as being ordinance of God, appointed thereunto in his Word.[1]

When the Massachusetts council of church representatives met in 1679, it was discovered that some churches had failed to send lay delegates and there was great dissatisfaction. The necessity of lay representation was debated and it was voted:

That not only elders (ministers), but messengers (lay delegates) also were to be delegated by churches and have their suffrage in a Synod, representing those churches; the primitive practice of the churches in the ages next following the Apostles.[2]

The early American Congregational councils were called by legal authority, usually on petition of ministers and interested lay people. The Court, in response to such a petition, called the council into being and in one at least, the Newtowne Synod of 1637, the expenses of travel and

[1] *Ratio Disciplinae; or the Constitution of the Congregational Churches*, Upham (editor), pp. 201–202.
[2] *Ratio Disciplinae; or the Constitution of the Congregational Churches*, Upham (editor), p. 202.

entertainment were cared for by the civil authority. The Court did not undertake to supervise deliberations, to judge the actions of the council or to revise or amend these actions; but served rather as the transmitting agent by providing for the printing and distribution of the actions of the council. A council was not altogether a new device in Congregational history. The gathering of the Mayflower Pilgrims in the cabin of the ship when they had reached Cape Cod might well be considered, if not the first Congregational council in America, at least the forerunner of our councils although no ministers were present. Whether or not it can be called a council, it is interesting as an example of a method to secure the common mind.

I

THE NEWTOWNE SYNOD, AUGUST 30, 1637—THE FIRST CHURCH COUNCIL

This first Synod was called by the General Court of Massachusetts at the request of the ministers of the churches then established, who presented a petition to the Court for such a council to consider "eighty-two erroneous opinions and nine unwholesome expressions."[3] The Synod included "the teaching elders" and "messengers from the churches," and, as Governor Winthrop wrote, "about twenty-five Godly ministers of Christ besides many other graciously-eminent servants of his."[4] "The diet of the assembly," Governor Winthrop continues, "was provided at the country's charge, as also the fetching and sending back of those which came from Connecticut,"[5] then a part of Massachusetts Colony.

This Council was truly a church council as delegates, both clerical and lay, were present from all the churches. When it assembled, they elected Rev. Peter Bulkeley and Rev. Thomas Hooker as moderators, and Rev. John Higginson as scribe. The Council proceeded in the order that has been followed since: discussions, reference to committee, report, discussion, and adoption of findings. "It marked the highest expression yet attained of that sense of comity and responsibility, of fellowship in churchly concerns, which had been growing in New England since the days of Fuller's ministrations at Salem, and distinguished American Congregationalism from English Independency."[6]

The Council considered the eighty-two opinions and nine expressions and agreed that the Scriptures had been "perverted." Having attended to these, the Council went further and recommended to the Court that the civil government:

[3] For a list of the "expressions" and "opinions," refer to John Winthrop (supposed author), *A Short History of the Rise, Reign and Ruin of the Antinomians, Familists and Libertines that Infected the Churches of New–England.*
[4] Winthrop, *History of New England*, vol. 1, p. 288
[5] Winthrop, *History of New England*, vol. 1, p. 288
[6] Walker, *The Creeds and Platforms of Congregationalism*, p. 143.

(1) "should prohibit any meeting in or near the meeting house of church people except under the regular call of the church." (Evidently in some of the communities the church people were holding "rump" meetings for the discussion of the pastor and his teachings.)

(2) "should instruct the churches not to issue letters of transfer to persons who held views contrary to the teachings of the church,"

(3) and state that "meetings of women for the discussion of doctrine are not expedient." (This had reference to the disturbance that was being caused by meetings held by Mrs. Anne Hutchinson. Inasmuch as so many members of the council were favorable to Mrs. Hutchinson's teachings, this last vote was not passed without considerable debate. When John Cotton, Mrs. Hutchinson's pastor, finally swung in favor of the prohibition, the matter was passed.)

The members had such a good time together, traveling and living at community expense and discussing the church and its doctrine that, as the meeting came to a close, they proposed a like meeting be held each year. The Governor agreed with the delegates that such a meeting might be in order regularly. The Governor adds, however, "This motion was well liked by all, but it was thought not fit to conclude it."[7] While the members of the Council wanted to make a Council meeting a regular occurrence, the General Court disliked the idea of a stated meeting of a council of the churches. Consequently, while this first Council voted in favor of regular, stated meetings, it was not until 224 years later, in 1871, that the reluctance to establish regularly appointed church councils was overcome by organization of the National Council under a constitution of its own writing and adoption providing for regular meetings.

One other interesting feature of this first Council of 1637 should be noted. There was great difference in the pay received by ministers in Colonial churches, and the magistrates asked the Council to advise concerning the equalization of salaries. Members of the Council looked at this proposition from all angles. They found many difficult questions they could not answer. So, with considerable dignity, the Council voted that it would not deal with this subject, lest it should be said that the assembly was gathered for the ministers' private advantage. This question has been considered by many councils since and is still on the agenda.

II

The Cambridge Synod, September, 1646—the Second Council

Although the magistrates did not approve the suggestion made by the Synod of 1637 that it should meet yearly, yet nine years later, in 1646, church questions of such urgency had arisen that another petition came to the General Court asking for a General Council or synod, and the

---

[7] Winthrop, *History of New England*, vol. 1, p. 287 ff.

Court, in response, issued a call for a synod to meet in Cambridge on September 1, 1646. The call for this Council stated as its purpose:

That there be a public assembly of the Elders and other messengers of the several churches, within this jurisdiction, who may come together, and meet at Cambridge, upon the first day of September, now next ensuing, there to discuss, dispute, and clear up by the Word of God, such questions of church government and discipline, in the things aforementioned or any other, as they shall think needful and meet, and to continue so doing till they or the major part of them shall have agreed and consented upon one form of government and discipline, for the main and substantial parts thereof, as that which they judge agreeable to the Holy Scriptures.[8]

In the great historic document, known as The Cambridge Platform, the churches of New England declared their independence of all European churches and set up a plan of church organization which, with few changes, was the guiding instrument of the churches for two hundred years and, in general, controls our church life today. Here we take notice of only that section which has reference to the nature and function of church councils:

Synods, being spirituall & ecclesiasticall assemblyes, are therefore made up of spirituall and ecclesiasticall causes. The next efficient cause of them under Christ, is the powr of churches, sending forth their Elders, (&) other messengers; who being mett together in the name of Christ (Acts 15:2,3), are the matter of a Synod; & they in argueing (vers. 6.), debating & determining matters of religion according to the word (vers. 7 to 23), & publishing the same to the churches whom it concerneth, doe put forth the proper and formall acts of a Synod; to the conviction of errours (vers. 31), & heresyes, & the establishment of truth & peace in the Churches (Acts 16.4.15), which is the end of a Synod. (Cambridge Platform c. XVI)

This doctrine as to the authority of a council or synod is the uniform testimony of the authorities through the years.

"All Congregationalists," says Increase Mather, "deny that Synods have any such ('judicial') power." "What is the power of a Council" says John Norton; "To declare the truth, not to exercise authority." Hooker "denies a Synod that hath a juridical power," but admits "one of counsel." "The sentence of a Council," says Richard Mather, "is of itself only advice, not of itself authority nor necessity." "It belongeth unto Synods . . . not to exercise . . . any act of Church authority or jurisdiction," says Cambridge Platform. "When a Church wants light," said Davenport, "she should send for counsel, but preserve the power entirely in her own hands." Cotton Mather's *Ratio* (himself rather bending towards Presbyterianism) says, "They pretend unto no judicial power, nor any significancy, but what is merely instructive and suasory." "When they (Councils) have done all, the Churches are still free," says Samuel Mather, in 1738, "To accept or refuse their advice." President Stiles says, "Churches universally hold a negative on the result of Council; the decision of a Council is of no force till

[8] Dunning, *Congregationalists in America*, pp. 145-6.

received and ratified by the inviting Church, nor does it render that Church obnoxious to community, if she recedes from advice of Council." "It is an acknowledged principle," says Upham's *Ratio*, "in respect to Councils, that they possess only advisory powers." "Congregationalists, however, agree in asserting that Councils have neither legislative nor executive authority over the Churches," says Punchard. Emmons is still more explicit.[9]

III

THE ASSOCIATION AND CONSOCIATION

The development of a national consciousness was preceded by the development of a state consciousness, and before a state consciousness there developed first a community consciousness, taking form in associations and consociations. The first type of association was that of ministers meeting for informal fellowship. Ministers' associations on an entirely voluntary basis were common throughout New England. Later they began to have stated meetings. The next step for these associations was to assume the duties of licensing, ordaining, and disciplining of ministers, and there are a few early records of the meetings of associations for ordination. These associations were

voluntary bodies, and their only relation to the churches is that they license men to preach, and in this way the churches have come to confide in them for the disciplination of ministers. One whom they recommend is accepted without further examination, and when they withdraw from a man their license, no church would employ him. They thus have in their own hands the keeping of the honor and integrity of their own profession.[10]

In Connecticut, following the Saybrook Conference (1708), the General Association of Congregational Ministers was organized, and is one of the oldest continuing ministers' organizations. The State Conference of Churches and Ministers of Connecticut was not organized until 1867. Of these early ministerial associations, others continue as, for example, the Essex North, of Boston. The oldest continuing ministers' association is the Ministerial Convention of Massachusetts, including both the Unitarian and Congregational ministers, which passed through the Unitarian controversy and continues undivided. This body was sufficiently organized by 1680 to have a moderator, a dinner, and a sermon.[11] There were no further movements toward colonial or state organization of ministers until after the Revolutionary War; and it was not until 1795, eighty-six years after the formation of the Connecticut General Association of Ministers, that the next state organization of ministers was formed, the General Association of Congregational Ministers in Vermont.

[9] Quint, "Councils," *Congregational Year Book, 1859.*
[10] *Boston Review*, Sept., 1864.
[11] Walker, *American Church History*, vol. 3, p. 201.

The consociation was the outgrowth of an idea going back to the early days of the Puritans in England and in New England and goes beyond the association in this particular: the consociation composed of ministers only had the right to pass final judgment on questions of church government, while associations composed of ministers and lay delegates had only advisory power. Some Massachusetts pastors supported the consociation form of government, as Richard Mather, who in 1639, nine years before the adoption of the Cambridge Platform wrote: "The consociation of churches in the synods we hold to be lawful and in some cases necessary, as namely, in things that are not particular to one church but common to them all."[12] It was in Connecticut, however, that the consociation idea had its fullest development. Thomas Hooker, a week before his death in 1648, said, "We must agree upon constant meetings of ministers and settle the consociation of churches or else we are undone."[13]

The Cambridge Platform did not provide for either associations or consociations. The Massachusetts Synod of 1680 had the matter up for discussion, but the members were so engrossed with the subject of baptism that consociations received scant attention, nor did the idea ever make any headway in Massachusetts. As will be noted later, when this form of local organization was adopted in Connecticut, Rev. John Wise, pastor at Ipswich, wrote so strenuously against it, and his writings were so widely read, that the Connecticut example was not followed. He contended that associations led to consociations; consociations to Presbyterianism; Presbyterianism to Episcopacy; and Episcopacy to Papacy.

IV

THE CONNECTICUT DISCIPLINE

In Connecticut growth of the consociation plan was stimulated by the differences that arose in the church at Hartford after Hooker's death. This long drawn-out controversy in the local church indicated the need of some agency to settle the trouble. As it was said, "there is no way of bringing troubles to a final issue."

The agitation for a college in the new settlement of New Haven brought the ministers together to discuss the project. In England, due to pressure put upon nonconformists after the Restoration, there had been in process the bringing together of Congregational (independent) and Presbyterian churches. The leaders of these two bodies had drawn up the famous document, "Heads of Agreement," in 1691, which outlined a plan

---

[12] *Congregational Order*, 1843, p. 25.
[13] Trumbull, *A Complete History of Connecticut, Civil and Ecclesiastical*, vol. 1, p. 479.

of consociation of Congregational and Presbyterian churches in England. This agreement had little influence in the church life of England, as the nonconformists after the Restoration were under increasing pressure and were soon suppressed. But when a copy came to America it was widely read. As Cotton Mather says in his *Magnalia,* "The brethren of the Presbyterian way in England are lately come into such a happy union with those of the Congregational that all formal names of distinction are lost in that blessed one of United Brethren."[14]

The New Haven ministers, having made a study of the "Heads of Agreement" and having in mind also the unsolved problems of some of the churches, petitioned the Court to assemble a synod to draft a form of discipline for Connecticut. The matter was before the Colonial legislation for several years, and in May, 1708, the upper house passed a vote requesting ministers and representatives of the churches to meet in the county towns and elect representatives to a meeting to be held in Saybrook to draw up a form of ecclesiastical discipline.

The following September, twelve ministers and four laymen met at Saybrook and drew up the Saybrook Statement. As far as doctrine was concerned, the Saybrook Synod followed the plan of the Cambridge Synod and also that of the "Reforming Synod" of 1680 by approving for "substance of doctrine" the statement adopted at the meeting at the Savoy, in 1658 (the Westminster Confession), with a few minor modifications. This Savoy statement had been adopted by the Massachusetts Synod in 1680. But in planning for the government of the churches, the Saybrook Synod followed the "Heads of Agreement" which influenced them to advise the formation of consociations. Thus the seed planted in England grew in America. The consociation was a permanent council including all the ministers in a certain district, usually the county. There were men of different minds in the Saybrook Synod, but as Trumbull writes, "they exercised great Christian condescension and amiableness towards each other."[15]

The Saybrook document provides "one or more consociations for each county which should be a standing, known, and responsible tribunal with final jurisdiction to which particular churches might refer cases too difficult to be well adjusted by themselves. The object was to avoid picked councils."[16]

This plan was adopted by the Legislature in 1708 and continued as the law of Connecticut until 1784 when it was dropped; the present State Constitution, adopted in 1815, granted no privilege to the churches. The

[14] C. Mather, *Magnalia Christi Americana,* book 5, p. 59.
[15] Trumbull, *A Complete History of Connecticut, Civil and Ecclesiastical,* vol. 1, p. 487.
[16] *Congregational Order,* p. 34.

consociation form of government continued in Connecticut; and today the consociation is usually the committee on license and ministerial standing of the association. In 1841 all but 15 of the 246 churches in Connecticut were consociated, but by 1892 only 71 out of 306 were so organized.[17]

The consociation idea was not too effective in solving the problems of the churches. Some found it too strict, as did the New Haven churches; others found it too liberal, as did the Fairfield churches. With the growth of associations of churches, the consociations of ministers declined. In the course of years the local ministers' associations grew into state ministerial associations, as will be noted later, but the next formal step towards a national consciousness came with the formation of the state conference of churches.

V

THE STATE CONFERENCE

The formation of the first state conference of churches, that of Maine, is of great historic interest. There had been considerable discussion in the county association of ministers of the possibility of a state conference of churches. An attempt was made in 1820 to form a state ministerial association comparable to those in existence in other states, but this was feebly supported because of the "fear that such an association composed of ministers only might somehow endanger the liberty of the churches."[18]

The first move to form an association of churches was taken at the meeting of the York County Association of Ministers which met at Alfred, Maine, in September, 1822. Two of the ministers, Rev. Levi Loring of Athens and Rev. Joseph Fessenden of Brighton were walking to the public meeting of the Association with Rev. Nathan Douglas, pastor of the church at York. As they walked, Mr. Douglas suggested that the idea of a meeting of ministers and lay delegates of the churches would interest the people and advance the interests of religion in the county. After the public meeting was over, the three returned to Mr. Douglas' home and this discussion resulted in presentation at the Association meeting the next day of a plan for a county conference.

The ministerial association voted that the churches in connection with members of the York County Association of Ministers be invited to appoint one delegate to unite with their pastor in attending an annual meeting to be held on every first Tuesday of October, and that the destitute (pastorless) Congregational churches of the county be invited to participate by appointing two delegates. The purpose of the meeting was to be "the promotion of the union and prosperity of the churches in the County and to this end a collection was to be taken to aid the destitute

[17] Dunning, *Congregationalists in America*, p. 226.
[18] Clark, *History of the Congregational Churches in Maine*, vol. 2, p. 401.

churches." The meeting was set to be called in Buxton at the home of Rev. Levi Loring, pastor of that church.

The meeting was held and the Conference organized, taking the name York County Conference. At this first meeting of a county conference (local association) ever held in the United States ten churches were represented, each by the minister and a lay delegate, except the church at Parsonfield which evidently was pastorless and was represented by a deacon. Rev. Levi Loring was the moderator and Rev. Nathan Douglas, the scribe. The sermon was delivered by Rev. Christopher March of Buxton. The number of church members reported at that time was 570 for the ten churches in the Conference. It was ordered that the Conference meet annually on the first Thursday of October.

Shortly after the organization of the York Conference, a meeting of representatives of the sixteen churches in Cumberland County was held at Gorham, December 24, 1822, where they organized the Cumberland Conference of Churches. Organization of the State Conference followed very quickly, for in sending out the notice for the Cumberland Conference meeting which was to be held in December, 1822, the following clause was inserted: "It may be proper to remark that representatives of other conferences will be received either as delegates to this conference, or as delegates meeting at the same time and place to form a general conference, according as their appointments have been made." [19]

Following this the York County Conference and the Cumberland County Conference took action towards the formation of a state conference. On December 28, 1824 the delegates appointed by the County Conferences met at Falmouth. A constitution was written and submitted to the County Conferences and with some amendments went into effect. The first meeting of the State Conference was held at Hallowell, June 26 to 28, 1827. The constitution as finally adopted contained one interesting provision: "Article 3. Ordained ministers, who may be present at the meetings of this body, may be invited to sit as honorary members, to take part in the deliberations, but not to vote." [20] This constitution adopted by the Maine churches was widely studied, and many of its provisions were later written into the constitution of other state conferences as they were formed.

VI

The Iowa Plan

A different method of procedure was employed in forming the State Conference in Iowa. There were no associations in the state but a group of Congregationalists who had gone into Iowa called a convention at

[19] *Congregational Quarterly*, vol. 6 (1864), p. 189.
[20] Clark, *History of the Congregational Churches in Maine*, vol. 2, p. 413.

Denmark, Iowa, November 5, 1840, and this group had the faith and courage to organize the Congregational Association of Iowa. A few years later the name was changed to State Conference.

The organization of this Association was a reversal of the policy pursued by the Congregationalists from the beginning of the century. A large majority of the people were from the West and South. Half of them had never heard of Congregationalism and many who had heard of it were indebted for this information to those who were opposed to its obtaining a foothold in Iowa. The strife between New School and Old School Presbyterians was at its height. The former claimed the Congregational element as their own; the latter, while charging Congregationalists with disorder and heresy of every description, never refused them admission into their churches. The custom so long prevalent among Congregationalists of throwing church polity of their fathers into the Hudson as they came to the West, encouraged all denominations to endeavor to draw them into their churches and feel a common interest in preventing the growth of distinctive Congregationalism. The organization of the Association settled the question whether Congregationalists would adhere to the Puritan polity. One result was that Congregationalists coming into the state, finding churches of their own order, were not disposed to join others and another result was that other denominations meeting little success in their attempts to proselyte, have gradually abandoned them.[21]

VII

INTERSTATE RELATIONSHIP OF MINISTERS' ASSOCIATIONS

With the growth of the state associations of ministers, there had been in the early 1800's a development of interstate interest. An agreement between the General Association of Connecticut and the General Convention of Vermont in 1802 provided that there should be two or three delegates sent by each of these organizations to the meetings of the other and these delegates should have "the right to discuss, to act and to vote, that union may be full and complete."[22] The Connecticut General Association later made similar arrangements with Massachusetts in 1809, New Hampshire in 1810, Rhode Island in 1821, Maine in 1828, and New York in 1835. Thus it came about that a meeting of the Connecticut Association would have representatives with the right to vote from six other states, making this Association meeting virtually a regional meeting. The Connecticut Association also entered into communication by letters with the Congregational Union of England and Wales in 1833 and later exchanged visitors and had correspondence with the Congregational churches in Switzerland. This was a significant move toward the development of international relationships.

[21] Douglass, *The Pilgrims of Iowa*, pp. 41–42.
[22] *Congregational Order*, p. 64.

VIII

THE INFLUENCE OF THE NATIONAL SOCIETIES

Further development toward national consciousness came through the organization of missionary societies, which brought together ministers and lay people from the various states. In 1810, the American Board of Commissioners for Foreign Missions was formed by the committee appointed by the Massachusetts State Ministers Association. This was approved shortly after by the Connecticut Ministers Association and soon included in its membership lay and ministerial members from most of the New England states. In 1816, the American Education Society was formed, which united other church leaders in a common cause.

In 1846 a Convention of Western Congregational Churches was held at Michigan City, Indiana, which was the antecedent of the Albany Convention held six years later.

The first impulse emanating from an official source looking toward greater recognition of the unity of Congregationalism, East and West, the removal of doctrinal prejudice, and a more aggressive assertion of Congregational claims, appears to have come from the then newly formed General Association of Michigan. In 1845, Rev. L. Smith Hobart, a Yale graduate of 1837, then pastor of the church at Union City, Michigan, and secretary of the Michigan Association, proposed a "General Convention of Western Congregationalists" to deliberate concerning denominational advancement; and, as a result of an approval of this recommendation by the body of which Hobart was secretary, such a "Convention" brought together representatives of the churches of the northwestern states and a few men from the East at Michigan City, Indiana, in July, 1846. The body declared the adherence of the western churches to the historic theology of New England, and discussed the feasibility of abrogating the "Plan of Union."[23]

IX

THE SLOW GROWTH OF NATIONAL CONSCIOUSNESS

The growth toward national consciousness was necessarily slow, because it went contrary to the plan of organization of the early churches, which were local institutions. A good analogy might be drawn from the present status of a local library. The town at town expense decides to maintain a public library. At town expense it constructs a building, buys books, organizes a library board, accepts gifts given toward this expense and perhaps orders that the library board shall be selected not at town meeting but by a group of interested citizens. The library is maintained by the town for all who care to use it. In a similar way, the early New England churches were established. The churches were built frequently at town expense on land donated by the town and were controlled either

[23] Walker, *American Church History*, vol. 3, p. 381.

directly by the town meeting or by a committee selected at town meeting of those particularly interested in the church. The town library would not consider itself responsible for the establishment of a library in a town ten or a thousand miles away. Although the librarians of the county might have an association for mutual helpfulness, as did the ministers of the town churches, yet no town library would be willing to accept more than advice from any agency originating outside the town. So it was with the early churches.

There was a growing need of churches in the West for persons coming from the East, who would not accept the advice of New England churches to affiliate themselves with churches denominationally organized and better fitted—so New England thought—to meet the necessities of a new and scattered population. This was causing much discussion throughout the country. As one New England writer stated, "the Congregational communion is not one great, imposing consolidated church; but a band of related Christian families bound together in a oneness of faith, affection, and aim, having the Bible for their direction and Christ for their common head."[24] The rest agreed, but desired means of keeping up the family connection.

At the same time, when western Congregationalists were planning at their Michigan City meeting for an assembly of representatives of the churches East and West, there was another and altogether independent movement originating in the East. This was the proposal of the churches of eastern Massachusetts in 1844 for a commemoratory council to meet in Cambridge in 1848 in observance of the 200th anniversary of the adoption of the Cambridge Platform. In the *Report on Congregationalism,* including a Manual of Church Discipline, published in Boston in 1846, there is an introduction written by Dr. Leonard Woods, the distinguished president of Andover Seminary. From this we learn that a committee was appointed May 29, 1844 charged to "take into consideration what measures are necessary for the reaffirmation and maintenance of the principles and spirit of Congregationalism." A special subcommittee which included Dr. Woods, Dr. Richard Salter Storrs and Rev. Parsons Cooke, appointed to consider a communication from the Worcester Central Association, stated that "a restoration of such harmony cannot be reasonably expected except at a convention of pastors and delegates from the churches. Such a convention or synod wisely called and not over-tasking itself might reasonably be expected to agree on principles and rules of discipline that would receive a cordial welcome in the bosom of the churches generally."

In commenting on this matter, Dr. Woods adds, "such a convention as that above named, has been spoken of with favor by many Congrega-

[24] Mitchell, *The United States Churches*, p. 43.

tionalists, both ministers and laymen. And it has been often suggested that, with proper attention, the way might be prepared for such a convention to meet in 1848, the second centennial from the time when the Cambridge Platform was adopted. The idea of a convention or synod of Congregational ministers and churches at that time has struck the minds of all, so far as we know, with peculiar satisfaction."[25]

These suggestions for a general council, offered by some of the leaders, were overborne by the fears of other church leaders who felt there would be danger in building up an overhead organization that would in some way restrict the freedom of the churches. Hence nothing came of this proposal for a commemorative council. The church magazines of the period reflect this spirit of fear in letters and editorial comment. It was argued that a Congregational church is responsible for religious leadership only in the community where it is situated; that to fulfill that function it must be absolutely free and independent.

Community life during this period was on a parochial basis and the range of interests of the people was severely limited by lack of newspapers and the difficulties of travel. Rev. John Wise still had profound influence through his writings, wherein he insisted on the need of the local church to confine its activities to its own parish. His fear of the consociation idea was still shared by many church leaders. In the years before the Revolution, and for more than fifty years after, his books were reprinted again and again, and his influence against general church organization was determinative. Even now a certain reluctance to participate in national church organizations can be attributed directly to John Wise. As his writings were instrumental in keeping the churches strong to safeguard their liberty, so was his influence powerful in building up before the Revolutionary War, among the masses of the people the same spirit of freedom and democracy which helped bring to that war the support of vast numbers of thinking people.

One other event delayed development of a national organization of the churches. When the proposal to form a foreign mission board was taken to the Massachusetts General Association at Bradford in 1810, it was indeed a challenge to the Association, then seven years old, whose membership was cautious and conservative. After long debate, swayed by Dr. Samuel Worcester of Salem, it was voted to authorize formation of an organization under joint auspices of the churches of Massachusetts and Connecticut. On September 5, 1810, the American Board of Commissioners for Foreign Missions came into being. It had nine members, five representing the Massachusetts Association and four the Connecticut Association.

[25] *Report on Congregationalism, Boston, 1846*, p. 13.

There was nothing in the constitution of the Massachusetts Association to authorize this action, taken in spite of the lack of authority to meet an emergency. There was considerable criticism of this assumption of power by the state conference. Many years later, Dr. Alonzo H. Quint, then secretary of the Massachusetts General Association and the outstanding authority on Congregational procedures of his generation, characterized the action as illegal. He wrote:

No church, or section of churches has a right to originate and determine a movement concerning, or involving the whole body of churches. Such cases all the churches are the parties to consider. Hence, the "Plan of Union" with Presbyterians, into which the General Association of Connecticut entered in 1801, and which the General Association of Massachusetts subsequently ratified, was wrongfully accomplished; whether advantageous or disadvantageous is not the question; a measure necessarily introducing a decided change into an ecclesiastical polity, was not a subject to be settled by the churches of one or two states, and far less by merely *clerical* bodies, in which the churches had no voice whatever. So, also, the method by which the churches were made morally tributary to the A. B. C. F. M., was a stretch of power on the part of the Massachusetts General Association; that it has accomplished vast good, renders it none the less true that, Congregationally, the churches who were to support, should have had a voice in forming and inaugurating its policy.[26]

The influence of the opposition to this emergency legislation was widespread, and the fact that a state conference had taken action without constitutional provision was used again and again to thwart any move toward development of a national organization, even though the missionary agency itself tended to become a common bond.

Another fact that worked against development of a national organization was the unfortunate results which had followed acceptance by the Connecticut State Conference of Ministers of the Plan of Union with the Presbyterians for the joint support of mission churches in the West. Massachusetts formally approved it; yet, as time went on and adverse criticism grew, the determination of the churches to confine their responsibilities to the local parish was greatly strengthened. Even though collective efforts were needed to remedy the conditions resulting from the Plan, the unfortunate outcome of this venture to mix in affairs outside the Northeast was discouraging.

Another influence which delayed formation of a national council was that the American Congregational Union (the first home missionary society) served in part as a national organization. This Union, made up of individuals who paid a membership fee, afforded many of the leading ministers an opportunity for exercising whatever interest they had in national church affairs.

[26] Quint, *Congregational Year Book, 1859*, p. 49.

What has been said in reference to the American Congregational Union could be said also in reference to the Tract Societies and the Publishing Societies composed of individuals, supported by individual givers, and governed by self-perpetuating boards. These free agencies, enjoying complete freedom, sometimes passing on board memberships to relatives and to friends, exerted a continuing and highly organized opposition to the formation of a central agency by and for the churches.

To summarize briefly, the growth of a national consciousness was retarded by:

1. The tradition that the duty of the local church was for the religious leadership in a local community;
2. The fear that a national organization would interfere with the freedom of the local church;
3. The continuing influence of the writings of Rev. John Wise in Massachusetts and other New England states;
4. The unconstitutional action of the Massachusetts General Association in establishing the American Board; and
5. The unfortunate results that followed establishment by the Connecticut Association of the Plan of Union.

The relationship of the early churches to local town government as often noted in this history influenced the church to confine its interests to its local community. This relationship is indicated in two instances, which can be multiplied many times. The Congregational Church received state subsidy in Connecticut until 1818 and in Massachusetts until 1834[27]. By a clause that was not formally repealed until 1877 the Constitution of New Hampshire provided that members of its legislature must be of the Protestant religion.

In spite of these hindrances the need of a national body representing the churches continued to grow.

X

THE ALBANY CONVENTION,

The calling of the first national convention at Albany, New York, in 1852 was a direct result of the plight of western Congregationalists who wished to be relieved from the provisions of the Plan of Union. This Plan of Union with the Presbyterians, entered into in all good faith in 1801, had been negotiated between the Presbyterian National Assembly and the Connecticut Association. The plan provided that all home missionary funds collected from the New England churches were to be used with funds from the Presbyterian churches to establish union churches in the West. The Presbyterians repudiated the Plan in 1837 by action of the General Assembly, which voted "that the act of the assembly in 1801 entitled 'The Plan of Union' be abrogated." Some of the middle west presbyteries continued to hold to the Plan of Union, and were known as the "new school." They were excluded from the General Assembly. This

[27] "Congregationalism," *Encyclopedia Americana*, vol. 5.

action caused a split in the Presbyterian Church which was not healed for many years. Under the best possible auspices the Plan was unsatisfactory, especially to the Congregationalists. All ministers who served the union churches (Congregational and Presbyterian) were required to belong to a presbytery and to the Congregational Association. But these churches (we would now call them federated churches) were required to acknowledge the presbytery even if the Congregationalists were in the majority. Thus, in fact, ministers of the union churches, having joined the presbytery, were to all intents and purposes Presbyterian.

The needs of Congregationalists, who were thus entangled in a system which was rapidly causing many union churches to become Presbyterian, eventually excited the interest of Congregational church people in New England. They were gradually deciding that Congregational salt need not lose its savor by being taken across the Hudson River, since some churches in different parts of the West organized as Congregational churches and not joining the Plan of Union had been able to maintain themselves without mission aid.

Other questions were agitating the minds of people East and West. The people in the West wanted to become better acquainted with the churches in the East; and people in the East had a great curiosity concerning the kind of Congregationalism that was growing up far from its ancestral home. The outcome was the call for a convention of Congregationalists to meet in Albany, New York, in 1852.

The official call was sent out by the General Association of New York inviting ministers and delegates of Congregational churches in the United States to meet in Albany on October 5, 1852 as a convention. The New York General Association asked a group of men to serve as a Business Committee and of this group Rev. Leonard Bacon, eminent pastor of Center Congregational Church, New Haven, was made chairman. This Business Committee sent out circulars before the convention assembled, announcing as main purposes of the assembly:

 1. The discussion of the Plan of Union between Presbyterians and Congregationalists agreed upon by the General Assembly of the Presbyterian Church and the General Association of Connecticut, in 1801.
 2. The building of church edifices in the West.
 3. The system and operation of the American Home Missionary Society.
 4. The intercourse between the Congregationalists of New England and those of other states.
 5. The local work and responsibility of a Congregational church.
 6. The bringing forward of candidates for the ministry.
 7. The republication of the works of our standard theological writers.[28]

[28] Hood, *The National Council of Congregational Churches of the United States,* pp. 41–42.

The new life which for years had been kindling found expression in the Albany Convention. The Plan of Union was declared at an end. "Congregationalists had discovered that their polity was adapted to the entire country, that they had a divinely appointed mission to give the gospel of Christ to the whole world, and in order to carry out this mission it was necessary that they should know one another and should become affiliated in one body in such a manner that they could act intelligently and unitedly in fulfilling their great work."[29]

The Albany Convention met to consider a definite crisis due to the breakdown of the Plan of Union and the need of the Western churches for help. This help was quickly given. The convention adopted a resolution calling for fifty thousand dollars with which to provide a fund for the assistance of churches in the West. In response to this resolution $61,891 was raised.

XI

The Council of 1865

There was no move at Albany looking toward another convention, for the churches East and West were busy organizing the anti-slavery movement. And many churches in the West were active in maintaining the underground railroad, which deserves far more attention from the student of American history than it has as yet received. [There is a voluminous and authoritative history of the underground by Professor Wilbur H. Siebert of Ohio State University.] When the war between the states was drawing to a close, the churches again faced a crisis. This was the challenge of several million liberated slaves in the South, a region considered by Congregationalists, especially those of Connecticut and Massachusetts, as a great missionary field. The American Missionary Association had been active in the South before the war with its schools and its churches. Now the New England churches felt a great responsibility for religious and educational work among these people.

The Cambridge Platform, the basic document in the churches for 200 years, contained certain provisions which had become obsolete. This is not surprising since the Cambridge Platform was written in 1648, eighteen years after the arrival in this country of the Puritan migration in 1630.

A problem of national importance was the lack of well-trained ministers, especially for the newly organized churches in the West. There was also need for continued assistance in church building.

These and other questions of growing intensity were receiving the consideration of conferences and associations throughout the country and everywhere it was realized that they could not be settled on the basis

[29] Dunning, *Congregationalists in America*, p. 333.

of state or county meetings. There was a growing national consciousness as a result of the Civil War, which had shaken people out of their narrow provincialism and compelled them to think in terms of national well-being.

Also a new sense of mission was being born in the thinking of the Congregationalists. They had survived the Civil War struggle feeling that the principles for which they had pioneered had been blessed of God; and though they were a small people, yet their ideas had emerged victorious in the strife. This sense of mission, crowned with victory, grew mightily and the new life demanded new expression.

Hence many church members, confronted with questions of national importance and thinking in terms of national concern, asked for a national gathering of representatives of the churches to take stock of the situation and plan for the future.

The first definite action toward calling a national council was taken at the Convention of the Congregational Churches of the Northwest at its triennial meeting in Chicago in April, 1864. This Convention was an association of churches from states within the Chicago area organized to sponsor the Chicago Theological Seminary. It became evident during the discussions of this Convention that if the scattered Congregational churches of the Northwest were to meet their pressing needs, help must come from the older churches of New England. The Western churches also felt the overwhelming task of ministering to the freedmen of the South. They voted that "the crisis demands general consultation, co-operation, and concert among our churches, and to these ends, requires extensive correspondence among our ecclesiastical associations, or the assembling of a National Congregational Convention."[30] The Convention of the Northwest also specified certain topics considered of primary importance.

The next month when the State Association of Illinois met at Quincy, Rev. Julian M. Sturtevant, president of Illinois College at Jacksonville, a national leader among Congregationalists (who was to be preacher for the 1865 Council) proposed a resolution which was adopted by that Association recommending that every orthodox Congregational church in the United States be invited to send as delegates "their acting pastor or pastors and one other member and to provide if necessary for paying their expenses to and from the convention."[31]

The Conference of Ohio, meeting in Springfield, June 10, 1864, endorsed the invitation of the Cleveland churches that the national coun-

[30] *Debates and Proceedings of the National Council, Boston, Mass., June 14–24, 1865*, p. 1.

[31] *Debates and Proceedings of the National Council, Boston, Mass., June 14–24, 1865*, p. 2.

cil be held there. Within the next month, nine other state conferences voted similar approval of a national convention; but the General Association of New Hampshire voted that it had "failed to appreciate the results for the call of such a convention especially in the present juncture of affairs and respectfully declined further action with respect to it."[32] However, one of the local associations did vote to approve the proposal and when the council was held, the New Hampshire churches were represented by delegates from that association.

In July the trustees of the American Congregational Union, present at the Yale commencement in New Haven, invited the state conferences to send representatives to meet in New York at the Broadway Tabernacle Church on November 16, 1864 to review the situation and to take such action as appeared wise.

Fifteen states sent representatives to this preliminary meeting. It was organized by electing Rev. Leonard Bacon of Connecticut, Moderator; Charles G. Hammond of Illinois, Assistant Moderator; and Rev. Philo Hurd of Michigan, Scribe. The roll of the meeting included many well-known leaders of Congregationalism. From Maine came Rev. George E. Adams and Rev. Alfred E. Ives; from Massachusetts, Rev. Alonzo H. Quint and Rev. I. P. Langworthy; from Connecticut, Rev. Leonard Bacon; from New York, Rev. Joseph Thompson, who served as temporary chairman, Rev. Ray Palmer, and Rev. William I. Budington; from Illinois, President Sturtevant; and many others. Many of these men took an active part in the Council and at least two of them—Quint and Budington—served later as National Council moderators.

The five men most influential in the development of plans for a national council were Messrs. Bacon, Sturtevant, Budington, Thompson, and Quint, who were appointed a committee to select the topics for the council and to nominate suitable persons to present matters for its consideration. The seven topics selected by this committee were:

1. The work of evangelization, in the West and South and in foreign lands.
2. Church-building.
3. Education for the ministry—in colleges, theological seminaries, or otherwise; and ministerial support.
4. Local and parochial evangelization.
5. The expediency of issuing a statement of Congregational church polity.
6. The expediency of setting forth a declaration of the Christian faith, as held in common by the Congregational churches.
7. The classification of benevolent organizations to be recommended to the patronage of the churches.[33]

[32] *Debates and Proceedings of the National Council, Boston, Mass., June 14–24, 1865,* p. 3.
[33] *Debates and Proceedings of the National Council, Boston, Mass., June 14–24, 1865,* pp. 7–8.

A committee was named also to formulate the Call for the council, sent to the various states in quantity for distribution throughout the fellowship. This letter missive, known as "the invitation," stated that the churches throughout the United States in fellowship with the associations, conferences, and conventions were "respectfully and affectionately invited."

It sought first of all to safeguard the autonomy of the local church and provided:

> Inasmuch as the Congregational churches acknowledge and hold that the local church is the only ecclesiastical body established by Christ and his apostles— a body complete in itself, and invested with an authority under Christ which can not be delegated; and at the same time, that the churches thus constituted are in relations of fellowship one with another, under which it is their duty and their privilege to meet for mutual counsel in cases of general interest and common responsibility; it will be universally understood that the National Council now proposed is destitute of all power or authority over individuals or churches, or over other organizations, and that the churches complying with this invitation will meet by their pastors and other messengers only for the purpose of considering the present crisis in the history of our country and of the Kingdom of Christ, and the responsibilities which the crisis imposes upon us who have inherited the polity and the faith of our Pilgrim Fathers.[34]

The invitation then mentioned the seven topics, emphasizing how these topics fitted into this growing consciousness of national responsibility. It also requested the churches to take a collection to be used for the traveling expenses of members who otherwise could not attend. A strong committee of Boston ministers, organized in January of 1865, sent out a letter seconding the invitation, emphasizing the growing national concern and renewing the pledge of autonomy to the local church. The churches were facing the great problem which is inherent in the very nature of democracy: how to maintain individual independence and still have sufficient coöperation to accomplish results in common enterprises.

There was much heart-searching throughout New England when the proposal for the calling of a national council came forth. As Rev. W. T. Savage of Franklin, New Hampshire, said, their hesitancy was not due to a lack of need for "a new infusion of energy in the ecclesiastical life of New England" nor was it because "the present grand period in the history of the Republic is not an appropriate time for the rallying of social and religious forces";[35] but the hesitation was whether or not there was enough unity among churches in the different sections of the coun-

[34] *Debates and Proceedings of the National Council, Boston, Mass., June 14–24, 1865,* p. 12.
[35] Savage, "The National Congregational Council," *Boston Review,* May, 1865, vol. 27, p. 285

try to make a thoroughly worth-while meeting; whether "the denomination wished for a national council."[36]

There had been an increasing realization of the lack of unity in the
churches. "As our ancestors, when they came to this country, brought
Congregationalism in the abstract, rather than in the concrete, we ought
not to be surprised if we should find many changes in their customs, as
the result of experience."[37] Many of the churches had outgrown the Cambridge Platform and the earlier documents. They had gone through two
great evangelistic experiences, "the Great Awakening" and "the Second
Great Awakening." They had suffered the shock of the Unitarian departure, but they had been united in support of the anti-slavery movement. The rigid Calvinism of the past was losing its uniting power, and
it was argued that such a great national body could not function unless
it had at basis one commonly accepted creed or statement of faith, which
it did not have and which many of the churches did not want. Each
church had its own covenant and there was no disposition on the part of
the churches to change their instruments of belief. There was a certain
amount of dissatisfaction with the looseness of the Congregational order;
and the statement of Jonathan Edwards, made a hundred years before
(1750), that "I have long been perfectly out of conceit of our unsettled,
independent, confused way of church government in the land," was
shared by a considerable number.

The New England churches faced the fact that the population in
New England was increasing more rapidly than church membership.
This unchurched majority caused church leaders to feel that they had
work enough to do at home without getting too much involved in western affairs. On the other hand, the demoralized condition of Congregational policy was urged by many of the leaders in pursuading the eastern
churches to accept the plan for a national gathering truly representative
of the churches, which should give evidence, if possible, of a national
consciousness. As one of the New England leaders phrased the need:

In what way will the Council best meet the demands of the world and of
Christ's kingdom? . . . it behooves the National Council, when assembled, to
define to itself, and clearly symbolize to others, what evangelical Congregationalism is, body and soul, organism and spirit, the earthly chalice and heavenly wine
contained in it. . . . This includes a statement of doctrine and polity—the
evangelic faith of the Fathers rendered with their full vigor, yet made clear to
the modes of thought of the present time. . . . But the most important work of
the Council will be to fling the power of the denomination, with greater directness and energy, on the field of action. . . . The preliminary Conference has

[36]Savage, "The National Congregational Council," *Boston Review*, May, 1865, vol.
27, p. 285.
[37]"Congregational Polity, Usages and Law," *Boston Review*, vol. 28, p. 329.

recommended many lines of effort to the consideration of the body. . . . The opening home field is immense. The South will soon task all capacities of effort. The world belongs to Christ, and must be conquered for him. May the Spirit of the Lord Jesus rest on the great Council, and the wisdom of his servant, Paul, that, with true and comprehensive Christian statesmanship, it may act aright for the present emergency and for the welfare of the grand future.[38]

When the council met in Boston, the roll included 502 delegates, 14 honorary members, and 16 delegates from foreign countries, a total of 532 persons. It proceeded in a businesslike way to deal with the topics listed in the Call. The Preliminary Committee had selected a small committee to draft a report on each of the seven topics. These reports were prepared with great care and were of considerable length; the report on Ministerial Education covers eighteen pages of close print, and the report on Parochial Evangelism, twelve pages. The committee that prepared the advance report presented it to the council, which received the report and assigned it without discussion to a new committee selected from the council members. This new committee received such instruction as the council saw fit to give and made a careful study of the report. In its own words it presented what it considered should be placed before the council, where general discussion on the topic took place.

These council committees took their responsibilities seriously, and in the council records there are many references to the long hours spent in drafting the final reports. For example, when the advance Committee on Statement of Faith presented its preliminary report, containing a recital and a declaration, it was referred under the rules to the new committee appointed by the council. This council committee worked several days, Professor Park of Andover, a member of the committee, remarking when its report came up for discussion, that he had been deprived of the benefits of the council by being confined for three days in the cellar (the basement room of the church used by the committee for its daily sessions). The council committee set aside the advance committee's report and brought in a new statement of belief and a declaration of faith. Thereupon a vigorous debate ensued. In the course of this debate, the leaders of the council moved one after the other into the discussion. Prominent among the debaters were Professor Bacon of Yale, Professor Park of Andover, President Sturtevant of Illinois, Dr. Barstow of New Hampshire, and Dr. Wolcott of Ohio, but many others also took part. The hour of adjournment was postponed twice, and debate continued. The final point of difference was whether as Calvinists the delegates should reaffirm their allegiance to Calvin or, on the other hand, the way should be left open for a more liberal interpretation of religious doctrine.

[38] Savage, "The National Congregational Council," *Boston Review*, May, 1865.

It was in this debate that Professor Park spoke those words which were given wide currency in the years that followed: "We are Calvinists, mainly, essentially, in all the essentials of our faith: and the man who, having pursued a three years' course of study—having studied the Bible in the original languages—is not a Calvinist, is not a respectable man."[39]

Dr. Leonard Bacon of New Haven spoke truly of the nature of Congregational beliefs:

I must say here, and I hope that I may be found in error, that I have had some apprehension that some of our brethren in some parts of the country have an idea of Congregationalism that it consists in believing nothing in particular. . . . I believe, furthermore—I am making something of a declaration of faith myself—that it is the right and duty of any such body of representatives as those representing the Congregational churches of the land, to stand up, and with one heart and one voice to say what we believe—what we unitedly believe, and not what this or that particular colleague believes or would like to have other people believe; not what a few perhaps would like to impose by some sort of force or coercion upon people that do not believe it, but what we ourselves believe; because we who are assembled know that, one and all, there is a great body of Christian doctrine upon which we are unanimous as to the substance of it, and which we know our churches hold as the basis of their special fellowship and communion, and cooperation in the advancement of the kingdom of Christ.[40]

The next day they went to Plymouth for a celebration. Dr. Quint, who had not taken too active a part in the discussion of the statement of faith, had a partially drafted statement, which embraced the essential teachings both documents previously presented. On the train to Plymouth, using his tall silk hat as a table, Dr. Quint finished this statement of common belief. He was asked by the Business Committee to read it to the delegates as soon as they assembled on Burial Hill.

This was one of the most dramatic moments in Congregational history. As the simple statement of the great underlying teachings of Congregationalism was read, the entire group was united in a deep experience of finding a common mind. The proposal was made that this statement be substituted for the two documents previously presented to the council. Rev. George Allen, of Massachusetts, protested, saying, "In the name of our fathers, I protest, from this consecrated hill, against that Declaration. It is sectarian."[41] The Moderator asked that he protest in writing and file it with the secretary. Dr. Leonard Bacon and Professor Porter, together with Dr. Eddy and Dr. Dexter, each spoke briefly, urging immediate adoption. It was adopted with two dissenting voices, and re-

[39] *Debates and Proceedings of the National Council, Boston, Mass., June 14–24, 1865,* p. 357.
[40] *Debates and Proceedings of the National Council, Boston, Mass., June 14–24, 1865,* pp. 350–351.
[41] *Debates and Proceedings of the National Council, Boston, Mass., June 14–24, 1865,* p. 363.

ferred to a committee of revision "to perfect the diction without affect-ing the sense."

The next morning the committee on revision presented its report. A few questions were asked and answered. Then the council paused for a period of prayer. The statement, now known as the Burial Hill State-ment of Faith, was read, this being the fourth reading. "The vote was then taken by rising upon the adoption of the above Declaration of Faith, and it was adopted, *nem. con.* (Applause)"[42]

This admirable epitome of modern Congregationalism was unanimously ap-proved . . . a Mather or a Cotton would have looked with astonishment on the statement that the duly established ministry implies "no power of government." Yet, in this the Statement reflects the position of present Congregationalism, that in matters of government the minister is at most but the moderator of the deliberations of the membership. The development of Congregationalism has carried its polity to its logical outcome in pure democracy, and this fact here finds definite expression . . . owing perhaps to the willingness of our churches to be a law unto themselves, and the distaste of the present age for minute pre-scriptions and elaborate definitions, this document sometimes known as the "Boston Platform" has never been widely known and has latterly been well-nigh forgotten. It has hardly merited this fate, but the days of elaborate plat-forms, like that of Cambridge, are as fully past as those of lengthy confessions.[43]

Discussion of the contents of this Burial Hill Declaration and its variation from the earlier statements of faith will be taken up elsewhere, but this brief recital illustrates the Congregational method of finding the common mind.

Another noteworthy session of this '65 council was that given to Min-isterial Education. To the New Englander, college and seminary gradua-tion were looked upon as essential prerequisites to entering the ministry. The delegates from the East desired that the council go on record that no candidate should be ordained who did not have this preparation. This proposal was opposed by Western delegates. One Iowa delegate told the council that in Iowa they had need of forty new ministers and there was but one seminary graduate available. It was necessary, therefore, for them to lay hands upon some of their own men and make ministers out of them, even if they did not have this required training. "But," said he, "what happens?" "Just as soon as one of these 'Iowa-made' ministers be-gins to demonstrate his ability, the long arm of some New England church reaches out and picks him up from his six-hundred-dollar church and finds him a two-thousand-dollar church in Massachusetts and makes him a Doctor of Divinity!" It was obvious that at this stage in the de-

---

[42] *Debates and Proceedings of the National Council, Boston, Mass., June 14–24, 1865,* p. 404.
[43] Walker, *The Creeds and Platforms of Congregationalism,* pp. 468–469.

velopment of Congregationalism uniform regulations were impossible.

There was great interest and sympathy for the freedmen. In the discussion on reconstruction of the South, however, there were wide differences of opinion and the council ended without making headway towards finding a common mind. One quotation indicates the difficulty of reaching unanimity on this question. Senator Pomeroy, of Kansas, said:

It is not supposed that in a single resolution or two resolutions the committee could report what would be acceptable to everybody. Our only effort was to hit upon some general topics on which we could all agree, and report them to the council. The fact is, the report (of the Committee on the State of the Country) would suit me better if we spoke out a little more plainly about hanging somebody. (Applause) I am very willing to mingle our justice with mercy to the common people of the South, as has been suggested by our friend Henry Ward Beecher; but it does seem to me that it is time somebody was hung. (Applause) Some wholesome hanging, I think, would have settled this question in the minds of the American people long ago; and I do not believe that a convention, even of this character, composed largely of clergymen—men who love forgiveness and mercy—would be harmed if it adopted a little stiffer resolution on this question.[44]

Nowhere in the records of the council is there evidence that the members had any idea of establishing an organization with stated meetings, nor was there discussion of a constitution, although it did instruct certain of its committees to complete their work and to publish a formal report on the denominational publications. For example, it was ordered "That the Committee on Church Polity be authorized, if they think best, to issue an epitome or digest of their large report for use and circulation among the churches, the copyright to be held in trust by the Directors of the American Congregational Association."[45]

There was, however, the statement of Dr. Wolcott, of Ohio, who said:

I thought it desirable, if we could, to come together as a National Council, for this practical work, without discussing the faith and polity of the churches; because, if that is understood to be the work of a National Council, we cannot meet oftener than once in a century; or, perhaps, two centuries; while, upon the other plan, we might secure the benefit of occasional, and, perhaps, stated meetings of this kind.[46]

In the closing moments of the council, the Moderator, Governor William A. Buckingham of Connecticut, announced that the Cambridge Synod in 1648 closed by singing "The Song of Moses and the Lamb"; and so, this council sang the old hymn:

[44]*Debates and Proceedings of the National Council, Boston, Mass., June 14-24, 1865,* pp. 244-245.
[45]*Debates and Proceedings of the National Council, Boston, Mass., June 14-24, 1865,* p. 496.
[46]*Debates and Proceedings of the National Council, Boston, Mass., June 14-24, 1865,* p. 349.

> Awake, and sing the song
>   Of Moses and the Lamb;
> Wake, every heart, and every tongue,
>   To praise the Saviour's name![47]

Dr. Rufus Anderson, of Massachusetts, then offered prayer, after which the Doxology was sung:

> To God the Father, God the Son,
>   And God the Spirit, Three in One,
> Be honor, praise, and glory given,
>   By all on earth, and all in heaven![48]

The Moderator declared the council adjourned. The council, having fulfilled its purpose as voiced in the original letter of invitation, adjourned *sine die* as had the Albany Convention, making no provision for future meetings.

Professor Williston Walker thus summarized the Albany Convention and the '65 council:

The Albany Convention of 1852 had clearly manifested the real unity of Congregationalism, East and West, and the abandonment of the *Plan of Union* gave impetus to the growing consciousness of the denomination. . . . This dawning sense of the continental mission of Congregationalism was strengthened by the war of the rebellion—a crisis in which national spirit in all its forms was aroused and in which the Congregational churches, unlike the Presbyterian, found themselves substantially united in support of the triumphant cause. Accordingly, when the failure of the rebellion became probable, and it was evident to far-sighted observers that the South and Southwest would be unbarred to Congregationalism as never before, and that a new epoch in national history had opened, movements began having for their aim the gathering of a representative Convention wherein the churches might deliberate as to the best methods of improving the opportunities of the hour . . . at the council of 1865 there came into being the only Declaration of Faith which a body representative of American Congregationalism as a whole had approved since 1648—a distinction it still retains.[49] As compared with the Puritan symbols of two centuries before, it shows great advance in simplicity and catholicity. . . . In a statement of broad principles, rather than specific beliefs, issued on a historic occasion as a memorial rather than as a formula for permanent local use, these characteristics are not necessarily demerits; but they have operated to prevent the adoption of the Burial Hill Declaration as the creed of individual churches, and have made it to be comparatively little known and little used.[50]

[47] *Debates and Proceedings of the National Council, Boston, Mass., June 14–24, 1865*, p. 499.
[48] *Debates and Proceedings of the National Council, Boston, Mass., June 14–24, 1865*, p. 500.
[49] This was written before the Kansas City meeting of the Council, in 1913, when a new Statement of Faith was adopted by the National Council.
[50] Walker, *The Creeds and Platforms of Congregationalism*, chap. 18, pp. 553–554, 564–565.

CHAPTER XIV

The Council: Its Formation and Changes in Its Structure

THE National Council of the Congregational Churches, officially organized at Oberlin in 1871, was the result of the normal growth of national consciousness. It had as its antecedents the gathering in the cabin of the Mayflower, the Newtowne (Cambridge) Synod of 1637, the Cambridge Synod of 1646–48, the Massachusetts Synod of 1662, the Reforming Synod of 1679, the Saybrook Synod of 1708, the Michigan City Convention of 1846, the Albany Convention of 1852, the Boston Council of 1865, and the Pilgrim Memorial Convention of 1870.

I

THE PILGRIM MEMORIAL CONVENTION

The Pilgrim Memorial Convention, which met in Chicago, April 27, 1870, was initiated by the Church of the Pilgrims of Plymouth, Massachusetts, for observance of the 250th anniversary of the landing of the Pilgrims. The original letter to the churches sent by the Church of the Pilgrims said in part: "On the approach of the two hundred and fiftieth anniversary of the landing of the Pilgrims, the Church of the Pilgrims at Plymouth, Massachusetts, invites the churches to meet by delegates at New York, to consider the appropriateness of particular action in celebrating this fifth jubilee." This meeting was held March 2, 1870 and a general committee of arrangements for a Memorial Convention was appointed.

This committee issued the Call for the Pilgrim Memorial Convention to meet in Chicago, April 27, 1870, stating that it would be open to delegates from each Congregational church in the United States. The Convention met, and while celebrating the landing of the Pilgrims with speeches, banquets, and formal resolutions of commemoration, it adopted the following resolution:

Resolved, That this Pilgrim Memorial Convention recommend to the Congregational State Conferences and Associations, and to other local bodies, to unite in measures for instituting on the principle of fellowship, excluding ecclesiastical authority, a permanent National Conference.[1]

[1] Walker, *The Creeds and Platforms of Congregationalism,* pp. 570–571.

When this resolution was broadcast over the country, a nationwide discussion followed. The *Congregational Review,* of Boston, led in supporting the proposal. In an editorial it said:

Shall we not have an annual or a triennial National Council of the Congregational Churches in our land? The Pilgrim Memorial Convention, at Chicago, in April last, proposed it. The General Association of Indiana has approved such a gathering of our churches. Dr. Bacon is reported to have said, "that though there might have been, thirty years ago, some danger of an assumption of authority by such conference, there was none now. Our churches need it, and one ought to be held." The General Conference of Ohio, in giving its assent, at its June meeting, at Oberlin, took an important step, it is hoped, toward the organization of such a conference, by appointing a committee of correspondence, to lay the matter before other State organizations and our denominational societies. . . . Maine, Vermont and Massachusetts have responded to the overtures from Ohio, approving the formation of a stated National Conference. . . . Massachusetts was especially emphatic in her action, suggesting the basis of representation; "that the National Conference be held once in two years," and directing her committee to "secure, if possible, the meeting of such a conference in the early autumn of the ensuing year," but if this be found impracticable, then to arrange "for the meeting of a General Convention of the Congregationalists in the United States, in the month of October next."

It was stated that a council composed of clergy and laity would safeguard rather than injure the liberties of the churches. As one writer stated:

Associations of ministers alone have tried to encroach on the completeness and independence of local congregations, but if conferences composed of pastors and laymen have tried it, the record is unknown to us. The admission to them of usually two laymen to one minister, is both a guarantee against usurpation, and a return to the apostolic and primitive model. For during the first centuries they were admitted; but after the fourth century, the lower clergy and the laity were entirely excluded from the councils, and bishops only admitted. Besides, the positive exclusion of all idea of authority or jurisdiction over individuals or churches from the conference by express provision, effectually secures the churches in their Divine liberties.[2]

It is interesting that at this time, 1870, the possibility of an ecumenical council, as now represented in the World Council of Churches, was presented as a goal toward which the churches would take a long step by organizing a regular national council. As The *Congregational Review* urged:

Has not a half century of successful experiment on a smaller scale, prepared our churches for a National Conference? Is not such an organization the next logical step in our progress towards the union of all believers? This taken, the final step remains, to gather, through Ecumenical Councils, all our churches in all lands into one body, a visible exhibition of universal Christian brotherhood, in harmony with the perfect autonomy of each local church.[3]

[2] *Congregational Review,* vol. 55, Sept., 1870.
[3] *Congregational Review,* vol. 55, Sept., 1870.

Those desiring a national council cited Pastor Robinson: "May not the officers of one or many churches meet together to discuss and consider matters for the good of the church or churches? I deny it not, so they infringe no order of Christ or the liberty of the churches." It was also felt that the churches should have the advantage of the resource of leadership that would be available if the leaders, lay and clerical, could be brought together to work in coöperation for common ends. As it was said, "the matured wisdom of the few will thus become the accepted wisdom of the many . . . at present we have no adequate way for making use of the true statesmanship found in the denomination."

There were some practical problems, the most pressing of which was, as one advocate of a national council phrased it, "The relation of our denominational societies to our churches should be readjusted."

II

The English Union

The leaders of American churches were encouraged by the experience of the English Congregationalists who had organized a national Union and maintained it for forty years without endangering the liberty of the churches. But there had been strong opposition to its formation. One writer had said it was "a most illegal, as well as an insulting, violation of the British Constitution," while another writer, fearing that this was the first move towards episcopacy, wrote, "It is wise to take precaution while the wind whispers; it may be too late when it roars."[4] Another wrote, "It is for us to profit by the past. Episcopacy arose out of the presidency of the more influential men in the assemblies of presbyters holding equal rand; and the churches lost their internal rights by appealing to the wisdom of such assemblies. . . . The pastoral chair of a single church became, in the end, a throne lifted high in supremacy over all the churches. Hierarchies have sprung from the most inconsiderable beginning."[5] And it was urged that if they formed a Union, the Congregational churches in England would become a sect.

In spite of these difficulties the Union was organized in the Congregational Library in London, May 13, 1831, with eighty-two ministers and nineteen laymen. The purposes of the new Union were to collect information, to publish a Year Book, to cultivate brotherly affection, to give advice as to the collecting of funds, to assist in maintaining the civil rights of dissenters, and to promote other worthy objects. The first article of the constitution contained a clause which in substance has been written into all constitutions, British or American, adopted since; viz.:

[4] Dale, *History of English Congregationalism*, p. 688.
[5] Dale, *History of English Congregationalism*, pp. 689–690.

I. That it is highly desirable and important to establish a Union of the Congregational Churches and Ministers throughout England and Wales, founded on a full recognition of their own distinctive principle, namely, the scriptural right of every separate church to maintain perfect independence in the government and administration of its own particular affairs; *and, therefore, that the Union shall not in any case assume legislative authority, or become a court of appeal.*

The American leaders had studied both the constitution and the work of the Union of English and Welsh Congregationalists and in the experiences of the English churches during the forty years the Second Union had been in existence, had found much to assist them in their plans for an American National Council.

III

THE CALL FOR A NATIONAL COUNCIL

In response to the resolution of the Pilgrim Memorial Convention, mentioned above, the New York Conference voted to issue an invitation to state conferences to send delegates to a preliminary meeting in Boston, December 21, 1870. This was approved by the Massachusetts Association. When the state representatives met in Boston in response to this invitation, the following resolution was passed: "That it is expedient, and appears to be clearly the voice of the churches, that a National Council be organized." Only one state, having seventy churches, voted adversely on sending delegates, and that by a majority of one.

The committee appointed a Provisional or Executive Committee[6] to issue the Call, or invitation; to prepare the draft of a suitable constitution; to select the time and place of meeting; and to designate the proper representation of the churches. The Call embodied the seed ideas which grew into the constitution presented to the council when it met and is worthy of careful attention. It states that it is expedient and appears clearly to be the voice of the churches that such a council shall be organized. It provides for the allotment of delegates and for a committee to prepare a proposed constitution; assumes the acceptance of the Burial Hill Declaration, and made very clear the metes and bounds of the council's work.

On the positive side it stated:

That a declaration be made of the two cardinal principles of Congregationalism, viz., the exclusive right and power of the individual churches to self-government; and the fellowship of the churches one with another, with the duties grow-

[6] The Committee, elected by ballot, included Reverend A. H. Quint, of New Bedford, Massachusetts; President William E. Merriman, of Ripon College; Professor S. C. Bartlett, Chicago Seminary; Deacon Samuel Holmes, Montclair, New Jersey; Major General Oliver O. Howard, United States Army; Reverend William Ives Budington, Brooklyn; and Honorable A. C. Barstow, of Providence. Other well-known men who shared in these deliberations were Reverend James G. Vose, Reverend Leonard Bacon, Reverend George Bicknell, President Israel W. Andrews, and Edward W. Gilman.

ing out of that fellowship and especially the duty of general consultation in all matters of common concern to the whole body of churches.

That the objects of the organization be to express and foster the substantial unity of our churches in doctrine, polity, and work, and to consult upon the common interests of all our churches, their duties in the work of evangelization, the united development of their resources, and their relations to all parts of the kingdom of Christ.

On the other hand, it set limits:

That the churches withhold from the National Council all legislative or judicial power over churches or individuals, and all right to act as a council of reference.

To provide as simple an organization, with as few officers, and with as limited duties as may be consistent with the efficiency of the Council in advancing the principles and securing the objects of the proposed organization.[7]

IV

THE FIRST NATIONAL COUNCIL

In response to this Call, a Council of the Congregational Churches assembled in the Second Church, Oberlin, Ohio, Wednesday, November 15, 1871.

A temporary organization was effected by the election of Hon. Erastus D. Holton of Wisconsin, as Moderator. The 3,100 churches, 3,000 ministers, and 312,000 members in the Congregational fellowship were represented by 276 delegates.

Morning and afternoon sessions of the first day were given to formation of a temporary organization and presentation of the constitution as drafted by the Preliminary Committee. In the evening, Rev. Leonard Bacon, of New Haven, preached from the text, "And hath put all things under his feet, and gave him to be the head over all things to the church" (Eph. I:22). During the meeting papers were read and discussed upon the following subjects: "Vacant Churches and Unemployed Ministers"; "Congregational Literature"; "The Supply of the Ministry"; "The Unity of the Church"; "The Relationship of the Boards to the Churches"; and "The Need of Better Missionary Support." The main business of this council, however, was the perfecting of a permanent organization.

Two days were given to discussion of the constitution presented by the Committee. The one provision which caused prolonged debate was the name for the national organization. Some timid folk in the group were afraid of the word "council." From earliest days the churches had held councils for a variety of purposes. These people thought that if the name "council" were adopted, the national body might assume duties and privileges in regard to national questions which local councils had

[7]Barton, *The Law of Congregational Usage*, p. 402.

sometimes assumed as to local questions. The debate on the question of name continued intermittently, when, in a thoroughly democratic way, each delegate was asked to write the name he favored. While "council" had the largest vote, the word "union" had many and there were enough scattered votes on other names to prevent a clear majority. The delegates then voted on the two names, and "council" had by far the majority of votes. Upon motion from the floor, the title was adopted unanimously. This was followed by a unanimous vote adopting the constitution. And the National Council of the Congregational Churches in the United States came into being.

The more important sections of the constitution were:

The Congregational churches of the United States, by elders and messengers assembled, do now associate themselves in National Council:

To express and foster their substantial unity in doctrine, polity, and work; and

To consult upon the common interests of all the churches, their duties in the work of evangelization, the united development of their resources, and their relations to all parts of the kingdom of Christ.

They agree in belief that the Holy Scriptures are the sufficient and only infallible rule of religious faith and practice; their interpretation thereof being in substantial accordance with the great doctrines of the Christian faith, commonly called evangelical, held in our churches from the early times, and sufficiently set forth by former General Councils.

They agree in the belief that the right of government resides in local churches, or congregations of believers, who are responsible directly to the Lord Jesus Christ, the One Head of the church universal and of all particular churches; but that all churches, being in communion one with another as parts of Christ's catholic church, have mutual duties subsisting in the obligations of fellowship.

The churches, therefore, while establishing this National Council for the furtherance of the common interests and work of all the churches, do maintain the Scriptural and inalienable right of each church to self-government and administration; and this National Council shall never exercise legislative or judicial authority, nor consent to act as a council of reference.

The Council proceeded to organize under this constitution, and elected officers by ballot. Rev. William I. Budington, of Brooklyn, was chosen Moderator. He remarked significantly in taking the chair, "We stand on the grave of buried prejudice." General O. O. Howard and Rev. George H. Atkinson were Assistant Moderators. Rev. A. H. Quint, New Bedford, Mass., was made Secretary, Rev. William H. Moore, Berlin, Conn., Registrar, and Hon. Charles G. Hammond, Chicago, Treasurer.

The Council completed its program and participated in laying the cornerstone of "Council Hall," the new building for the theological school. For sixty years this Hall, now replaced by new buildings, was to be the home of successive generations of students preparing for the ministry.

One of the significant actions of this first Council was the following vote:

"Voted, That many requests having come that a manual of doctrine and polity be prepared . . . ," a strong committee be appointed to this work "whose sanction may give currence to the manual, not as a book of binding authority, but as a means of general instruction, commended to the churches for its real merits." From meeting to meeting similar votes have been taken and manuals written providing guidance for the churches.

V

STRUCTURAL DEVELOPMENTS

The early constitution is, in its spirit, purposes, and prohibitions, to a large extent embodied in our present constitution. With the continuing growth of a national consciousness; the realization of the responsibility of the churches to take a worthy part in the highly organized society in which they exist; and the desire for mutual advice and counsel, the national organization has grown in its outreach and influence.

The changes that have been made in the constitution, and there has not been a single Council which failed to add some amendment to the constitution, have always been within the framework of the original document. The votes of the Council have never been considered binding on the local churches but only as advice which churches are free to accept, modify, or reject as they deem best. Nor have the votes of one Council been considered as binding precedents for the next Council. Each Council has felt itself free and able to observe, ignore, amend, or repeal the actions of previous Councils.

The structural changes of the Council through the years may be considered under four heads: (1) the Executive Committee, (2) the Moderator, (3) the Secretary, and (4) the standing committees and commissions.

VI

THE EXECUTIVE COMMITTEE

The Executive Committee is the Council *ad interim*. The growth of the place of the Executive Committee in the denomination registers more clearly the outward manifestation of the growing national consciousness and unity than any other denominational agency. The development of its place and function in the denominational life is worthy of careful study.

The constitution of 1871 did not provide for the appointment of an

Executive Committee but did provide for a Provisional Committee as follows:

The Provisional Committee shall consist of seven persons by appointment, with the addition of the Secretary, Registrar, and Treasurer, *ex officiis*. The committee shall specify the place, the precise time, at which sessions shall commence; shall choose a preacher of the opening sermon; may select topics regarding the Christian work of the churches, and persons to propose and present papers thereon; shall do any work which shall have been referred to them by the Council; and shall make a full report of all their doings—the consideration of which shall be first in order of business after organization.

The Provisional Committee may fill any vacancies occurring in any committee or office in the intervals of sessions, the person so appointed to serve until the next session.[8]

There was no printed report from this committee in the minutes of the next regular meeting of the Council in 1874, although it is evident from the minutes that the Provisional Committee had arranged the Council meeting. In the period 1874 to 1877, however, the Provisional Committee functioned as a continuing agency to the extent of appointing fraternal delegates to other church bodies; filling vacancies on committees; conducting correspondence and, as originally provided, arranging for the 1877 Council. Through the next twenty years the Provisional Committee was assigned more and more duties by the Council. The Committee fixed the salaries of the Secretary and Treasurer, made appropriations out of the limited Council funds to other bodies, supervised the printing of the *Year Book* and had the responsibility for raising the denomination's share toward expenses of the Federal Council of the Churches of Christ in America.

The Provisional Committee wrestled with the perennial difficulty of councils: the relationship of business to the devotional and inspirational features of the meeting which has not yet been adjusted to the satisfaction of all concerned.

The constitution, as approved by the Kansas City Council, provided that the name of the committee be changed from Provisional Committee to Executive Committee and given the status of the Council *ad interim.*

VII

THE EXECUTIVE COMMITTEE AND THE COMMISSIONS

The development of the functions of the Executive Committee in relationship to the commissions was of slow growth. In earlier years there were various committees appointed, some being standing committees from council to council without executive responsibilities. Each commit-

[8] "By-Laws," *Minutes of the National Council, 1871*, pp. 66–67.

tee was expected to make a careful study of the particular field assigned
and to report its findings to the Council, but without any authority for
action. Beginning with 1913, some of the continuing committees were
given the name commissions. For the first few years these commissions
worked independently of one another and of the Executive Committee
and made their reports only to the National Council at its regular meetings. The first step towards coöperation between the Executive Committee and the commissions was the vote of the Council in 1917 that the
Executive Committee be instructed to aid the commissions in "developing and coördinating their work," but that "the Executive Committee is
assigned no authority over the commissions." The same Council voted
that the Executive Committee be authorized to invite the chairmen of
the various commissions to be present at one meeting for a discussion
of their problems and programs. There was no requirement that the commissions should confide to the Executive Committee what their proposals to the Council would be.

VIII

THE COMMISSION ON POLITY

One interesting development was the transfer to the Executive Committee of the responsibilities of the Committee, later on the Commission, on Polity. From the early days of the Council there had been a Committee on Polity which sought to bring some general system out of the
varied practices and usages of the churches. This Committee had prepared a manual for the churches and had presented several learned reports. Authority for the Committee was the vote of the Council of 1904,
which provided "that a committee of nine be appointed to do what may
be done, on its own initiative and in conference and coöperation with
local and state bodies, for the better adjustment of our Congregational
order to existing conditions." The phrase "on its own initiative" should
be noted. Later, this Committee was made a Commission and became a
sort of "supreme court," passing judgment on all questions relating to
procedure in the churches. The chairman of the Commission, usually a
man well learned in Congregational practice became the chief spokesman
on denominational procedure. The detachment of this agency from the
Executive Committee and also from the office of the Secretary caused
many complications. The constitution of 1913 had specifically provided
that the Secretary should conduct the correspondence of the Council and
the question was raised continually as to whether or not the letters written by the chairman or other members of the Commission on Polity were
Council correspondence. To simplify matters, the Council in 1923 voted
that the Commission on Polity be discontinued and the interests previously committed to the care of this commission be transferred to the

Executive Committee. Since that time the Council office, with the assistance of the state Superintendents, has served as a source of information on matters concerning polity and procedure.

IX

The Constitution of 1931

The new constitution adopted at the time of the merger with the General Convention of the Christian Church contained most of the provisions of the Congregational constitution relating to the function of the Executive Committee: (a) to appoint any committee or commission authorized by the Council but not otherwise appointed; (b) to arrange for the next meeting of the Council and have charge of expenses; (c) to continue as the Council *ad interim;* (d) to fill vacancies and "between meetings of the Council . . . represent the Council in all matters not otherwise provided for"; (e) to "determine questions of polity not clearly defined by the Council." At that time, the Executive Committee membership was increased from twelve to fifteen and provided that the Secretaries should be corresponding members without vote, but that the Moderator should be a full voting member.

At the 1936 meeting of the Council at South Hadley it was voted that "the Committee may submit to the Council for consideration any recommendations it may deem useful for the development of the efficiency of the organization, life, and work of the denomination."[9] At this time, on recommendation of the Strategy Committee which had made a study of the denominational structure during the preceding two years, a forward step was taken committing to the Executive Committee "the duty to consider the work of the organizations named in By-Law Number 4 (the national societies) to prevent duplication of activities and to effect all possible economies of administration." To the Executive Committee was committed by this vote the responsibility of correlating all publicity and promotional activities so as to secure maximum efficiency with minimum expense. The Committee was directly charged with recommending to the Council adjustments in the work of the national societies. Further attention will be given to this particular extension of the duties of the Executive Committee, in Chapter 8, in the treatment of the relationship of the Council to the national societies.

X

The Executive Committee as the Business Committee

The Council of 1936 made one other change in the structure of the Council for efficiency and cooperation. The Council of 1865, which met without a constitution and no continuing responsibilities, found so many

[9] *Minutes of the General Council, 1936,* p. 171.

different interests to be presented that a steering committee was needed. Therefore one of the first committees to be elected was the Business Committee, with Rev. Alonzo H. Quint as chairman. The duties of this Committee were not defined by action of that early Council, but the Committee presented reports and recommendations to the Council concerning action on resolutions and suggestions submitted to it, arranged reference to special committees, and attended to various details concerning the Council program.

The constitution provided that all proposals from the floor of the Council should be referred to this Business Committee; and if in its judgment they were worthy of the Council's consideration, the Business Committee reported them to the Council with or without recommendation. The members of the Business Committee, not being members of the Executive Committee, sometimes lacked information as to what was involved in questions which came before them.

It was the judgment of the Strategy Committee, reporting to the Mount Holyoke Council in 1936, that it was an unwise provision that one group should provide the program for the Council and conduct the Council business through the biennium, and then the responsibility for the consideration of this business be turned over to an entirely new group of persons assembled after the opening of the Council. To remedy this situation, the Strategy Committee recommended that the Executive Committee should appoint out of its membership a subcommittee to serve as the Business Committee of the Council. The provision making this change was very carefully safeguarded by providing that this Business Committee (now a subcommittee of the Executive Committee) should have no relationship to the following items: (1) the annual report of the Executive Committee; (2) the work of the Nominating Committee; (3) the work of the Resolutions Committee; and (4) the appointment of any new commission. It further provided that matters of business suggested on the floor of the Council which were pigeon-holed by the Business Committee could be brought to the floor by direct appeal to the Council. With these provisions in working order, the Executive Committee has become in reality what it had been in name for many years—the Council *ad interim,* and its business as the central agency in the denomination has multiplied many times.

That the Executive Committee may carry forward its work with full knowledge, it has adopted the method of inviting persons responsible for our various denominational interests to sit with the committee as corresponding members. This virtual enlargement of the Executive Committee has not yet been validated by Council action; but the Executive Committee is being helped in its work by the representatives of the Boards and by five state superintendents representing the different sections of the country.

The Executive Committee has three standing committees to facilitate its work: the Finance Committee, which has care of the expenditures of the Council and general responsibility for the raising of funds for its modest budget; the Survey Committee, which has the responsibility for the needs of the various Boards and for determining the apportionment percentages; and the Advisory Committee, which meets between sessions of the enlarged Executive Committee to transact routine business and matters definitely referred to the Advisory Committee.

XI

THE MODERATOR

There was considerable discussion in the first Council over the office of Moderator. Congregationalists had been accustomed to moderators from the day when John Cotton and Thomas Hooker were joint Moderators of the Newtowne Synod, in 1637. But it was a well-established principle that Councils were called for a particular purpose and, having completed that purpose, they adjourned *sine die*. The Moderator of the Council was in office only during the life of the Council, which was the period of its meeting. Under the constitution adopted in 1871, the Council became a continuing body and the question arose as to whether or not the Moderator was to be a continuing officer whose duties and responsibilities extended beyond the meeting of the Council. The constitution of 1871 provided: "At the beginning of every stated or special session there shall be chosen, from those present as members, a moderator and one or more assistant moderators, to preside over their deliberations."

For thirty years the Moderator laid aside all "honors, responsibilities, and functions" with the pronouncement of the final adjournment, although, of course, a man thus honored had achieved a certain distinction among his brethren. But with the election of Rev. Amory H. Bradford as Moderator of the Council in 1901, there came a change in procedure.

Dr. Bradford had long been a leader of the Congregationalists. He had served as Assistant Moderator the previous triennium and was widely known as a preacher and leader. When the Council of 1901 adjourned, Dr. Bradford was importuned by the churches to visit them and to speak before their associations and conferences. He accepted as many of these appointments as his time and strength would permit, with the understanding, however, that the inviting body should always care for his expenses so that it would not be a charge on the National Council treasury.

When the Council met in 1904 in Des Moines, Iowa, the Wichita Association of Kansas presented the following memorial:

We humbly request the National Council of Congregational Churches to make it plain that the Moderator of the Council is the presiding officer during the meeting over which he is elected to preside, but that he has no advisory powers over the Churches between the sessions of the Council.[10]

The minutes of the Council state that this memorial was received and "the same matter having been brought to the attention of the Council by others," the Council voted to refer the memorial and suggestions to a special committee. This committee brought in a well-considered report which stated that there were two positions concerning the office of Moderator: first, the historical one, which "identifies it with the presiding functions holding that in these it exhausts its intent"; and the second, or "advanced" position, which would admit the entire time and attention of the Moderator. There was also a third, or intermediate, position which "would make the position more flexible than the historical and less extreme than the advanced, and would conceive this high office liberally and entrust its interpretation to the wisdom and loyalty of its incumbent."[11]

The committee called attention to the fact that the Council had previously given slight intimations of the growing opportunity of the Moderator and cited two instances: first, that in the period following some Councils the Moderator had been *ex officio* member of the Provisional Committee which had in charge the preparation of plans for the next Council meeting; and second, that at a previous Council the Moderator had been asked to prepare an address for the opening session of the Council following the one over which he was the Moderator. Both of these acts, taken perhaps without thought of the implication, had pointed the way towards the Moderator's having some "semblance of office" during the period immediately following the Council over which he presided. The committee drew from these actions that "the idea of moderatorship has more significance than merely that of a presiding officer having some representative character and individual initiative." Having said this, the committee stated clearly that "such representative privilege is absolutely unattended by any ecclesiastical authority, and that any slightest departure from our invariable principle in this respect would be impoverishment of the Spirit, and an infringement upon the rights of our free churches."[12]

The committee proposed the following resolution:

Resolved: That, in view of the widening opportunities of Congregationalists and the increasing desire for fellowship through denominational representation,

[10] *Minutes of the National Council, 1904,* p. 412.
[11] *Minutes of the National Council,* 1904, p. 412.
[12] "Report of the Committee on Sphere of the Moderator," *Minutes of the National Council, 1904,* p. 413.

it is the sense of this Council, that the Moderator interpret his position, generously, as having in addition to presiding duties, a representative function; that visiting upon invitation, churches and associations, so far as he may be able and disposed; addressing the churches, if in his judgment occasion requires it; and, in general, serving the churches be regarded as his prerogative.

But it is understood, that all his acts and utterances shall be devoid of authority and that for them shall be claimed and to them given only such weight and force as there is weight and force in the reason of them.

The resolution was approved and became a by-law of the constitution. This vote, adopted in 1904, continues with slight modification in the present constitution. From time to time there have been different provisions as to assistants and associates, and for the period 1925 to 1929 there were co-moderators. The vote providing for this change specified that there should be a minister and a layman elected Moderators who would have equal standing in the denomination. But this did not work out too happily and the next Council returned to the former plan of electing a Moderator with assistant moderators to represent interests and agencies.

XII

THE MODERATOR'S RESPONSIBILITIES

The Council at different times has added to and taken from the Moderator's powers during the Council sessions over which he presides. For the Council meetings prior to 1886 the Credentials, Business, and Nominating Committees were always named by the Council after it had organized. But in 1886 the Provisional Committee went so far as to nominate these three important committees in advance of the meeting. A discussion arose in the Council as to whether the Provisional Committee had exceeded its prerogatives and the general feeling was that it had. To avoid this irregular practice, a by-law was adopted which provided that the Moderator who had served as a presiding officer of one Council and who, by the regulations of the day, called the next Council to order and presided during the election of a new Moderator, should be given the responsibility of appointing these three important committees. With considerable satisfaction, no doubt, they voted that he should appoint these committees as his last official act. The committees were not to serve with him but with the new Moderator.

This plan was not effective. At the next meeting of the Council, at Worcester in 1889, the duty of naming the Committees on Business and Credentials was taken from the Moderator which left him only the appointment of the Committee on Nominations. At Syracuse, in 1895, the right to appoint this Committee was taken from the Moderator, but he was given the right to nominate the Nominating Committee subject to approval by vote of the Council.

This continued to be the practice until the meeting of the General Council at Beloit in 1938. Then, in response to a resolution presented by the Superintendents at the opening of the Council, this last remaining vestige of authority was taken from the Moderator. The present by-law was adopted which provides that the Nominating Committee shall be nominated by a committee composed of the Moderator, the Assistant Moderator, the President of the Superintendents' Conference, and the chairman of Women State Presidents.

The moderatorship, having all vestige of authority removed, continues to be an office of high dignity and great opportunity. The Moderator's words are listened to by churches and denominational officials everywhere, and as far as his judgment and recommendations are considered wise they are adopted by the churches. The Moderator is welcomed as a brother beloved by the churches and his advice and counsel and inspiration and Christian faith enrich the life of the fellowship.

In 1923, the Council meeting in Springfield, Massachusetts, elected President Calvin Coolidge as Honorary Moderator. President Coolidge graciously accepted the honor. Dr. S. Parkes Cadman was so elected at the Oberlin Council of 1934 and President Mary E. Woolley, of Mount Holyoke College, at the Mount Holyoke Council of 1936.

XIII

THE SECRETARY

The first constitution adopted in 1871 provided that

At each triennial session there shall be chosen by ballot a secretary, a registrar and a treasurer, to serve from the close of such session to the close of the next triennial session.

The secretary shall receive communications for the Council, conduct correspondence, and collect such facts, and superintend such publications, as may from time to time be ordered.

The earlier councils and synods, including the Council of 1865 and the Pilgrim Memorial Convention, had elected a scribe with assistants who kept the records of the meeting and whose work was completed with the publication of the minutes.

Dr. Quint, the church historian and editor, was elected the first Secretary and served from 1871 to 1883; he was followed by the Rev. Henry A. Hazen, who served until 1900. The Rev. Asher Anderson succeeded Dr. Hazen and served until 1913. During this period the secretarial office was looked upon as a part-time position and the Secretary carried on the work of the Council in connection with other employment.

In the early years the annual statistics had been published under the auspices of the American Congregational Union, which issued a general

Year Book. In 1854, the American Congregational Union appointed Rev. T. Atkinson as editor of the *Year Book* and under his supervision *Year Books* were published by the Union from 1854 to 1860. In 1860 the *Congregational Quarterly* began publishing statistics of the churches, usually in the January number, but adding to the January statistics other figures received later in the year. This added much to the value of the *Quarterly* and increased its circulation. In 1877, the National Council voted "that the annual compilation of the statistics of our churches throughout the country and especially an accurate and complete list of ministers in the fellowship should be published under the sanction of this Council."

The Secretary of the Council, as elected under the constitution of 1871, was responsible for collecting the statistics of the churches, although these were printed in the privately-owned *Quarterly*. By 1877 the Council assumed the publication of the *Year Book* as a Council enterprise under the Secretary's supervision. He also was responsible for the preparation of the minutes of the Council meetings and their publication.

From time to time the Council voted that the Secretary should assume other duties. In 1886, the Secretary was instructed by the Council to prepare a list of ministers and was given suggestions as to cooperation with the church clerks. Thus as the Council grew in influence as a continuing agency in the denomination, the office of the Secretary increased in work and responsibility. The men who served as secretaries in those years from 1871 to 1913 were consulted frequently by both churches and ministers. They were men familiar with the life and work of the churches and informed as to prevailing trends in religion.

By 1910 the Council was ready to take a forward step, for "the office of Secretary had become mainly an editorial office . . . and it was desirable that the Secretary of the National Council should be our recognized leader in promoting the great issues of the denomination, the organizer of our national forces for world-wide enterprise." There had been much discussion previous to 1910 as to whether or not the American churches should follow the Congregational Unions in England in the election of a salaried Moderator. But the Council of 1910 voted that "it is better to have a salaried secretary than a salaried moderator." This Council of 1910 studied the structure of the Council and its relationship to the mission boards and voted "that the committee appointed to provide for the developing life of the denomination should work under the general instruction of the Secretary."

It further approves of a broader interpretation of the office of secretary which shall provide not merely for existing editorial and office functions, but include the active management of such interests as are placed in charge of the Council and not otherwise provided for, and the general function of leadership among the churches, counseling with conferences and associations, and promoting the great issues which our churches are working out.[13]

Upon motion, the committee appointed to study the relationship of the Boards to the churches, the so-called Committee of Nineteen was instructed, "to be prepared to nominate a general secretary who would be able to carry forward such a program for which the committee would provide."

The Council meeting of 1913, in Kansas City, marked a high point in the history of the denomination. The Committee of Nineteen, which had worked diligently since the previous Council, presented a report consisting of three sections. The two sections relating to polity and to the Boards will be considered elsewhere. We are concerned here only with that section pertaining to the structure of the Council and, in particular, to the expansion of the secretaryship.

The presentation of the section on the secretaryship received immediate and cordial acceptance. Dr. Hubert C. Herring, who was serving effectively as the Secretary of the Home Missionary Society, was elected the first General Secretary of the denomination. The duties of the office, as provided in the action of the Council of 1913, were as follows:

The enlargement of the duties of the secretary now proposed is the direct consequence of the enlargement of the duties of the Council whose representative he is. Its aim is to secure the more effective performance of the tasks to which the Council has set itself in its endeavors to achieve a "more efficient Congregationalism."

First, as Secretary of the Commission on Missions, he would serve it and, through it, the churches in the two great tasks immediately confronting them: (1) the work of coordinating and readjusting our missionary activities; and (2) the more efficient financing of those activities, through the Apportionment Plan and other plans which may be devised.

Second, as one widely acquainted with the interests of the churches, the secretary would be in a position, when invited, to give helpful advice in their problems and to make suggestions looking toward their greater efficiency. In this work, as far as permitted by the churches themselves, the secretary would be the representative of the Council.

Third, to enlarge his acquaintance with the churches and their needs, the secretary should, as far as possible, respond to invitations to be present at state conferences and other gatherings of the churches. Like the Moderator, he may also represent the Congregational churches in interdenominational relations— a matter of increasing importance in these days when cooperation between Christians of various names is constantly coming into greater recognition.[14]

By-law IV concerning the Secretary, which was adopted at this meeting, provided that:

[13] *Minutes of the National Council, 1910,* p. 286.
[14] *Minutes of the National Council, 1913,* pp. 337–339.

The Secretary shall keep the records and conduct the correspondence of the Council and of the Executive Committee. He shall edit the Year Book and other publications, and shall send out notices of all meetings of the Council and of its Executive Committee. He shall aid the committees and commissions of the Council and shall be Secretary of the Commission on Missions. He shall be available for advice and help in matters of polity and constructive organization, and render to the churches such services as shall be appropriate to his office.

On the death of Dr. Herring in 1920, Dr. Edward D. Eaton, former President of Beloit College, served as Secretary *ad interim* until the meeting of the Council of 1921 when Dr. Charles E. Burton, who had succeeded Dr. Herring as secretary of the Home Missionary Society, was elected Secretary of the Council.

In the constitution adopted at the time of the merger with the Christian Churches, the office of Secretary was continued practically on the same basis. On Dr. Burton's retirement in 1938, Rev. Douglas Horton, pastor of the United Church of Hyde Park, Chicago, was elected General Secretary. It was considered advisable to give constitutional recognition to the changing status of the General Secretary, who had become not only an administrator for the Council but also a leader of religious life with increasing responsibilities. The constitution was amended in 1938 to provide an additional title that the General Secretary should also be the Minister of the denomination and assume a pastoral relationship to the churches and agencies of the fellowship.

Very early in the history of the Council, the Secretary appointed assistants who served during the period of the Council meeting. Later the Executive Committee was authorized to employ an Assistant Secretary. In 1921, the position of Associate Secretary was created and Rev. Frederick L. Fagley was chosen for this new position. In the constitution of 1931 it was provided that the Council should elect the Associate Secretary and an Assistant Secretary if there be need for such an office. Rev. Warren H. Denison, who had been Secretary of the General Convention of Christian Churches, was elected Assistant Secretary of the General Council of the Congregational and Christian Churches following the merger in 1931 and served until his retirement in 1938. Under the present arrangement the Secretaries share responsibility for the work of the commissions and other interests in the province of the Council.

The secretaryship may be interpreted as bringing to the Congregational churches effective administration without infringement upon either the freedom of the local church or upon personal leadership.

The Congregational system or ideal is not a mere theory of Church politics or government, but fundamentally a doctrine of religion, a way of apprehending and realizing the Christian faith. Its ecclesiastical polity is but its doctrine applied to the exercise and cultivation of the religious life. Catholicism is a splendid system, even without the religious idea that fills it; but Independency, apart from its religious basis and ideal, is at once mean and impotent, impracticable and visionary. Our fathers held that legislation, civil or ecclesiastical, could not create a church; conversion and converted men alone could. All were kings and priests unto God, and could exercise their functions only as they stood in open and immediate relation with him. In his Church Christ did not reign, while officials governed; he both governed and reigned.

This Council speaks of an independency that is ceasing to be an isolation and learning to become a brotherhood. There is nothing that has so little solidarity as an autocracy. It may secure cohesion, but cannot realize unity; its weapons are the mechanical forces and clamps that may aggregate and hold together atoms; they do not represent those vital principles and laws which can build up a living and productive and complete organism.[15]

XIV

OTHER OFFICERS OF THE COUNCIL

The constitution of the Council from the beginning provided for the election of a Treasurer and the by-law concerning the Treasurer and his responsibilities has continued practically unchanged through the history of the Council.

It never was the purpose of the Congregational leaders to build up a large permanent endowment for use of the Council. They had in mind evidently the old French saying, "Men alone enjoy democracy; men plus money, however, equals autocracy." The income and outgo of the Council in its earlier years was a very modest sum of from ten to fifteen thousand dollars a year, most of this expense being represented by the cost of publishing the *Year Book*. In recent years the expenses of the Council have been approximately $50,000 per year, $10,000 of which represents the expense of the *Year Book*. No appeal has ever been made for endowment of the Council, although it has received a few small bequests.

XV

THE CORPORATION

When the Council was organized in 1871, no one would have favored the organization of a corporate body and the first constitution was a "limitation of power rather than a grant of power."[16] But the responsibility of the Council increased rapidly, especially in connection with the Board of Ministerial Relief. When the Knowles legacy was received in 1883, it was necessary to form a legal body to receive the bequest. The National Council petitioned the Assembly of Connecticut in 1885 for authority to form a corporate body to be known as the "Trustees of the National Council of the Congregational Churches of the United States."

[15] Barton, *The Law of Congregational Usage*, p. 405.
[16] *Minutes of the National Council, 1923*, p. 61.

This body was organized as the law provided. By this law the trustees were not permitted to hold property exceeding $60,000. In 1907 this board of trustees which had been primarily organized for the purposes of ministerial relief, became by legal authority the Congregational Board of Ministerial Relief. With this change, the Council was again without a corporate body.

At the 1907 Council meeting the question arose as to whether or not provision should be made for the creation of a corporation which could act as custodian of funds for the Council and other denominational agencies. A special committee, of which Governor Simeon E. Baldwin of Connecticut was chairman, studied this question. The committee advised against incorporation of the Council but recommended that a Committee of Five, three of whom should be Connecticut lawyers, be appointed to study the situation and prepare a draft of an organization to be known as the Corporation for the Council, to be a separate corporation but subject to the Council. This committee was duly appointed and at the 1910 Council the Committee on Incorporation reported a proposed bill for presentation to the Connecticut Assembly which would authorize the formation of a corporation as follows:

Resolved by this Assembly:

Section 1. That Charles A. Hopkins, Thomas C. MacMillan, Charles L. Kloss, Dan F. Bradley, Charles L. Noyes, Francis L. Hayes, William H. Day, Charles W. Osgood, Alexander Lewis, Asher Anderson, Joel S. Ives, and such other persons as may be associated with them, and their successors, are hereby constituted a body politic and corporate, by the name of the Corporation for the National Council of the Congregational Churches of the United States.

Section 2. The object of said corporation is to do and promote charitable and Christian work for the advancement of the general interests and purposes of the Congregational churches of this country, and to receive, hold, and administer, in trust or otherwise, funds and property for the uses of said National Council, or of churches of the Congregational order, or of any particular church of said order, and all in accordance with resolutions and declarations made from time to time by the National Council of the Congregational Churches of the United States, or by any body which may succeed to the functions of said council; and said corporation may cooperate with any other corporation or body which is under the charge and control of churches of the Congregational order in the United States, or churches at the time affiliated with said order. . . .

Section 4. Said council, or its successor as aforesaid, may, from time to time, make and alter rules, orders, and regulations for the government of said corporation, and said corporation shall at all times be subject to its direction and control. . . ."[17]

This report was presented by a committee composed of Simeon E. Baldwin, Charles E. Mitchell, Verrenice Munger, Joel S. Ives, and Asher Anderson. The report was referred to the Committee of Nineteen.

The Committee of Nineteen, in its report of 1913, had to decide

[17] *Minutes of the National Council, 1910*, pp. 234–236.

whether or not to accept the proposals of the Baldwin Committee. The discussion narrowed down to the question: Should there be a Corporation *of* or *for* the Council? The lay members were strongly in favor of the corporation *for* the Council, and it was so voted by the Committee and later by the Council.

The Corporation was duly created by act of the Connecticut Assembly and has continued with slight changes. It is now the Corporation for the General Council of Congregational Christian Churches and holds in trust funds for the Council, for the Annuity Fund, and for other agencies. Its record of careful investments is in every way praiseworthy.

CHAPTER XV

Concern for Education

INTEREST in education, from the beginning one of the foundations of the whole free church movement, came to its high point in official action at the Los Angeles Council in 1921. This interest is inherent in the very nature of Congregationalism. The founding fathers not only went back to the New Testament for their doctrine but were familiar with the development of early Christianity.

When Christianity first came into touch with Greek learning, there were fortunately two leaders, Clement of Alexandria (150–217) and Origen (185–253), who believed and taught that the system of philosophy developed by the Greeks found its completion in the teachings of Christianity. The Christian church early in its history joined forces with the cultural life of the world and drew from the contemplation of truth wherever it could be found further confirmation of God's revelation of himself to man.

The Reformation was primarily an educational movement in its insistence on right goals and worthy educational materials and techniques in harmony with the nature of man's intelligence. The Reformation "in defiance of dogma, tradition, custom, and self-arrogated authority of the Church, stoutly defended the right of spiritual freedom and came to the most definite expression in the type of thought and life known as Puritanism, and signally and very logically in the most unique development of Puritanism now designated as Congregationalism."

The concern of the New England colonies for education has been repeatedly noted, as have the forces which combined to create and maintain that concern. Migration itself is always a selective process. It appeals to the more vigorous and adventurous, and when a migratory body is urged to its adventure by social and religious idealisms or when the people choose exile for conscience' sake—they have been, by every test, outstanding in force and quality. The first two or three generations of New England immigrants were like that, unmatchedly like that. (The Huguenots are their only peers, but they were sadly sown broadcast in their exile.) By the English educational standards of the time there were the literate at the bottom and university-bred at the top. Arthur Norton believes that the majority of the twenty-one thousand of the first immigrant groups had some schooling before they left England, could read the catechism and English Bible, write in one of the twenty-eight styles then in vogue, and knew enough arithmetic to add and subtract. Three or four hundred of them had probably attended a Latin grammar school in England. There were no less than 135 university-trained men amongst them (mostly Cambridge). These men read and spoke Latin fluently. Their libraries were awesome with theological books in Latin. They were vigorous thinkers, at home in the Hebrew Old Testament and the Greek New. One man was equal to writing a treatise on church government in Latin. These gave the colony, New Haven included, "a cultural tone unique in the history of civilization." The first Bay churches had at one time fifteen pastors and teachers; thirteen were graduates of the University of Cambridge, two of Oxford.

I

The Educational Purpose of the New England Settlers

The Pilgrims came by way of Leyden, one of the most cultured cities in Europe. John Robinson and Elder Brewster had the freedom of the faculty of Leyden University. The Puritan ministers were "men of generous education and intellectual tastes." They inherited the spirit of the "New Learning" which leavened the English Reformation and continued the humanistic impulse in their new world. One must not read back into Seventeenth Century New England the perfected philosophy of a democratic society, but the leaders of the little commonwealth knew by sound instinct that "if people were to follow the dictates of conscience, that conscience must be enlightened. If people were to govern themselves in church and state, opportunity for education must be provided."[1]

They laid the foundation of a public school system which was to continue in later years across the continent and become, perhaps, the finest single aspect of American life. The vital and organic unity of the "Congregational Way" and the New England Commonwealth has also been sufficiently stressed—perhaps over-stressed—in this narrative. What New England did for education was, therefore, done by Congregationalism. The political assemblies founded public schools for the common good. The clergy led the movement and urged the founding of colleges both to secure a trained ministry and to provide for the education of leaders and teachers. The intimate relation between the early New England colleges and the Congregational churches was organic rather than official.

The famous Massachusetts Law of 1647 which applied to the settlements around Boston is generally marked as the beginning of popular

[1]There is an admirable résumé of Congregationalism and Education in the published *Proceedings of the Fourth International Congregational Council, Boston, 1920.* It is a group contribution and authoritative. This section is in its debt.

education in America. This law directed that every town of fifty dwellings should have a primary school and every town of one hundred dwellings should have a grammar school. The primary purpose of this Colonial educational system was that there should be an educated citizenry, but another important reason was that the Colonies needed learned ministers. The ministers at first were practically all trained at Oxford or Cambridge, and the people felt a great urgency to provide an educated ministry "when our present ministers lie in the dust." The churches officially did not found the college or the school system, but no one could vote except church members and the ministers were leaders in the discussions and plans for all public measures. Governor Winthrop said that what John Cotton preached in his pulpit soon found its way into the legislative acts of the General Court. The influence of the pulpit was nowhere more determinative than in the establishment of schools. The church did not dominate the school; rather, it insisted that the freedom which the church demanded for itself should likewise be enjoyed by the school, and the schools were in fact as well as in name, free schools.

II

HARVARD

They needed a college. That, amongst other things, was what they had crossed the ocean for. Winthrop had advanced the possibility of securing an uncorrupted college as one of the defensible reasons for the Plantation. "The fountains of learning and religion" (he meant Old Cambridge and Oxford) were hopelessly polluted. The Puritan rod would smite the rocks of New England and release a purer spring. Harvard College was the answer to such faith, though not itself, as the issue would prove, entirely free from earthstain.

The fascinating story of its founding need not be told in detail. Salem wanted it; Newtowne (now Cambridge) got it; private benefactions and grants from the General Court financed its beginnings. John Harvard, lately come to the colony (1637) with his young wife, gave it his library of four hundred weighty volumes, Latin, Greek and Hebrew, containing writings of Ames and Calvin, then under suspicion or interdict in England. He died in 1638 and besides his books, left the College half his fortune. His was a prophetic vision, the first of the benefactions to education which ennoble our history and a perpetuity of remembrance he could not have anticipated. For six months after his death this entry, still legible, was written into the orders of the General Court: "It is ordered that the College agreed upon formerly to be built at Cambridge shall be called Harvard College. The Committee appointed "to take order for the College at Newtowne" became in 1642 the Board of Overseers. It has continued as one of the two chief governing bodies of the University. A printed account of the College (the earliest) appeared in London in 1643, apparently written after the first Commencement (1642). It is a quaint and flowery document rehearsing every detail of organization and the Rules and Precepts. The discipline was stern, the courses and hours of study precise. And one wonders what wisdom there was in the faculty to teach them all they were expected to know.

III

YALE

The people of Connecticut also wanted a college. The founding of Yale was a project close to the hearts of the ministers. Rev. John Davenport, first pastor at New Haven, agitated for a college so continuously that dissatisfaction arose in his church. One of the reasons why he left New Haven for Boston was that the people of New Haven could not or would not proceed to the establishment of a college. His successor, Rev. James Pierpont, was more successful. He enlisted the cooperation of other ministers and a college was established first at Bramford, then at Saybrook, and finally at New Haven in 1701. Here again it cannot be said that the churches officially founded the college, although it is true that the founding fathers were clergymen. Nine of the ten trustees of the college were Congregational ministers, delegates to the Saybrook Synod which met, one might almost say, jointly with the trustees, for nine of the thirteen members of the Saybrook Synod were trustees of the college. "The meetings of these trustees at once became the most important ministerial gatherings in Connecticut."[2]

IV

THE NEED OF EDUCATED MINISTERS

As the leaders, in founding both Harvard and Yale, felt the great need of an educated ministry, so did the leaders two hundred years later in the Council of 1865 put emphasis upon the need of an educated ministry to insure the permanence of the churches and the future of religion, and the Council of 1865 adopted the following statements:

1. As it is an admitted fact that in the providence of God the high religious character, the Christian energy, the sound and intelligent patriotism, and the wide and salutary influence of New England in the past have depended to a large extent upon the existence and continuous work of an educated and devoted ministry, so it must be admitted, that in the future within New England the perpetuation and enlargement of such character and influence, and beyond New England the training of communities to a similar character and influence, depend, and will ever depend, upon the existence and continuous work of a minister in like manner devotedly pious, and generously educated.

[2] Walker, *The Creeds and Platforms of Congregationalism*, p. 206.

2. Inasmuch as the present emergency is pressing, and the condition of the West and South imperatively demands immediate attention, it is eminently desirable that our theological seminaries should provide for the education of earnest-minded and vigorous young men whose hearts are in the Lord's work, by arranging a course of instruction not requiring a previous collegiate training, in order that, with as little delay as practicable, they may engage in preaching the gospel to the many thousands who wait for it in our land.[3]

Professor Park, from the Committee on Collegiate and Theological Education, reported the following resolution:

Resolved: That in order to the raising up of an educated ministry for the supply of the churches of the new States, now becoming filled by the advancing tide of population, and to meet the large demands of those States which recent events have opened to Christian influence, it is a fundamental necessity that well-endowed and well-manned collegiate and theological institutions should be established, and that, too, in the best positions.[4]

In the first regular meeting of the Council under the new constitution at Oberlin in 1871, it was voted "that it was the duty of the pulpit systematically and thoroughly to instruct the whole people touching the indispensable necessity of Christian education, and the consequent necessity of sustaining these institutions."[5]

The Council also declared that "the distinctively Christian college still stands, as it ever has done in this land, in the front of the means God has pointed out and blessed for the production of the choicest and best Christian laborers."[6]

In harmony with this sentiment, the Council went on record as commending the American College and Education Society, approving the work and urging the churches to make regular contributions to it.

The next meeting in 1874 approved the merger of this Society with the American Education Society for the more effective development of a national plan of education.

The American Society for Educating Pious Youths for the Gospel Ministry was organized in 1815. Later there had been organized in New York City the Society for the Promotion of Collegiate and Theological Education in the West. In 1874 these two united under the name of the American College and Education Society. The Council of 1874, while not assuming responsibility for the work done by these Societies, approved the merger. The minutes of the 1877 Council show that there was considerable discussion of the granting of aid to poorly prepared students:

That, hereafter the American College and Education Society will, as a rule,

---

[3] *Minutes of the National Council, 1865,* pp. 470–471.
[4] *Minutes of the National Council, 1865,* p. 484.
[5] *Minutes of the National Council, 1871,* p. 50.
[6] *Minutes of the National Council, 1871,* p. 50.

receive upon its lists only those who are pursuing the full collegiate and theological course of study. All others will be regarded as exceptions, and, if taken
upon the list at all, each case must be considered separately and decided upon
its own merits.[7]

This is one of the earliest evidences of the Council's concern with the
administration of a society. This action was taken at the suggestion of
the Society, which in its report to the Council stated:

The action of the Directors of this Society, making it a rule, *with proper exceptions,* "to receive upon the lists only those who are pursuing the full collegiate and theological course of study," seems to be eminently wise and worthy
of the indorsement of this Council. The fact that there are exceptions must be
recognized; and we have confidence that the officers of the Society will not fail
to treat them fairly.[8]

Thus the Council, while approving the report, added its own interpretation. Back of it was a discussion of whether or not the ministry was
to be closed to men without a full college training, and the action of the
Council was a liberal interpretation of the requirements.

The Council of 1892 considered the merger of another organization
with this Society. This time it was the New West Education Commission, formed some years previously to establish free Christian schools in
that section of the country dominated by the fast-growing Mormon
Church. Its purpose appealed strongly to the sympathies and interests
of the Councils of 1880 to 1889. The union of the New West Education
Commission with the American College and Education Society, approved
by the Council of 1892, resulted in formation of the Education Society.
This Society continues its beneficent work as the Christian Education
Division of the Board of Home Missions.

During this period the denomination, through its educational agencies, and after 1892 through the Education Society, developed a program
of education; and through the Publishing Society continued to supply
the churches with books, magazines and papers of a very high quality.
The Publishing Society was administered by a board chosen by the members of that Society and, like other societies, was not subject to Council
supervision except that the Society presented a report of its work for the
commendation of the Council and recommendation to the churches.

V

THE EDUCATIONAL SURVEY COMMISSION

Interest in education, especially in Christian colleges and in ministerial education, continued; and, as mentioned above, the interest grew

[7] *Minutes of the National Council, 1877,* p. 96.
[8] *Minutes of the National Council, 1877,* pp. 32–33.

in the two years preceding the 1921 Council at Los Angeles. The cause of the unusual revival of interest in education at the 1921 meeting of the Council goes far back into history. Its immediate cause, however, was the work of a Committee on Educational Institutions appointed two years earlier by the Commission on Missions, at the request of the Congregational World Movement, which in turn was influenced by the work being done under the Interchurch World Movement. The title of this Committee later was changed to the Educational Survey Commission, and included in its membership President Henry Churchill King of Oberlin College, Chairman; Dr. Luther A. Weigle of Yale; Dr. Marion Burton, later president of Smith College and the University of Michigan; President Edward D. Eaton of Beloit College; President Donald J. Cowling of Carleton College; Rev. J. T. Stocking; and Rev. Charles F. Carter. Dr. Arthur Holt of the Education Society was appointed secretary of the Commission. Its purpose was defined "to work out the denominational policy to cover the relationship between the schools and the churches";[9] and its duty, (1) to survey the educational situation, and (2) to work out an inclusive policy.

The boards and various committees and commissions of all the denominations were thinking in large terms at this time. The Interchurch Movement had been launched for the purpose of unifying the missionary and benevolent work of churches of many denominations and financing this united work by the total benevolent giving of the millions of Protestant church people in America, and planned to include a large sum for colleges. The Budget Committee of that organization had made a preliminary study of the relationship of colleges to the churches. "This had proved to be a very knotted question," and no definite action was taken. The Congregationalists then appointed their own commission and the extended report made by this commission covers forty-six pages in the minutes of the 1921 Council and is accompanied by many statistical tables and graphs. This report clearly states what is the relationship in Congregationalism between the colleges and the churches:

1. In almost every case the colleges were brought into existence by the organized activity of the churches.

2. The church groups were the largest organized source of financial support for the colleges.

3. The churches were the recruiting centers for college students.

4. The churches were the chief consumers of the college products. Training for the ministry was a major task in the plans of the colleges.

5. The churches furnished the greater part of the personnel on the boards of control and ministers supplied a large part of the teaching force.[10]

[9] *Minutes of the National Council, 1921*, p. 126.
[10] *Minutes of the National Council, 1921*, p. 275.

VI

THE FREE COLLEGES

The colleges founded by Congregationalists were never church institutions as Oxford and Cambridge, England, were Anglican. The American denominational college was, and is, something else and dates from a later period. The control of Harvard, Yale, Dartmouth, Williams, Bowdoin, Middlebury, and Amherst (these were the first seven New England colleges in chronological order) was from the first "in the hands of a self-perpetuating Board of Trustees." They could not be controlled or reached by any ecclesiastic body nor, as the Dartmouth case finally determined, could their charters be modified without their consent or revoked by the State. The significance of this for free thought and sound scholarship cannot be overstated.

And yet these sovereign, self-governing and self-continuing corporations must have trustees, presidents, and a faculty; and all of them drew upon the Congregational ministry for leadership. That was almost automatic. Their principal concern in the early period was the training of a ministry which was, just as automatically, Congregational. Both in theory and practice they were non-sectarian; but they were rooted in Congregational soil and they perpetuated the order which created them. The result was, well into the Nineteenth Century, a predominant affiliation of Congregationalism with higher education in the United States. The older colleges trained the presidents of the newer colleges and these presidents were, until the institutional promoter or the specially trained educator displaced them (with results open to some question), ordained clergymen. No one American denomination has furnished so many distinguished college and university presidents as Congregationalism—and shining constellations of educators in addition. A confessedly Congregational historian may seem a special pleader, and probably is to a degree, when he suggests that the disciplined freedoms which have always characterized the Congregational Way are also the vital breath of any right education and that this historic relation between them is of their mutual essence.

The early northern colleges—and this includes the first women's colleges—were fortunate in situation, priority, and resource. Their resources grew with the resources of their alumni and their always mounting endowments magnified their prestige as they made possible an always widening range of educational efficiency. They proved with great satisfaction to themselves that to him that hath, it shall be given. They became, therefore, able more and more to detach themselves, not only from anything which savored of denominationalism, but from any religious affiliation. As far as Congregationalism goes, they are attended in their final phases by a tradition which begins to be only the ghost of a tradition.[11]

College founding (already noted) attended the westward extension of all denominations. All these (the colleges) were quite literally denominational and so known. They sought support for denominational reasons, appealed to denomination pride and loyalty, and in highly centralized communions were under denominational control. Their contributions to the nation have been immeasurable. They were clearings in the forests to begin with, or lonely groups of poor buildings on the prairies, but they were indwelt by the heroic and the devoted, their pathetic campuses inherited the traditions of the humanist—and the Christian missionary since Columba and Iona. They were near enough for aspiring youth everywhere to reach them; they reduced the cost of education to its bare bones and where all were poor together, all were equally rich. Their low towers were guide posts to opportunity, their doors opened upon the boundless future of America. They lived or died as fortune favored and, finally, there were too many of them. Those that won out have repeated the history of the older institutions, created loyal alumni, multiplied their resource, adorned their physical equipment and asserted in turn their independence of sectarian control.

Congregationalists carried their colleges as stepping-stones to the shores of the Pacific. The Minutes of the International Council (previously cited) lists forty-six colleges and universities whose early history was closely related to the Congregational churches. The *Year Book* for 1940 catalogues forty-four institutions, some of which are now undenominational, but all of which have had some historic relation to Congregational or Christian churches.

The Educational Survey Commission in its report to the Council of 1921 called attention to the fact that in the early years there had been no need of formal relationship between the churches and colleges, for the informal relationship was close and intimate. The college was the child of the church, to be helped but never to be dominated. Now (1921) the situation in the colleges had radically changed from the days when the churches were the chief sources of students and funds and the chief field of activity for college graduates. The colleges had become independent of the churches and had extended their work over a wide field. The same conditions which had developed years before at Harvard and Yale

[11] This is true of the older colleges which like Brown were more professedly and organically denominational. President Benjamin Andrews of Brown is reported to have said that his difficulty in getting money was to persuade Baptists that his University was Baptist and non-Baptists that it wasn't. The Carnegie Pension Fund also led Boards of Directors to plead and effectuate the non-sectarian character of their institutions.

were being reproduced at Oberlin, Grinnell, Carleton, and other colleges.

As time went on benevolent men and women other than Congregationalists began contributing largely to these institutions, which were never sectarian; it was but natural that when vacancies occurred in the boards, representatives of these non-Congregational givers should be included in the management. In the course of time, the colleges with boards of trustees on which the Congregationalists were sometimes in the minority did not consider themselves Congregational except in spirit and tradition. The churches had only the same friendly interest in the colleges that they had in other community agencies.

There were many reasons why the colleges went their own independent way. The churches were not the main recruiting grounds for the colleges. High schools and private schools furnished the best fields. The churches took but a small percentage of the graduates, and the number of courses of instruction had been greatly increased from the days when the chief work of the college was to prepare young men for the ministry.

Perhaps the most potent consideration that caused the Congregational colleges to be wary of Congregational influence was the care taken by college administrators to prove that the institution was thoroughly undenominational in its appeal for students and support. To be able to qualify for the benefits provided for the retirement of professors by annuities from national educational foundations, it was required that the applying school give evidence that it was undenominational.

Another influence was the indifference of many college teachers to the religious life of their students. In some cases the religious life of the professors themselves was not quite in harmony with the ideals of religion as held by the churches. So, while perhaps eighty per cent of the students in colleges traditionally Congregational came from religious homes, many found, in the college atmosphere and in the teachings they received, attitudes towards the church that did not strengthen their home church ties. These factors did not lead to a spirit of antagonism so much as of indifference.

Neither did the church people have a strong feeling of responsibility for the financial well-being of these institutions. The Foundation for Education discovered, when it was formed by this Council of 1921, that unless the giver felt somewhat responsible for the management of the institution his gift was apt to be only a nominal amount.

This Educational Survey Commission went into considerable detail as to the state of religion in the colleges. From a questionnaire sent to the colleges, the following results were received:

Twenty-three of our colleges were asked the question, "Do you require Christian character and influence on the part of your teachers?" Twenty-two answered, "Yes," and one answered, "Desired, but not required." The same colleges were asked the question, "Do you require, in addition, church membership?" Seven replied, "No." One replied, "Ordinarily," and the rest replied, "Yes." The same colleges were asked the question, "Do you give preference to some particular church?" Two replied "Yes," and twenty-one replied, "No."[12]

The answers to this survey indicate that the colleges were established on a broad and liberal basis. At the same time it must be recognized that support of these colleges by the churches was not strengthened by the indifference on the part of some colleges to their relationship to the churches. It was quite clear that, if the churches were to become more interested in the colleges, the colleges would need to become more interested in the churches, or at least in religion. The desired cooperation could not be a one-sided affair.

The attitude of parents towards the colleges, according to this report, was: "We do not send our children to a college just because it is Congregational." It also showed that Methodist schools were graduating quite as many young men who went to seminaries to prepare for the Congregational ministry as were Congregational colleges.

The conclusions of this carefully studied report balanced cause and effect very nicely by saying that the colleges, to win the support of the churches, must demonstrate their value to these churches by providing well-trained workers and leaders; and, on the other hand, that the churches should make use of well-trained leaders and workers.

The extensive report of the Educational Survey Commission ended with the following conclusions:

> The hope of the church for a larger number of religious workers lies in the cultivation of the colleges to which the masses of Congregational students go. . . . It should be a first charge upon the church to guarantee favorable religious conditions in the situations where the Congregational students are to be found.
> The colleges should more and more find their place in the total educational program of the church . . . and should be the source from which leadership and the training staff can come.
> . . . We should look upon our Christian colleges as training schools for religious education in the same way as the public school system now looks upon the normal schools.[13]

This report was printed and sent to the delegates in advance of the meeting of the 1921 Council. Dr. King, who had been chairman of this Survey Commission, was also the retiring Moderator. In his moderatorial address on the topic, "A National Educational Policy for the Denomination," he called attention to the underlying principles that govern the relationship of religion to education. He quoted Dr. Robert Horton's

---

[12] *Minutes of the National Council, 1921*, p. 291.
[13] *Minutes of the National Council, 1921*, pp. 300–302.

warning, "It is the unhappy delusion of the church that it knows the teaching of Jesus." Dr. King emphasized the need of church support for an educational program in order that religion might have solid foundations. He insisted that the obligation resting upon Congregationalists was not for control of the institutions of learning, but that it was their responsibility as it had been of the founders of Harvard and Yale, that there should be well-educated leadership for church and state, and that the permanence of these institutions rested not so much upon law which is necessary but in the last analysis upon the determination of the people that there should be effective, yet free, coöperation between church and college. He presented the recommendation from the Educational Survey Commission, which had been endorsed by the Commission on Missions, for the establishment of a Foundation for Education.

VII

THE FOUNDATION FOR EDUCATION

Following presentation of the report of the Educational Commission, the Council voted, after public hearings and a general discussion, to organize a new denominational agency, the Foundation for Education:

a. To promote the ideals of the churches of the Congregational fellowship through institutions of secondary and higher education which possess those ideals and share in that fellowship.

b. To make available the resources of our fellowship for the counsel and encouragement of these institutions in the realization of our common purpose.

c. To establish a permanent fund, the income of which shall be used to aid the upbuilding and maintenance of these institutions.

d. To provide an agency for the study of the educational problems of these institutions and for the administration and distribution of these funds in such ways as shall best further the common interests and ideals of these institutions and our churches, by the maintenance in these institutions of high standards of educational efficiency and moral and religious purpose.[14]

The Council further instructed the Commission on Missions to set aside seven per cent of the apportionment for the operating expenses of the Foundation for 1922 and charged the Foundation with the duty of organizing a campaign for a large sum of money to assist the colleges in their present needs and to add to the endowment of colleges traditionally of Congregational origin.

The Foundation established offices in Chicago and Dr. George W. Nash was elected president. Dr. Nash had been Commissioner of Education in South Dakota and had held other responsible positions as an educator. When the campaign got under way to secure money for these

[14] *Minutes of the National Council, 1921*, pp. 382–383.

colleges, Dr. Nash discovered how true were the findings of the Education Survey Committee as to why the churches were not manifesting the old-time interest in the financial well-being of the colleges. When the Commission on Missions set aside seven per cent for the expenses of the Foundation, it was necessary to take that percentage from the existing boards. Many of the churches felt that the financial situation which affected the colleges, while lessening their service and causing serious problems, was not so serious as the financial situation which affected some of the Boards, and that the colleges were in a better financial condition to do their work than were many of the smaller churches. Dr. Nash and his associates and later, when Dr. Nash resigned, his successor Dr. William R. Kedzie, worked faithfully to carry out the instructions of the Council; but the enthusiasm which had waxed strong at Los Angeles and had carried the denomination to this high point was not sufficient to carry the proposals into execution. Six years later the Foundation became a department of the Education Society. Later it was discontinued as a separate department, but the Education Society inherited the unfinished task for which the Foundation for Education was set up.

VIII

Development of the Education Society

Although the Foundation for Education did not succeed in its task, the interest created strengthened greatly the work of the Education Society. Two promising features of that program as it is now being carried forward are: First, the development of the Pilgrim Fellowship, which is to some extent an outgrowth of the original Society for Christian Endeavor and brings young people in the churches and in many educational institutions into closer touch with the life and work of the churches. Under this department of the Education Society a large number of summer conferences for young people are held throughout the country. Second, the development of a program of adult learning. Here is a great open field for the churches. Our own churches have been leaders in analyzing this problem and publications of the Education Society in this field are accepted by other denominations as of unusual merit. The churches have only begun to study the problem of interesting adults in a program of continued learning which will bring enjoyment and profit to multitudes of church people.

In the other departments of leadership training, the children's department and missionary education, the Education Society is carrying forward a useful work headed by consecrated individuals who are giving splendid leadership.

IX

EDUCATION IN THE CHRISTIAN CHURCHES

Concerning the interest of the Christian Churches in education, Dr. Frank G. Coffin, long President of the General Convention of the Christian Churches, wrote:

The Christian Church was from the beginning sympathetic toward education, yet feared dogma-producing institutions. Its ministry was a student ministry. The larger number were at some time school teachers who gave parttime service to the church. Most of the theological schools were of a kind they did not want; therefore, they established their own. Of these there were many. They were too small and resourceless financially to survive. As early as 1811, Rev. Barton Stone established a school at Lexington, Kentucky.

Some of the other institutions were: Rittenhouse Academy (Ky.), Wake Forest-Pleasant Grove (N.C.), Junto (N.C.), Christian Academy (N.H.), New England Manual Labor School (Mass.), New England Christian College (Mass.), Christian College, (N.Y.), Honeoye Falls School (N.Y.), Wolfborough Christian Institute, Starkey Seminary (N.Y.), Graham Institute (N.C.), Lafayette University (Ind.), Suffolk Collegiate Institute (Va.), Elon College (N.C.), Kansas Christian College, Union Christian College (Ind.), Antioch College (O.) (of which Horace Mann was president and which is said to be the first college of high rank in the United States open to students of both sexes on conditions of absolute equality), LeGrand Christian Institute (Ia.), Christian Biblical Institute (N.Y.), Weaubleau College (Mo.), Palmer College (Mo.), Defiance College (O.), Franklinton College (N.C.) for colored, Jireh College (Wyo.), Bethlehem College (Ala.), and Kirton Hall (Can.).[15]

X

THEOLOGICAL SEMINARIES

Theological Seminaries and Schools of Divinity have been more intimately associated with their denominational founders and sponsors, being established to train the ministers of their supporting communities. Ministerial training was not at first specialized in the United States. The general college courses were sufficient for Greek, Hebrew, dialectics, and, one hopes, though Edwards questions it, for professional piety. In addition a winter or two with a recognized theologian were indicated. In due course regular professorships of divinity were added to the college faculties. Andover was the first New England specifically theological school. (The Seminary at Brunswick, New Jersey antedated it.) Bangor was chartered in 1814; Yale Divinity was opened in 1822. Twelve years later Hartford Seminary was founded to correct, in the intention of its founders, lapses in New Haven orthodoxy. Oberlin and Hartford are of an age. Lane Seminary (Cincinnati) forbade its students to discuss slavery. Most

[15] Fagley, *The Congregational Churches*, pp. 132–133.

of them left that institution in a body and migrated to Oberlin on condition that Charles G. Finney be made theological instructor.

Chicago Theological Seminary was chartered in 1855, organized and controlled by the churches of the six interior states whose interests converged upon Chicago. It has shared the fortunes of that city and region and, in its affiliations with the University of Chicago and allied institutions, is now an honored member of an educational group second to none. The Congregationalists of California organized the Pacific School of Religion in 1866. Three years later it began its work. A prescient foresight located it at Berkeley, destined also to be a strategic educational center. Its buildings now crown a hill above the campus of the University of California and its western windows open upon the Golden Gate.

The Fathers and Brethren who constituted the Council of 1865 entertained bright hopes of Congregational extension in the South, but as Massachusetts Bay had discovered two hundred years earlier, that region was not hospitable to Congregational overtures. In 1901, however, conditions seemed to warrant the establishment of a Congregational theological school in the South, and Atlanta Theological Seminary was founded. It carried on valiantly but could not overcome adverse conditions. It was later moved to Nashville, Tennessee and associated with the Vanderbilt University School of Religion.

Many forces and conditions began early in the Twentieth Century to affect adversely the smaller detached theological schools which had played, for a hundred years, so necessary a part in the training of American Protestant ministers. Old stations rich in memory were surrendered and the seminaries moved in on outstanding educational centers. Andover was finally consolidated with Newton Theological Seminary after a pilgrim's progress via Harvard campus. The affiliation has met with distinguished success. It is likely that the apparatus of theological education for Congregationalism is now stabilized. The surviving institutions have accumulated endowments, housed themselves generously, continue their services, and proudly rehearse their pasts.

XI

EDUCATION THROUGH RELIGIOUS JOURNALISM

In 1896 *The Congregationalist* published an eightieth anniversary number whose remaining copies are now historical documents of great value. Contemporary religious journals recognized the significance of the issue—and the anniversary—and extended their congratulations through their editors. Denominational religious journalism was then at its peak, and the congratulatory letters, with their headings and signatures, recall a brilliant and vanished past.

There are in these letters engaging differences of opinion about the value of denominational organs, depending upon the status of the editor. William Hayes Ward generously thought that denominational journalism "if not sectarian in spirit, offers a field for beneficent influence which cannot be surpassed." Lyman Abbott, naturally, subtly qualified his appraisal of the denominational journal but thought *The Congregationalist* admirable in its catholic spirit; all of them saluted the then *Congregationalist* as, in direct succession, the senior publication.

A compact, authoritative paragraph in the 125th anniversary number of *Advance* (Dec. 1, 1941) traces the main and continuing lines of Congregational religious journalism down to date:

"When Nathaniel Willis in 1816 founded the Boston *Recorder,* he began a stream that, with other main branches and many contributing rivulets, has gone on uninterrupted to the present day, and is continued in *Advance.*

The main branches of that stream are easily distinguished. They consist of *The Recorder,* the original source, and *The Congregationalist,* founded in 1849, which came together, continuing the name *The Congregationalist,* in 1867. In that same year *The Advance* was established in Chicago, continuing as a separate stream until 1917, when it became merged with *The Congregationalist.* In 1930 *The Herald of Gospel Liberty,* which had begun in 1808, also flowed into this main stream. The unwieldiness of the use of the dual name upon which there had been insistence led to the adoption of the simple name *Advance* in 1934, and the following year the paper became the present monthly. Up to that time, however, from *The Recorder* to the *Advance* there had been a continuous flow manifested in an issue every week."

XII

The Development of *The Congregationalist*

The Congregationalist had been founded by Galen James and Edward W. Jay in 1849. There had been a growing feeling that the *Recorder* "had come to be somewhat narrow in its outlook, particularly antagonistic to what was known as the new-school theology and consequently obnoxious (strong word) to a large and increasing element of ministers and laymen." The younger men complained that the *Recorder* would not accept their contributions. "There was a strong feeling, too, that the *Recorder* was not outspoken enough against slavery." The movement for another journal "crystallized" around prominent and influential "divines," with every confidence that the denomination had "sufficient editorial and literary ability" to sustain a paper. Deacon Galen James, a retired ship-builder, underwrote the enterprise financially and the new paper appeared May 25, 1849 with an imposing editorial staff. Two years later (October 1851), Dr. H. M. Dexter's name appears as editorial contributor. What became of the some-time *Recorder's* theological conservatism is not on record. Dr. Dexter became editor-in-chief in 1867. The paper had been shrewdly managed financially, and C. A. Richardson, who would probably be called managing editor, had a flair for what the average reader wanted of a Sunday afternoon. *The Congregationalist* became a family paper. Dexter's incisive style and astounding erudition made its editorial page famous. During the peak period, Dr. A. E. Dunning who succeeded Dr. Dexter in 1889 maintained the high editorial tradition. The list of contributors during these years is awe-inspiring. Getting something accepted by *The Congregationalist* became an accolade for young writers, and getting one's picture on the cover was a ministerial D.S.O. The editors were always present in the larger denominational gatherings, and their influence was acknowledged. Altogether, those were happy days.

Dr. Howard A. Bridgeman (for thirty-five years associated with the publication) succeeded Dr. E. A. Dunning as editor-in-chief in 1911 and held that office for ten years. The paper was no longer self-supporting and became the responsibility of the Congregational Publishing Society. Dr. William E. Gilroy was made editor-in-chief after Bridgeman's resignation and, since 1922, has filled a difficult and demanding duty with wisdom and grace. A period of experimentation followed during which the official title of the old paper was so often varied that it might have been puzzled as to its own identity. In April 1934 it became the *Advance,* surrendering (one must believe sadly) its time-honored denominational designation. It is now (1942) a fifty-two-page monthly. It remains only to add that a judicious digest, with the right touch, of the issues of *The Congregationalist* from 1849 to 1934 would be a better history of Congregationalism—and many other things—for almost ninety years than any one will ever write.

XIII

The Society Magazines

The Denominational Boards, American Board of Commissioners for Foreign Missions, Home Missionary Society, and American Missionary Association had their own promotional literature. (Of these the *Missionary Herald* was oldest and most honored.) They rendered a distinct missionary and educational service, and as they have faded out of the picture, nothing since has quite taken their place. They were usually subsidized in part by the specific Boards which maintained them, and reflected in their various and somewhat uncorrelated way the want of unified control in Congregational policy.

CHAPTER XVI

The Growth of Social Concern

THE Pilgrims were essentially religious. Religion was the flag under which they marched. When they landed at Plymouth, they established their community on the basis of First Century Christianity, where each one made his best contribution to the common store.

It was soon discovered, however, that the more industrious members were being penalized because of the indifference of some to the pressing needs of the new community, and in 1623 there was a division of property among the settlers.

The temporary division of land in 1623 was, in 1624, continued until the end of the Adventurers' contract (in 1627). The plan of leaving each individual to work as he pleased, and have the proceeds, but no more, had been highly successful, even the women and children eagerly sharing the lighter field-work —a thing before unknown. The result was an abundant crop.[1]

While this first experiment in applied socialism did not succeed as a plan according to their expectations, it left the settlers with some understanding of the problems of providing for the common good.

I

SOCIAL ATTITUDES OF THE COLONISTS

Another evidence of social concern was the attitude of the settlers towards the Indians. Many and grievous wrongs have been done through the years to the Indians by the whites, but the Plymouth settlers came with high ideals of helpfulness. Yet even in the Mayflower group there were "adventurers" who did not share these ideals.

In November, 1621, just a year after the arrival of the first settlers, the "Fortune" brought thirty-five new colonists—a welcome addition—among them a son of Elder Brewster and a brother of Edward Winslow, but most of them apparently picked up by the merchant-partners in England and, as Bradford describes them, "wild enough."

In July, 1623, about sixty additions were brought to the colony by the "Anne," "some of them being very usefull persons . . . and some were so bad, as they were faine to be at charge to send them home againe ye next year." That these less desirable elements came with the better was due to the somewhat discordant aims of the partners in the Plymouth undertaking. On the one hand, the Leyden Pilgrims desired first of all the maintenance of Congregational institutions and the preservation of the moral tone of the community; on the

[1] Goodwin, *The Pilgrim Republic*, p. 258.

other hand, the merchants of London, who had furnished the chief part of the money for the adventure, cared little save for a flourishing trading colony which should yield satisfactory profits. A divergence of wishes speedily manifested itself. The Pilgrims desired to bring over their Leyden associates as speedily as possible, but bound as they were to their partners, they could not well raise the money for such an end. On the contrary, the merchant-partners preferred to send active young men, picked up where they could get them, who might make good hunters, fishers, and tillers of the soil. . . . They felt that if something could be done to minimize the Separatist characteristics of the colony it would grow more rapidly.[2]

Reference has been made to Morton who established headquarters at Merrymount where liquor and firearms were sold to the Indians. The Indians, thus wronged, wrought vengeance upon the whites indiscriminately, whereupon the Pilgrims defended themselves and inflicted heavy discipline. This brought grief to the church leaders. John Robinson, hearing of these troubles, wrote, "Oh, that you had converted some before you had killed any!" There were frequent wars between the Indians and the whites, yet many of the settlers tried to adjust the difficulties with the Indians. Efforts were also made to ameliorate the conditions of the Indians at Plymouth. The first festive Thanksgiving had the Indians as guests of honor. Roger Williams, Elliot—"The apostle to the Indians," —the Mayhews, father and son, and in later years Jonathan Edwards and many others were active in bettering relations with the Indians. But the record as a whole does not bring credit to the colonists. Later on the imprisonment of Indians and the greater wrong of selling Indian captives into slavery are among the darkest pages of Colonial history. The Puritans took the Bible as their guide and in the record of the Israelites taking the land in Palestine, killing and enslaving the natives, some of the colonists found justification of their attitude towards the Indians.

Of the colonists' relationship to the Indians, Rev. John Cotton said, "Let us be mindful in our dealing with the Indians that as we share their temporalities we share with them our spiritualities, and as we share their bread, let us share the Bread of Life with them."

The scattered settlements, forced to depend upon themselves, with means of communication so difficult, became individualistic. The Revolutionary War forced a certain amount of cooperation between the colonists, but it was grudgingly given and was withdrawn as soon as the emergency passed. The adoption of the Constitution in 1787–1789 was a hard-fought victory against individualistic attitudes. Vermont withheld its approval and was a separate republic for some years, so strong was the individualism of the people and the towns of that state. The New Englanders, however, contributed one great doctrine to social well-being

[2] Walker, *American Church History*, vol. 3, pp. 69–70.

—the essential nature of democracy, the foundation of social reconstruction. While this principle of democracy was hedged about by many restrictions and limited in its applications, still the idea grew by the continued "searching of the word of God" for fuller directions for fashioning the community under the will of God into a political state.

The town organization with its annual meeting where all citizens met to decide questions of public concern was the foundation of their social life. The town looked upon the church as part of itself, for in many cases the town had set aside land, built the meetinghouse, and provided the stipend for the minister. The church naturally felt its responsibility for the well-being of the town. There have scarcely ever been communities where the poor and needy were more carefully, though frugally, looked after, or where prices were better regulated and fair business conditions established than obtained in the New England towns under the rule of the democratic town meetings. In these town meetings church people have always taken an active part in behalf of justice and social well-being.

"It is quite certain that they copied largely in their formation of the scheme of town government from the form of church government. . . . One example is that the title 'Moderator' applied alike to the presiding officers of both town and church meeting."[3] Out of this cooperation between New England town and church grew many of our ideas of civic freedom, education, wise laws, and benevolent institutions. Hence, with this background and with perfect freedom to follow the light, the democratic polity of the Congregational churches encouraged the growth in social concern. A second fact of perhaps equal weight is that the church in New England was not an end in itself but existed for what was considered to be community well-being. It followed that the fellowship of the churches, when established, did not exist for the promotion of denominational prestige but did have for its mission the cure of injustice and the lifting of the level of the whole of life.

II

SOCIAL PIONEERS

The modern development of social concern of the churches, which was climaxed at the Oberlin Council by the establishment of the Council for Social Action, had its primary source in the life and work of Rev. Horace Bushnell (1802–1876). "Bushnell's *Christian Nurture* did more than any single factor to break down the extreme individualism of the old Puritanism."[4] He redeemed the theology of the time from a narrow,

[3]*Proceedings of the Fourth International Congregational Council, Boston, 1920,* p. 324.
[4]McGiffert, *The Rise of Modern Religious Ideas,* p. 277.

legalistic expression and broadened the concept of the place of religion in modern life. This made possible the development within Christianity of a clearer meaning of Christ's definite teachings. He criticized the individualism of the churches, emphasized the shortcomings of revivalism, and opened the field for the whole modern development of religious education. Rev. Theodore Munger, in his *Life of Bushnell,* says that Bushnell's influence "was sure to reach all forms of thought, as in time to come it will reach all forms of social life." While his lasting reputation rests on his proclamation of the need of Christian nurture, he also preached on such topics as "How to be a Christian in Trade," "The Christian Church," "The Pattern of Society," "Amusements," etc. Dr. Bushnell opened the door and there entered a young poet-pastor-preacher, Rev. Washington Gladden, whose ministry to the churches and whose moderatorship of the National Council in 1904 brought the social gospel to its first high peak and laid the foundation of the movement which made possible the formation of the Council for Social Action thirty years later.

As individualistic as the New England churches were in many aspects of their life and work, they were most active in the anti-slavery movement. Since 1790, the date of the founding of the Connecticut Anti-Slavery Society by President Stiles, through 1832, when Dr. Lyman Beecher and Dr. Leonard Bacon formed an American Anti-Slavery Society, there had been a continuous growth of sentiment against slavery. The organization of the American Missionary Association "for the propagation of a pure and free Christianity from which the sins of caste, polygamy, slave-holding, and the like shall be excluded" marked a great forward movement in behalf of freedom for the Negroes. For years the interest of many churches was centered in this anti-slavery movement. Lincoln said it was the reading of Dr. Bacon's book against slavery which gave him his foundation ideas concerning the iniquity of human slavery. The success of the anti-slavery movement gave the churches a feeling of great confidence in their power to lead in righting civil wrongs.[5]

Rev. Horace Bushnell's writings and the stirring of the "New England conscience" in connection with the successful anti-slavery movement slowly led to concern about social injustice in other fields. Dr. Gladden and his associates knew of the privations and abuse heaped upon early leaders of the anti-slavery movement, and they knew the price they would have to pay as pioneers in the field of social justice. Dr. Gladden was opposed, ridiculed, threatened, driven out of more than one position, but to the end of his life he remained deeply Christian and a lovable per-

[5] See "The Congregational Conscience and Slavery," *Proceedings of the Fourth International Congregational Council, Boston, 1920,* pp. 328–330.

son, surrounded by an ever-increasing group of loyal men and women dedicated to the high interpretation of true Christian teachings. Dr. Gladden and his associates were called "rampageous preachers," as if such a characterization answered their cry. Dr. Gladden was conscious that the social movement born in the anti-slavery agitation must go forward. He said "now that slavery is out of the way, the questions that concern our free laborers are coming forward; and no intelligent man needs to be admonished of their urgency. They are not only questions of economy, they are in a large sense moral questions; nay, they touch the very marrow of that religion of good-will of which Christ was the founder. It is plain that the pulpit must have something to say about them."[6]

Dr. Gladden, the pioneer in this field of social concern, was strongly supported by Rev. Theodore Munger, pastor of the Center Church, New Haven, who emphasized that the new theology "holds that every man must live a life of his own . . . and give an account of himself to God; but it also turns our attention to the corporate life of man here in the world. . . . Hence, its ethical emphasis . . . holding that human society itself is to be redeemed."[7] Munger asserted that you cannot isolate the individual from society but that the state, family, commerce and all other phases of man's activity were "areas wherein God manifests himself."[8]

Another supporter of this gospel was Rev. Richard S. Storrs, for many years pastor of the Church of the Pilgrims, Brooklyn. Storrs attributed the abolition of slavery to the influence of the Sermon on the Mount, the ideals of the fatherhood of God and the brotherhood of disciples, and the Christian conceptions of mutual duty and common immortality. These were the beginnings of a true social gospel. Christianity had always attacked the problem of reform from within the individual. This gospel, if preached in its fullness, would nevertheless in time produce a far better society which would be just and harmonious.[9]

Another influential worker for the social gospel was Rev. Amory Bradford, pastor of the First Church of Montclair, New Jersey, and Moderator of the Council of 1901. He urged that "whatever the inheritance, it may be changed by good environment; Christianity must, therefore, provide helpful surroundings as well as correct doctrines for those it would aid." Dr. Bradford conducted a survey to discover how close was the relationship between the working man and the church. The results of this inquiry were published in *The Christian Union* and may be summarized:

To the first question, "How large a proportion of the artisan classes in your

[6] Gladden, *Working People and Their Employers*, p. 3.
[7] Munger, *The Freedom of Faith*, p. 25.
[8] Munger, *The Freedom of Faith*, p. 25
[9] Storrs, *The Divine Origin of Christianity*, p. 151.

region are regular attendants at any church?", the answer was for Protestants, a range of one-half per cent to ten per cent. Answers to the second query concerning church attendance indicated that such attendance was decreasing in all cases but one. The third question as to whether non-attendance was caused chiefly by "unbelief in Christianity as taught by Christ," the response was a unanimous "No." But "unbelief in Christianity as practiced by the churches" was given as a significant cause, along with the statement that "ministers of the gospel do not practice what they preach," and "Christians do not possess what they profess, or at least manifest it in their lives and conduct."[10]

About this time, Rev. Lyman Abbott who had succeeded Rev. Henry Ward Beecher as pastor of the Plymouth Church, Brooklyn, and who was a widely known editor, brought his great power to bear in behalf of a better understanding of the working man's problems, saying that if he were a working man, most assuredly he would be a member of a union. His attitude may be summed up in these words: "The object of Christianity is human welfare; its method is character-building; its process is evolution; and the secret of its power is God."[11]

Dr. George A. Gordon, pastor of the Old South Church, Boston, added his voice to the discussion of this problem, asserting that "above and beyond history, God dwells in the processes of human society, giving man his ideals and sending the race to its highest achievements."[12]

Dr. Newman Smyth, pastor of the Center Church, New Haven, was defining Christianity as "the unfolding and application to human life in all its spheres and relations of the divinely human ideal which has been historically given to Christ."[13]

The development in social responsibility was largely outside official church organization. It is surprising how little emerges in the records of the early Councils. Those meetings were concerned primarily with the inner life of the church, its polity and its extension. While it is true that temperance and prison reform both received a fair amount of attention in the early Councils, it was not until the Council of 1889, at Worcester. Massachusetts, that the theme of social concern appears on the Council program. This was in an address by Dr. Washington Gladden on the topic, "Christian Socialism." He opened his address with the question: "Is Christianity in any sense socialistic?" He answered in part by saying: "It begins to be clear that Christianity is not individualism. The Christian religion has encountered no deadlier foe during the last century than that individualistic philosophy which underlies the competitive

[10] Bradford, "Why the Artisan Classes Neglect the Church," *The Christian Union,* 7/2–9/85.
[11] Abbott, "What Is Christianity?" *Arena,* 1891, 3:46.
[12] Gordon, "The Theological Problem for Today," chap. 4 in *The New Puritanism,* pp. 156–157.
[13] Smyth, *Christian Ethics,* p. 57.

This address surveyed the whole field of the church's responsi-
r community life and for the welfare of the state. He was insistent
ᴧ social rebuilding "we must not only mean well, we must know
It is not enough that our hearts are right; our heads must be clear
ᴧ our methods wise." [15]

During the next biennium little attention was given to the specific
problems that were perplexing the people. There were, however, certain
ventures by individual churches and pastors. The churches became interested in the immigrant problem, which was intensified by the rapidly
increasing number of foreigners in America. This was partly due to the
influence of Rev. Henry A. Schauffler, whose name and influence is perpetuated in Schauffler College in Cleveland.

When the committee was preparing for the Council meeting in Minneapolis in 1892 it ignored all public questions, and the report is significant for its brevity: "No papers appointed to be read." It was not because
there were no social questions pressing for answer, but rather that the
leaders hesitated to enter so complicated a situation. The country at large
was deeply concerned about the growing tensions in industry and the
church was reluctantly coming to the conclusion that religious interests
were involved. Everyone had been shocked by the Homestead (Illinois)
strikes which terminated while the Council was in session at Minneapolis.
The first official action in the field of social concern by the Council was
taken at this meeting—the appointment of a Committee of Five on Capital and Labor to report in 1895.

This first committee was composed of Rev. Washington Gladden, of
Ohio, chairman; Rev. Henry Hopkins of Missouri, Rev. John L. Scudder
of New Jersey, President David Starr Jordan of California, Rev. Robert
Newell of North Dakota. When the Council of 1895 met at Syracuse, Dr.
Gladden presented the report, a document of great historic value which
could be read today with profit by church people. The Committee affirmed that:

A society which cannot settle rates of wages and terms of work between employers and employed without constant resort to the sword is in a perilous condition. . . . The Christian Church is not required to take either side of this
quarrel. Manifestly, the right is not all on one side. . . . The Church is called
to bear one clear word of testimony. It must declare and proclaim that all this
bitter strife, which constantly tends to break out in acts of violence, is needless
and wicked; and that some way must be found of putting an end to it. The
Church may lack the power to solve economic problems, but it knows that the
kingdom which it is here to establish is a kingdom of peace and good-will. . . .
It will be seen that the solution of the labor problem here suggested consists,

14 *Minutes of the National Council, 1889,* p. 338.
15 *Minutes of the National Council, 1889,* p. 351.

fundamentally, in the recognition of the Christian law as the law of business, and the regulation of all our industrial life by Christian principles. It is, therefore, a solution which begins with the motives and purposes of men; which must spring from new ideas of business and new standards of conduct.[16]

The report was well received, but as the country was enjoying a lull in labor controversy, no action was taken except the reappointment of the Committee on Capital and Labor. At this Council Rev. Joseph H. Twichell of Hartford presented a paper on "The National Council and Civil Liberty," which introduced this subject into the discussions of the Council. In the course of his remarks, Dr. Twichell was asked to be more specific, whereupon he replied in a phrase which has since been widely quoted: "I am referring to those to whom I allude."

By the time the next Council met in 1898, business conditions had become so critical because of the depression that employers could hardly keep factories and mills going, and working men accepted employment under any conditions. There was not even a report by the Committee on Capital and Labor, which may have been due to Dr. Gladden's absence. But this silence was not to continue, for by the next Council in 1901 at Portland, Maine, the Massachusetts Conference sent a memorial that a Committee on Labor be appointed, and Rev. Frank W. Merrick of Massachusetts, Rev. Washington Gladden of Ohio, Rev. William J. Tucker of New Hampshire, Rev. David N. Beach of Colorado, Rev. William A. Knight, of Massachusetts, were appointed by the Council as the Labor Committee.

The Council meeting in 1904 in Des Moines witnessed a significant upsurge in social concern. Following are excerpts from the report of the Labor Committee: "Apparently unionism is something more than that valuable phase of present-day industry, collective bargaining, for unionism stands for the introduction of democracy into industry, the right of representation in the conduct of business."[17]

Your committee has a two-fold conviction out of which issues an inference vital to the spiritual problem of our churches: First, that this question has come to stay; that it cannot be blinked or waved aside, that no amount of religious activity or of practical religious helpfulness can solve it; that nothing short of justice—justice by and justice to capital and labor alike—can reach the case. But on the other hand, and second, that only by the principles of the Gospel— its ethics, its love, its law of respect for every human soul as a son of God, and a brother of Jesus Christ, and its foundation stone of sacrifice—can the ends properly sought by all true employers and workers be attained. In these circumstances, since hearts must be reached and the inmost man changed in order to supply any adequate motive for all this, one crowning inference follows,

[16] *Minutes of the National Council, 1895,* pp. 147, 148, 159.
[17] *Minutes of the National Council, 1904,* p. 417.

namely, that the present industrial-economic crisis constitutes a supreme motive for that fundamental revival of religion in all our churches for which the hearts of our people are looking, and longing, and praying.[18]

The Council adopted the recommendations of this Committee:

Whereas, the industrial problem has been given fitting place on the program of this Council, and deep interest therein shown by the public response to the sectional meetings provided, and

Whereas, the local Trades and Labor Assembly courteously invited the members of this Council to its meeting on Sunday afternoon last, and provided a rare occasion in inviting Professor Graham Taylor to address it, and also in giving free opportunity for question and conference,

Resolved, that this Council thank the local Trades and Labor Assembly for its courtesy, and recognize in this mutual interchange of opinion and purpose, and in the formal proceedings of these meetings, evidence of the existence of a social, religious spirit prophetic of a better day both for labor and the church.[19]

At this Council the plan of presenting controversial questions through speakers representing different points of view was introduced. Dr. Graham Taylor of Chicago, Mr. E. E. Clark of the Railroad Brotherhood, Mr. A. L. Ulrich, and Judge Henry M. Beardsley of Kansas City, later Moderator of the Council, presented various aspects of the labor problem.

In the opening years of the Twentieth Century a whole group of new leaders came forward. Among these was Dr. Graham Taylor whose address, "The Church in Social Reforms," given before the International Council in Boston in 1920, was an analysis of the present and a chart for the future in social building. About this time there came a second *Uncle Tom's Cabin* in the world-circulating *In His Steps,* written by Dr. Charles M. Sheldon, pastor of the Central Congregational Church in Topeka. This book has been criticized because it did not carry an adequate scholastic philosophy, but the readers of the more than thirteen million copies were aroused by the injustices in the industrial world in the same way that the emotions of mankind had been aroused by the injustices of human slavery. The conditions against which Dr. Sheldon wrote were complicated and he did not pose as a social engineer, but he saw clearly and felt deeply the social wrongs and shared this concern with his readers.

Other activities which evidence the rising social interest of the churches was the establishment by Chicago Theological Seminary of a chair in Christian Sociology in 1892. Before this there had been a course in Social Ethics and Sociology in Andover Seminary since 1887; and a course in Sociology had been a requirement at Hartford Seminary since 1880. The Chicago Seminary established a Department of Social Training in 1890 under the direction of Dr. Graham Taylor, who had been a pastor at

[18] *Minutes of the National Council, 1904,* p. 420.
[19] *Minutes of the National Council, 1904,* pp. 540–541.

Hartford, Connecticut and a professor in Hartford Seminary. Yale Divinity School at the same time established a distinct professorship in Social Ethics.[20]

Another evidence of growing interest was the establishment by Congregational agencies of three social centers. St. George's Church in New York (Episcopal) had established a social center on the East Side of New York City. The second social center founded in the United States, however, was the South End House of Boston (first known as Andover House) which began its work under Congregational auspices in 1892. Following this was the organization of the Chicago Commons by Dr. Graham Taylor.

The American Missionary Association, the Home Missionary Society, and the American Board were continually sending out literature and speakers preaching the Christian's responsibility for social conditions at home and abroad. These agencies placed great emphasis on the need of changing the social conditions of the masses. As the churches became interested in providing right living conditions in the foreign mission field and for Negroes, Indians, and immigrants at home, they naturally became interested in social conditions in their local communities. It was often easier, however, to interest a church in a slum condition in Bombay than in its own city.

The schools and colleges also aided in the development of better understanding. Of the leaders of this group no one was more influential than Dr. Henry Churchill King, whose interest in social welfare paralleled his interest in education, already noted in Chapter III. Dr. King's books, *The Ethics of Jesus* and *The Moral and Religious Challenge of Our Times* were supported by the writings and work of Dr. Edward S. Parsons, long president of Colorado College.

The move toward social concern, although originating in the churches, extended far and was taken up so enthusiastically by many secular organizations that it appeared to some that social rebuilding had outgrown its original religious impulse and was becoming theoretical, and that the leaders in social planning were becoming technical. This tendency was noticed and the workers were called to order sharply by Dr. Graham Taylor in his epoch-making book, *Religion in Social Action*. Its thesis is that social action, to be soundly established, must be a true manifestation of religion. Dr. Taylor rightly calls attention to the lack of permanent results when social action is based only on humanitarian impulses and emphasizes the place of religion in all social planning.[21]

---

[20] "The New Theology and Social Ethics," *Proceedings of the Fourth International Congregational Council, Boston, 1920*, p. 332.
[21] *Minutes of the National Council, 1904*, Dr. Taylor's address, pp. 87–99.

III

THE SOCIAL CRISIS

The Council of 1907 at Cleveland was made memorable by the moderatorial address by Dr. Gladden on "The Church and the Social Crisis." Dr. Gladden referred to the "swift and tumultuous" times in which "our faiths, our philosophies, our social conventions, our political and industrial institutions, are tossed upon its plunging flood." He continued:

It is idle, it is fatuous, to hide from ourselves the fact that we are facing, here in the United States of America, a social crisis. . . . The tendencies which have been gathering strength since the Civil War—the tendencies to the accumulation of power in the hands of a few; the tendencies to use this power predaceously; the tendencies to boundless luxury and extravagance; the tendencies to the separation and the antagonism of social classes—must be arrested and that speedily, or we shall soon be in chaos. . . . These swollen fortunes that many are gloating over are symptoms of disease; the bigger they are, the deadlier. They are not the reward of social service; they are the fruit of plunder. We have made them possible only by permitting the gate of opportunity to be made narrower and the burden of toil more unrequiting for millions of the poor. They exist only because by our acts we approve or by our indifference we consent to monumental injustice.

A society which tolerates such conditions cannot live. . . . Ever since we got rid of absolutism and feudalism and paternalism we have been trying to build our civilization on the basis of moral individualism . . . self-interest has been recognized as the regulative principle of the social organism. . . . Instead of its being true that democracy will transfigure egoism, we have found that no form of society can march hellward faster than a democracy under the banner of unbridled individualism. . . . Such was the challenge of Jesus Christ to the social order which he found existing, which was, in its fundamental principles, the same social order that exists today. . . . He condemned it as radically wrong; he called for its reconstruction upon a ruling idea which would *change the direction of human conduct* . . . the Church of Jesus Christ is called to replace this principle of selfishness and strife with the principle of good-will and service. It is called to organize industrial and civil society on Christian principles. This is its business in the world, a business too long neglected. . . . The thing which we have most to fear is . . . disintegration of life. The sentiment which we most need to cultivate is not suspicion of encroachments on our liberty, it is rather a sense of our solidarity, an enthusiasm for the interests that are common to all.[22]

Dr. Gladden's address has been frequently quoted in the church and in secular books and papers as embodying a sound basis for Christian rebuilding. Dr. Gladden said, speaking of workers' societies, "They have a perfect right to deliberate together concerning the wages they are receiving, and to unite in refusing to work unless their wages are increased. The law gives to capital an immense advantage in permitting its consolidation in great centralized corporations and neither law nor justice can forbid laborers to combine."[23]

[22]*Minutes of the National Council, 1907*, pp. 1–21.
[23]Gladden, *Working People and Their Employers*, pp. 137–138.

This Council of 1907 voted for the appointment of an industrial secretary on the recommendation of the Industrial Committee. The vote was "that we approve the recommendation of the Industrial Committee that an Industrial Secretary be appointed, and that the necessary steps, appointee, support, etc., be left to the Executive Committee of the Congregational Home Missionary Society in cooperation with the Provisional Committee of the National Council."[24]

In January, 1909, the board of directors of the Home Missionary Society voted that it was "an utter impossibility under present conditions to contemplate the engagement of an industrial secretary." The Industrial Committee then requested the Provisional Committee to appropriate money to secure a secretary, but the "Provisional Committee by vote declined to comply with this request, both on account of lack of funds to appropriate for such a purpose, and on account of setting the precedent other committees of the Council would demand to have followed."[25]

While this proposal was not carried into effect in the way the Industrial Committee had proposed, its main object was accomplished by the development of the Brotherhood Movement, initiated in the Congregational churches by a group of business men and ministers in Chicago.

The Council was requested to recognize this Movement and to provide it with a secretary. The Council approved the project and left it to its promoters to secure the necessary funds. The Brotherhood Movement, thus approved, had difficulty in securing finances. When the Council met in 1910, a report was made that the proposal for a labor secretary had been referred to the Home Missionary Society with a suggestion that the Society accept this responsibility for the welfare of the churches and that the Society found this "utterly impossible." The Brotherhood Committee had a secretary but no funds for promoting its program, while the Industrial Committee marked time because of its inability to finance a labor secretary. Dr. Henry A. Atkinson, now secretary of the Church Peace Union, was elected as the Brotherhood secretary. He had great interest in social concern. Hence, at the 1913 Council the Brotherhood Movement virtually absorbed the program of the Social Service Committee, and the two movements were merged with Dr. Atkinson as the general secretary.

The Brotherhood Committee gave a report of its activities since the Council of 1910. This report is significant as the first venture of the Congregational Churches to carry into action the social ideals that had been slowly developing:

The Brotherhood has become the instrument for the development of the

[24]*Minutes of the National Council, 1907,* p. 407.
[25]*Minutes of the National Council, 1910,* p. 230.

service of our churches, both in their direct relation to the claims of the social forces of the day, and in their cooperative relation to the kindred agencies of other Christian bodies. The rising tide of the social consciousness, the truer conception of the church's obligation, the abounding opportunities for social service and the reflex influence of social evangelism upon the life of the church itself, all combine to give largest significance to this department of the Brotherhood service. In social service the field of the Brotherhood's activity is growing continually. Its objective here is:

1. To know the principles of social Christianity.

2. To arouse the spirit of social service in our churches.

3. To secure the cooperation of our churches with all other agencies doing social service work.

4. To outline programs for our churches in their work for community betterment.

5. To interpret the gospel of Jesus Christ and the new purpose of the church to industrial workers.

6. To represent the denomination in official capacity at all meetings where labor and social service subjects are discussed.[26]

The Brotherhood Committee, led by Dr. Atkinson, established an office in Chicago and wrestled with the perennial question of finance. It was proposed that the National Council raise one half of the budget of $6,000, and that the boards be asked to contribute the other half; one half of the membership of the Commission to be appointed by the Council and the other half by the boards. The boards vetoed the proposition and the Council was left to finance the Social Service and Men's Work Commission.

Dr. Hubert C. Herring, who had been elected Secretary at this (1913) Council meeting and who had received encouragement by the Council for an enlarging denominational program, proposed that one-half the cost of the project be borne by the Council budget, provided the other half be raised by subscription. Dr. Atkinson's office was moved to the National Council office at Boston and again the difficulty of financing denominational activities outside of the regular missionary giving of the churches proved too difficult. Dr. Atkinson assisted for a year in various denominational activities of the Council. For the year 1914 he supervised the editing of the *Year Book*.

Meanwhile, the interest of the churches in their relationship to problems of community and national life was growing, although most of the denominational leaders and board officials felt these problems were too controversial for the established agencies to become too closely related to them. The plan to organize the Social Service Department under the National Council office having proved impossible, the Education Society, after considerable hesitancy, organized a special Department of Social

[26] *Minutes of the National Council, 1913*, pp. 235, 241, 242.

Service and in 1915 Dr. Atkinson was transferred to the staff of the Education Society to develop a social program within that structure and under the official sanction of an organized denominational board.

This historic move was made possible because the World War was placing new and unexpected social responsibilities upon the churches, requiring an agency through which they could cooperate. The national Fosdick Commission was relating camp communities to army life and was concerned with other aspects of social and religious work for the soldiers. Dr. Atkinson was loaned to this Commission and became the connecting link between the Congregational churches, the Fosdick Commission, and other agencies dealing with national issues.

The war and its problems shook the churches out of their complacency. Action by the churches in social concern usually follows a period of confusion. They are seldom ready to initiate a program of social amelioration until the community, local or national, reaches a critical condition. Then the churches are aroused sufficiently to overcome their traditional individualistic temperament. Through the years before the World War the churches had gradually opened their doors to such men as Washington Gladden, Graham Taylor, and Judge Henry M. Beardsley; but the problem of how to wield mass influence in behalf of measures and ideals that are universally approved by prophetic individuals has not yet been solved by the democratically organized churches.

At the close of the war Dr. Atkinson was elected General Secretary of the Church Peace Union and of the World Alliance for International Friendship through the Churches. Dr. Arthur E. Holt, who had had a distinguished career as pastor and leader in social concern, was elected social service secretary of the Education Society. Under Dr. Holt, the department proposed to the churches an educational program of social emphasis. The churches' next high peak of corporate activity in social concern was adoption by the 1921 Council of a statement in regard to social and industrial questions, which contained these principles:

We believe in the application of the gospel to all the affairs of men. We realize both the need and difficulty of clearly defining the principles of Christ in terms applicable to the vexed and complicated conditions of today. Therefore, we urge upon the ministers and churches of our order the careful and earnest study of social and industrial questions that the church may attain effective leadership in teaching through its clergy and in action through its laymen.

To this end we commend the suggestions and provisions made by our Social Service Commission.

We record our conviction that in the contest between labor and capital, wherever either party is striving for a position from which to dictate terms to the other, such effort is contrary to the spirit of Christ. A victory for either side carries defeat for humanity and a perpetuation of strife. An industrial order pervaded by the sense of brotherhood must be achieved.

We look with favor and hope to those instances happily increasing in number where the principle of representation is being introduced into the conduct of business affairs, whether by the method of dealing with unions, by shop councils or other systems of organization. We believe that the human status must be recognized as the essential factor in the problem. Our confidence of progress is based on God working in our midst and in the integrity of human nature ever responding increasingly to his spirit.[27]

Dr. Holt resigned in 1924 to become professor of Social Ethics in Chicago Theological Seminary, and Rev. Hubert C. Herring, Jr., who had been pastor of the United Congregational Church in Wichita, Kansas, and like his father had a broad interest in all phases of social concern, was elected social service secretary. Through Mr. Herring's pioneering work, the social service department enlarged its education program to include not only interest in industrial affairs, but also gradually developed a program of social activity which included interracial as well as international relations.

The 1925 Council meeting in Washington adopted on recommendation of the Commission on Social Service, a Statement of Social Ideals. There was considerable debate and several amendments made to the original report. But with the exception of the vote of Section II of the report, there were no negative votes registered. The preamble of the Statement is:

We believe in making the social and spiritual ideals of Jesus our test for community as well as for individual life; in strengthening and deepening the inner personal relationship of the individual with God, and recognizing his obligation and duty to society. This is crystallized in the two commandments of Jesus: "Love thy God and love thy neighbor." We believe this pattern ideal for a Christian social order involves the recognition of the sacredness of life, the supreme worth of each single personality and our common membership in one another—the brotherhood of all. In short, it means creative activity in cooperation with our fellow human beings, and with God, in the everyday life of society and in the development of a new and better world social order.

Then followed sections on Education, Industry and Economic Relations, Agriculture, Racial Relations and International Relations.

IV

THE COUNCIL FOR SOCIAL ACTION

In the years previous to the Oberlin Council in 1934, interest in social subjects continued to increase rapidly. The movement began officially with Dr. Gladden's address at the Worcester Council in 1889 and reached a high point of interest in the Council of 1901. It had progressed in 1913 with the calling of the first secretary; in 1921 and in 1925 with the adoption of the two statements of social ideals. Now it came to its peak in the establishment of the Council for Social Action at Oberlin in 1934.

[27] *Minutes of the National Council, 1921*, pp. 393–394.

Preceding the Oberlin Council, much attention had been given to the churches' relationship to various social problems. It was the general opinion that while the four commissions working in the social field under the Council evidenced and stimulated an interest they did not create a unified program. Also, the department of social service, functioning as a part of the Education Society, felt that its activity was unduly restricted and that the program should include more than the educational aspect since it should also provide the churches with active leadership in social amelioration. The board of the Education Society was selected not on the basis of special interest in social concern, but rather for the knowledge of and interest in the religious educational program of the churches. It was urged that the interest in social concern had become so keen that to give the program the attention it deserved required the full time and thought of a group free from other responsibilities.

The plan to set up a Council for Social Action was presented to the General Council at its Oberlin meeting, the members to be elected by the General Council on the nomination of its nominating committee and the Council for Social Action to take its place as one of the denominational agencies supported by the apportionment. Dr. Carl Patton, the retiring Moderator, in his address at the opening session of the Council, gave a masterly analysis of the ills of society, saying that the "question is, from top to bottom, a religious question. The trouble with war, and cutthroat competition, and long hours, and low wages, and child labor, and privileges and exploitation and widespread poverty is not merely that they leave people hungry and cold, but that they leave them angry, disillusioned, and bitter. They make it easy to hate mankind and hard to believe in the goodness of God."[28]

Some of the more conservative members of the General Council were fearful lest the enthusiasm of the leaders of the Council for Social Action would embarrass the churches in their own communities. The Council proposed to pioneer in the study and analysis of the points of social tension. It was granted that these points of tension existed in church groups as well as outside the church; and that equally sincere men, while holding fast to the purpose of religion to lift the whole level of life, yet differed radically as to means and methods to be used to reach these ends.

There was no disposition to urge the General Council to take hasty action. Hearings were held day after day. All realized that the Council was making history. Not since 1810, when the Massachusetts Association of Ministers voted to approve the organization of a Board of Foreign Missions and thus give denominational standing to the agency which was to become the American Board of Commissioners for Foreign Missions,

[28] *Minutes of the General Council, 1934*, p. 136.

had the churches been asked to give official sanction to the organization of a denominational agency of such importance.

One act of the Council, not sponsored by the group working for the Council for Social Action but a natural result of the discussions held at Oberlin, was the introduction by a delegate of a "non-profit motive" resolution. Most of those who had worked for the formation of the Council for Social Action had taken no public position on the "profit motive" in industry and were no little embarrassed by the passage of this resolution. The Oberlin Council had 764 voting delegates. The resolution was introduced during a "thin house" and came to a vote when most of the leaders in the formation of the Council for Social Action were absent from the hall. It was adopted by a vote of 130 to 17. Not more than one-fourth of the voting membership of the Council expressed themselves on the subject. The vote was taken in the midst of routine business and other resolutions and its implications were not immediately grasped. It was the one thing seized upon by the newspapers for publicity and as it was passed by the same Council which had set up the Council for Social Action, it was taken by the public as evidence that the new Council for Social Action was prepared to pontificate on controversial subjects and to work for the revolutionary resolution.

The full weight of the burden placed upon those advocating social education by the passage of the "non-profit motive" resolution was not fully sensed until the Council had adjourned. In spite of all that could be done for the next three years to explain the origin of this resolution, and the conditions under which it had been passed, it injured not only the standing of the Council for Social Action but prejudiced many sincere laymen towards the denominational agencies as a whole, and the work of the Council for Social Action was greatly handicapped.

The historic vote at Oberlin, establishing the Council for Social Action, stated:

Stirred by the deep need of humanity for justice, security, and spiritual freedom and growth, aware of the urgent demand within our churches for action to match our gospel, and clearly persuaded that the Gospel of Jesus can be the solvent of social as of all other problems, we hereby vote:

"That the General Council create the Council for Social Action of the Congregational and Christian Churches of the United States of America.

"That the purposes of this Council for Social Action shall be to help the churches to make the Christian gospel more effective in society, national and world-wide, through research, education, and action, in cooperation with the Home and Foreign Boards, Conferences and Associations, and local churches. It is proposed that the Council shall increasingly cooperate with the Federal Council of Churches in the creation of a program which shall be genuinely interdenominational. In its research, the Council will aim to be impartial, its only bias being that of the Christian view of life; its educational efforts will be directed primarily toward the local churches but will also envisage the cultivation of public opinion; in action, the Council may, on occasion, intercede directly in specific situations. . . .

"That in launching this Council for Social Action we envisage a new kind of churchmanship which, enlisting the volunteer services of a group of eighteen outstanding men and women of social vision, wisdom, and Christian purpose, and commanding the services of five or six strong leaders in the fields of international relations, race relations and economic statesmanship, will carry the campaign of education and action based on careful research out among our entire constituency at home and abroad. Believing that the church will find itself as it loses itself in the struggle to achieve a warless, just, and brotherly world, we launch this venture, dedicating ourselves to unremitting work for a day in which all men find peace, security and abundant life."

Oberlin, which had seen the formation of a National Council in 1871, and had been a center of social interest from the days of its founding, witnessed also this outstanding development of social interest in the churches.

The General Council, in setting up the Council for Social Action, went beyond the churches' existing interest in social problems. It was not so much the outcome of a unanimous demand from the churches as of the keen interest and deep concern of a very devoted minority. The General Council voted that it should be included in the apportionment at a figure which would yield a sum sufficient for a modest budget. Here again the unfortunate "non-profit motive" resolution and the fact that the churches had not reached a level of social concern equal to its program led to discrimination against the Council for Social Action by many churches and by individual givers. The financing of the organization was a difficult problem from the start. As the churches have awakened to the necessity for the kind of work the Council for Social Action is doing, the financial problems tend to become less acute, being no more serious, relatively speaking, than those of the older boards, all under the pressure of lowered income.

In the 1934 Council, it was provided that the Council for Social Action should have a quasi-administrative relationship to the Board of Home Missions and that the apportionment percentage assigned to the Council for Social Action should be listed in the *Year Book* under the total receipts of the Home Board work.

Since 1934 the structural relationship of the Council for Social Action to the total denominational program has been that of an autonomous agency functioning as an integral part of the Missions Council. In the seven years since the founding of the Council, it has developed its program, overcome many objections, and won many friends.

What happened in this group has been demonstrated again and again —that opposition has been changed to tolerance, and, in many instances, tolerance has given place to cooperation. The change in attitude towards the Council is traceable in part to a widespread use of *Social Action,* a very effective magazine published monthly and dealing in a broad Christian way with many aspects of social concern, thus enlarging the Council's sphere of usefulness.

In 1939 Mr. Herring resigned as director of the Council and Rev. Dwight J. Bradley, professor of Social Ethics at Andover Newton Theological Seminary and pastor of Union Church in Boston, was elected director. At the 1940 Council meeting in Berkeley, the Council for Social Action was given the added responsibility of sharing in the denomination's effort in the aid of war victims.

The purpose and program of the Council for Social Action as it faces the world today may be summed up in the words of Rev. Alfred Wilson Swan, president of the Council:

"The central imagery of the Church is of special assistance in illuminating the pattern of our economic life. The Body broken and the Blood shed, that we might have life—that is the eternal symbol. But now, what is money, if it is not a negotiable symbol of personality? The dollar in my hand is someone's sweat and blood. The shirt I wear was stitched by someone's patience; the food I eat produced for me by someone's body bent. In every exchange of goods and services a sacrament takes place.

"The exchange counter is the realistic communion table of our common life. On it our bodies are broken and our blood is shed for one another. If this exchange be forced by violence, it is no better than any other form of paganism. But if in this daily transaction a mutual and voluntary sacrifice be recognized and acknowledged, all life becomes illuminated with a sacrament, as it here speaks to us with the eloquence of a universal tongue. And it is to apply the sacramental grace at precisely that point where the mind of the age is most confused and the hearts of men are most sore.

"It is the faith of the Church that sacrament saves, in its recognition of a common bond, and that it does so by realistically transforming life, in either its individual or its corporate appearances. In this confidence the Church holds this imagery before itself and before the world as a true representation of the nature of the economic process. When it is so seen, men may sit at the Table of Life, where each shall eat and all be filled, and none go hungry away."[29]

[29] Fagley (editor), *The Gospel, the Church and Society: Congregationalism Today,* p. 167.

CHAPTER XVII

Evangelism and Worship

T HE Congregational churches grew out of a movement at heart evangelistic. The early leaders broke away from institutional religion as represented in the established church and conditioned full participation in the life and work of this fellowship on the individual's personal relationship to God. To the early Separatists and Puritans this relationship was so all-engrossing, so satisfying, that it did not need the support of any national institution or the authority of another human being.

It was no easy matter for a person to maintain a place in the fellowship. From day to day the "elect" went their way towards God through all discouragements and bafflements and had ever in mind Bunyan's pilgrim, whose chief purpose in life was to win his soul's salvation.

They believed there were great spiritual values in fellowship and that Christ was present in their meetings, imparting to each one the measure of help needed. The basis of their fellowship was the covenant and those so covenanted formed the church. They were convinced that the way to salvation, while based on the individual's personal relationship to God, was to be found in the fellowship of covenanted believers. They were ever mindful that their lives should be under severe discipline and, as they disciplined themselves, so they disciplined their children. Seldom in history has family life been so filled with religious teaching and practice as was that of the early Congregationalists.

When it came to reaching those outside the church, they suffered from the difficulties of their theological assumptions. They were Calvinists and believed that God in his own time and in his own way would speak to the unconverted. It was the responsibility of Christians to show the fruit of their religion in their lives, but they were reticent in inviting those outside the covenanted group to participate in their religious services or to share in their religious understandings until God in his own way had spoken.

They early provided that "they that carry themselves holilie and religiouslie" would be received in the fellowship. So strict were the requirements for church membership that not more than twenty per cent of the people of the early New England colonies were in communion with the church. While there is not much evidence that the church sought to increase its membership by bringing outsiders into its communion, still there is considerable evidence that the early settlers wished to extend the privilege of the gospel to the Indians, provided they were "good Indians" and would accept the whites as superiors entitled to rule.

This missionary motive was written into the original documents. After the colonists had been in America a few years, they wrote of their labors on behalf of the Indians in the famous book, *The Day-Breaking, if not the Sun-Rising, of the Gospel with the Indians in New England,* published in 1647; and also in *Some Helps for the Indians Showing That They Improved Their Natural Reason to Know the True God and the True Christian Religion,* published in 1658. These efforts to evangelize the Indians unfortunately had no enduring effect.

Reception into church membership was a solemn rite. We are told in *Plain-Dealing and its Vindication Defended* something of the process:

Persons wishing to join such a Church made known that desire to the Ruling Elders and were examined—sometimes in presence of members of the Church— by them as to "the worke of grace upon their soules, or how God hath beene dealing with them about their conversion." The Elders being satisfied, one of them on some convenient occasion would give notice that the applicant wished to unite with them, desiring any who might be aware of objection from any cause to notify the Presbytery. If objection were made, it was duly considered.

Then, usually on a Sunday after afternoon service, but sometimes on a week-day (all the Church having notice to be there), the candidate being present, a Ruling Elder would give notice that nothing (or nothing which had not been fairly explained) had been alleged against the party thus duly propounded, and call once more upon any person present knowing anything in the way of the proposed admission, to give testimony thereof. No response being made to such appeal, the Elder would then desire any parties who have "anything to speak for his receiving" to testify as briefly as they may. The way being thus prepared, the candidate, if a man, "in a solemn speech, sometimes a quarter of an houre long, shorter or longer, declareth the work of grace in his soule, to the same purpose, as that before the Elders formerly mentioned"; and "by questions and answers, if the party be weake, or else in a solemn speech," made profession of his doctrinal faith and personal experience of God's grace. If a woman, this confession was usually read by the Pastor, although sometimes she was received on the testimony of the Elders of their satisfaction before gained "without any more adoe."

This being finished, the Elder asked any who might remain dissatisfied to use their liberty and declare their minds, and, none doing so, requested those who were ready to receive the candidate to manifest it by the "usuall signe, which is erection and extension of the right hand." The covenant was then proposed to the neophyte, "the summe of which" was "to this effect":

"To give up ourselves to the Lord in all duties of holinesse; then to the Church, and the Officers, in all love and submission, according to the will of God; and this they doe not trusting in their owne strength, but in the name and by the grace of Christ himselfe."

"Then the Elder in the name of the Church responded, covenanting also with the new confessor to perform the like duties back again. Prayer followed, after which 'they depart away with a blessing'."[1]

When the civil government was established with suffrage limited to church members it gave them added dignity, as the civil state was maintained by their votes. These colonists came to America to set up the kind of church they believed offered the true way of salvation and not primarily to set up a new kind of civil government. The civil state was a necessary development but not the primary objective, and to guard the church's interest there was a strict supervision of the admission of church members from outside the families of the church people. Again and again in the early writings we find words of caution uttered by ministers and laymen that great care be taken lest unworthy people be granted suffrage by being admitted to church membership.

There was much discussion, even from the beginning of the Half-Way Covenant period, as to whether or not the churches were weakened by the great number of people who lived under this Covenant—people who were baptized and attended church but could not take the sacrament— or whether the church should hold to its strict standards and thus preserve the purity of religion. The greatest difficulty was that often the most conscientious persons who gave evidence of Christian living could not testify "the day and the way" when the glories of the mercy of God had been revealed to them. Those who advocated the value of the Half-Way Covenant were known as the advocates of "Large Congregationalism." The churches were vexed with this discussion for several generations.

There were those who considered participation in the Lord's Supper not as a testimony to a conversion already achieved, but rather as a regenerating experience. Rev. Solomon Stoddard, pastor at Northampton, was the leading advocate of this doctrine. When Jonathan Edwards came forward with his interpretation of "Calvinism at its best," the Half-Way Covenant was forever abolished, for he eliminated the family relationship as a prerequisite for church membership as shown above. He insisted that converted persons, regardless of relationship to present members, should be admitted to church membership.

The legalistic pattern which controlled church life for generations was broken by the evangelistic emphasis of the Great Awakening. The early pattern mentioned above required that a child presented for baptism must have been born into a family of baptized church members. Limitation of church membership to those families within the church was relaxed to permit the baptism of grandchildren of church members, and this continued until the Great Awakening when all regulations were swept away and any person professing the Christian experience was wel-

[1]*Plain-Dealing and its Vindication Defended.*

comed into church fellowship regardless of the standing of parents or grandparents.

The Great Awakening turned their thought to the problem of conversion of unbelievers who were, by this time, in a vast majority. The church was disestablished and church membership was no longer a prerequisite for voting. Without tax support the church had to depend upon its own members and realized it must recruit new members or suffer a decline and possible extinction.

Rev. Charles G. Finney, pastor of the Broadway Tabernacle Church of New York and later president of Oberlin College, and others during the first half of the Nineteenth Century led in a renewed emphasis on evangelistic services. His method was used by many evangelists through the years following but lacking Finney's deep religious understanding and his respect for personality, they violated many of the principles of good taste and sound psychology and brought the revival meeting into disrepute. With the development of revivalism under Dr. Finney there was a corrective movement led by Rev. Horace Bushnell of Hartford, whose writings on *Christian Nurture* have profoundly influenced religious thought through the years. In the main the churches followed the lead of Dr. Bushnell rather than of Dr. Finney.

I

PAROCHIAL EVANGELISM

From denominational records it is evident that in the early synods little thought was given to evangelism and none whatever to worship. Not until the National Council met in Boston in 1865 did worship and evangelism receive official attention. This Council, called because the churches, having pursued a more or less individualistic course, were now shocked into a realization of the need for national planning which was everywhere recognized, was most carefully prepared for. A committee was appointed well in advance to present a report on Parochial Evangelism, composed of Rev. Daniel P. Noyes and Rev. Henry M. Dexter, editor of *The Congregationalist*.

When the Council assembled, this committee presented a report which covers fourteen pages of the Council records, and from its wording it is evident that the report was written by Dr. Dexter. This report, covering all phases of the program of evangelism and worship is so clear, penetrating, and comprehensive that it should be in the required reading of every person preparing for the ministry. The report outlined a program for the local church to meet the needs of the parish. It stated as a first principle that each church is responsible for the evangelization of its own community and that the responsibility for this program rests with the pastor of the church as the authorized leader. As to method, this report states: "The first great duty of the church is worship" and the second is "the edification of its members in Divine Love."

The instructions for worship in gaining religious understanding include the use of music, Scripture reading, and prayer. The place of worship in evangelism is "to bring all souls into communion with God; and the Church maintains these public acts of communion, in part, from the hope that the spirit of devotion may spread, like leaven, from soul to soul, till all be leavened. But, that the leaven may spread, it must be real, and real at the time which is its opportunity."[2]

The second method is by instruction. This instruction ought "to unveil eternity; to unfold the mind of God; to take divine things, and show them unto men; to make plain the ways of a heavenly life here on earth; and to breathe something of the dignity native to souls regenerate and sanctified—the dignity of a love like Christ's. While considering the methods of parochial evangelization, neither the ministry nor the churches may forget this."[3]

The committee put great emphasis on the necessity of organizing church work so that those quickened into new understandings might be given an opportunity to practice their religion, and advised the church to plan definitely that each member should engage in some form of Christian service in the community.

The third section emphasizes the importance of maintaining fellowship and being faithful in observance of the sacraments and is followed, significantly enough, by the section on conversion. This is important, as it indicates the progress of the churches since the early days when all emphasis was placed upon a definite miraculous experience which the recipient recognized and the church acknowledged to be conversion. This prerequisite to acceptance into the fellowship of the church was held so rigidly by the early churches that some persons with a deep religious life and whole-hearted devotion to the Christian cause, but without the experience of definite conversion, were denied membership. This was true of Mrs. Jonathan Edwards, who could not tell the exact way and day of her conversion, and so was never considered a full member of the church. With meek resignation, she said "if it was God's will that she be damned she was willing for the glory of God so to be."

The section of the report of the 1865 Council on conversion is worth quoting in full:

The third great end of the church remains, namely, the bringing into a state of reconciliation the souls that are alienated from God.

[2] *Minutes of the National Council, 1865,* p. 212.
[3] *Minutes of the National Council, 1865,* p. 213.

We have, it is pre-supposed, a church composed of believers—persons who have begun to love with a love like Christ's; organized a brotherhood; worshipping God; instructing and edifying its members in the wisdom, the power, and joy, of divine love; entering into sacred bonds of communion in the sacraments.

But the chief labor of Christ's militant church on earth has ever been the reconciliation of alienated souls, the saving of the lost. Not only do our churches find their principal work here, but they cannot even be faithful toward their own members unless they engage them in efforts for the spiritual benefit of those who are still out of personal covenant with God. Very properly, therefore, is the inquiry urged home upon us: How can a church be faithful and successful in this momentous work?"[4]

This is followed by sections on lay evangelism, the home prayer meeting, and membership recruiting. The churches are urged to plan their work so as to reach these groups in the community:

(1) the members of the church; (2) members of the congregation and regular attendants who are not members of the church; (3) those in some sense connected with the congregation, but not regular or frequent attendants at the sanctuary; (4) families and individuals having no real connection with any Christian congregation, and who come under no stated religious influence.[5]

The report also gives attention to the need for better Scripture instruction, saying:

"In respect to the religious training of our youth, it is a question for those competent to decide, whether more pains may not wisely be taken to exhibit the gospel in its glory, so that the young, who are easily kindled with enthusiasm, may not be led to feel that nothing else can possibly be so glorious as the truths and realities contained in this 'gospel of the blessed God.' Also, whether, in addition to general instruction, special teachings for the purpose of guarding against prevalent errors might not be of use. Whether succinct catechisms might not be formed for this purpose; and whether lectures upon portions of church history, and the history of opinions, could not be turned to advantage. Whether the influences of 'society' may not be made more uniformly benignant and wholesome? Whether pastors are really faithful in following up with personal labors the effects of their preaching."[6]

The report concludes with definite proposals:

That, when possible, every church, taking counsel if necessary with neighboring churches, define for itself the territory embraced in its parish, and recognize a special responsibility to labor for the spiritual benefit of all Congregational and all neglected families and individuals within those bounds.

We recommend to all churches to devote one prayer-meeting every month (or, perhaps, in the case of the feeblest country churches, one in each quarter), to the special object of the church and its work, giving to this meeting the name of The Home Prayer Meeting.

That all ministers of churches (1) take special pains to instruct their people in the true doctrine of the church; bringing into special prominence (a) the

[4] *Minutes of the National Council, 1865*, pp. 214–215.
[5] *Minutes of the National Council, 1865*, p. 217.
[6] *Minutes of the National Council, 1865*, pp. 217–218.

character of its material—believers; (b) the form of its organization—a brotherhood; (c) the dignity of its threefold end—God's glory in conversion, holiness and worship; (d) the several methods whereby it accomplishes its end, making especially prominent the duty of each church to be, within itself, a veritable family of God, and, for those without, a band of loving missionaries, and sedulously inculcating the doctrine of church responsibility for communities. (2) That the ministers systematize the work of their churches, apportioning it so that none of it shall be overlooked and none unnecessarily neglected; and aiming to secure the effective employment of as many church-members as possible in some form of Christian effort.

We suggest whether it may not be wise to test, by trial, whether a State ministerial association cannot be of service as a professional body for professional ends, a college for the promotion of Christian fellowship and of the knowledge, wisdom, and skill requisite for the inculcation of the truth, the sagacious conduct of necessary controversies, and the successful administration of the pastorate, thus rounding out, in full symmetry, our Congregational organization.[7]

This report was adopted and referred, as was the rule at that time, to a new committee appointed by the Council from its membership. This new committee was instructed to study the report and to submit the results to the Council for action. This review committee, in making its report, stated: "Your committee is more and more impressed with the importance of this work. They have carefully examined and considered the report submitted to their inspection. They indorse substantially the recommendations appended at the close, and commend the report as a whole to the earnest and prayerful consideration of the churches represented in the Council."[8]

One unusual feature about the Congregational fellowship is that the representatives of the churches at national gatherings often register decisions which are not carried beyond the door of the Council. In the chapter on missionary relationships there will be found many illustrations of this fact, but in all Congregational history there is no better illustration than the work of the Council of 1865. This Council gave much time and thought to the report on parochial evangelism, which provided the churches with a modern, comprehensive, and truly religious program, but there is no evidence that the report was carried to the churches or that it affected their manner of work. It was not until more than fifty years later, with the organization of the present Commission on Evangelism and Devotional Life, that the idea of parochial evangelism, re-phrased as "parish evangelism," became the accepted plan which has been carried forward during the last twenty years.

Following the 1865 Council, the churches attempted to join in the emotional revival movement being promoted in some denominations,

[7] *Minutes of the National Council, 1865*, pp. 221–222.
[8] *Minutes of the National Council, 1865*, p. 487.

without realizing that such emotionalism was contrary and foreign to the spirit, the traditions, and the temperament of the Congregational churches.

Following the constitutional organization of the National Council in 1871, the leaders were so concerned with its structure and its relationship to the churches and to the missionary organizations that evangelism does not appear in the Council discussions until thirty-six years later.

II

BEGINNINGS OF PRESENT PROGRAM

At the 1907 Council meeting Dr. Edward I. Bosworth, dean of the Oberlin Graduate School of Theology, an acknowledged leader in interpreting the New Testament to meet the needs of the Twentieth Century, gave an address on "The New Day for Congregationalism in Evangelism." Dr. Bosworth defined evangelism as follows:

Such publishing of the good word from God brought to all men in Jesus Christ's personal experience with and revelation of the Heavenly Father, as will make them conscious disciples of Jesus Christ. . . . The evangelistic message has Jesus Christ as its central feature. It reports the possibility of a personal connection with Jesus Christ and the results in character and social relationships that will follow. In this message Jesus Christ stands out as a great personality, having an unparalleled revelation of the Heavenly Father. . . . Two great propositions, therefore, underlie the evangelistic message: (1) Jesus Christ is such an adequate, enduring, ever-present revelation of God in terms of human life, death, and deathless spiritual presence as make it possible and right for every man to yield to Jesus Christ the absolute control of his life—to accept his lordship; (2) A life so controlled by Jesus Christ will be lifted by him into an increasing share of his own vital fellowship with God and men. . . .

The Church, in so far as it is an evangelizing agency, must do several things. First, it must find a method of securing the somewhat prolonged attention of the non-churchgoing adults in the community to the character and teaching of Jesus. He must be made to live before them as he lived before the Jews of Jerusalem and Capernaum. Second, it must find a method of following up this prolonged attention to the life and character of Jesus Christ with a suitable appeal for action, with the opportunity for a definite acceptance of Jesus Christ as Lord. . . . In the third place, the evangelistic method must be one that will make large use of capable laymen.

The new evangelism is a simplified, rational, and incisive message with Jesus Christ as its central feature. An evangelistic spirit is being developed that is respectfully tolerant, but enthusiastically confident of the supreme value of the discovery made in its own Christian experience, and is eager to share it with all men.[9]

When the present Commission on Evangelism and Devotional Life was organized ten years later, Dr. Bosworth was a member and greatly assisted in formulating its program. He was instrumental in setting the

[9] *Minutes of the National Council, 1907,* pp. 120–132.

pattern both for the method and for the message of modern evangelism.

In 1917, considering how best to observe, in 1920, the Tercentenary of the landing of the Pilgrims, the council appointed the Tercentenary Commission to arrange for a fitting observance. This Commission recommended to the churches a five-point program. One recommendation was that there should be established a functioning department on evangelism and worship to assist the churches in a workable program. A committee on evangelism was appointed by the Tercentenary Commission to cooperate with the Commission on Evangelism of the National Council, a nominal commission in existence for a number of years.

III

The Commission on Evangelism and the Devotional Life

The Tercentenary Commission, with the assistance of a grant from the Congregational Home Missionary Society and with approval of the Council's Commission, provided for establishment of the work of evangelism and worship and the calling of Rev. Frederick L. Fagley to be the executive secretary of the new Commission on Evangelism. The action of the Board of the Home Missionary Society in making the original grant of $12,000 per year to a commission of the National Council was due largely to the efforts of Dr. Charles E. Burton, then secretary of the Society. He urged the grant to the Commission on the same basis as a grant made to an aided church. This grant was continued annually until the Springfield Council Meeting in 1923, when the per capita denominational dues were increased by vote of the Council to finance the work of the Commission from the National Council treasury.

The Commission on Evangelism was enlarged by the 1919 Council to include members of the Tercentenary Commission. The new Commission was made up of some of the strongest leaders of the denomination; Dr. William Horace Day, who had just finished his term as Moderator of the Council, was selected as chairman; other members were Dr. Bosworth, Dr. Charles E. Jefferson, Dr. Ozora S. Davis, Dr. Ernest Bourner Allen, Dr. Robert E. Brown, Dr. Charles E. Burton, Rev. Dwight M. Goddard, Professor Eugene W. Lyman, Rev. George M. Miller, Dr. J. Edgar Park, Rev. Harry E. Peabody, Rev. E. S. Rothrock, and Dr. Jay T. Stocking. The laity was represented on the Commission by Charles K. Calhoun of White Plains, New York; H. W. Darling of Wichita, Kansas; Judge A. C. Shattuck of Cincinnati, Ohio; and Maurice E. Preisch of Buffalo, New York.

From the beginning the Commission emphasized parish evangelism. It sought to discover where in the denomination the most effective work was being done in building a truly Christian church as the center of community life; to study methods and materials being used to achieve this result; and to make known to ministers everywhere both the materials and the methods that had been found most effective.

IV

The Christian Year

In the program announced by the Commission, tentative recognition was given the Christian year. It was suggested to the churches that there were certain values in the January-to-Easter period. The first year the word Lent or Lenten was not used, but the program was organized to begin the first of January and come to a climax at Easter. The second year the Commission went a step farther and used the words "Lenten season" and certain publications were made available for that period. There were mild protests over the use of Ash Wednesday. *The Fellowship of Prayer* was issued in 1919 for use in Lent as an aid in building the devotional spirit during these significant weeks. To avoid controversy the first issue of this booklet began with the first Sunday in Lent, not with Ash Wednesday. The Commission felt that it was making a rather bold step forward when in 1920 *The Fellowship of Prayer* began with Ash Wednesday. But step by step the churches, with few exceptions, realized the unusual opportunities for a devotional program in Lent.

V

The Fellowship of Prayer

The Fellowship of Prayer was the first daily guide for devotions published by a religious denomination. It soon reached a large circulation being used in churches of many denominations. Separate editions were provided for such organizations as the Federal Council of the Churches of Christ in America, the National Council of the Y.M.C.A., the United Church of Canada and others. Since then different denominations have issued their own guides, but *The Fellowship of Prayer,* which has always been non-denominational and broadly Christian, continues its wide circulation year after year.

Along with the publication of *The Fellowship of Prayer* for the Lenten season, the Commission on Evangelism developed a program for the culture of the prayer life. Its literature for private devotions and for public church worship has had an increasingly nationwide circulation. Through conferences and writings by leaders in this field, the whole denomination has become worship-conscious. This growing interest in worship has led to extension of the study of worship in the seminaries, to assist those preparing for the ministry to a better understanding of the principles and purposes of worship. When the Commission began its study of worship there were only a few books available in this field and these were more or less concerned with details of the worship service rather than with principles and purposes. So great has been the rising tide of interest in worship in all denominations that in recent years there has been a steady stream of books on worship.

VI

The Pastor's Class

The pastor's class for the preparation of young people for church membership is another field in which this Commission pioneered. In 1919 the office of the Commission conducted a nationwide survey by questionnaire to discover how many pastors in the denomination were giving special attention to the preparation of their young people for church membership in instruction classes. From this survey it was apparent that there were very few. These pastors were pioneering in this work unknown to one another, each man following his own method and using material he himself had prepared. Dr. William Horace Day, chairman of the Commission, and Dr. Robert Elliott Brown, then pastor of the Second Church, Waterbury, Connecticut, were among those who conducted a pastor's class. They were asked to collaborate in an outline for the instruction of young people in church membership in a pastor's class, and *A Brief Text Book for the Pastor's Class,* written in catechetical form, was the first publication of the Commission. From this small beginning the pastor's class spread rapidly as a recognized part of the work of the church, and was heartily endorsed by the Education Society. As new text books develop in quality, more attention is being given to this important feature of the church program. The movement is towards more definite instruction—not that the church wishes to force an authoritarian doctrine upon young people, but rather to present with some fullness those truths of religion which are commonly accepted. A few churches practice a regular confirmation service.

The Commission on Evangelism and Devotional Life has conducted many institutes for pastors and published much material to aid in recruiting new members, using as a basis those assurances of faith that have come down through the ages and have been attested by acceptance and value in the daily life. The purpose of its work is, as Dr. Bosworth early stated, "Building men and women into an everlasting fellowship with Jesus Christ, the leader and saviour of those who put their trust in him."

VII

The Advent Season

In 1935 the Commission's program was expanded by introduction of the observance of the Advent Season. Lent as a time when the church emphasized the development of faith and worship had proved so helpful that now it seemed wise to put a like emphasis on the Advent Season that people's hearts and minds could be prepared for a truly Christian observance of the coming of Christ into the world and that Christmas might be protected from commercialism. Foundation for this observance was laid by publishing "A Devotional Guide for Advent" and other material.

The latest feature of the program recommended by the Commission on Evangelism and Devotional Life is participation with other denominations in the observance of World-Wide Communion Sunday, the first Sunday of October. This observance began in 1938 and has become a regular part of local church programs. Thus Christians of all denominations in all lands testify to their oneness in faith and discipleship, signal testimony of the unity of Christians. This observance also serves in a very fine way to emphasize the opening of the church year with a service which is vital in the life of the church.

The work of evangelism and worship in churches today shows many significant changes from practices of the earliest days. Those early churches had a carefully restricted membership of highly moral and introspective people who were strict disciplinarians. They were much given to church trials, with resultant excommunication of those not meeting their standards. They were in the grip of a Calvinistic theology and this theology, although modified, was the dominating ideology for 200 years and made the churches first of all custodians of Calvinism. Both their theology and their discipline "softened" as years passed and changes came rapidly in the period from 1840 to 1865. The churches were then becoming conscious of their national responsibility to assist in making a Christian nation, and they set themselves to meet the problems of a great and expanding people. Religion was interpreted in terms of Christian missions and the modified Calvinism of the past became practically a tradition.

In the period from 1865 to 1910 changes in basic thought continued. The publication of Dr. Henry Churchill King's *Reconstruction in Theology* signalized the extent of the change. During these formative years a thoroughly evangelistic mood became evident. This has made possible the program of parish evangelism which follows the natural sequence of the Christian year and gives great promise for development of more effective work in the years to come.

VIII

EVANGELISM IN THE COUNCIL

Evangelism reached one peak in 1865. It came to a second peak in the Council of 1919 with the organization of the Commission on Evangelism and Devotional Life and the publication of *A Program of Parish Evangelism*. It came to its fullest expression at the Council meeting held in Berkeley in 1940, for that Council gave itself primarily to the deepening of the religious life through prayer and worship, led by the Minister of the General Council, Rev. Douglas Horton.

At the Berkeley Council meeting in 1940, in addition to the services of worship conducted by the chaplain, Rev. Theodore K. Vogler, pastor of the Bryn Mawr Church of Chicago, there were communion services for men and for women, evening prayers and morning prayers. The evening session of addresses on various themes were dispensed with, and under a Board of Preachers" a service of worship and a sermon were presented each evening. The Council felt a deepening religious consciousness. Thus the careful work that has been going on through the years came to this high peak in Berkeley in 1940.

The changing attitude towards evangelism and worship in these years can well be illustrated by the growth of the chaplaincy of the Council and the introduction of the Council lectureship. From the very beginning Council meetings have opened with a prayer and a hymn. Beginning with the Council at Omaha in 1927, the devotional services were committed to the Commission on Evangelism and Devotional Life. A series of devotional services was planned under the direction of a chaplain, and Dr. Oscar E. Maurer, pastor of the Center Church, New Haven, served as the first chaplain of the Council. Following introduction of the chaplaincy by the Council, the state conferences, the local associations, and the Mission Board meetings now appoint chaplains who are given adequate opportunity for true worship services. The plan for the worship of the Council under the leadership of a chaplain has been continued and additional features have been added, making the Council meeting truly worshipful.

These three distinct peaks in evangelism and worship are thus climactic: the peak of 1865, with the acceptance of the plan of parochial evangelism; that of 1919, with establishment of the Commission on Evangelism and Devotional Life and adoption of the plan of parish evangelism; and the high peak of 1940, when true and vital religion dominated the Council from the opening session until the final closing hymn.

IX

WORSHIP AND HYMNOLOGY

The final creation by the National Council of the Commission on Evangelism and Devotional Life with which this chapter has so far concluded is significant. Two great concerns of the religious life which have, during long periods of church history, taken their independent ways have thus finally in Congregationalist procedure been reassociated to the manifest gain of both. Interpretations are always hazardous but this attempt, officially, to recover for worship in Evangelical Protestantism the values which it had largely lost in the Reformation is at least a recognition of the winning and converting power of worship and an endeavor to secure for Congregational churches a broader basis for the culture of the spiritual life.

There has been, naturally, a considerable examination of worship forms in the earlier narrative chapters of this history, but the authors after consultation have felt that a relatively brief summary might be added here even at the risk of some repetition, with a brief notation of the historic sources of Calvinistic worship, with a particular though equally brief consideration of the place of music and hymnology in colonial and later worship.[10]

There are many ways of classifying and describing religions, but they come in the end to almost this: What do the worshippers of any religion see, hear, do, and think about when "they go to church." The entire action of the Protestant Reformation may be better understood by this deceptively simple test than by the entire literature it created. The profoundest differences between Catholicism and Protestantism are just this for anyone to see and feel directly he goes through a church door—Sunday or week days. All the variants within Protestantism itself are equally there to be seen and felt, Sundays and week days. If an historic cathedral like Canterbury or Notre Dame or St. Peters could write its own autobiography, the sequent movements of the Christian centuries would all be there.

For the purposes of this history, in any examination of Congregational worship the autobiography of the old Cathedral of Geneva, on its hill above the lake and reached by narrow, winding streets, would be the most significant. For there within its walls and in one long generation Christian worship suffered its most far-reaching and dramatic recasting and redirection. The Calvinistic Reformation decentralized inherited worship and focused it upon a new center. A single sentence says it all: The Pulpit displaced the altar, though that sentence needs a library to interpret it. For Catholicism the sacraments had been—and continue to be—the means of that communion with God, which is the essence of all worship. Protestantism found its means of communion with God in the Word.[11] The sermon, therefore, supplanted the mass.

---

[10] This résumé as originally written by one of the authors was intended as a semi-detached section of another chapter. This explains a somewhat abrupt and retroactive transition.

[11] *Christian Worship*, edited by Nathaniel Micklem. Particularly chaps. 10 and 11, by J. S. Whale and A. G. Matthews.

The mass itself had almost a thousand creative years behind it and for its support, seen and unseen, the whole structure of medieval society —indeed of the whole medieval mind. Its administration had evoked philosophies and theologies. It was maintained by an interlocking system of sacerdotal authority. Its conduct was attended by majestic liturgical sonorities of chanted Latinity in a multicolored and jewelled drama of visible action in which every movement, every gesture had a symbolic meaning. Cathedrals and churches had become the efflorescence in stone and pictured glass of the worship they sheltered. Their walls echoed ceaselessly prayer and praise. They were star-lit with candles, dim with incense, and all this for so long that it seemed beyond the power of time to reach or change. Then almost in a day it was gone in Geneva and there was left only a preacher in a black gown, a pulpit—and the Bible.

To go to church in reformed Geneva was only to go to the sermon. Farel called his Genevan liturgy, in a free translation, "how to behave when the people are assembled to hear the Word of God." Participation in public worship, Calvin said himself, was "to frequent the sermons." Actually, he never reduced his services to any such bare-bones (he never preached over a half hour either), and worked out a liturgy which even now would be thought rather high church.[12]

Early English Congregationalism simplified even the Calvinistic liturgy, would have nothing but the Word itself. For them the "written Word of the Everlasting God" was the only rule of and for worship and the devout must be on their guard against "the imaginations and devices of men or the suggestions of Satan." Both their temper and their situation thus constrained them. They had not even the barest of churches in which to worship, nor a pulpit for the preacher to stand in. They were compelled to elemental simplicities; they could worship only in spirit and in a truth for which they pledged their very lives. Time and growth brought fuller and patterned forms of worship. In the final New England fusion of Puritanism and Congregationalism there were five main ele-

---

[12] Calvin's position has of late been more carefully and justly examined, not only for its form but for its historical sources. Farel, who laid the burden of Geneva upon Calvin, had reduced reformed Genevan worship to a lesson and a sermon. Calvin had, therefore, bare foundations upon which to build. It is now known that his liturgy goes back to Bucer and Strasbourg. There was a thorough and carefully documented study of this. L. R. Hill, in the *Revue d'Histoire et de Philosophie Religieuses,* published by the Protestant Faculty of the University of Strasbourg, November–December, 1938. Bucer translated and simplified the mass. It was to be followed by communion and was, therefore, liturgically, a pre-communion service. (The worship offices, Whale maintains, were conducted by the minister from the table, the sermon from the pulpit. Calvin, himself, wanted weekly communions but had to compromise on four observances a year, and said that "par règârd pour les rigoristes genevois" he renounced the absolution. Puritanism took all this over and modified it variously in its controversies with Anglicanism, holding fast to one principle: there should be nothing in public worship not enjoined and supported by the Word of God. The full development of all this belongs specifically to the histories of Protestant worship.

ments in public worship.[13] Prayer with thanksgiving, the reading of the Scriptures, sound preaching, singing of Psalms, and receiving of the sacraments. Solemn fastings and thanksgivings were marginal. Prayer of course must be free, with no books. There would be no fixed lessons, exposition was allowed and expected, the sermon must be unfettered, and being unfettered, tended to usurp the whole service. The administration of the sacrament was occasional and marginal. All this has already been seen in actual operation in the general course of this history, and its variants are studies in themselves.

New England singing has furnished the specialist an inexhaustible and fascinating field. Since only the Psalms could be sung, something must be done to make them singable in verse and tune. Result: successive metrical versions of the Psalms of various and sometimes astonishingly uncouth literary values. Sternhold and Hopkin's really noble version served the English Church after the Reformation, but the Separatist and Puritans wanted Psalm books of their own. The Plymouth Pilgrims took Henry Ainsworth's version with them. Massachusetts Bay doubted whether the Psalms were veraciously translated in Sternhold and Hopkin's and achieved (the word is quite right) the Bay Psalm Book (now a collector's treasure). There was no closed season, however, for Psalm books and other versions followed, consequential or unconsequential.[14]

Getting the Psalms sung was another matter. There would be few books and the worshippers were not all able to read. Therefore, line them out—let a leader announce a line and the Congregation sing it. The final deliverance of the congregation from "lining" is a little epic in itself. And tunes? There were only a few to begin with of a primitive though moving quality, and most confusingly scored; and the more rigid found, even in the use of such musical notation as there was, the menace of popery. It would be difficult at best to carry any tune with a consistent pitch when it all had to be begun over with every line. There was also the important matter of getting the tune rightly pitched to begin with. Pitch pipes began to be surreptitiously used—accompanied by alarums and excursions.

The situation grew distressful and the ministers began to take it in hand with decisive consequences. The first aid was to get those who could sing together in one place in the sanctuary. This was done with extreme caution, the singers were experimentally given the back pews. In 1756

[13] For a compact and scholarly examination of the whole subject, see an address on the "Congregational Idea of Worship" by Williston Walker before the Connecticut Congregational Club, December 18, 1894.

[14] Alice Morse Earle, in *The Sabbath in Puritan New England,* covers a wide field here with a scholarship her bright touch adorns. As the strain between the colonies and the crown increased the colonial divines began to dislike the deference to the King in the British versions. Therefore, they made their own.

the Visible Saints in the Kittery (Maine) Church voted "that the petitioners for a singing pew have liberty to sit in the hind seat but one, and
to move the hind seat three inches at their own cost." (Sprague's *Annals*.)
Occasionally the singers were given a front pew. Instrumental support
was gradually introduced against much opposition. The bass viol was
allowed when the violin was forbidden. Puritanism had destroyed most
of the organs in the old English churches. There would be none in New
England churches. The first "pair of organs" were sent to America in
1713. Thomas Brattle gave them to the Boston Brattle Street Church.
The church voted to refuse the gift. King's Chapel accepted them, but
hesitated to unpack them. Organs came slowly into use during the first
quarter of the Nineteenth Century.

Meanwhile English Protestant hymnology began its great course, and
the Psalms were supplemented by "Pious Songs derived from the Scriptures by Dr. Watts and others." Colonial architecture made it difficult
to place the organ in buildings where there was no means of egress for
the minister in any extremity save by the front doors. The back gallery
was most convenient and beginning to be empty, so the organ and the
choir went up the back stairs.[15] Later highly experimental church architecture put the organ and the choir in the front corners, on shelves above
the pulpit—anywhere the architect fancied. A period of paid quartettes
followed. The more prosperous churches made generous appropriations
for their music, spoke proudly of it, began to depend upon it to attract
congregations, especially to their evening services. Occasionally the "quar-
tette" was more famous—locally—than the minister. The anthem began to
be cultivated and a noble development of church music put a wealth of
material at the services of the churches. For all that, Protestant worship
toward 1900 was too easily "assembled." There was no controlling principle of integration and the service was "enriched" rather than unified.

The last phase of Congregational worship contemporary with the
date of this history is too familiar to need detailed treatment. Vested
choirs and gowned ministers are the rule rather than the exception.
Prayers are increasingly "read" and litanies begin to be said. Hymn books
are creatively edited and draw their content, both of hymn and music,
from wide sources. The Communion table begins to simulate an altar;
Candles are lighted again and the Cross reflects their light. For all that,
the ancient freedoms are maintained. Congregationalism still worships
in spirit and in truth.

No study of Congregational worship would be complete without some
consideration of the distinctive contributions of Congregationalists themselves to hymnology, and when an important contribution to a little

[15] So late as 1892 the congregation in Jaffrey, New Hampshire, turned around to sing.

considered aspect of American Congregationalism is made by a highly accredited authority—himself a musician—in a compact form, it is both courtesy and economy of effort to let that authority speak directly. We are, therefore, incorporating here a study of Congregational contributions to hymns and hymnology made by Professor Henry Hallam Tweedy of Yale Divinity School at the request of the authors. It is only skeletal—that was the request—but its compactness is part of its virtue and Dr. Tweedy's sources are included for the benefit of any who might care to make their own studies.

"Here," Dr. Tweedy wrote, "are the results of my search thus far; and as you plan to give only a page or two to the subject, I wonder whether these are not sufficient for your purpose. I need hardly say that this is miles away from an exhaustive study—exhaustive for the investigator as well as for the investigations—nor have you asked for it. I have, however, used the following books: Ninde, The Story of the American Hymn; Brown and Butterworth, The Story of the Hymns and Tunes; Robinson, Annotations Upon Popular Hymns; Hatfield, The Poets of the Church; Louis F. Benson; Stories of the Hymns. (2 Vol.); Our Hymnody—Companion Volume to the New Methodist Hymnal; Handbook to the Hymnal—Companion Volume to the Presbyterian Hymnal; John B. Pratt, Present Day Hymns; Julian, Dictionary of Hymnology. There were also several other lesser volumes from which I gathered either a scant harvest or none at all.

"As for hymnals I consulted the following: The Pilgrim Hymnal; The Hymnal—Presbyterian; Hymns of the Christian Life; the Methodist Hymnal; The Student Hymnary; The New Church Hymnal; Christian Worship and Praise.

"I have found very few names during the early years of our history. Our forefathers were entirely content to sing only 'inspired words,' even though those metrical versions of the Psalms were for the most part utterly devoid of any poetic inspiration and it was a long time before they were heretical and daring enough to attempt any compositions of their own. However, the editions by Englishmen—Tate and Brady, for example —wrought into their translations such direct reference to the British Empire and the King that some of our good Congregationalists brought out editions from which these offensive passages were omitted. As for collections of hymns, Ninde recounts the story of several:

Hartford Collection of Hymns, by Nathan Strong, minister of The
    First Church in Hartford; page 107.

Dr. Samuel Worcester edited another collection in 1815; page 111.

Village Hymns, by Asahel Nettleton, in 1824; page 114.

"I have found no hymns written by these men themselves, though I must confess that I have not searched very hard for them. Before their time Joel Barlow, another good Congregationalist, brought out a version of Watt's "Hymns and Spiritual Songs" in 1785 (see Ninde, page 31 ff.), while Timothy Dwight gave the churches another. In recalling these it may be interesting to mention some modern Congregational editors who brought out the Pilgrim Hymnal and others:

Edward Dwight Eaton: The Hymnal of Praise; The Student Hymnary.

Milton S. Littlefield: Hymns of the Christian Life.

Henry H. Tweedy: Christian Worship and Praise.

Dr. Dawson's American Hymnal—he was a Congregationalist—must be credited to an Englishman, I suppose."

LIST OF HYMNS[16]

(Where no abbreviations are cited the Pilgrim Hymnal is indicated)

Hymnals consulted, with abbreviations

C. W. P.	Christian Worship and Praise.
H.	The Hymnal (Pres.).
H. C. L.	Hymns of the Christian Life.
M. H.	Methodist Hymnal.
P.	Pilgrim Hymnal.
S. H.	The Student Hymnary.
N. C. H.	The New Church Hymnal.

LEONARD BACON

O God, Beneath Thy Guiding Hand. Page 347.

WILLIAM G. BALLANTINE

God Save America. Page 360.

KATHARINE LEE BATES

Dear God, Our Father, at Thy Knee Confessing. M. H. 361.
O Beautiful for Spacious Skies. Page 350.
The Kings of the East are Riding. M. H. 101.

FERDINAND Q. BLANCHARD

Before the Cross of Jesus. Page 194.
O Child of Lowly Manger Birth. C. W. P. 299.

JOHN W. BUCKHAM

O God Above the Drifting Years. Page 342.

WILLIAM M. CRANE

Dear Lord, Who Dwellest with Us Now. H. C. L. 365.
Lord Jesus, Son of Mary. C. W. P. 298.

[16] All the readers of this history will join with the authors in their gratitude to Professor Tweedy.

ALLEN EASTMAN CROSS

As Stars Come With the Night They Come. S. H. 309.
What Doth the Lord Require of Thee. N. C. H. 326.
Jesus, Kneel Beside Me. C. W. P. 345.
America, America, the Shouts of War Shall Cease. Page 453.
Though Fatherland Be Vast and Fair. C. W. P. 568.
Mount Up with Wings as Eagles. C. W. P. 670.
More Light Shall Break from out Thy Word. H. C. L. 395.
Guide of My Spirit. S. H. 222.

OZORA STEARNS DAVIS

At Length There Dawns the Glorious Day. Page 390.
We Bear the Strain of Earthly Care. Page 312.

HENRY M. DEXTER

Shepherd of Eager Youth. Page 471.
    (He translated hymn, probably by Clement of Alexandria, abbreviating
    and altering it).

CHARLES A. DICKINSON

Blessed Master, I Have Promised. M. H. 244.

WILLIAM E. DUDLEY

Dear God of Life, the Truth, the Way. Page 290.
The City, Lord, Where Thy Dear Life. Page 341.

TIMOTHY DWIGHT

How Pleasing Is Thy Voice. S. H. 384.
I Love Thy Kingdom, Lord. Page 404.

JAMES G. GILKEY

Outside the Holy City. C. W. P. 311.
O God, in Whose Great Purpose. S. H. 317.

WASHINGTON GLADDEN

Behold a Sower, from Afar. Page 422.
O Lord of Life, to Thee We Lift. N. C. H. 192.
O Master, Let Me Walk with Thee. Page 291.

S. RALPH HARLOW

O Young and Fearless Prophet. C. W. P. 516.

HUGH HARTSHORNE

Come, Ye Thankful People Come. Page 454.
    (Merely made alterations and arranged. Hymn is by Henry Alford).

WILLIAM DeWITT HYDE

Creation's Lord, We Give Thee Thanks. Page 316.

SHEPHERD KNAPP

Dear God, the Sun Whose Light is Sweet. S. H. 333.
Lord God of Hosts, Whose Purpose. Page 365.

WILLIAM ALLAN KNIGHT
Come, My Heart, Can'st Thou Not Hear It. Page 77.

THEODORE B. LATHROP
On This Glad Day We Dedicate. Page 443.

ERNEST F. McGREGOR
Before the Cross of Jesus I Bow In Reverent Awe. Page 135.
O Blessed Day of Motherhood. C. W. P. 614.
Lift High the Triumph Song Today. M. H. 131.

DANIEL MARCH
Hark, the Voice of Jesus Calling. Page 504.
(Ninde, *Story of the American Hymn.* Page 363).

LOWELL MASON, COMPOSER
For list of tunes see Methodist Hymnal, Index. Page 680.

IRVING MAURER
Father, In Need of Thee I Pray. Page 414.
O God, Hear Thou the Nation's Prayer. Page 344.
O God, We Pray for Faithful Wills. S. H. 238.

OSCAR E. MAURER
Brother Man, Awake. Page 311.
The Son of God, the Prince of Peace. S. H. 252.
(Mrs. Maurer shared in this).

CHARLES S. MILLS
Lord, Thou Hast Known Our Joy. Page 440.

HARRIET O. MUNGER
O My Father, I Would Know Thee. H. 395.

ALICE FREEMAN PALMER
How Sweet and Silent Is the Place. Page 416.

RAY PALMER
Come, Holy Ghost, in Love. M. H. 176.
(Founded on Veni, Sancte Spiritus).
Jesus, These Eyes Have Never Seen. Page 217.
Take Me, O My Father Take Me. C. W. P. 350.
My Faith Looks Up to Thee. Page 498.
Jesus, Thou Joy of Loving Hearts. Page 415.
(Translated and Arranged from Latin Hymn).

J. EDGAR PARK
O, Jesus, Thou Wast Tempted. Page 107.
We Would See Jesus. C. W. P. 305.

EDWIN P. PARKER

Come to Jesus, Ye Who Labor. C. W. P. 346.
Hail, Holy Light! The World Rejoices. Page 40.
Lord, As We Thy Name Profess. Page 269.
Master, No Offering. Page 334.

ROSSITER W. RAYMOND

Far Out on the Desolate Billow. Page 208.

MARGARET E. SANGSTER

O Christ, Forget Not Them Who Stand. H. 387.

ERNEST W. SHURTLEFF

Lead On, O King Eternal. Page 251.

JAY T. STOCKING

O Master Workman of the Race. Page 328.

HARRIET BEECHER STOWE

Abide in Me, O Lord. H. C. L. 236.
Still, Still with Thee. Page 50.
When Winds Are Raging. C. W. P. 390.

WILLIAM B. TAPPAN

'Tis Midnight; and on Olive's Brow. M. H. 133.
    (Ninde, page 143).

LUCIUS H. THAYER

The Church of God Is Stablished. Page 392.

HENRY H. TWEEDY

All Ye Who Love the Lord Draw Near. C. W. P. 173.
Eternal God, Whose Power Upholds. Page 368.
O Gracious Father of Mankind. Page 229.
O Holy Spirit, Making Whole. C. W. P. 264.
O Spirit of the Living God. M. H. 182.
Lord of Starry Vasts Unknown. C. W. P. 354.
True Lovers of Mankind. C. W. P. 520.

SAMUEL WOLCOTT

Christ for the World We Sing. Page 369.

VERY EARLY WRITERS

Mather Byles, born 1706. (See Ninde, page 49).
Samuel Occam, born 1723. (See Ninde, page 52).

For a bibliography, see "Our Hymnody," the companion volume to the new Presbyterian Hymnal, page 585.

CHAPTER XVIII

Later Development of Congregationalism

There are two principles in our polity. One is the entire completeness of each local church for its own government; and the other is the principle which relates to all those duties and privileges which grow out of the relation of one church to another. Everything that conforms to those two principles, everything consistent with them, is good Congregationalism; everything opposed to either of them is bad Congregationalism.

ALONZO H. QUINT

CONGREGATIONALISTS from the beginning have looked upon the Bible as the source not only of belief but also of the basic principles of the organization and work of the churches. It was early stated and emphasized that neither the local church nor any group of churches was ever given any right to legislate. Basic legislation was to be found in the Scriptures and the church's task was that of administration.

The relationship of the Lollards and Wycliffe and the Waldensians to the beginnings of Congregationalism has been presented in earlier chapters. It should be mentioned that "Francis Lambert had, indeed, as early as 1526, proposed a Congregational system for the Hessian churches, and a synod, called by his patron, Philip the Landgrave, to consider the plan, had heartily endorsed it. But upon the advice of Luther, who seems to have thought it right in theory but, for the time being, impracticable, it was postponed till a more convenient season, and never revived."[1]

Although the leaders of the early New England churches profited by the writings of Richard Hooker, Barrowe, Greenwood and many others, they were pioneers and their main purpose was to develop a church organization which would have all the advantages of Separatism with none of its disadvantages and would have in it some of the elements of stability which characterized Presbyterianism without the danger of an aristocracy, which to their minds Presbyterians tended to support. Hence Cotton and Hooker developed what was then called the "middle way" between Independency and Presbyterianism and their writings were published in England and extensively read (in both England and New England).

---

[1] Huntington, *Outlines of Congregational History*, p. 43.

287

I

THE WAY OF THE CHURCHES

Congregationalism was spoken of in old England as the "way of the New England brethren." Many of the records of those early years are lost and we are not able to discover whether the word "Congregational" was first used in America or in England, but it is quite evident that the Congregational system originated in America and that the English churches, first as Separatist and then Independent, did not acquire a denominational plan of organization until long after such a plan was working in America. The slowness of the development of English Congregationalism will be noted later in the section on ordination.

The foundation principles of Congregationalism which dominated the thought of the great majority of churches were clearly stated in the debate held in the Council of 1865. The Cambridge Platform adopted in 1648 was the result of only a few years of practice in America, where the churches had been free to develop their own systems of church government. The men participating in that Synod, as far as we know, were all English-educated, and there were only a handful of them. Yet the Church which they planned was far different from the Separatist churches they had known in England. Although certain sections of the Platform never came into universal use (for example, the section on ruling elders), yet the principles of a fellowship of autonomous churches were there and were so clear that they guided the churches for two hundred years. Two principles, the autonomy of the local church and the necessity of fellowship of the churches, did not receive equal attention in Massachusetts and in Connecticut. In Massachusetts emphasis was placed on the first principle, autonomy, and this has continued through the years; while the Connecticut churches, especially after the Saybrook Synod of 1708 with the introduction of the consociation idea, placed more and more emphasis upon the second principle, that of fellowship, and sought to implement that principle in their group activities through the consociation of ministers.

II

THE 1865 STATEMENT

In preparation for the 1865 Council, the presentation of a statement on church polity was assigned to a committee of three: Rev. Leonard Bacon, pastor of the Center Church, New Haven; Rev. Alonzo Quint, pastor of the church at New Bedford and later a recognized authority on Congregational usage; and Rev. Richard S. Storrs, pastor of the church in Cincinnati, later of Brooklyn. Dr. Storrs was absent and the report on polity was written by the venerable Leonard Bacon. It covers thirty-one closely printed pages, and was printed in advance. When the time came for presentation of the report, a delegate suggested that they proceed to discussion of it as printed and in the hands of the delegates. Thereupon Dr. Bacon said, "My impression upon that subject is that the report ought to be heard by the hearing of the ear, and then it should be distributed so that every member of the Council could read it through at his ease and get access to it through another medium." This notable report covers a study of the origin and development of Congregational polity from its very beginning. It emphasized that the difference between church polities (as Episcopalianism, etc.) could be noticed not so much from the study of the principles as by tracing the application of those principles in the organization of society. If they were to come to an understanding of Congregational polity, it was necessary that the application of these principles should be traced in the expanding life of the churches. The committee argued that a statement of polity in Congregationalism was altogether different from the canons established by other religious bodies. It insisted that all a Council could do was "to inquire, to deliberate and to testify," but that the testimony of such a group of Congregationalists as were then assembled, representing "all those Congregational churches in the United States which are in recognized fellowship and coöperation through the General Associations, Conferences and Conventions in the several states," would have both interest and value to the churches as testimony but in no sense as law.

The report defined the church as "that *Association of believers* for united worship and spiritual communion, in order to the visibility, the purity, the advancement, and the perpetuity of Christ's kingdom, which God has prescribed by the teaching of the Holy Spirit in the Scriptures. . . . Under the Gospel, the organized church is a congregation of faithful or believing men, dwelling together in one city, town, or convenient neighborhood."[2]

This is perhaps the best statement of the fundamental ideas of a Congregational church to be found in our literature. Dr. Bacon said that the study of the Cambridge Platform was of interest primarily because it showed how little the churches had departed from the principles of their fathers in the 200 years that had elapsed since its adoption. It should be noted that the churches have changed very little in principles and methods in the years since 1865.

There have been changes. Congregationalism is not a static order but a live and growing thing. It roots deep in the past, but its growth is affected by the atmosphere and environment of the times and by the changing emphases on various aspects of the Gospel. As the understanding of

[2] *Minutes of the National Council, 1865*, p. 105.

theological truths broadens and deepens, so does the polity of the churches reflect this growth.

On the doctrine of the Church, this report states:

1. Church power, under Christ, resides primarily not in the officers of the church, nor in any priesthood or clergy, but in the Church;

2. Church power is not legislative, but only administrative. It extends no further than to declare and apply the law of Christ. As no church may lawfully add anything to the sum of Christian doctrine, or take anything therefrom; so no church may lawfully add anything to, or take anything from, the rules of Christian living, and the conditions of Christian fellowship, which the Scriptures prescribe."[3]

After the report had been presented to the Council by the committee on organization, it was referred to a new committee for study and report at a later session. Eleven of the twelve on this committee reported that the task assigned was too much to accomplish in the short period at their disposal. They did not disagree with the fundamental principles; they found the Quint-Bacon report "a generally correct statement of the principles of Congregational polity . . . well correlated for use in our churches and for insertion in our church manuals." They realized that whatever might be adopted by the Council in the language of Richard Mather of the first generation, "hath so much force as there is force in the reason of it,"[4] but they did not want this statement adopted by the Council as presented by Bacon and Quint. They proposed that a general committee of twenty-five be appointed by this Council, of which Quint and Bacon would be members, to expand the report and include explanatory material to clarify some questions now in the minds of this special committee.

A very illuminating minority report was also presented by Rev. Joshua Leavitt of New York, who insisted that the report of Bacon and Quint looked too much to the past, described what had been and was then the practice of the churches, while the present need was a chart for the future. Dr. Leavitt urged the Congregationalists to adopt a platform which would draw all Christian churches into a fellowship as one great ecumenical brotherhood. He said, "Let us now realize our opportunity, raise ourselves up to the height of our privilege, look beyond the narrow field of denominational aggrandizement, and see what we can do in giving to the great fundamental principles of Congregationalism the influence they deserve, and which the interests both of religion and of the country so perilously need."[5] He also felt that churches should be propagandists for the polity they believed and should abandon the traditional church atti-

[3]*Minutes of the National Council, 1865*, p. 108.
[4]R. Mather, *Church-Government and Church-Covenant Discussed*, p. 62.
[5]*Minutes of the National Council, 1865*, p. 435.

tude, "We have something that we enjoy; you are welcome to it, if you want it, but we will not urge it upon you." He urged that "it is our duty now to assume the sufficiency of our ecclesiastical system by boldly commending it to others as tried and trustworthy; to commend our way to the confidence of others by writing as if we believed it ourselves; to spend as little time or strength as possible in the indulgence of cavils and fears; and, in the assurance that we are right, to go forward in the most unreserved manner to give the widest influence to our principles, and aim to secure at the earliest period the universal adoption of our ecclesiastical order by all churches of every name and diversity that have a right to be called Christians."[6]

A debate ensued which enlisted the authors of the original report and many other men of independent mind and of great individual power and leadership. In the annals of our church there is nothing more illuminating than the twenty-five pages of *verbatim* report of this debate. Surely nothing more could be said as to the origin of Congregational order—its strength and its weaknesses, its handicaps and its freedoms. They went back to the very beginnings for, as Dr. Quint said, "a little spice of antiquity will not hurt us." The purpose of the Council was summarized:

Why then, we must still ask, do we need a platform of discipline, emanating from this National Council, and the product of its combined wisdom? It is that the polity which now exists may be distinctly *enunciated,* with all the modifications which an experience of more than two centuries can give. More than all, it is that the polity which is so abhorrent of the letter which killeth, and so instinct with the spirit which giveth life; the polity which is so tolerant of minute variation, and so flexible in its practical details, may yet live in its *great principles.*[7]

Under the various heads, the report may be summarized as follows:

1. Ecclesiastical polity, or church government, is that form and order which is to be observed in the Church of Christ.

2. The Holy Scriptures are the sufficient, exclusive, and obligatory rule of ecclesiastical polity. Church powers, therefore, are only administrative, not legislative.

3. For government, there is no one visible, universal church; nor are there national, provincial, diocesan or classical churches; but only local churches, or congregations of believers, and responsible directly to the Lord Jesus Christ, the one head of the Church universal, and of every particular church.

4. Each local church is complete in itself, and has all powers requisite for its own government and discipline. But all churches, being in communion one with another, have such mutual duties as grow out of the obligations of fellowship.

5. Although churches are distinct and equal, yet they ought to preserve fellowship one with another, being all united to Christ, their head.

[6] *Minutes of the National Council, 1865,* p. 436.
[7] *Minutes of the National Council, 1865,* p. 441.

6. When a company of believers propose to unite in a distinct church, it is requisite that they ask the advice and help of neighboring churches; particularly that those churches, being satisfied with their faith and order, may extend to them the hand of fellowship.

7. Fellowship should be withdrawn from any church which is untrue to sound doctrine, either by renouncing the faith or continuing to hear a teacher declared by council to be heretical; or which gives public scandal to the cause of Christ, or which wilfully persists in acts which break fellowship. When one church finds such acts in another, it should admonish, and, if that fail, invite a council to examine the alleged offense.

8. When ordination of a pastor is to be performed, the Church in which he is to bear office invites a council to examine as to faith, grace, and ability, that, if he be approved, they may extend the hand of fellowship. If the ordination be in view of any other sphere of labor, the request for a council ought to come from the church of which he is a member.

9. In case a pastor offend in such a way that he should no longer be recognized as a minister, the church should request a council to examine the charges, and if it find cause, to withdraw all fellowship from him, so that his ministerial standing shall cease to be recognized.

10. Associations of ministers are useful for mutual sympathy and improvement. They can exercise no sort of authority over churches or persons, save to prescribe the rights and duties of their own membership. But common consent has recognized that their examination of candidates for introduction to the churches is a wise safeguard.[8]

III

THE PROPOSED MANUAL

The committee of twenty-five was composed of one representative from each of seven seminaries, pastors and laymen representing different sections of the country. The plan was that this committee by correspondence and otherwise would complete the report and print it, not as a statement adopted by the Council but as a statement approved by those signing it. When the National Council was formally organized with a constitution six years later, in 1871, the question arose as to what had happened to this report and it was announced that it was still in preparation, and it was voted: "That the committee appointed by the Council of 1865, on a declaration of church polity, be urged to complete their work as speedily as possible."[9] This 1871 Council also voted for preparation of a manual for the churches based on the statement of this committee. But neither statement nor manual was prepared and it was not until 1892, twenty-one years later, that question of the need of a manual again arose. At that time the Council appointed a committee of seven to prepare a manual and to report at the next meeting. In 1895 the committee presented a manual following the pattern set by the 1865 Council.

[8] *Minutes of the National Council, 1865,* pp. 129–133.
[9] *Minutes of the National Council, 1871,* p. 41.

The Council did not adopt this manual but authorized the committee to have it printed, with an introduction signed by the members of the committee, and to offer it to the churches as the testimony of these individuals. Interestingly enough, the chairman of this committee was Dr. Quint who, as a young man thirty years before, had assisted the Rev. Leonard Bacon in preparing the report on polity, which, in final form, never saw the light of day.

The development of Congregational polity may be traced from the Cambridge Synod, with its Platform in 1648, the Reforming Synod supplementing this in 1668, and the Saybrook Synod emphasizing its interest in the consocation idea in 1708, to a peak in the Council of 1865. We have only the records of the proposals and the debate, but from these records the development is seen.

The vote of the Council of 1895, authorizing publication of a manual, was framed in these words: "The manual is to be signed by the members of the committee and by such other persons as may be joined in consultation and will carry, it is hoped, such weight as may be found in character, learning and practical wisdom of the brethren whose names should be thus appended."[10] By this vote the Council dissociated itself from the publication of a manual lest the churches feel that this joint "testimony" was legislation being imposed upon them.

This fear of legislation grew out of the problems of the earliest colonists, who were faced with the question whether or not they should use English laws. They had left England to escape some of these harsher laws and so they took what appeared to them as a higher law, namely, the law of the Scriptures. In so doing, they felt in good conscience that they were not rebelling against the laws of England but were placing themselves under the fundamental laws of the Bible.

IV

THE MANUAL PUBLISHED

The publication of the manual prepared by the Quint committee, which had been submitted to the Council of 1895, received tacit approval, in spite of a desire of the members to dissociate themselves, for it was printed in full in the minutes of that Council. It was published the next year and continued as the standard guide until 1907.

V

THE POLITY COMMITTEE

When the Council again turned its attention to polity it was to formulate answers to questions which had been received by the Polity Com-

[10] *Minutes of the National Council, 1895,* p. 27.

mittee. The Kansas City Council of 1913 which adopted the revised constitution included in its vote the acceptance of the following brief statement of polity: "We believe in the freedom and responsibility of the individual soul, and the right of private judgment. We hold to the autonomy of the local church and its independence of all ecclesiastical control. We cherish the fellowship of the churches, united in district, state, and national bodies, for counsel and cooperation in matters of common concern."[11]

In 1931, the year of the merger between the Congregational National Council and the Christian General Convention, notice was taken of divergent practices in the Christian churches, and in the Council of 1940 further attention was given to the status of ministers.

VI

SUMMARY OF POLITY DEVELOPMENT

In viewing the development of polity in our churches over a long range of years, we find that interest manifested in the Cambridge Synod, the two Massachusetts Synods of 1662 and 1680, and the Saybrook Synod in 1708 continued within the main lines stated by these bodies until the Council of 1865. While polity was one of the most interesting topics under discussion, no statement resulted. A widening interest was created, however, and the search for a common statement continued until twenty-five years later, so long was the period of incubation.

John Robinson in his writings had said:

And for the gathering of a church I do tell you that in what plan soever, whether by preaching the Gospel by a true minister, by a false minister, by no minister, or by reading and conference, or by any other means of publishing it, two or three faithful people do arise, separating themselves from the world, into the fellowship of the Gospel, they are a church truly gathered, though never so weak.

When it came to organizing the churches in the colonies there were always more than "two or three." They had observed "that a rule of church discipline in the eighteenth chapter of Matthew cannot well be reduced into practice by any number under seven."[12]

VII

THE ORGANIZATION OF A CHURCH

One of the earliest records of the organization of a church is that of the church at New Haven where seven men were selected as the founders of the colony by vote of those who wished to become covenanted mem-

[11] *Minutes of the National Council, 1913*, p. 341.
[12] C. Mather, *Ratio Disciplinae Fratrum Nov-Anglorum.*

bers of the church when established. These seven having covenanted together chose John Davenport to be pastor and Thomas Hooker to be
teacher.

Then, by vote, this original group of seven admitted others to the
covenant. John Davenport was a man of great character and distinction.
The ill-fated ship which sailed from New Haven in January, 1637, in a
first commercial venture with old England, carried the manuscript of
Davenport's book, *The Power of Congregational Churches*. This ship
was lost. This was one of the earliest known uses of the term "Congregational." The ship also carried Hooker's *A Survey of the Summe of
Church-Discipline*. Both manuscripts were rewritten and published later.
The spirit of Davenport is illustrated by the oft-quoted sentences: "If we
build God's house, God will build our house. While we are attending to
our duty, God will be providing for our safety." [13]

The covenant of the early churches was usually brief. For example,
the covenant of the second church founded in New England, the church
at Salem, contained only one sentence: "We Covenant with the Lord
and one with another; and doe bynd our selves in the presence of God,
to walke together in all his waies, according as he is pleased to reveale
himself unto us in his blessed word of truth."

The "Congregational Way" came into being providing for establishment of a church with the cooperation of a council representing neighboring churches. "Not that they claim an entire independency with regard to other churches; for they agree that in all cases of offence, the
offending is to submit to an open examination by other neighbor churches; and, on their persisting in their error or miscarriage, then they are to
renounce all Christian communion with them, till they repent; which is
all the authority or ecclesiastical power which one church has over another. This they call a middle way between Browneism and Presbytery." [14]
This spirit of fellowship grew and was evidenced in the founding of new
churches. The method can be illustrated by quoting a "letter missive,"
dated January 22, 1829, from a group desiring to form a Congregational
church. This letter was sent out signed by the moderator and scribe of
the group desiring to be organized as a church. The main part of the
letter reads: "To the Congregational Church in L————. Greeting.
The undersigned, being, some of them, members of separate and distant
churches, and all of them hoping to live as the renewed and humble followers of our Lord Jesus Christ, ask leave respectfully to represent, that
there is no Congregational church in the town of N————, where
they reside. . . . Accordingly, after much consideration and prayer, they

[13] Bacon, *Thirteen Historical Discourses*, p. 150.
[14] Neal, *History of the Puritans*, p. 492.

esteem it to be a duty, and are desirous to be gathered into a new church, according to authorized and scriptural order. . . ."[15] This was followed by information as to time and place.

In the 1865 Council there seemed to be perfect agreement as to the method of founding a church and the nature of the church. As stated by Leonard Bacon, the prevailing ideas were: "A church is made simply by the members of it agreeing—expressly or impliedly agreeing—to walk together in one assembly, under the rules of the New Testament, trusting in Christ, doing his work together, helping one another, administering the Word and the sacraments. We hold that. Do we also hold the communion of churches? . . . if a church, falling back on its reserved rights, its extreme powers, says: 'We will have nothing to do with other churches, we will elect whom we please to be our minister and we will turn him away when we please,' we say, 'Very well, only you don't ride in our troop, that's all.' "[16]

The churches were not averse to pronouncing this polite form of banishment. The ancient records of the old associations and conference meetings show that more than half the sessions was given to a discussion of discipline and the dis-fellowshipping of churches and individuals. No noteworthy change has taken place in this usage except the abandonment by an increasing number of churches of the so-called dual organization of Church and Society.

In colonial days the church was a part of the town organization and its field of service was the town. When a second church became necessary, it was located at a distance from the first church in order to serve people in its vicinity and the town was divided into two sections as parishes. In many of the early towns the title to church property rested with the town and the voters determined its financial policy. When the church was disestablished, or no longer part of the town organization but a free and independent group in the community, it was not given the right of incorporation. Therefore, not being a "body corporate" but being a "body religious," it had no legal or financial standing. Those who had been supporters of the church under the old parish or town system usually organized as the "Society." This could be legally incorporated, and could hold property. Many persons belonged to both the church and the society. There were often leading citizens without too active a part in the religious work who had a benevolent attitude towards the church, and who insisted that the society maintain its separate identity. The relationship between the two bodies was usually on a cordial, cooperative basis and each group knew the metes and bounds of its own jurisdiction.

---

[15] Upham (editor), *Ratio Disciplinae, or the Constitution of the Congregational Churches,* pp. 63–64.
[16] *Minutes of the National Council, 1865,* pp. 452, 455.

As the number of "friendly citizens" decreased, the churches found that the society was almost exclusively made up of members of the church acting in a dual role. To avoid such duplication, the society united with the church which, under modern laws, is competent to become incorporated and thus hold title to property and funds. There are, however, throughout the East a few churches still maintaining a dual organization both for sentiment and for practical reasons. In this way they bring into relationship with the church those who, because of reticence or reluctance to assume church vows, would, if the society were abandoned, lose official touch with the church.

VIII

CHURCH OFFICERS

From the first, church members had the duty of electing officers, which were usually the pastor, the teacher, the elders, and the deacons. The elders had somewhat the responsibility of the present trustees, although the deacons in the early churches were responsible for collection of funds and one usually served as treasurer. Soon the election of elders fell into disuse. Later the churches discovered that the election of two men, the pastor and the teacher, with practically the same requirements and duties, was unnecessary. "The pastor's special work is to attend to exhortation, and therein to administer a word of wisdom; the teacher is to attend to doctrine, and therein to administer a word of knowledge; and either of them to administer the seals of that covenant unto the dispensation whereof they are alike called; and also to execute the censures, being but a kind of application of the word: the preaching of which, together with the application thereof, they are alike charged withall."[17]

Once a month, as now, the Lord's supper was celebrated at the close of the morning service, in precisely the same forms which we observe, the pastor, teacher and ruling elder sitting together at the communion table. One of the ministers performed the first part of the service, and the other the last, the order in which they officiated being reversed at each communion.

The assembly convened again for the exercises of the afternoon at about two o'clock; and the pastor, having commenced as in the morning with prayer, and a psalm having been sung as before, another prayer was offered by the teacher, who then preached, as the pastor did in the morning, and prayed again.[18]

The usual custom was that the teacher would conduct the service one Sunday and offer the prayer, and the pastor would preach. At the next service the duties would be reversed. The ordinary officers in the church today are pastor, deacons, clerk, treasurer, and trustees. The one change

[17] *Cambridge Platform.*
[18] Bacon, *Thirteen Historical Discourses,* p. 45.

made in recent years has been in electing deacons for a term of years rather than for life, as was the custom in the early churches.

IX

CHURCH MEMBERSHIP

The early churches maintained a high quality of church membership, and the examination was a serious transaction from which no one was excused. When the eminent John Cotton came to Boston and was to be received into the membership of the First Church, the church officials proceeded to examine him as to his religious faith and practice, exactly as they would any other person. The earliest churches, as stated in Cotton's and Hooker's writings, looked upon the members of the church as "saints, by calling." For example, Cotton in his *Holiness of Church Members* says: "The church . . . cannot lawfully receive members . . . but such as are, in a charitable discretion, esteemed saints by calling." The church considered that those received into membership had reached a high state in personal experience in religion. The examination of women, however, was not usually held in public but one of the officers of the church was delegated to present the testimony of the woman who applied for membership or it was submitted in writing.

After the first few years very few people coming to the community could satisfy the requirements, and the custom grew that the "weakest measure of faith was to be accepted." In his great convention sermon President Stiles said, "There was never an instance of admission to the churches without the votes of the brethren." In the years since, this customary practice has continued in form.

The most pressing unsettled question concerning church membership is grounds on which and whereby names can be removed from the roll. Some state laws provide that members of the church are joint owners of property and as such they cannot be deprived of that right except by "due process." The Council of 1877 recommended a uniform system to deal with the following classes of persons:

1. Those who have been long regarded as nonresidents, and concerning whose whereabouts the church has no knowledge.

2. Those who have requested and received letters of admission, and yet as to their connection with any other church the church has no knowledge.

3. Those who have been for a long time absent, and refuse to request letters of dismission.[19]

The report of this committee laid down the principles which underlie the usage in the Congregational churches in a statement quoted widely through the years and which remains standard:

[19] *Minutes of the National Council, 1877*, p. 51.

. . . The New Testament idea of the local church is that of a local congregation of believers, able by residence to meet together for worship, sacraments, and discipline. A permanent resident in one city where there is a church, with nominal membership in a city far off, seems entirely abnormal. A church now should consist of residents, with, of course, some exceptions; such exceptions as a case where the absent member does not find a church such as he can properly apply to, or where certain ties of a tender and affectionate nature may be indulged. Such exceptional cases are, of course, to be within the scope of church indulgence. But the church cannot be bound forever to continue its responsibility for persons over whom it cannot exercise watch and care.

Those who have been long regarded as non-residents, and concerning whose whereabouts the church has no knowledge; it is unfortunate that any church should allow such a lack of loving oversight as to allow any considerable number to disappear without notice. A common and good course is to place such names upon a separate list, cease enumerating them as members, but being able thus by a simple vote to replace the name on the common list, if occasion should enable it to be done.

A person receiving a letter is still a member of the church voting the letter, until he is received by the church to which he is dismissed.

The church has the right, we have seen, to relieve itself of the watch and care of persons who are not resident within its convenient territory. It can do this, not summarily, but first by a rule requiring such absentees to remove their connection in an orderly manner, or by special vote suggesting it in given cases.

But it should be remembered that the object of church discipline is to *save*, not to cut off and get rid of. Pastoral and other care should be a loving, gentle, and faithful helpfulness. It is related of Cotton Mather that he kept a perfect list of the members of his church and of his congregation, and that he used, at regular times, to pray to God in behalf of each member in turn, calling his name aloud to the Lord who calleth his sheep by *name;* and with this asked God and himself. "What good can I do to this soul?" Great results were his constant reward. Had any one asked Cotton Mather how many were his church members, and how many resided in Boston; if the questioner had gone further and asked how many had confessed Christ before the world in the preceding twelve months, or had come from other parts to his fold, or how many had gone to other flocks, or from the church militant to the church triumphant; or how many children he had commended to him who took the Judean babes in his loving arms, doubtless Cotton Mather would not have shuddered at a spectre of "statistics," for he had counted these souls upon his knees.[20]

As stated by Dr. William E. Barton, long the leading authority on Congregational polity, "You are not required to become a Congregationalist in order to unite with a Congregational church. A Congregational church is not a church of Congregationalists, but a church of Christians in which the congregation governs. It has absolutely no sectarian tests. To belong to a Baptist church one must be a Baptist, submitting to a particular rite administered in a particular form. To belong to an Episcopal church one must be an Episcopalian. Congregationalism has no such divisive tests."

[20] *Minutes of the National Council, 1880,* pp. 131–133.

CHAPTER XIX

The Council and the Boards

BEFORE 1871

THE relationship between the National Council and the Benevolent and Mission Boards has had a slow but continuous growth. The Boards with few exceptions were organized by groups of individuals, and in the earlier years were supported almost entirely by individual gifts. They have exemplified in their organization and work all the attributes of Congregational independency. The American Board, the Education Society, the original Home Board, and the American Missionary Association all were well established and doing a most significant work before the urgent need of a national representative body became evident.

I

THE BOARDS BEFORE 1865

The Boards were organized to meet certain definite needs. As the Boards were located in different centers (for example, the American Board in Boston, the Congregational Union in New York, and the New West Educational Society in Chicago), they tended to become localized in their management and in their support.

By 1865 there were also agencies interdenominational or nondenominational in nature which appealed then as now to the church people for support. These included the two Tract Societies, one in Boston and one in New York, the Bible Society, and the Sabbath School Society.

There was competition for support and as there was no intersociety planning agency, there was overlapping in the different fields of work. The societies depended on their own representatives for raising funds, so that the stronger churches especially were embarrassed by more appeals for personal presentation than they could grant. These problems emphasized the need of an agency which would serve as a clearing house for discussion of the work and support of these agencies.

It was the pressing need for more active support of missionary work by the churches that led to the calling of the first truly national Congregational convention in Albany in 1852. The need among the scattered western communities for aid in church building was especially urgent. The eastern churches felt also a growing need for some organized agency that would administer their gifts to the churches in the West. The Plan of Union which had provided the channel for the gifts of New England, especially of Connecticut, to the western churches, had been officially abrogated by the Presbyterian General Assembly (1837); and though some western Presbyteries served as agents for New England Congregational churches, yet the situation had become quite unsatisfactory.

The Albany Convention gave careful thought to the needs of western communities for help in church-building, and after passing strong resolutions endorsing the missionary and benevolent societies which appealed to Congregational churches for support the Convention adjourned, leaving no continuation committee, and providing for no future meetings of a similar body. The results of this Convention were so favorable that the way was prepared for future meetings, and the net result of the Albany Convention for the existing Boards was that they were given endorsement for their work by the representatives of the churches and funds had been raised for the specific work of church building.

II

AT THE 1865 COUNCIL

The next national meeting of representatives of the churches was the Council of 1865. The immediate occasion for this Council was the crisis faced by the churches due to the Civil War. Another reason was that there were so many agencies appealing to the churches for support. Some of these were denominational in origin, some were interdenominational, and others were non-denominational. From all these agencies the Council selected those which seemed to be closest to the churches in organization and purpose, and indicated their relationships to the churches by a brief statement of the history of each organization. The early history of these Boards, as presented to the '65 Council, may be summarized briefly as follows:

A. *The American Board*

The Massachusetts General Association of Ministers at its meeting at Bradford in 1810 received a petition from "the Brethren," five young men who had participated in the famous Hay Stack meeting at Williams College and now, having completed the course at Andover, desired to become foreign missionaries and needed the backing of an organized agency. The Massachusetts Association granted their request and appointed a committee of nine, five from Massachusetts and four from Connecticut, to serve as an organizing committee for a foreign missionary society. The next year the Connecticut Association appointed its own representatives. In 1811 this group which had been organized by the state associations received a notable bequest, and asked the Massachusetts General Court for incorporation as a Board.

After long discussion in the legislature a charter was granted in 1812 to "the American Board of Commissioners for Foreign Missions as an independent, self-perpetuating corporation." This was the first foreign missionary society in North America; and as was natural it appealed to a wide constituency, including among its early supporters members of Presbyterian and Dutch Reformed churches.

After some years the Old School Presbyterians withdrew and formed their own board; the Dutch Reformed withdrew in 1857, and the New School Presbyterians in 1870. When the 1865 Council was held, the American Board was still receiving funds from the members of other churches, although it was no longer officially recognized by other denominations as their agency. The Council in its report stated that the "American Board is the child of the Congregationalists of New England, and although instituted in the comprehensive spirit of catholic Christianity, and common to us with the Presbyterians . . . it has all along been the favored of our people." The report continued: "Your Committee, therefore, recommends that the Council, as representative of the churches, do testify their deep sense of the importance of Foreign Missions, and their unabated devotion to the prosecution of the enterprise. We need it for ourselves. The work will die at home, if it languish abroad. It is the sign of our fellowship with Christ. It is the condition of his blessing. We need it in every sense, and for every reason."[1]

B. *The Education Society*

The 1865 Council also reviewed the development of educational programs and gave special attention to the education of ministers. It noted the formation of the American Society for the Education of Pious Youth for the Gospel Ministry, organized in Boston in 1815 and incorporated in 1816, which later became the American Education Society; also the organization of the Society for the Promotion of Collegiate and Theological Education in the West. It urged that these two societies should work in close harmony, and forecast their merger into the American College and Education Society, which took place later (1874).

C. *Home Missions*

In its review of home missions the '65 Council stated in brief: For many years there had been state missionary societies in the states of Connecticut, Massachusetts, and New Hampshire. In 1822 there was formed in New York a United Domestic Mission Society. The students at And-

[1] *Minutes of the National Council, 1865*, p. 232.

over and some Massachusetts ministers desired that this United Society should become national and petitioned the Society to organize on a national basis. In response to that petition a meeting was held in the Brick Presbyterian Church in New York on May 10, 1826, of representatives from four denominations (Congregational, Presbyterian, Reformed Dutch and Associated Reformed) who organized a national, interdenominational home missionary society.

This society had the same experience as the American Board. The other denominations withdrew to form strictly denominational bodies, until only Congregationalists were left. The society then changed its name and purpose in order to serve the Congregational churches, adopting the name Congregational Home Missionary Society in 1893.

D. *American Missionary Association*

The Civil War had just come to an end so the American Missionary Association and its work received special attention in discussions of the Council. This Association had been formed in 1846 from three parent organizations "to conduct Christian missionary and educational operations, and to diffuse a knowledge of the Holy Scriptures in our own and other countries." The American Missionary Association represented the anti-slavery sentiment in the churches, which required an agency whole-heartedly devoted to it, since the backers of the older societies had not taken so firm a stand against slavery as the American Missionary Association supporters had desired. Because of the critical need of the great multitude of newly freed Negroes, the 1865 Council placed added responsibility upon this society.

The remote genesis of the A. M. A. is a now almost forgotten drama, unless it be sought in the first ship which brought a slave to these shores. In 1839 a United States brig took in charge a Spanish slave ship off the coast of Long Island. There were then on board the Amistad forty-two Africans who had mutinied, killed the Captain, imprisoned the crew, and ordered the ship back to Africa—all this off the coast of Cuba. They were betrayed by their navigators and the Amistad, after her capture, was taken into New Haven harbor and there the Africans were imprisoned on the charge of mutiny. Difficult questions of international law were involved, but mutiny was mutiny. A distinguished group of citizens organized together "for the purpose of protecting the legal interests of the accused and making provision for their care during the trial." John Quincy Adams, onetime President of the United States, acted as one of their lawyers. After two years' litigation the Supreme Court pronounced them free. They were returned to Africa in 1841 under the care of three missionaries.

The Amistad committee had found a cause and it merged with the "Union Missionary Society of Connecticut," pronouncedly anti-slavery. There were also other societies conceived for the Indians and emancipated Negroes. All these finally merged and became the American Missionary Association. The charter of the Association was unusually inclusive. It permitted almost any form of missionary or education work anywhere and for anybody. Its founders believed in human equality without racial bias, and the injustice of human slavery. There was only one limitation to membership. Its members must "not be holders of slaves or engaged in the practice of any other immoralities." It was nonsectarian. It aided John G. Fee in the founding of Berea College which admitted white and colored students and "taught them in the same classes without contamination and reproach."

The Association found its really appointed work at the end of the Civil War. It began the "Contraband School" for Negroes freed by the northern armies at Hampton, Virginia—which became Hampton Institute. Its missionaries followed the Union forces along war-rutted roads. They were fearless, dreamers of a new human order, accepting social ostracism as the dust of the day's task. Their schools were pathetically poor, their students were men and women for whom "Massa" Lincoln had broken down bolted doors. The romance and the pathos of it all are beyond words, but it was washed with a great and prophetic light. In 1865 the National Council, from which American Congregational history began to be redated, made the Association its agent for the missionary activity of the denomination in the South. Thereafter the relations between the American Missionary Association and the Congregational churches of America were increasingly intimate.

E. *Publishing and Other Interests*

The Council of 1865 gave considerable attention also to the two Tract Societies which were pouring out books and pamphlets for use in the churches; and to the American Bible Society, "too well-known to need any special mention." The American Seamen's Friend Society was highly commended, as was the American Congregational Association with its plans to raise money for a Congregational House, and to provide a home for the Congregational library.

F. *In General*

After passing these agencies in review the Council stated: "We see no necessity for any new organization, and it is not new machinery which we want, but to give greatly increased efficiency to the machinery which we have by supplying a vastly greater moving power."[2] The Council suggested that this need be considered under three questions:

1. How can the requisite spirit of earnestness and self-consecration be imparted to the churches?
2. How can our young men be induced, by thousands, to consecrate their lives to this holy cause?
3. How can we raise the requisite pecuniary resources for a religious enterprise so vast, and so imperatively demanding immediate action?[3]

The Council recognized that there should be a more systematized plan of benevolent giving, saying:

To what causes shall our churches contribute? To what organizations shall they intrust the expenditure of their money? These are questions always important, always pertinent. Is there anything in the peculiar circumstances of our country, or the world, that makes them specially important and appropriate at the present time? Has there been any change in the relative importance of different organizations? Even if nothing be said of the honesty, fidelity, and ability with which these organizations have been conducted, has not the progress of events, or rather the providence of God, rendered the claims of some more imperative, of others less so, than formerly? Has not this Council been convened to consider anew the fields of Christian labor, and to inquire how the work of Christian benevolences can be most successfully carried forward?[4]

This statement might well have been adopted by the three reorganization committees appointed in the seventy years that were to follow, for each committee has faced these identical questions. It was realized that the churches and the societies were laboring toward a common end, and that the societies were agencies of the churches. The churches frequently faced great problems that did not fall specifically within the program of any of the existing societies. They felt that no new society should be established without the most careful planning, but to meet the new needs as they arose there should be some agency to aid the societies in planning their work with neither overlapping nor overlooking.

In planning for better support for the Boards, the Council adopted a statement which has been honored perhaps more in the breach than in the observance. "It is our conviction that a clear, businesslike statement of the condition and operations of a society, occupying ten or fifteen minutes, would be more potent with the men who give the money than an impassioned appeal of an hour."[5]

The Council closed its consideration with these words:

If Congregationalism has no mission except to add one to the number of religious sects, which divide and distract the household of faith, then far bet-

[2] *Minutes of the National Council, 1865,* p. 145.
[3] *Minutes of the National Council, 1865,* p. 147.
[4] *Minutes of the National Council, 1865,* p. 224.
[5] *Minutes of the National Council, 1865,* p. 230.

ter confine itself within the limits of New England, and consign at once all its emigrant population to the care of those centralized church governments which always stand ready to receive and assimilate them. But if the Congregational conception of the church is true and precious—if it is as well fitted to all latitudes and longitudes as to New England, and is really an important element of American civilization, and of the brighter and better ages of the promised future— then these Congregational churches are bound to be true to their fundamental principles.[6]

FROM 1871 TO 1913

I

CONSTITUTIONAL PROVISIONS AND CHANGES

The general effect of the Council of 1865 on the missionary giving of the churches was so helpful that the movement for a regular national meeting of elected representatives of the churches developed rapidly. When the Council met at Oberlin in 1871 it adopted a constitution providing that the voting members should be delegates from associations and conferences, but that "Congregational general societies for Christian work, as may be recognized by this Council, may be represented by one delegate each, such representatives having the right of discussion only."[7] The phrase, "such representatives having the right of discussion only," was stricken out by the Portland Council in 1901, thus giving the delegate of each society regular voting privileges.

By-law III of the Council defined the meaning of "Congregational" to be:

The term "Congregational," as applied to the general benevolent societies, in connection with representation in this body, is understood in the broad sense of societies whose constituency and control are substantially Congregational.[8]

In 1883 the by-laws were amended by insertion of the clause, "A committee shall be appointed on each of the national Congregational societies, to which severally may be referred any statements from, and any communications relating to, said societies,"[9] but the amendment was repealed in 1892. The 1883 Council also provided, by a revision of the by-laws, that "the afternoon and evening of Saturday and the evening of the Sabbath shall be assigned to hearing from such Congregational general societies as may be recognized by this Council, the time to be equitably divided between them and no other portion of the time of the Council is to be occupied by them."[10] This provision was eliminated three years later, in 1886.

6 *Minutes of the National Council, 1865*, p. 136.
7 *Minutes of the National Council, 1871*, p. 148.
8 *Minutes of the National Council, 1871*, p. 66.
9 *National Council Digest, 1930*, p. 123.
10 *National Council Digest, 1930*, p. 123.

In 1889 an amendment was made to the by-laws that the statements from the general benevolent societies should be in print, and copies placed in the hands of the delegates two weeks before the meeting of the Council. This was modified in 1892, by giving the Provisional Committee of the Council the right to decide whether or not any statement should be printed from the societies, and how much; and the representative of each society was to be given twenty minutes for a statement by the delegate. The 1892 Council added the provision which has been continued, admitting to the Council as corresponding members the missionaries in the service of the American Board of Commissioners for Foreign Missions present in this country on furlough.

II

DEVELOPMENT OF RELATIONSHIPS

It was not alone through constitutional provision or legal enactment that the members of the Council showed their interest in the work and support of the Boards. At the first regular Council of 1871 after adoption of the constitution, much time and discussion were given to the project of the American Congregational Association to erect a Congregational House in Boston. It voted that this should be built as a home for the benevolent societies and the library. It refrained from any discussion of relationship of the Boston Tract Society or the New York Tract Society to the churches, which had occupied so large a place in the 1865 Council; but did urge increased support for the Congregational Publishing Society and commended it heartily to the churches. The first appearance of the movement which led later on to the Apportionment Plan is noted in the acts of the Council recommending "systematic and regular contributions to the societies."

The troubles resulting from the Civil War and the freeing of the Negroes received special attention at the 1871 Oberlin meeting of the Council, as had been the case in the 1865 Council. The Congregational churches had always been active in behalf of the anti-slavery movement. The great majority of the officers and workers of the American Missionary Association had come from Oberlin College. It was but natural that the Oberlin Council should give special attention to the condition of the freedmen, and should seek greatly increased funds for the Association.

The consolidation of societies was considered at this 1871 Council meeting, and the vote was as follows:

In view of the number of existing organizations for benevolence that claim contributions from our churches, some of which organizations are so closely affiliated in purpose and method that they contemplate essentially the same work; therefore,

RESOLVED, That a committee of seven be appointed to consider and report at the next session of this Council whether any consolidation of such organizations is practicable, with a view to the promotion of great unity and efficiency of operation, and the reduction of expenses that are felt to be needless and therefore burdensome.

RESOLVED, That this committee be requested, when desired to do so, to investigate the merits of such special objects and institutions as are to be generally presented to the churches for aid, and give the churches the advantage of their judgment on their merits and importance.[11]

In the 1874 Council occurred the first vote directly affecting the affairs of a missionary agency. The Council voted that the churches be advised that the funds they were accustomed to give to the American and Foreign Christian Union (an interdenominational missionary society) "be added to the contributions ordinarily made to the American Board."

The report of the Committee on Consolidation, appointed in 1871, was very carefully prepared. The Committee had invited the secretaries of all the Boards to their meetings, and had conducted an extended correspondence. In their report they stated that independent benevolent organizations had been formed to meet certain specific needs; and that the wisdom of the organizers and directors had been vindicated by successful work accomplished. The report pointed out the difficulty arising from differences in incorporation and from legacies and made this observation: "Consolidation is easily reached in resolution, but, practically, presents problems which are not so readily solved."

Furthermore, the report stated: "It is difficult and maybe dangerous business to lay the hand of change upon any of them." The Committee advised the Boards as to spheres of influence and work. It approved the consolidation worked out by some of the societies; advised that the Congregational Publishing Society should be organized "as a strictly business enterprise"; and recommended that the missions of the American Board among the North American Indians be transferred to the care of the American Missionary Association, and the foreign missions of the American Missionary Association be transferred to the American Board. These foreign missions of the American Missionary Association had grown out of the necessity to provide for religious and educational facilities for the freed Negroes who had returned to Africa.

Perhaps the most historic vote of the Council of 1874 was that relating to the consolidation of the magazines. The vote was:

RESOLVED, That, in the judgment of this Council, the consolidation of our various misisonary and benevolent magazines into one, is desirable; and that the officers of the different societies are respectfully requested to consider the practicability of such a consolidation.[12]

[11]*Minutes of the National Council, 1871,* pp. 46–47.
[12]*Minutes of the National Council, 1874,* p. 28.

This recommendation which was passed in 1874 and renewed again and again through the years accompanied by hours of discussion, was not finally accepted until sixty-four years later at the meeting of the Council in 1938 in Beloit.

In 1877 the first move was made to organize a ministerial board; and in 1883 the New West Education Commission was approved.

In 1889 there was also presented a memorial from the General Conference of the Congregational churches of Connecticut on the relations of the national benevolent societies to the churches. The memorial called attention to the fact that the mission boards, "though vitally related to the Congregational churches in every point of *fact,* are nevertheless wholly *independent* of them in law and management; and that these facts not only discredit our polity, but threaten our peace." While the Connecticut Conference was not ready to recommend any solution, it petitioned the National Council to give this matter careful study. It also stated that the American Board had appointed a Committee of Fifteen on better relations with the churches "holding out its *olive branch* in the face of the churches" and that this venture on the part of the Board should receive due consideration by the Council.

Another significant vote was that instructing the secretary of the Council "to enter into correspondence with each mission of the Board, with view to having some person appointed to act as a medium between this body (the Council) and the mission to which he belongs, who shall receive, translate, and distribute the papers and doings of this Council as having a bearing upon Christ's Kingdom." This provision did not come into effect, for the American Board advised that all correspondence with missionaries should originate with the Board and not with the churches or the Council.

The Council also authorized appointment of a committee to study relationships of Boards to the churches; another committee to consider the relationship of missionary societies one to the other; and a Committee of Five to attempt a merger of the missionary magazines.

Having made all these moves toward closer relationship, the Council passed a strongly-worded resolution in behalf of increased support to Mission Boards; and commended the observance of Children's Day in the churches by a general offering to the Sunday School Society.

In 1892 the Council reviewed the development of systematic benevolences, and laid the groundwork for what developed later into the Every Member Canvass in the following vote:

That this Council suggest and urge that this subject of proportional giving be made a special order of the day for consideration in every local association and conference at the next meeting; and that such action be taken as may secure this year a contribution from every church to each one of our several national benevolent societies; and, so far as possible, something from every individual member proportionate to his ability.[13]

Meanwhile, the societies were beginning to take the churches more closely into their plan of organization, and the American Board had greatly expanded its list of corporate members, so that the Council could vote:

> That this Council, appreciating the importance of the unanimous action of the American Board at its last meeting in adopting measures looking towards the representation of the churches in the Board, expresses its gratification at such action; and the Council further expresses the earnest hope that the Board, through its committee already appointed, will devise such measures as will secure such desired representation; and that these measures may be such as will show the confidence of the Board in the churches, and result in increased confidence of the churches in the Board.[14]

III

THE COMMITTEE OF 1892

The committee appointed in 1892 to study the relationship of the societies to the churches recommended that any measures looking toward accomplishment of this purpose should "originate in the societies themselves, and be such as commend themselves to those who have had long experience in the management of our affairs"; it commended the efforts made by the societies to draw closer together and to interrelate their work, and to open the management to the representatives of the churches. The Council of 1892 asked the churches to contribute in the largest possible measure to the work the societies were doing.

By the 1898 Council meeting, however, discussions of Board and church relationships were again under way, and continued through the next fifteen years. They eventuated in the report of the Commission of Nineteen and adoption of the Kansas City draft of the constitution of the Council, defining the relationship of the Boards to the churches and to their representatives in the National Council. To better the relationship between the Boards and the elected representatives of the churches in the Council, a plan was made for union meetings of the Boards at the same time and place selected for the Council meeting.

This plan had been urged by resolutions received from various associations and ministerial bodies. After carefully studying the situation, the Committee on the Relation of Benevolent Societies to Churches summarized the arguments against union meetings of Boards and Council under four heads: (1) the meeting would be too large for accommoda-

---

[13] *Minutes of the National Council, 1892*, p. 22.
[14] *Minutes of the National Council, 1892*, p. 26.

tions; (2) there would be a confusion of thought and interest; (3) each society would lose by joining the others; and (4) their own constitutional provisions.

On the other hand, there were four arguments for such a meeting: (1) the reduction of expense; (2) a broader and more consistent view of the work; (3) deeper spiritual power; and (4) the opportunity offered to the smaller societies to present their work before the larger group. The Committee concluded by saying: "There are evident reasons that any proposition on the part of your present committee would be indelicate and presuming." Having heard the report, the Council voted to request the societies to study further what was known as the "Council plan" for holding the meetings of the societies in connection with the meeting of the Council.

When the Council met in Portland in 1901, its Committee of Fifteen presented a brief report that the question of the relationship of missionary societies to each other and to the churches had been continually before the churches, and that there was a desire on the part of the churches that a better understanding be reached. The committee placed its greatest emphasis upon the duty of each church "by personal canvass [to] reach as far as possible every one of its members with a direct personal appeal for some gift to each of our six missionary societies." They again urged the five homeland societies to constitute "an advisory committee of their own choosing, which would consider questions affecting the work of the societies"; and requested the homeland societies "to try the experiment of a united annual meeting." Once more they resolved that there should be one missionary publication.

It was at this Council that announcement was made by the Publishing Society of the purchase of *The Congregationalist,* thus putting under denominational auspices. the paper which up to this time had been privately owned.

IV

The First Secretary for Promotion

During the next three years (1901–04), the Boards established the Advisory Committee, with one member from each of the seven Home Boards and two from the American Board. This committee employed Rev. Charles A. Northrup, pastor at Norwich, Connecticut, as "secretary for the promotion of systematic benevolence," his salary and expenses being secured not from the Boards but from private sources. The Committee expressed the hope that so successful would be his work as a general promotional agent that missionary giving would become "systematic beneficence." The Committee, defining the work of the new secretary, said he was not to raise money for any one society, but was to cultivate the field in the interest of all, "to secure a definite pledge from each member of our Congregational churches, to support each one of our societies." Mr. Northrup, in a brief address, presented the first joint appeal for missionary giving.

The principle on which he was to work, he said, was "that every Congregational church should recognize our six-sided, six-fold work of missionary enterprise as practically one organic whole, and make a place for every one of the six societies in its scheme of benevolence."[15]

This 1904 meeting of the Council at Chicago followed the meeting of the American Board which had just been held in Des Moines, and many persons who had attended the American Board meeting came also to the Council meeting. The meetings of the Home Boards were to be held in connection with the Council, different organizations being given special sections for their own meetings. This was so helpful that it was proposed that the Council change its constitution to provide for a biennial instead of a triennial meeting; and to provide for the appointment of a new committee to formulate a plan which would bring the churches and the societies into closer relationship. This proposal was not carried into effect.

At the next Council meeting in Cleveland in 1907, the American Board held its meeting in connection with the meeting of the Council. Here appeared the first report of what might be called the predecessor of the Commission on Missions, for the Advisory Committee, reappointed by the Boards, had been functioning for five years and had begun to develop a program. The secretary of promotion, Mr. Northrup, had served two years when the office was discontinued in 1906, as the private funds provided for his salary were no longer available and the Boards were not ready to finance a joint undertaking. The main reason for failure of the plan was that the agencies which were to benefit from the work of a joint secretary preferred the former method of promotion whereby each Board was entirely independent.

V

THE APPORTIONMENT PLAN

At this meeting of the Council, Dr. Hubert C. Herring, then secretary of the Home Missionary Society, gave a report stating the need for an apportionment plan:

The churches have too long laid upon the societies the burden of collecting funds at great labor and expense. In so doing they have also forced the societies into at least the appearance of competition with one another. Let the churches now, by joint and thoughtful effort, gather from their ranks whatever

[15] *Minutes of the National Council, 1904,* p. 444.

amounts they are able to contribute to these causes, setting their representatives free to give undivided attention to the doing of the work for which they exist. The attainment of this ideal may be long postponed, but none the less it is an ideal toward which we all should work.[16]

This is a significant statement and ten years later, when Dr. Herring had become secretary of the National Council, he considered his major responsibility the development of the Every Member Canvass as a great joint enterprise of Council, Boards, and churches.

So happy had been the results of the combined meetings of Council and Boards, bringing together more than a thousand members, that the Council voted "that we invite and urge the affiliated societies to unite with the National Council of 1910." Later it voted a strong endorsement of the apportionment as recommended by the Advisory Committee, and urged the state and local bodies to do their utmost to secure the full amount, as indicated by the Advisory Committee.

Two other significant actions of this Council relating to the organization of Congregationalism were: first, the Council accepted the statement:

The functions of the local, state, and national bodies may safely be defined and enlarged so long as they remain advisory and directive and involve no authority save as the wisdom of their action secures the assent of the churches.[17]

and second, it advised the development of the state conference system:

That the state organizations become legally incorporated bodies; and that under a general superintendent and such boards as they may create, and acting in cooperation with committees of local associations and churches, they provide for and direct the extension of church work, the planting of churches, the mutual oversight and care of all self-sustaining as well as missionary churches, and other missionary and church activities, to the end that closer union may insure greater efficiency without curtailing local independence.[18]

This transference of responsibility for missionary work within the state from the Home Boards to regularly established state conferences marked a long step forward in bringing responsibility for home missionary work closer to the churches. Thus far the steps towards closer relationship had been restricted by fidelity of the Boards to their original constitutions and to the wishes of donors making certain specifications concerning funds put in trust for the Boards. The Boards had to preserve their identity in order to keep faith with these donors. At the same time the expanding work of the Boards required continually increasing funds. If the churches were to respond to these appeals, they needed to be assured that there was no money being used unnecessarily for administra-

---

[16] *Minutes of the National Council, 1907*, p. 205.
[17] *Minutes of the National Council, 1907*, p. 344.
[18] *Minutes of the National Council, 1907*, p. 346.

tion and promotion. They were inclined to react unfavorably to the appeals of so many independently organized agencies for the support of different enterprises which the churches looked upon as one missionary enterprise. This caused increasing pressure from the churches on the National Council, a representative body all of whose members were elected by the churches, and none of them appointed by any central agency. While some members of the Boards were nominated or suggested by state conferences or associations, yet these Boards reserved the right to nominate the larger part of their membership. This was considered wise because the agencies had become custodians of large funds which required a continuing body.

VI

The "Together Campaign"

The work of the Boards had so outgrown their resources that by 1907–8 debts were accumulating. In 1909 the societies agreed on what came to be known as the "Together Campaign" which was so successful that the accumulated indebtedness of the missionary societies was greatly reduced. The success of this first great missionary effort was due, according to the report of the Moderator, Hon. Thomas C. MacMillan, to the fact that

the entire group of our Missionary Societies entered into the canvass of the church membership upon an agreed and equitable basis. Thus united, they carried through a program marked by entire freedom from rivalry, and in a spirit of cooperation as fine as it was successful.

Gratifying and helpful as were its financial results, it produced at least three important effects:

1. The "Together Campaign" gave an impressive exhibition of the essential unity of all the mission work in the denomination.

2. It did much to promote and establish unity and cooperation between the missionary societies.

3. It resulted in the bringing into existence of a larger consciousness of the importance and of the claims of the missionary cause than had been had in many years, if ever.[19]

In the report of the Advisory Committee again appears the discussion of the need for one magazine rather than several. The Committee stated it had conducted a country-wide survey, and of the replies seventy per cent favored the publication of one magazine; but the Committee voted "that as it is not now feasible to have a single missionary magazine for all the societies, the Advisory Committee recommends that the home societies unite in publishing one Homeland Magazine to be issued on and after January, 1909."[20]

[19] *Minutes of the National Council, 1910*, p. 21.
[20] *Minutes of the National Council, 1910*, p. 378.

The Council itself was becoming something more than a convention. It had up to this time maintained a small office with a secretary, whose chief task was to edit and to publish the *Year Book,* with a budget for his salary and office expenses of about $3,000 a year. In addition to this budget the Council raised a fund for the printing and mailing of the annual *Year Book,* which amounted to considerably over $6,000 per year. But with this small budget, the Council was more and more serving as the central clearing house for the state conferences and for the churches.

The report of the Committee of Twenty-five, appointed to study these questions, contained the following statements:

We find that the National Council is already an administrative as well as an advisory body. This is seen in the organization and administration of the Board of Ministerial Relief, in the organization of the National Brotherhood through the Council's Committee of Twenty-Nine, and in the creation of the Advisory Committee which has given us the Apportionment Plan.

. . . the Council acts as counsellor and servant of the Boards so far as they are willing to avail themselves of such aid. We find that there is a large and growing sentiment favorable to administrative relations between the Council as our national representative body and the benevolent societies. . . .[21]

These statements were followed by this vote:

Resolved, that this Council is in favor of developing administration relations between the Council and the National Societies, that it believes the next step in such development consists in constituting the delegates of the Council the voting membership of the several societies with the addition of such members-at-large as may prove to be necessary, and that it refers the practical working out of these new relations to the Commission of Fifteen on Polity, hereinafter mentioned, report to be made to the next regular or special or adjourned session of this Council.[22]

VII

THE COMMISSION OF NINETEEN

The appointment of the Commission of Nineteen by the Council of 1910 is one of the historic acts in Congregational history. The field of study for the Commission is indicated, in part, by this section of the vote:

The movement for more efficient and more economical administration of home missionary work suggests that the missionary department of this (the Sunday-School and Publishing) Society might be wisely merged with the Congregational Home Missionary Society as a special department of the latter's work. The splendid traditions of the work under its present auspices arguing against this change, as also the difficulties involved in such a readjustment are fully recognized, and it is easily possible that the merger would be undesirable, but it is recommended that the Sunday-School and Publishing Society and the

[21]*Minutes of the National Council, 1910,* p. 387.
[22]*Minutes of the National Council, 1910,* p. 388.

Home Missionary Society take the question under careful consideration with a view to such readjustment if that shall seem wise.[23]

Anticipating the adoption of articles of agreement by the Council and Boards at the next Council meeting (to be held in 1913) the Council set up the National Council Apportionment Commission composed of one representative from each of the Boards and six members at large. Thus for the first time public interest was to be represented by the six members appointed by the Council. The duty of this Commission was:

(1) to adopt a general budget containing the amounts to be asked for the several Benevolent Societies;

(2) to employ such means as may seem desirable in administering the Apportionment Plan so as to secure from the churches adequate support for Congregational Missionary and benevolent enterprises.[24]

In the appointment of the Commission of Nineteen and in the assignment of its duties the Council went beyond an advisory relationship to the Boards and became to this extent administrative. Great care was taken that the selection of the Commission of Nineteen should represent all sections of the country, all shades of opinion, and each of the various Boards. The Commission included President Frank K. Sanders, Kansas; Rev. Henry A. Stimson, New York; President Charles S. Nash, California; Rev. William E. Barton, Illinois; Rev. Oliver Huckel, Maryland; Lucien C. Warner, New York; Rev. Charles S. Mills, Missouri; Rev. Rockwell H. Potter, Connecticut; John M. Whitehead, Wisconsin; Frank Kimball, Illinois; Professor Williston Walker, Connecticut; Henry M. Beardsley, Missouri; Rev. Henry H. Kelsey, Ohio; President Edward D. Eaton, Wisconsin; William W. Mills, Ohio; Samuel B. Capen, Massachusetts; Arthur H. Wellman, Massachusetts; Rev. Nehemiah Boynton, New York and Rev. Raymond Calkins, Maine.

Between the Council of 1910 and that of 1913 the Commission of Nineteen held many meetings, conducted wide correspondence and published in 1911 a tentative report. Before the meeting of the Council in Kansas City it published also a revised report, that the churches and their representatives might become familiar with the problems and the measures proposed for meeting them.

One proposal on the early drafts of the report was for a united Home Board of Missions. This met with a storm of protest. Each of the Home Boards had a loyal constituency which felt particular responsibility for the welfare of that Board. Also, the churches generally were not prepared to consider the work of the six homeland societies as a united national enterprise. Therefore, the Commission withdrew that recommendation.

[23] *Minutes of the National Council, 1910*, p. 395.
[24] *Minutes of the National Council, 1910*, p. 404.

The report as adopted by the Kansas City Council included two major reforms affecting the societies. One provision made the voting members of the Council voting members of each of the societies by virtue of their office as official delegates to the Council. This had been approved in principle by the Council of 1910. Each of the societies however was to continue the practice of having a group of corporate members appointed by itself thus giving the society in its business session a group well informed as to the work of the particular Board and alive to its needs and interests. The corporate members elected by the Boards had no special rights and duties, for all the members of the Council were also elected corporate members by each of the Boards. This plan has worked out most satisfactorily. The elected representatives of the churches function for the days when the Council is in session as voting members of the Council; and on days when the various Boards hold their meetings, as voting members of those Boards. This arrangement does not "bring the Boards under the domination of the Council" any more than it brings the Council under the domination of the Boards. It usually happens, however, that votes relating to the work of the Boards are first considered by the members sitting as a Council and then the same persons vote as members of the Board, having previously voted as members of the Council. Or the order may be reversed. By this provision unity of action has been achieved without placing one body under the direction of another.

The other major reform recommended by the Commission of Nineteen, while adopted with unanimity, did not work so harmoniously. It provided for a Commission on Missions having "advisory supervision" over the work of the societies. The report provided that:

On nomination by the standing Committee on Nominations, the National Council shall elect fourteen persons, and on nomination by the several national societies, home and foreign, shall also elect one person from each society, and on similar nomination one each from the whole body of Woman's Boards of Foreign Missions and from the Woman's Home Missionary Federation, who, together with the Secretary of the National Council *ex officio,* shall constitute a Commission of Missions.[25]

The duties of this Commission, as outlined in the report may be summarized as follows:

1. To prevent duplication of missionary activities.
2. To effect all possible economies in administration.
3. To seek to correlate the work of the several societies for maximum efficiency and minimum expense.[26]

[25] *Minutes of the National Council, 1913,* p. 351.
[26] *Minutes of the National Council, 1913,* p. 338.

To accomplish these purposes, it was given the following rights:

1. To examine the annual budgets of the several societies and have access to their books and records.
2. To give advice to the societies regarding problems involved in the work.
3. To make recommendations to the societies when their work can be made more efficient or more economical.
4. To examine present conditions and recommend to the National Council such simplification and consolidation of the home societies as shall seem most expedient.[27]

It also provided that all the expenses of this Commission should be paid by the treasury of the National Council, and that the new secretary of the Council should be the secretary of the Commission on Missions. The provision of the report relating to the secretary has been treated elsewhere; but it should be mentioned here that the secretary of the Council as secretary of the Commission on Missions should "serve it and through it the churches in the two great tasks immediately confronting them: (1) the work of coordinating and readjusting our missionary activities; and (2) the more efficient financing of those activities, through the Apportionment Plan and other plans which may be devised."[28]

Each Board had a representative on this Commission of Nineteen and when the report was presented to the Council it was a unanimous report; that is, the representatives of the various societies concurred in the recommendations. There was much questioning on the part both of the members of the churches and also of the societies as to whether or not the plan proposed would meet the objectives in mind. The following statement was presented to the Council by the American Board, in advance of the consideration of the report of the Commission of Nineteen:

Your committee rejoices in this attention which is being given to the administration of our denominational missionary work, feeling that the more churches can concern themselves in what all must regard as their leading interest, the better will they be able to perform their part in establishing Christ's kingdom in the earth. As in the past, the Board on its own account has from time to time sought to bring itself into closer relations to the churches, so now that the matter has, in a measure, been taken out of our hands and thrown into the arena of general denominational debate, the members of the Prudential Committee and the officers of the Board, speaking for themselves, stand ready to favor such further changes as the churches may desire, in so far as these changes are found to be legal and practicable.[29]

[27] *Minutes of the National Council, 1913*, p. 338.
[28] *Minutes of the National Council, 1913*, p. 338.
[29] *Minutes of the National Council, 1913*, pp. 102–103.

Not since the meeting of the Council in Boston in 1865 had there been a Council having such an array of responsible leaders of the denomination as was present at Kansas City. Dr. Nehemiah Boynton was the retiring Moderator, Dr. Charles E. Jefferson was the Preacher, Dean Charles R. Brown was the new Moderator, and Dr. Carl S. Patton, Dr. Newman Smyth, Governor Simeon E. Baldwin and many others came to this Council meeting aware that the denomination, which had come to self-consciousness in the Council of 1865 and had organized in the Council of 1871, now was to work in real earnest on a main task long deferred.

Anticipating the discussion which would occur over the report of the Commission of Nineteen, Dr. Boynton in his moderatorial address prepared the delegates for serious consideration of the task before them. This masterly address should be considered in part:

Permit me to affirm that putting our denomination in effective play through the readjusted institutions is just as much a spiritual task as prayer and preaching. . . .

Nor are we to be deterred because of the fear that such adjustment will throw our denominational interests into the hands of ecclesiastical politicians. The politician in Congregationalism is usually a short-lived individual. He is like the grass; in the morning flourishing and growing up; in the evening, cut down and withering. . . .

The autonomy of the local church is, and will always be, the slogan of our American Congregationalism. Every local church, free and independent in its pulpit and in its pew, a law unto itself; cordially conceding all this, it still remains true that there is no reason why the autonomy of the local church should destroy the Congregationalism denomination. The principle of the fellowship of the churches is just as truly Congregational as the other. They are the foci of our Congregational ellipse . . .

Congregationalism never hesitated to match a necessity with an efficiency. In this way we have provided ourselves with conferences, associations and national councils. In this way we have established societies for the prosecution of home and foreign missions. In this way we have approved an apportionment plan for raising our benevolent funds; in this way, it is to be hoped, we shall at this Council find ourselves inclined to meet new occasions with new efficiencies . . . The adjustment of a principle, so far from being an abandonment, is the accentuation of it. It is efficiency or exit, for Congregationalism.[30]

Dr. Jefferson in his sermon said:

What is the mission of Congregationalism? To keep alive a theory of church government? No; to keep the soul alive to God. It is often said that Congregationalism is a theory of church government; that it is foundationed on two principles—the independence of the local church and the equal sisterhood of these local churches. But these principles are not foundations. They rest on something deeper. The fundamental thing in Congregationalism is a doctrine of God . . .

[30]*Minutes of the National Council, 1913*, pp. 11-13.

Our doctrine of independence grows out of our faith. Our polity is foundationed on our conception of God . . .

We are free men in Christ. We are not bound by the traditions of the second
century, or the dogmas of the fourth, or the doctrines of the sixteenth, or the
customs of the seventeenth, or the practices of the eighteenth, or the methods of
the nineteenth, but are at liberty to build the church along the lines indicated
by the Eternal Spirit speaking in the intelligence and conscience of our day, so
it shall become more and more an effective instrument in the hands of God for
the promulgation of his gospel and the extension of his kingdom.[31]

From the opening day of the Council interest centered around the
report of the Commission of Nineteen. The great day came on Saturday,
October 25, when Dr. Raymond Calkins and Dr. Rockwell H. Potter
conducted the devotional service. At 9:30 Dean Brown took the chair,
and the report was presented as a whole by the chairman, Dr. Frank K.
Sanders of Washburn College, Topeka. Dr. William E. Barton, secretary
of the Commission, presented the section on the revision of the constitution for the Council; Rev. Charles S. Nash the section on the secretaryship; and Prof. Williston Walker the section relating to missionary societies. After a full discussion approval was given on the various sections,
and the report as a whole was adopted. The Council then sang, "Praise
God from whom all blessings flow." Dr. Albert J. Lyman led in prayer.
The hymn, "I love Thy kingdom, Lord," was sung. The benediction was
pronounced by Rev. Sidney L. Gulick, eminent missionary from Japan.

This is reminiscent of the closing session of the Cambridge Synod in
1648 which in the words of the *Magnalia* was on this wise:

They went on comfortably, and after many *"filing* thoughts upon it," settled
down substantially upon Mr. Mather's draught of a Platform; after which they
broke up with singing the Song of Moses and the Lamb, in the fifteenth chapter
of the Revelation, "adding another sacred *Song* from the nineteenth Chapter
of that Book; which is to be found metrically paraphrased in the *New England
Psalm-Book*."[32]

FROM 1913 TO 1925

Tracing the progress of other interests through the denominational
life from 1865 to the present shows that each interest appears to come
to a peak in certain years and to predominate in certain Council meetings. The main interest of the Council of 1913 was the adoption of the
new constitution with its proposals for closer relationship of the boards
and Council. The Council of 1925 registered high interest in this same
subject, and also the Council at Mount Holyoke College in 1936.

The task was to determine if the new constitution was workable.
When the Council of 1915 met in New Haven the Commission on Mis-

[31]*Minutes of the National Council, 1913*, pp. 36–37.
[32]Dexter, *Congregationalism as Seen in Its Literature*, p. 438.

sions was able to report that "The American Board, the American Missionary Association, the Congregational Home Missionary Society, and the Congregational Church Building Society have made the necessary changes in their constitutions, and that the other societies have not yet completed action but are in process."[33]

The report of the American Board by Rev. William E. Strong, the editorial secretary, states:

As the American Board makes report once more to the National Council, it is to be recognized that it now does so as clearly and organically one of the agencies of the Council. When it was founded, 105 years ago, the American Board was not formally linked with the Congregational Church machinery. It was not uniformly approved of by those churches or supported by them. It was left to find its own constituency and to create its own membership. It had to devise methods for its continuance and its upkeep. It kept close to the churches; its friends belonged to them; but it was not itself within the fold.[34]

This Board has been set up by a committee appointed by the General Association of Massachusetts; but later when it was incorporated by the State, it became a self-perpetuating, closed corporation. This cut its official connection with the Association first sponsoring it. "It should be noted that at that time neither the ministers or the churches of Massachusetts wished to assume responsibility for it, though the Association was willing to give the venture its blessing."[35]

The report on the Home Boards written by Dr. Charles E. Burton, then general secretary of the Home Missionary Society says, "The Home Missionary Society has been listening carefully for the voice of the churches on the question of the realignment of our missionary forces in the homeland. . . . Finally, its Committee felt no reluctance in voicing its opinion that the entire home missionary constituency could be depended upon heartily to cooperate under any plans which the churches formulate through the wisdom of their National Council."[36]

I

THE COMMISSION ON MISSIONS

The Commission on Missions under Dr. Herring's leadership began publishing material for the Every Member Canvass. Dr. Herring became national protagonist in the next Council for the Canvass, in which he was ably supported by Mr. E. C. Capen.

Dr. Donald J. Cowling, chairman of a subcommittee on organization,

[33] *Minutes of the National Council, 1915*, p. 268.
[34] *Minutes of the National Council, 1915*, p. 163.
[35] Letter from Dr. Fred Field Goodsell to the writer, dated Nov. 10, 1941. In Congregational Library.
[36] *Minutes of the National Council, 1915*, pp. 174–175.

presented a report on the relationship of agencies working for the local churches. He advised closer affiliations of three Boards, the Home Missionary Society, Church Building Society, and Sunday School Extension Society, to lead naturally in time to the formation of one board; or to operation under a common board of directors.

The churches were approaching the three hundredth Anniversary of the landing of the Pilgrims and the matter of greatest interest at this 1915 Council was planning for the proper commemoration of this Tercentenary. Dr. Herring and his committee saw a great opportunity here for strengthening the loyalty of the churches to the Boards and to the Council.

As a first step in planning a great national program, Dr. Herring desired to have the united support of Council officials, Board officials, state conference officials, pastors, and church members. Replying to questions many people were asking, Dr. Herring said that in the beginning of Congregational history there were no Boards; John Eliot constituted himself a missionary board and got church support. John Harvard set up a private organization as a college and the churches accepted it. In the early days when the churches felt a great missionary impulse, they had left such enterprises to interested individuals.

II

THE TERCENTENARY

The Council of 1915 approved the plans for the Tercentenary and the Commission on Missions was charged with their development and with the promotion of the apportionment for the Boards. One portion of the plan for the Tercentenary was the project to raise an adequate sum for a ministerial pension fund. This was carried forward with great vigor in the years between the Council meeting of 1915 and that of 1919.

The Council at Columbus, Ohio in 1917 gave most of its attention to war service and the relationship of the churches to problems raised by the war. The Commission on Missions had been studying the necessary readjustments of the Boards, transfer of work, and study of the field. At this Council a noteworthy report was presented on Congregationalism in the South, prepared by a small committee composed of Dr. Hastings H. Hart of the Russell Sage Foundation, Professor E. C. Norton of Pomona College, Mr. Charles W. Davison of Newtonville, Massachusetts and Dr. Herring. The report has for its objectives:

1. To convey to our fellow Congregationalists in the South the greetings of the denomination and to assure them of its sense of the significance of the work they have done and are doing.
2. To gather impressions concerning local situations, general tendencies,

unmet needs, questions of policy, et cetera, and so far as these impressions should be deemed relevant to the work of our mission agencies to report them to the officers and directors of those organizations.

3. To communicate to our constituency at large the committee's judgment concerning the progress of our Southern work with some appraisal of its importance and estimate of its possibilities.[37]

This report presented a plan for the church agencies working in the South which has become the basis of their program through the years. This study served to emphasize the usefulness of the Commission on Missions as an agency to reduce possible overlooking and overlapping.

The Commission on Missions had a second report on the national plan of benevolence based on stewardship, proposing a Pilgrim Covenant of Stewardship as a basis for nationwide enrollment in proportionate giving.[38]

III

The Care of the Ministry

The Council of 1917 was made historic by adoption of the plan for the Annuity Fund. The plan had been inaugurated at New Haven in 1915, had been well organized, and a vigorous campaign was in progress to raise the endowment fund for ministerial annuities.

The Council for many years had placed the care of aged ministers in the forefront of the churches' interest. The National Council from the meeting in 1886, when the need for relief for aged or incapacitated ministers had been made in an overture from Ohio, had continued to give attention to this cause. Some states had state relief societies, but were without sufficient funds to meet their needs.

A Committee on Relief had been appointed in 1889, which administered funds held by the trustees of the National Council. In 1907 the trustees of the National Council organized the Congregational Board of Ministerial Relief, the members being elected by the Council. This became a permanent Board.

In 1910 Ohio proposed a pension system for ministers which would so safeguard the ministry that there would be fewer calls for relief. Results followed. Other states joined in this memorial, notably Southern California and Wisconsin. The campaign for an endowment had been approved by the Council of 1915 and at the meeting in 1917, Dr. Charles S. Mills presented a plan for the Annuity Fund which with the endowment in hand was adopted and put into effect. The Annuity Fund under the statesmanlike leadership of Dr. Charles S. Mills, ably assisted by Dr.

[37] *Minutes of the National Council, 1917*, pp. 160–161.
[38] *Minutes of the National Council, 1917*, p. 205.

Lewis T. Reed, who succeeded Dr. Mills as general secretary in 1928, soon became the highly efficient Pension Board.

IV
THE INTERCHURCH WORLD MOVEMENT

The 1919 Council meeting at Grand Rapids, coming at the close of the war when there had been enormous outpourings of funds for charitable and welfare interests, had before it a proposal from an influential interdenominational group in New York for the formation of an Interchurch World Movement. The proposals were breathtaking in their sweep and range. The Movement proposed the enlisting of 50,000,000 Protestants in America to support the united world-wide religious and educational program of all the churches. This interdenominational committee solicited the coöperation of the Congregational agencies.

To allay the fears that this Movement would involve too great expense to the Boards, the Commission on Missions stated that it was proposed that the expense of the Movement would not rest on the boards but would be raised from friendly citizens who were not regular contributors to the mission boards.

With much questioning and some misgivings, the Council finally decided to coöperate. Dr. Herman F. Swartz was appointed secretary of the Congregational World Movement, with Rev. Lloyd Douglas of Ohio and Rev. Frederick L. Fagley, associate secretary of the National Council, as assistants; and with the service of all promotional secretaries of the boards at the disposal of this Movement, the denomination went forward in a great educational program which, it was confidently expected, would be of great service to the boards and all other religious agencies.

While these great plans were going forward, a discussion claimed the immediate attention of denominational leaders, concerning the relationship between the state conferences and the boards. The Commission on Missions had already asked the state organizations to take a larger share in the raising of funds for the Boards, and to raise funds for their own work along with those raised for the national agencies. There were almost as many different plans in operation as there were state conferences, a plain illustration of Congregational independence. The superintendents had been meeting annually the last of January in Chicago in what had become known as the Midwinter Meeting. Here they discussed all phases of their work. Through processes of group thinking they defined their problems and found certain solutions. The questions relating to state work and its support came before the Council of 1915 for discussion and were assigned to the Commission on Missions for study during the next biennium, for report at the next meeting of the Council.

In all these activities Dr. Herring, the Council's secretary, was busily engaged. His advice was being received more and more by the boards, the churches, and the state conferences. His untimely death by drowning at Martha's Vineyard, Massachusetts, August 6, 1920, brought an irreparable loss to the whole national fellowship.

When the Council met in Los Angeles in 1921, one of the first tasks was election of a successor to Dr. Herring; and again the Council looked to the Home Missionary Society and selected Dr. Charles E. Burton for Council secretary. Dr. Burton had succeeded Dr. Herring as Home Missionary secretary when Dr. Herring had become secretary of the Council in 1913, and had been Dr. Herring's close associate through the years.

By this time the Interchurch World Movement had passed into history. After carrying forward a great nationwide program of education, it was not able to finance itself and came to a sudden end, leaving the participating denominations with considerable debt. The denominational organization known as the Congregational World Movement, which was related to the Interchurch World Movement, was successful beyond all expectations. The table of apportionment giving shows, in 1910, the average giving per member to the apportionment in the denomination was $1.70 per year. This had been raised to $3.98 by 1920, in part as a result of the educational work of the Congregational World Movement.

The time had come to return to normal after the venture into great interdenominational plans, and the Council voted:

> That the Commission on the Congregational World Movement be instructed to transfer to the Commission on Missions the executive organization now maintained by the Commission on the Congregational World Movement, together with its property, and also the undistributed funds in the hands of the Commission on the Congregational World Movement, at the date on which the transfer is made; and further that the Commission on Missions assume the obligations standing against the Commission on the Congregational World Movement at the date of the transfer.[39]

V

The Foundation for Education

This Council of 1921 also established the Foundation for Education and voted that it should receive seven percent of the apportionment to provide for its first year's activities. This seven percent out of the total apportionment virtually made the Foundation a charge against the receipts of all the societies. As it was expected that this arrangement should last only for one year, objection did not go beyond a discussion stage.

The next year the Foundation not receiving sufficient funds for its expenses and likely to become a permanent charge on the apportion-

[39] *Minutes of the National Council, 1921*, p. 378.

ment, objection developed. The Foundation's activities were reduced and in 1927 it was made a department of the Congregational Educational Society and its work integrated with the work of that society.

VI
THE DEVELOPMENT OF JOINT PROMOTION

The Congregational World Movement had raised thousands of dollars. It had received grants for expenses in the sixteen months from December 23, 1919 to April 30, 1921, of $166,658; had spent $62,000 for administration, $58,000 on a field department, and $32,000 on a publicity department, a total of more than $150,000; but had received directly from donors gifts of approximately $1,100,000, in addition to what the boards had received in their treasuries. When the World Movement was concluded and its work and personnel turned over to the Commission on Missions, serious questions arose as to the future. The Commission on Missions had been financed by the National Council, but this expense seldom went beyond $600 a year, usually for expenses of Commission meetings.

The Apportionment Committee, financed by the boards and related to the Commission on Missions, seldom spent more than $2,000 a year on Every Member Canvass material. The Commission on Missions now raised the question whether (1) there should be joint promotion by the Commission on Missions which would function somewhat after the plan of the Interchurch World Movement—that is, be organized under the Council but financed by the boards, to raise money from the churches and individuals for the work of the boards; or (2) the boards should continue their independent promotion and develop this feature of their work, now somewhat disorganized following the raising of the Pilgrim Memorial Fund and the joint efforts of the Congregational World Movement.

Dr. Herman F. Swartz, who had been most successful in management of the Congregational World Movement, resigned as promotional secretary. Dr. Burton assumed the major portion of the responsibility for a part of the year; when Rev. William S. Beard, who had distinguished himself first as a leader in raising the Pilgrim Memorial Fund, and later as promotional secretary for the Church Extension Boards, became the secretary of the Commission on Missions.

In his report to the Council at Springfield in 1923, Dr. Burton called attention to this unexpected development of the program of the Commission on Missions of which he was, by constitutional provision, the secretary. The Kansas City plan made the Commission on Missions a consultative and advisory body under the National Council. Its work was limited to holding a few meetings each year with expenses seldom over $600 per year. When the Commission on Missions became the chief promotional agency succeeding the Congregational World Movement with a budget three times that of the National Council and a staff of employees, a different situation arose. Dr. Burton in his report to the Council of 1923, said:

In addition to the work of promotion, the Commission on Missions, as the agency of the denomination for coordinating the work of the various boards has called for much more of the secretary's time and energy than any other department and possibly more than all the others. Perhaps this is as it should be in view of the fact that our missionary and educational work constitute the bulk of the things we do together. Nevertheless it is doubtful whether the secretary would have been made secretary of the Commission had the present plan of making it a promotional agency been contemplated in its original organization. So soon as and if the present or similar plans are determined as permanent the Council should face the question as to whether the Commission on Missions should not have its own secretary in the person of another than the secretary of the Council.[40]

The Commission on Missions in its report stated what it considered to be its tasks under the new arrangement:

It is the judgment of your Commission that under the constitution of the National Council it is the duty of the Commission on Missions in the field of promotion to initiate and to direct the common appeal of the Congregational Missionary Societies to the Congregational Churches and their members for the support of the missionary work of these societies, and to correlate and coordinate the special individual promotional work of the several societies one with another and each with the common appeal and all with the appeals of the several states for the particular missionary work within their borders and under their charge.[41]

It gave the difficulties of the situation in these words:

These centered in the fact that the Council had commissioned an organization of its own to raise money for corporations which already have boards legally appointed for that purpose, and in the further fact that under the apportionment plan and the desire of the churches to subscribe their benevolences in a single budget the national organization retains a system of competitive promotion directed by six general boards and two woman's organizations besides the Commission on Missions.[42]

The question arose as to whether the concentration of the promotional activities for missions under the control of an agency primarily directed by the National Council was not dividing the responsibility which naturally belonged to board and members, thus making for confusion.

[40] *Minutes of the National Council, 1923,* p. 24.
[41] *Minutes of the National Council, 1923,* p. 30.
[42] *Minutes of the National Council, 1923,* p. 28.

Another question arose, whether it was possible for an agency like the Commission on Missions, without responsibility for the administration of the Boards, to promote their interests and raise funds as effectively as the Boards themselves. Many insisted that if the Commission on Missions raised the money, (it) would soon concern itself with problems of administration, and imperil the Boards' traditional independence.

Other problems needed solution. The first was in the field of promotion, where an adequate plan for bringing the states into the promotional picture had been developed. The Council had advised the Church Extension Boards to turn over to the state conferences as much of the work in the various states as was possible, and for this work the state conferences needed funds. The conferences depended very largely on promotional literature and leadership of the boards' secretaries for raising these funds.

The second problem concerned the closer affiliation of the boards; and the third was the desire of many for more simplified promotion. Not only was the Commission on Missions appealing to the churches for the support of the Every Member Canvass, but it was also developing its program on the year-round basis for individual gifts. Separate appeals were being made by the seven societies. Thus eight agencies were asking the churches for funds. The apportionment to the churches contained eleven items, and this multiplicity of demands created general confusion.

A collateral problem concerned the denominational publications. The request that had been made from time to time for fifty years that there be a combining of the various magazines was renewed.

VII

THE COMMITTEE OF TWELVE

The Commission on Missions was instructed to set up a Committee of Twelve to study these multiplied problems. This Committee consisted of Rev. William Horace Day, Bridgeport, Connecticut, Chairman; Mr. Henry M. Beardsley, Kansas City, Missouri; Rev. Hugh Elmer Brown, Evanston, Illinois; Rev. Harry P. Dewey, Minneapolis, Minnesota; Mrs. Ernest A. Evans, New York, New York; Mr. Elbert A. Harvey, Boston, Massachusetts; Rev. Horace C. Mason, Seattle, Washington; Mrs. E. A. Osbornson, Oak Park, Illinois; Mr. Dell A. Schweitzer, Los Angeles, California; Mrs. Lucius H. Thayer, Portsmouth, New Hampshire and Mrs. Charles R. Wilson, Detroit, Michigan.[43]

The committee was given instructions, including these items:

1. The simplest and most efficient machinery for raising the necessary funds for the state work and the work of the Boards.

[43] *Minutes of the National Council, 1925,* p. 131.

2. Economy.

3. Efficiency. "On the foreign field in some missions there are two sources of administrative authority; in some three; and in some even four; involving separate sets of books, inflexibility of budgets and complications in administration. There is also real overlapping in the work of the home societies."[44]

4. Simpler relationships.

5. The continuing of unification. Consolidation was to take into consideration the legal restrictions, efficiency and service, and nothing to be done in any way to prejudice any society's vested interests.

In general, the committee was to plan for such a change in status that the result would be "A row of friendly but unrelated societies become departments of a single enterprise, resulting in no loss of efficient detailed attention to the departmental program but in a new unity of outlook in the accomplishment of the entire task."[45]

When the Council met in Washington in 1925 the Committee of Twelve presented its proposals. Again, as in 1913, the Council was truly a meeting of "many men of many minds."

The Committee of Twelve realized it was dealing with a delicate situation: "Your Committee is aware that the desire of the churches for changes in organization often grows out of impatience with the multiplicity of appeal, which is a purely promotional problem."[46]

The Committee stated that if there was to be simplicity in promotion and unity in the appeal to the churches, it was necessary that there should be unity in leadership. It stated that in foreign missions there were four separate boards, the American Board and the three women's boards; that each board worked in the closest cooperation, yet each had its own budget and its own administrative and promotional problems, also its own missionaries. In some extreme situations abroad, there would be in the same station missionaries appointed by and responsible to three different American Congregational agencies.

The Committee realized that each Board had its loyal supporters who would resent changes in the status of their particular interest, and if changes were made this might immediately be followed by loss of contributions.

The discussion of the Committee of Twelve's report occupied practically half of the Council's sessions. Practically every proposal was the result of a compromise. Because of its very multiplicity of detail, all of which was perhaps necessary, the report was most difficult to comprehend. Some members expressed the opinion that this was a case where "tinkering with the machinery" had gone beyond reasonable limits.

[44] *Minutes of the National Council, 1925,* p. 69.
[45] *Minutes of the National Council, 1925,* p. 70.
[46] *Minutes of the National Council, 1925,* p. 57.

After the final report was adopted by the Council the various boards met *seriatim,* according to the constitution, which provides that the voting members of the Council shall also be voting members of the various societies; and each board adopted the report.

When the Prudential Committee of the American Board met in Boston following the Council meeting and the minutes of this special meeting were read, the question was raised whether the Washington meeting, held on the closing day of the Council, was a legal meeting. It was ruled not legal, as the meeting had not been called according to constitutional provision. Therefore, the vote of approval in Washington was not a legal vote. The matter thus being open, the Board felt that much more time was necessary for the study of the report of the Committee of Twelve, which was now before the American Board simply as proposals. This situation in the American Board brought great confusion into the whole plan. Whether or not the plan of the Committee of Twelve could have been carried into successful operation is a moot question; but with this handicap the confusion that had existed was not lessened but increased.

The Home Boards adopted the report, and proceeded to put into operation measures to carry out the various consolidations, leaving the home work divided into four separate agencies. The states were given more control of their own work. The Board of Ministerial Relief became one of the Home Boards. The new Commission on Missions was organized to include the entire membership of the Prudential Committee of the American Board, the entire membership of the Board of Directors of the Home Boards, plus nine members at large elected by the National Council. This enlarged commission was directed to set up a Promotional Council of sixteen, five from each Board, three state superintendents and the secretaries of the Council, the Commission on Missions and the Layman's Advisory Committee. It was thought the Boards would have confidence in the plan now that promotion had been unified under an agency which the Boards controlled. The public interest was represented by the nine persons elected at large. As the Boards each had thirty-six members in the Commission, the nine at large were a very small minority.

One unusual provision was that the Board secretaries on the Promotional Council were to be elected also as promotional secretaries for all the Boards, the purpose being that each secretary thus elected should be as responsible for securing funds for the other Boards as for his own Board. It was understood that each man would have more information about his own Board, but unitedly the secretaries would have responsibility for support of all the Boards. Also, the secretaries were to feel responsible for raising money for the states and the states for raising money for the Boards. This put a tremendous burden on the secretaries, many of whom had spent long years familiarizing themselves with the need of one particular phase of the whole program. Now the total work of the churches at home and abroad, carried forward by the eight administrative agencies and by the states covered so wide a range that each secretary faced an almost impossible problem of presentation. The plan was based on the idea that administration and promotion could be separated and thrive, when in reality they are the "two legs that carry the body." These provisions affected only the promotional secretaries. The Boards classified some secretaries as "educational," and these were not under the immediate direction of the Commission on Missions.

The Commission on Missions in its report to the Council for 1923 had reported total receipts of $725,173, and total expenses of $122,867, or 19 percent. The total receipts on the apportionment for the same year were $3,186,803, indicating that only one-sixth of the money contributed to the apportionment was passing through the Commission on Missions' receiving treasury.

The anticipated value of the whole plan as adopted may be summed up in the words of the Commission on Missions under two heads:

1. *Simplification.* "We conceive that with a single promotional agency embracing all the contacts it will be possible to deal personally with any church which desires it and to establish contacts with many times the number of individuals now interested. Where any one society on a limited budget and for a limited contribution could not afford such relationships, and where now they would not be possible because of the forbidding number of approaches, one body with a large appeal and correspondingly large resources can establish these connections effectively."[47]

2. *Democracy.* "The proposals contemplate an organization in which the representatives of the churches would have direct voice in a feasible way for the control of the entire missionary activity. As it is, the representatives of the churches face an organization which is so complex that expression of opinion is not attempted, and if it is expressed, the number of organizations involved is so great that it becomes lost before it reaches the final authoritative group."[48]

This marks the second peak in the relationship between the Council, the churches, and the Boards. Of the two proposals adopted at Kansas City in 1913, the first, common voting membership, continued unchanged. The second, joint or unified promotion, had been the field in which the experiments had taken place, and which it was hoped would be regularized by adoption of the report of the Committee of Twelve.

[47] *Minutes of the National Council, 1925*, p. 127.
[48] *Minutes of the National Council, 1925*, p. 127.

VIII

THE STRATEGY COMMITTEE

These hopes were doomed to disappointment. Through the next ten years the whole denomination and the Boards continued somewhat in a state of ferment, with much discussion, many resolutions by conferences and Boards and committees. There were valiant efforts to work the plan, but there were too many intangibles. This situation caused a nationwide demand for a thoroughgoing restudy of the problems, and resulted in the appointment of a third committee, the Strategy Committee. This Committee made its report after long and careful study, to the Mount Holyoke meeting of the Council in 1936. In the intervening years there were developments worthy of note.

In 1927 it became necessary for the states to increase their share of the apportionment by three and one-half percent to take care of the work taken over from the Home Boards, and also because of the increase of work and demands within the states. This meant that an equal percentage must be deducted from the income of the Boards, which raised new problems. The Commission on Missions reported it had not been possible to commit all the promotional work of the Boards to the Commission on Missions, as ordered.

It was during this period that Mr. Beard resigned, and Associate Secretary Fagley was assigned to the Missions Council *ad interim*. During this interval Mr. Fagley led in the organization of regional committees which were first composed of small groups of responsible officials, clergymen, and lay people meeting in different sections. So helpful was this plan of acquaintance between board representatives and church officials that it became a regular feature of denominational work. The regional meetings have become great consultative conventions for the whole field of missionary work.

At the meeting of the Council in 1927 the Commission on Missions reported eight "departures" from the Washington action, made seventeen recommendations for action by the Council, and then listed in a paragraph "matters to be considered later on." Dr. Lucius Thayer, chairman, who had so wisely guided the Commission through this turbulent year, closed his report by saying: "In conclusion, the Commission records with gratification the fact that in these years of reorganization the treasuries of the societies have not suffered from decreases, such as many of the other denominations have suffered from. This is genuine cause for gratitude to the Giver of all good gifts."[49]

By the time of the meeting of the next Council in 1929 in Detroit,

[49] *Minutes of the National Council, 1927*, p. 45.

Dr. Burton, in his report on the development during the four years since the Committee of Twelve reported, said: "Without doubt some momentum was lost in turning aside for a little to repair the machinery. It is for us now with the improved organization to more than regain the lost momentum."[50]

The American Board was able to say in its report:

The particular point of emphasis in the present biennium of the American Board has been the increased cooperation within the denomination with the other missionary societies. Under the leadership of the Promotional Council and Secretary Merrill, the denomination has attained the highest degree of partnership and the spirit of sharing that we have ever known. The text might almost be used: "looking also on the things of others."

This biennium has also seen a number of interesting developments in the reorganization of the Board's work, due to the merger of the three Woman's Boards with the American Board.[51]

But the report continued with the statement that this cooperation and reorganization had affected adversely the income of the Boards. "The merger has laid an extra burden upon the treasury of the American Board, and the effect of this is still revealed in the treasurer's report."[52]

The 1931 Council meeting at Seattle was made memorable by the merger of the General Convention of the Christian Church with the National Council of the Congregational Churches to form the General Council of the Congregational and Christian Churches, with the merger of the denominational organizations and Missions Boards. No insurmountable problems were found in merging the two churches, including the various missionary boards. The secretaries of the Christian Boards found employment in the merged organizations. Dr. Warren H. Denison, the secretary of the General Convention, became one of the secretaries of the General Council. Rev. Wilson P. Minton, secretary of the foreign board of the Christian Church, became one of the assistant secretaries of the Commission on Missions. Rev. A. W. Sparks, secretary of the Christian Home Missionary Society, joined the staff of the Town and Country Department of the Board of Home Missions. Mr. Herman Eldredge of the Christian Education and Publishing Society became connected with the Pilgrim Press and the new denominational paper; and Miss Lucy Eldredge, young people's secretary of the Christian Church, became a secretary of the Young People's Department of the Education Society.

Discussion continued as to the function of the Commission on Missions as instituted by the report of the Committee of Twelve at Wash-

[50] *Minutes of the National Council, 1929,* p. 18.
[51] *Minutes of the National Council, 1929,* p. 96.
[52] *Minutes of the National Council, 1929,* p. 96.

ington in 1925. It was found that this all-inclusive agency was assembled with great difficulty and at great expense. It included all members of the Home Board (thirty-six); of the Prudential Committee (thirty-six); ten members at large, and the moderator and secretary of the Council, a total of eighty-four members. The report of the Commission states what was considered its task and its staff:

> The chief function of the Commission is the promotion of income for our missionary and educational activities. Associated with this is the general work of education in missions and the furnishing of information concerning all departments of work.
>
> The Commission maintains a staff of six fulltime Secretaries and two on parttime, the chief dependence for the total work being upon the Secretaries of the several societies and the officers of the state conferences. The General Secretary of the National Council serves as General Secretary of the Commission without salary from the Commission.[53]

While this was going forward in connection with the Commission on Missions, the Boards were strengthening their own educational departments. The question was continually arising as to how far the Commission on Missions was responsible for the missionary education work cared for by the Boards, and where the line was drawn between missionary education and promotion. It became generally accepted that what the Boards wished to do in their own name was education, through the work of the Education Secretaries.

The situation that developed was quite adequately described in the report of the Home Boards:

> It may not be generally recognized that the Home Boards, despite their independent origin and the retention of their individual names, are very closely unified both in administration and in promotion. Among the factors which tend to produce this unity are: substantially common corporate membership, similar by-laws, common Board of Directors and general officers, interlocking Administrative Committees, joint Cabinet and receiving treasury. The work of the Project Secretary, operating on behalf of all the Boards, further tends to bring their interests into conjunction, while the unified Annual Meetings, which have been held ever since 1924, more and more emphasize aspects of the common task rather than division of work as carried on by separate societies. In promotion, too, the Home Boards are directly unified under common leadership, the issuance of a joint magazine and the preparation of joint advertisements. Consolidation of practically all our New York denominational offices on the eighth and ninth floors of the United Charities Building, effected May 1, will make for cooperative efficiency. Underlying and enveloping all this joint activity on the part of the Home Boards is a spirit of cordial, mutual interest and good fellowship both among the Directors and general officers as well as among the employed official staff. It is doubtful whether any business or industrial organization could show a better spirit of mutual understanding and fraternal regard than is evidenced

[53] *Minutes of the General Council, 1931*, p. 27.

in the frequent personal contacts of those who are charged with the carrying on of both administrative and promotional activities.[54]

It will be noted from this paragraph that so far as the Home Boards were concerned, the Commission on Missions and its office were not in the thought of the officials who wrote that biennial report. They were trying to bring the various Home Boards into a closer relationship, and to build up an educational agency with literature and magazine, to parallel the corresponding department of the American Board, which included educational and editorial secretaries.

The Commission on Missions had been charged with responsibility for promotion but was finding a restricted field of activity. The Boards now having seventy-two out of eighty-four members of the Commission on Missions, followed their own best judgment, which was to strengthen their individual educational and editorial departments rather than to build up a joint agency for which they had not asked, and which they felt was costing increasingly large sums of money. Dr. Charles C. Merrill, secretary of the Commission on Missions, resigned, and other staff officials withdrew. When the Council met in Oberlin in 1934 the Commission on Missions made a proposal for reorganization; presented the results of an appraisal committee set up some years before, and made the following statement: "The Commission is eager to be the faithful servant of the churches and solicits the freest discussion of these questions and others and covets the leading of the divine mind through our common thoughts and aspirations."[55]

IX

THE APPRAISAL COMMITTEE

The Council, acting upon the recommendation of the Commission, set itself to restudy the whole problem under the guidance of an enlarged committee. The following were named as the committee: Dean L. A. Weigle, Connecticut; Rev. H. Paul Douglass, New York; Rev. Oscar E. Maurer, Connecticut; Mrs. Helen V. Morse, Ohio; Rev. Frank M. Sheldon, Oklahoma; Mr. Walter Gilpatric, New York; Rev. John C. Schroeder, Maine; Mr. Elbert A. Harvey, Massachusetts; and Professor W. A. Harper, Tennessee.[56]

X

THE COUNCIL FOR SOCIAL ACTION

At the meeting in 1934 the General Council created a new agency, known as the Council for Social Action as has been noted in the chapter on "Social Concern." It should be mentioned here that when a new

[54] *Minutes of the General Council, 1931*, p. 85.
[55] *Minutes of the General Council, 1934*, p. 45.
[56] *Minutes of the General Council, 1934*, p. 103.

need was recognized the Council, without question of its authority or its capability, provided for the establishment of this denominational agency, elected a board of control, and voted it a share in the denominational apportionment.

This vote of the Council was passed the more easily because of the support of Rev. Fred Field Goodsell, executive vice president of the American Board, and Rev. William F. Frazier, who later became executive vice president of the Home Boards, and many state superintendents.

The new Strategy Committee began its work immediately following adjournment of the 1934 Council. It followed the plan of two previous committees, the Commission of Nineteen and the Committee of Twelve, in seeking the advice of Board officials, pastors, and lay people from all sections of the country. As a result, it could report "these studies have made it clear that our denominational agencies have been and are doing the important work with which they are charged with a high degree of efficiency, so that the task of the Strategy Committee has not been that of designing a plan of rescue from failure, but rather that of adding efficiency to efficiency by any improvements it might be able to suggest."[57]

Dr. Burton summed up the situation in these words:

The Commission on Missions is a creature of the General Council, which draws together the membership of the responsible Boards for the purpose of unifying promotion. The members of the Boards have constituted nearly 90 percent of the Commission on Missions membership. Its meetings are therefore practically joint meetings of the Boards, nevertheless the Commission on Missions is technically an outside agency, and the Secretary of the General Council is its General Secretary. This set-up has dulled somewhat the sense of responsibility of the Boards for the Commission and their feeling of dependence upon it for promotional effectiveness.[58]

That the Boards might have a keener sense of responsibility for the Commission on Missions the Committee proposed, in the South Hadley Council in 1936, a new arrangement whereby the boards would have a one hundred percent membership rather than the previous ninety percent by eliminating Council appointees. This proposal was adopted.

Our suggestion means that the members of the Boards continue to meet in joint session, without additional representatives named by the General Council, to do just such things as they have been doing in the field of promotion and education, but doing these things in the name of the responsible Boards under the executive leadership of the officers of the Boards.

We recommend that the General Council amend its by-laws to the effect that it shall relinquish direct responsibility for the promotion of income and leave that responsibility with the Boards themselves.[59]

[57] *Minutes of the General Council, 1936,* p. 30.
[58] *Minutes of the General Council, 1936,* p. 33.
[59] *Minutes of the General Council, 1936,* p. 33.

XI

THE NET RESULT

By this action the denomination had virtually completed a circle in the field of promotion, where differences of opinion had caused a confused situation for more than sixty years. It should be emphasized again that the Strategy Committee, like the Committee of Twelve, made no proposals for a change of the first of the two principles adopted at Kansas City in 1913, namely, that the relationships between the Council and the Boards should be on the basis of practically identical voting membership, and secondly, that the churches, through their representatives in the Council should have more responsibility in determining the promotional and educational work of the Boards.

Now adopting the report of the Strategy Committee the Council was divesting itself of all responsibility for the Every Member Canvass, and missionary promotion and education, and was committing these various interests to a joint committee of the two Boards, plus a representation of the state superintendents. The state conferences called for increasing consideration in relation to the national set-up, as the missionary and administrative work in the states required practically one-third of all the benevolent giving. As a matter of fact the chief responsibility for maintaining the financial health of the Boards was placed on the two executive vice presidents, Dr. Fred Field Goodsell, executive vice president of the American Board, and Dr. William F. Frazier, newly elected executive vice president of the Board of Home Missions.

The Council, however, in its approval of the report made the net gain that missionary promotion and missionary education of the Boards and of the states were to be carried on in cooperation, and that the total needs were to be presented to the churches in a unified program. In 1913 there were many societies with separate appeals, and as late as 1925 there were eleven items in the apportionment. After 1936 there was to be one joint appeal and the apportionment was to carry three items: the Board of Home Missions, the American Board, and state work. The basic percentage of the apportionment assigned to the American Board was thirty-two percent, to the states thirty-two percent, and to the Board of Home Missions thirty-six percent, of which four percent was voted to the Council for Social Action. The evident purpose of the Council in adopting the detailed plan as proposed by the Committee was to insure, as far as possible, that the executive secretary for promotion was to have a unique place in the denominational set-up. He was to be promotional secretary in charge of each Board's promotional unit, and also chief executive of the joint promotional program. It was intended that this should result in complete unification of the approach of the Boards to the churches.

The Committee attempted to do the impossible. The promotional staff of each Board is chosen by that Board on recommendation of the executive vice-president of that Board, and the secretaries on that staff look to him for primary instructions. It was planned, however, to place these promotional secretaries under the direction of an executive secretary for promotion, not responsible to the chief executive officer of either Board. Such divided responsibility, even with the best of intentions on all sides, caused endless discussions and hampered the work.

The most revolutionary recommendation of the Strategy Committee was that section relating to the Executive Committee of the Council. This recommendation was adopted, and provided:

> That under amendment of the By-Laws the Executive Committee be enlarged from fifteen to eighteen; be elected in three classes for terms of six years each, members being ineligible for re-election for a two-year period. The Secretaries of the Council should be non-voting members in attendance at all meetings.
>
> That the By-Laws of the General Council be amended so as to transfer to the Executive Committee of the Council the functions therein committed to the Commission on Missions other than promotion, those now carried temporarily by the Strategy Committee and also the functions of the Survey Committee and approval of apportionment percentages.[60]

Following the precedent of the Committee of Twelve, the Strategy Committee ended its report with a list of questions for further study, thus laying the groundwork for the appointment of a fourth committee.

It should be noted that through all these changes the great corporations have come into closer relationship to the Council, guided by two principles: (1) the maintenance of the work they are doing and (2) closer coordination of their work with that of the churches generally. While there have been many discussions as to methods, both Board members and church representatives have been united in the purpose to strengthen the work at home and abroad.

The two Councils at Beloit in 1938 and at Berkeley in 1940, registered a growing spirit of cooperation between the old established Boards and the state conferences in the development of cooperative activities.

The Council for Social Action, set up by the Council at Oberlin, developed its program as an independent agency. Since the work of the Council for Social Action was related to the work of the Board of Home Missions in many ways, especially to the Educational Division, a closer official relationship seemed desirable. It was therefore decided at the

[60] *Minutes of the General Council, 1936*, p. 42.

Beloit meeting that the General Council divest itself of the responsibility of electing the members of the Council of Social Action, and that the board of directors of the Home Boards assume this responsibility with the understanding that the largest possible measure of freedom should be retained by the Council for Social Action in its administration and program. That change has not proved satisfactory and further adjustments are in prospect.

XII

THE DEBT OF HONOR

Adequate provision had not been made to pay in full the $500 annuity to ministers who had qualified under the "original plan." It was hoped that contributions from the churches would make good the deficit necessary to pay these annuities, but in order that these annuities might be paid in full, an increasing amount had to be taken from the benevolent contributions of the churches. Hence, at the 1938 Council meeting in Beloit, a Debt of Honor Commission was authorized on the recommendation of the Executive Committee which, in its report, said:

In April, 1937, the Missions Council, supported by the Prudential Committee of the American Board and the Directors of the Board of Home Missions, asked the approval of the Executive Committee to a plan for raising a fund to care for the portion of annuities under the Original Plan of the Annuity Fund which is not already provided for.[61]

Then followed the recommendations for the organization of the Debt of Honor Commission under the General Council to raise funds to meet this deficit. This Commission, under the chairmanship of Dean Charles R. Brown, with the effective leadership of Dr. Lewis T. Reed and after his retirement of Dr. Frank J. Scribner, the general secretary of the Pension Boards, is carrying forward the campaign for funds sufficient to make full payment to the original fund members.

[61] *Minutes of the General Council, 1938*, p. 13.

CHAPTER XX

Church Union

THE Congregational pioneers did not accept the term "Separatists" or the term "schismatics" often applied to them, their contention being that it was the Anglican Church that had departed from true Christianity and that they were the upholders and restorers of it. They hoped to effect a reformation within the church. Robinson said, "Study union with the Godly people of England where you can have it without sin rather than in the least measure to effect a division or separation from them." Some of the writers of the Established Church also sought to unite Christians of different beliefs in worship in the church. For example, Edward Polhill, a layman in that church in the late 1600's said, "The unity of the church is a divine thing and does not consist in human rights, liturgy, episcopacy, nor the civil law; in the first golden age of the church there was little of ceremony but much of unity." Neal describes meetings of the ministers of various bodies in England during the Protectorate where, by agreement, "they abstained from discussion of political questions but where the fellowship was very helpful and the general effect was most happy."[1]

The Congregational churches have never been hampered by loyalty to creedal statements in their efforts towards union. What creed they have has been accepted for "substance of doctrine." Professor Bartlett, who had much to do in the framing and adoption of the declaration on unity in the Council meeting in 1871 said of the Congregational attitude towards creeds and the implications of the phrase, "for substance of doctrine":

True, our denomination has never done more than to accept for *substance,* any Confession; but that awkward word "substantially," is a very hard word to make people understand, particularly if they do not want to understand it. Doubtless a man, in any church of any denomination, who accepts literally, just as a plain man would understand it, every phrase in the Westminster, would be a rare specimen. The churches have never proposed to do it. They have never, in any synod, imposed a creed on any man's conscience. But every troubler has felt at liberty to insist that our laborers shall defend every sentence of Confessions which were never adopted by sentences. For ourselves, we can continue to believe and teach that "no mere man since the fall is able in this life perfectly to keep the commandments of God,"—and to hold to this "substantially," that is, just as it means.

[1]Neal, *The History of the Puritans,* vol. 2, p. 137.

The history of the ventures towards union by the Congregational churches makes clear certain principles which have controlled and directed the movement.

I

CONGREGATIONAL PRINCIPLES

The first principle is that the only official Congregational church is a local congregation which enjoys complete autonomy; whatever organizations there are beyond the congregation, as the association, the state conference, or the National Council, are only advisory organizations. Most of these have written into their constitutions words similar in effect to those of the first national constitution: "The churches, therefore, while establishing this National Council for the furtherance of the common interests and work of all the churches, do maintain the Scriptural and inalienable right of each church to self-government and administration; and this National Council shall never exercise legislative or judicial authority, nor consent to act as a council of reference."[2] This, with minor changes, has continued to be the official statement of the Council.

Hence, as the agencies outside the local church are neither legislative nor judicial, but only administrative, any proposal for church union affects only the agency taking action. For example, when the National Council has voted to merge with the national organization of another religious body, it has not followed that the local units of either body were merged but that the cooperative agency of the Congregational churches— that is, its National Council—united with a similar agency in some other body for coordination and mutual enrichment of both.

This principle is illustrated by the fact that when mergers have been proposed in the National Council there has never been any move to refer these proposals to the associations, conferences, and local congregations for official consideration previous to the vote by the Council. The Council has always considered itself competent to decide by its own vote whether or not it would affiliate with a corresponding body in some other denomination. This principle is illustrated by the latest merger between the National Council of Congregational Churches and the General Convention of the Christian Church, which was the corresponding body in that denomination. The action was taken by the National Council without reference to the churches. The state conferences and local associations, however, have accepted the Council vote and have welcomed into their fellowship uniting groups.

The second principle concerning church union is that members of Congregational churches have never looked upon themselves as sectarian.

[2] *Minutes of the National Council, 1871*, p. 30.

From the beginning it has been the idea that a Congregational church is not made up of Congregationalists as a Quaker congregation is made up of Quakers, but that a Congregational church is a group of Christians associated together for a definite purpose, not because of peculiarities of belief. Concerning this phase of the life of the churches of New England, Cotton Mather stated, "The Churches of New England make only vital piety the terms of communion among them and they all with delight see Godly Congregationalists, Presbyterians, Episcopalians, Antipedo-Baptists, the Lutherans all members of the same churches." These nondenominational community churches in New England opposed the establishment of other churches, saying they feared "the coming of sects lest they themselves should become sectarian." Today as in Cotton Mather's day a church with perhaps a thousand members may have but a small percentage of its membership who grew up in a Congregational church. Thus the local church is in truth a union of Christians who are not asked to renounce their previous denominational teachings but are asked to join in a simple covenant pledging cooperation and fellowship.

Perhaps no other religious body in America has made as many gestures toward union with other religious bodies as have the various National Councils. The members of these Councils have always felt perfectly free, acting in their own name, to make a proposal to any particular group that appeared willing to receive it. They have never felt any restriction as to what might be the attitude of the local church, association, or state conference, because it was always clearly understood that these bodies would accept the proposed merger if it were consummated only as far as it was to their interest to do so.

The attitude making possible independent and immediate action is based on two ideas. First, the basic idea of union with all Christians which works out so happily in most Congregational churches could be worked out just as well on a national scale. And secondly, local churches have never felt any particular responsibility for the actions of the National Council.

For almost a century Congregational churches in increasing numbers have been inviting ministers of other denominations to serve as pastors. Some of these "guest" pastors transfer their standing to the Congregational association, but often as many as five hundred churches have continued under the pastoral care of ministers who belong to other denominations, with the natural result that these churches consider themselves quite interdenominational. A few Congregational churches feel as closely allied to the Federal Council of the Churches of Christ in America, an interdenominational agency, as to the General Council. That affiliation may mean more to them than their membership in an association or a state conference which in turn is a member of the General Council. In the interdenominational organizations the local church has individual though associate membership, while in the Congregational Council it has a representative membership through delegates elected by the conferences.

THE EFFECT OF THE PLAN OF UNION

The experience of the churches with the Presbyterians in the Plan of Union in the first half of the nineteenth century is quite illustrative of the attitude and method of Congregationalists towards church union. The churches of Connecticut entered into the Plan of Union with the Presbyterian General Assembly and on both sides there was good purpose and fellowship in service.

The opposition to the Plan of Union which came to expression in the Albany convention did not arise because the New England churches were dissatisfied that Presbyterian churches were absorbing so many Congregationalists who went from New England to the West. It arose rather in the West when those western Congregationalists wanted the support of the eastern churches in establishing Congregational churches. The New England people felt that having their own Congregational church for free worship, in their own community, they had no particular responsibility for the kind of church the residents of a town a thousand miles away should have. If they cared enough for a Congregational church they should organize and maintain it themselves. Here and there throughout the western country were groups of former members of Congregational churches in New England who persisted in their attachment and did not become members of the Presbyterian order. By the time of the Albany Convention there were enough of these independent western churches to make a strong appeal. They aroused enough sympathy and understanding to create a consciousness of national Congregationalism, and then the eastern churches assumed responsibility for the fostering of Congregational churches through the West.

At the Boston Council of 1865, thirteen years after the Albany convention, there were debates on the need of granting help for church building, and the need of supplying western churches with a trained and educated ministry. This Council gave a great deal of attention to the Tract Society, the Bible Society, the Sunday School Union, and other nondenominational agencies working in their midst. They put the financial needs of these interdenominational agencies on practically the same basis as those more nearly related to the life of the Congregational churches. This spirit of broad interest was greatly strengthened by the attitude of the missionary boards. These boards sought to maintain an interdenominational membership and to have an interdenominational relationship to the National Council. Thus the Boards would have the maximum of endorsement and support from the churches, but would not be functioning as agencies of the Council. This interdenominational attitude of the Boards was a helpful influence towards Christian unity in the churches.

II

THE DECLARATION OF UNITY

When the National Council met at Oberlin in 1871, the constitution presented by the Provisional Committee included a declaration on the unity of the church. No part of the Committee's proposals received more hearty commendation than did this declaration, which for almost fifty years was printed in the. *Year Book* between the Constitution and by-laws. The declaration read:

The members of the National Council, representing the Congregational churches of the United States, avail themselves of this opportunity to renew their previous declarations of faith in the unity of the church of God.

While affirming the liberty of our churches, as taught in the New Testament, and inherited by us from our fathers, and from martyrs and confessors of foregoing ages, we adhere to this liberty all the more as affording the ground and hope of a more visible unity in time to come. We desire and purpose to cooperate with all the churches of our Lord Jesus Christ.

In the expression of the same catholic sentiments solemnly avowed by the Council of 1865, on the Burial Hill at Plymouth, we wish, at this new epoch of our history, to remove, so far as in us lies, all causes of suspicion and alienation, and to promote the growing unity of counsel and of effort among the followers of Christ. To us, as to our brethren, "There is one body and one spirit, even as we are called in one hope of our calling."

As little as did our fathers in their day, do we in ours, make a pretension to be the only churches of Christ. We find ourselves consulting and acting together under the distinctive name of Congregationalists, because, in the present condition of our common Christianity, we have felt ourselves called to ascertain and do our own appropriate part of the work of Christ's church among men.

We especially desire, in prosecuting the common work of evangelizing our own land and the world, to observe the common and sacred law, that in the wide fields of the world's evangelization, we do our work in friendly cooperation with all those who love and serve our common Lord.

We believe in "the holy catholic church." It is our prayer and endeavor, that the unity of the church may be more and more apparent, and that the prayer of our Lord for his disciples may be speedily and completely answered, and all be one; that by consequence of this Christian unity in love, the world may believe in Christ as sent of the Father to save the world.[3]

The learned Professor Bartlett in his report analyzing this declaration, said:

"Instead of throwing away the substance of any Confession, we really recognize the essential faith of the Christian church which is in all Confessions. We

[3]*Minutes of the National Council, 1871*, pp. 31–32.

refuse to be a sect, and we are loyal to the common faith. This is a great step, therefore, towards Christian union. It tells all Christian people that we will not make our peculiarities a bar to the union of the separated parts of Christ's divided church. We can welcome them on the simple basis of the common faith. Whatever the immediate result may be, an act like this of a powerful denomination must eventually bear fruit, and in the meantime we have the satisfaction of knowing that our churches have done the right thing for Christian union."[4]

On the basis of this declaration, church leaders were on the alert for any opportunity to carry these principles into effect.

III

The Free Baptist Proposals

The first definite Council action concerning church union was at Chicago, October 13–20, 1886. A proposal was before that Council regarding cooperation with the Free Baptist churches. It had been referred to a special committee of which Dr. Alonzo H. Quint was chairman. This committee presented a report which sketched briefly the history of the Free Baptists, saying: "No denomination is nearer to us than that of the Free Baptists, perhaps none so near. That denomination began its existence in New Hampshire, by the organization of its first church in the year 1780. It seems strange that two bodies so near alike could not be one, and thus remove one of the confusions of our Christendom. The principle is, at least, worth commending, and we do commend it."[5]

The Council accepted this report and seven resolutions were adopted bearing upon the proposed merger. These resolutions representing the mind and temper of the Congregational churches more than fifty years ago are of unusual interest. They emphasize the desirability of such a union as "an evidence to the world of the oneness of the church of Christ" and especially desirable would be the union of separate and weak local churches into one. The Council provided for delegates from the Free Baptists to the National Council and instructed the committee not only to advance this proposed union but "that it also be made the duty of this committee to seek and promote fellowship or union with any kindred bodies of Christians, and to report thereon at the next meeting of the National Council; and that we rejoice to acknowledge the fact that all Christians are members of the *one* church of Christ, whatever be the form of their organization, and that we will gladly cooperate in every effort to make this fact visible to the world."[6]

The Free Baptists had originally separated from the Congregational churches following the George Whitefield revival. They accepted prac-

---

[4] *The Congregational Quarterly,* 1872.
[5] *Minutes of the National Council, 1886,* pp. 351, 352.
[6] *Minutes of the National Council, 1886,* p. 35.

tically all the current teachings of the Congregationalists with the exception of baptism of infants, which they rejected on doctrinal grounds. According to the report of Dr. Quint's committee, the first minister and founder of the Free Baptists had been a lay member of the Congregational order; that he left "Standing Order," as the Congregational fellowship was called in New Hampshire, in protest against the relationship of the church to the civil society. The reason for this protest against conditions in the early churches had passed away long before the merger was proposed, for all the churches in New England had become free churches. Both denominations practiced what was known as "open communion." This report contained one sentence of great insight: "Denominations are not made, they grow; if they unite it is because they grow towards each other and together. Formal attempts may mutually repel."[7]

The committee at the next meeting of the Council could only express its appreciation of the work of the Free Baptist Churches, a cordial sympathy with doctrine and policy, and express regret that churches so closely allied could not form one body. Evidently objection had developed among the Baptist group to the proposed merger.

Three years later, no progress having been made to bring this proposed merger into effect, the Council in 1892 adopted a general resolution which has become one of the historic actions of the Council. This brief resolution reads as follows:

"Resolved, That affiliation with our denomination of churches not now upon our roll, should be welcomed upon the basis of the common evangelical faith, substantial Congregational polity, and free communion of Christians, without regard to forms or minor differences.

"Resolved, That this Council heartily agrees with the unanimous declaration of the International Congregational Council, held in London, in 1891, in favor of a federation without authority, of all bodies of Christian churches, as soon as the providence of God shall permit, for the manifestation of the unity of the church of Christ upon the earth, and for harmonious action in advancing the kingdom of Jesus Christ."

In commenting on this resolution Rev. Charles M. Lamson of St. Johnsbury, Vermont, said in his Council sermon: "That church is most profoundly religious today and will receive and deserve extension and honor that learns from its Lord that true living is now a movement from 'freedom to unity,' from Christ in the individual to Christ in society. This is Congregationalism in its idea, self-control as a church by means of the divine control, submission to the control of its Lord, autonomy for the sake of service, the fellowship of the churches for the sake of the Church, independency for the sake of unity."[8]

[7] *Minutes of the National Council, 1889*, p. 254.
[8] *Minutes of the National Council, 1892*, p. 64.

As the years went by however the Free Baptists found their fellowship growing stronger with the Regular and General Baptist churches, many of which were looking with kindly favor on open communion, one of the chief teachings of the Free Baptists. Nothing further developed from the discussion of this proposed merger, but the attention of many church leaders was focused on the problems involved in church union. One of the leaders said, "the smaller the denomination, the bigger the problems." It was just as difficult, if not more so, to discuss church mergers with small groups as with large ones.

IV

THE CONGREGATIONAL METHODIST

The Council of 1892 welcomed into the fellowship a group of Congregational Methodists from Georgia and Alabama.

"The Congregational Methodist Church was organized at Forsyth, Georgia, in May, 1852, as a protest against certain features of the episcopacy and itinerancy. The organization was formed for the purpose of securing a more democratic form of church government. The congregational form of government was adopted, although modified by a degree of connectionalism. The movement extended into Georgia, Alabama, Florida, and Mississippi. In 1887 and 1888 nearly one third of the churches of this body joined the Congregationalists. . . . Its polity is congregational, constituting the chief distinction between it and other Methodists." [9]

The union of these churches was not a merger of national denominational bodies, but rather the Congregational Methodist churches in a few states united with the Congregational associations and became to all intents and purposes Congregational churches in good standing. In later years some of these churches have withdrawn from the Congregational associations and established connections with other bodies, but some of these Congregational Methodists remain in our fellowship.

V

THE CHICAGO LAMBETH QUADRILATERAL

When the Council met in 1895 at Syracuse, New York, the whole Christian world had been stirred by a statement of four principles proposed by the Episcopalians meeting in Chicago and stating the basis on which they would be willing to discuss the union of Protestantism. These statements were later adopted by the Bishops meeting at Lambeth Palace and became known as the Chicago Lambeth Quadrilateral.

This world-wide interest in church union is reflected in the records

[9] Watson, *Year Book of the Churches, 1921–22*, p. 146.

of the Syracuse Council in 1895. The reports of the two committees, one on church union and the other on Christian unity, cover twenty-seven pages in the minutes of that Council and were widely discussed in the Council meeting. The address by the retiring Moderator, Dr. Alonzo H. Quint, who had been a directing genius of the National Council in 1871, also dealt with this subject. In it he developed the basic ideas for Christian unity. Dr. Quint, in his address, said:

> Congregationalism is almost ashamed to be distinctive, and gladly it would be merged in the undivided Church, if it found the undivided catholic Church in which to lose its name. . . . What Congregationalism signifies to us is the absolute supremacy of the Lord Jesus Christ; the equality of all Christians in their relation to him; the responsibility and discipline of brotherhood in government. . . . The Pilgrim principle of a spiritual kingdom, free and unshackled, carried forward by spiritual forces, and dependent upon the divine power vouchsafed to a willing church is the hope and prophecy of victory.[10]

The "longing for the unity of Christendom," which dominated that Council, found in current developments much to discourage it. There is nowhere in our records a better presentation of the whole problem of church union and its relationship to Christian unity than is contained in reports to this Council. Not only was the committee on church union compelled to report that negotiations with the Free Baptists had reached a standstill, but they also reported that the Chicago Lambeth Quadrilateral which had been before the churches for a number of years and which, on its face, seemed to be a possible basis for church union, had now been so interpreted by the Bishops that the committee reported "it is clear that these Chicago Lambeth proposals may now be considered as withdrawn by the Bishops."[11]

The Episcopal bishops had so interpreted the term "historic episcopate" so that it "would require all other denominations to accept the order of bishops as officially superior to that of the ministry to receive ordination through bishops who claim uninterrupted apostolic succession. It became equally clear that the Protestant Episcopal Church would refuse to allow its clergy to recognize the clergy of other denominations either fraternally or officially as possessing a valid ministry."[12]

In accepting the bishops' interpretation and considering the Chicago Lambeth Quadrilateral as outside the range of possibility, the Congregationalists were following the lead of the Presbyterian Assembly, which "after some ten years of courteous and laborious correspondence and con-

---

[10] Watson, *Year Book of the Churches, 1921–22*, p. 81.
[11] *Minutes of the National Council, 1895*, p. 284.
[12] *Minutes of the National Council, 1895*, p. 284.

sideration, had excused its committee from further considering the subject."[13]

VI

THE CLEVELAND PROPOSAL

There had been close relations between Presbyterian and Congregational churches in the Western Reserve dating back to the Plan of Union in the early 1800's, which had survived the troubles in the Presbyterian Church when it was split into two groups over some implications in the Plan of Union. In 1923 this good relationship found expression in proposals for organic union between the Cleveland Presbytery and the Cleveland Union of Congregational churches. This proposal was presented to the Synod of the Presbyterian Church of Ohio where it was "looked upon with favor." On the basis of this tentative action a Plan of Union was worked out and addressed to the General Assembly of the Presbyterian Church of the United States and to the Congregational National Council. The Congregational Council in 1927 viewed the proposal "with sincere approval" and authorized its commission to work toward its fulfilment. No further actions were taken by either the Presbyterian or the Congregational group and this venture ended in failure.

VII

THE CONCORDAT

Another gesture towards closer relations with the Episcopalians came to nought. This is the famous Concordat proposal. A group of Congregational ministers under the leadership of Dr. Newman Smyth and Dr. William E. Barton, some twenty years after the adjournment of the discussion over the Quadrilateral, started negotiations to make it possible in small communities where the Episcopalians had a church and the Congregationalists did not or vice versa, for the minister of the existing church to minister "legally" to the members of the other fellowship. The proposal aroused much discussion but was abandoned because Episcopalian law required anyone administering communion to an Episcopalian to have Episcopal ordination.

Congregational ministers believe that their ordination is valid as ministers of the whole Church of Christ. They would not accept re-ordination if it brought into question their Congregational ordination. Many were prepared to take a second ordination if in so doing their previous ordination would be accepted as valid, and the second ordination considered simply as a means of conforming to an old-time law. The Episcopalians would not accept this interpretation. They insisted that if a Con-

[13] *Minutes of the National Council, 1895*, p. 284.

gregational minister submitted himself to the bishop it would not be for re-ordination or a supplemental ordination but for a "valid" ordination. This, of course, implied that Congregational ordinations were not valid. The Council of 1923 laid the whole proposition on the table, the motion being made by Dr. Smyth, seconded by Dr. Barton, and unanimously carried.

VIII

THE DISCIPLES OF CHRIST

The committee also reported on a proposal from the Disciples of Christ. This has historic interest, as negotiations are still being continued. The Disciples, meeting in Alleghany City in 1891 and having before them the Lambeth Quadrilateral, were moved to issue a "Triennial" as a basis upon which they proposed organic union. The three items in this "Triennial" were (1) The original creed of Christ's Church, that Jesus is "the Christ, the Son of the living God," as first formulated by Peter, then approved by Christ, as the basis of his Church; (2) the ordinances of Baptism and the Lord's Supper, the former defined as "the immersion of penitent believers in the name of the Lord Jesus, and into the name of the Father and of the Son and of the Holy Spirit"; and (3) "the life which has the sinless Son of Man as its perfect exemplification."[14]

Thereupon the Congregational committee adopted a statement which has become historic because it presents so clearly the fundamental attitude of Congregationalists toward church union:

> It may be sufficient to say that a plan which makes the imposition of the form of a rite essential can no more be the basis for the union of the Christian world, than one which makes the particular form of church organization essential. Unity can never be achieved on the basis of any sort of formalism, for the insistence on formalism, whatever it may be, is of the same essence as that strict Judaism which our Lord came to replace by a spiritual faith and life. No union is possible based on submission of the intelligence of one party to that of another. Union can take place only on a spiritual basis which allows liberty for conscientious differences.[15]

IX

FIRST PROPOSALS FOR MERGER WITH THE CHRISTIANS

Still greater interest is aroused by the fact that the larger portion of this historic report of 1895 is concerned with proposals for merger with what the committee called the "Christian connection." This venture did not come to completion until thirty-six years later at Seattle, when the Christian General Convention and Congregational National Council united to form a General Council of the Congregational and Christian Churches. The report gives a brief history of "the Christians" and their

[14] *Minutes of the National Council, 1895,* p. 285.
[15] *Minutes of the National Council, 1895,* p. 285.

origin; also of their religious journal, *The Herald of Gospel Liberty*, which was first issued at Portsmouth, New Hampshire and "claims to be the oldest religious paper in the United States."

The summary of the characteristics of this body of Christians, whom the Congregationalists were to know much more intimately later on, contains this paragraph:

They are a very earnest body of believers, passionately devoted to the Bible only, earnestly rejecting all doctrinal creeds and statements, proclaiming Gospel liberty against all imposition of dogma, and protesting against all sectarianism which divides Christians into followers of this or that human leader, they having no leader but Christ. Their rejection of all man-made formulas and creeds has sometimes led to the idea that they are Unitarians, because they will not adopt the word *Trinity* which they do not find in the Bible. They prefer to express their dependence on the Holy Spirit and their faith in our and their Lord and Saviour in nothing but Biblical terms. At one time the Unitarians made an agreement with them to help their college at Antioch; but the results were such that the Christians broke away from the alliance believing that it endangered the faith of their people in the Word of God. In their worship of our Lord they do not differ from us, even although some of them still protest against being called Trinitarians.[16]

The report gives the history of the movement for the union of these two bodies, which had originated in the New Jersey Christian Association with a proposal that such a merger be arranged. On the invitation of the Convention of the Christian Church which met in Haverhill, Massachusetts, in October, 1894, the Congregational committee was represented by a delegation and held a two-day discussion of all phases of the possible merger. It was voted by the Christian General Convention that "the ultimate ideal of Christian union is the union of all the followers of Christ in one body, in an organic union, inspired with the spirit of the Master, existing and acting with single reference to carrying on his work, building up his kingdom, and bringing the world to Christ; and we would encourage and cooperate with any and all measures looking to this end."[17]

Following this the Christian Convention appointed a Commission of Twelve to deal with the Congregational committee and voted also

"that the Church of Christ is *one*; that it consists of all those who are the disciples of the Lord Jesus Christ, accepted of him into his fellowship, regardless of personal beliefs or denominational relations; and that no conditions of fellowship should be held that will not *include* all and *exclude* none of those who stand in vital fellowship with Christ. Here we stand. We cannot reject overtures that come to us in harmony with this position. We cannot turn a cold shoulder on any Christian or body of Christians who propose to join us in work

[16] *Minutes of the National Council, 1895*, p. 291.
[17] *Minutes of the National Council, 1895*, pp. 292–293.

for Christ and the building up of his kingdom on ground of our own choosing. To do so would be to repudiate our own professions and turn our back on all for which we have all these years contended. On the other hand, we have nothing to yield of the fundamentals of our position." [18]

No further action was taken by either denomination until August, 1897 when Dr. Summerbell invited Dr. Ward, editor of the *Independent*, and the leader of the Congregational committee, two other Congregational representatives, and four representatives of the Christian Churches to meet at his cottage in Craigville, Massachusetts. There this joint committee worked out what came to be known as the Craigville proposal. This was as follows:

Resolved, that a union of the two bodies be recommended on the following basis:

1. Mutual recognition of the Christian standing of each other's churches and ministers, with no doctrinal test beyond the acceptance of the Bible as the only standard of faith and practice.

2. One name for the highest representative body, such as the General Council of Christian Churches.

3. Present organizations, institutions and usages not to be disturbed by this action.

4. That there be maintained between the churches and ministers of the two denominations such a fellowship and mutual understanding that when members of a church of one body remove to a place where there is no church of their own, but is one of the other, they be encouraged to take letters to such church of the other body; and that if a minister of one body accepts a call to the church of the other he shall not thereby impair his membership or good standing in his own body.

The Committee recommends the local or state associations or conferences in which delegates to the National Council or American Christian Convention are chosen, to authorize such delegates to act in a General Conference of Christian Churches, in case such a conference be advised by the National Council and by the American Christian Convention. [19]

When the proposal came before the Christian Convention meeting at Newmarket, Pennsylvania, in 1898, it was vigorously opposed by southern and western delegates who asserted that New England representatives of the Christian Churches were "selling out to the Congregationalists." The proposal was not approved. Although Dr. Ward and Dr. Washington Gladden for the Congregationalists and Dr. Martyn Summerbell and Dr. J. B. Weston for the Christians continued to work for a merger, there was so much opposition in the Christian churches that the matter was dropped. It was the contention of representatives of the Christian churches that any merger with a church bearing a denominational name was

[18] *Minutes of the National Council, 1895*, pp. 300–301.
[19] *The Christian Annual*, 1899, p. 65.

departing from their principles, as they considered the name "Christian" the one name under which all churches could unite. They contended that their churches ought not to become affiliated with a "sect" which they considered the Congregationalists to be and which by its very sectarianism was less than wholly Christian. Here the matter rested.

When the proposals to unite the two churches were made in 1923 no reference was made to the previous attempt and few if any of the participants of the 1923–31 negotiations seem to have known of the long discussions of twenty-five years earlier.

X
The Congregational Quadrilateral

After all the discussion of various aspects of church union the most significant action taken by the Council of 1895 was adoption of "the Congregational Quadrilateral." This was an acknowledged summarization of the declaration on the unity of the church which had been adopted in 1871 and was still published annually as the official declaration of the Congregational churches. The Congregational Quadrilateral included these four principles:

1. The acceptance of the Scripture of the Old and New Testaments inspired by the Holy Ghost to be the only authoritative revelation of God to man.
2. Discipleship of Jesus Christ, the divine Saviour and Teacher of the world.
3. The Church of Christ, which is his body, whose great mission it is to preach his Gospel to the world.
4. Liberty of conscience in the interpretation of the Scriptures and in the administration of the church.[20]

XI
The Act of Union with the Methodist Protestants and the United Brethren

Discussions concerning a merger with the Methodist Protestant churches began as early as 1898 and were continued through the next three Councils. In the Council of 1898 it was voted "Whereas, in various ways there has been expressed a desire for a closer fellowship of these churches with our own. . . ." This would indicate that various feelers had been put out but without definite proposals. The Council appointed a committee for conferences with the Methodist Protestants. These conferences went on for the next six years. Then the United Brethren churches were invited into the discussions. This led to appointment by the three denominations of delegates who met in Chicago in March, 1907 and after much preliminary correspondence and discussion drafted an "Act of Union," an historic document in the history of Ameri-

[20] *Minutes of the National Council, 1895,* p. 294.

can Christianity. Although not approved, it serves as a statement of the essential basis of church unity. It included a declaration of purpose, a declaration of faith, and the articles of agreement which were in effect a constitution for a new body to be known as "The United Churches." The "Act of Union" did not propose an immediate union of churches in the local communities but a union of the national organizations representing these churches. The United Churches would be a joint agency, a limited interdenominational holding body, to be supported by the local churches of the three denominations, which in time would merge in the communities as provided in the Act of Union:

We recognize in the Act of Union adopted by the General Council of The United Churches at Chicago the fundamental principles by which such union must be accomplished. The aim of that act is the desire of our churches, combines their benevolent activities, and conserves their vested interests. It makes provision for the gradual amalgamation of their state and local organizations, leaving the people of each locality free to choose their own times and methods for the completion of such unions. It contemplates, as the result of a continued fellowship of worship and work, a blending of the three denominations into one. This is the end to which the Act of Union looks forward, and these are essential means of its accomplishment.[21]

When the Act of Union came before the Congregational Council, the committee in charge including Dr. Washington Gladden, Dr. Henry Churchill King, Dr. William Horace Day, and others, approved most highly its purpose. They proposed however that the section on the autonomy of the local church should be strengthened; that it should be made very clear that this national organization was made up of delegates from the local churches of the Congregational, United Brethren and Methodist Protestant groups; and that the local churches should maintain their autonomy unchanged; and that the local associations continue without any interference whatsoever as to their autonomy or their work. The Committee asked the other church bodies to restudy the "Act of Union" and to grant this added security to the autonomy of the local church. It soon became apparent that the idea of autonomy of the local church among the Congregationalists was considerably different from that of the other bodies. When the request of the Congregational group was received the other denominations declined to restudy the "Act of Union" and this venture, which had extended over many years, came to an end.

XII

THE EVANGELICAL PROTESTANT CHURCHES

At the meeting of the National Council at Springfield in 1923, there were present, on invitation of the Committee on Comity, Federation, and

[21] *National Council Digest, 1930,* p. 196; *Minutes of the National Council, 1910,* p. 397.

Unity, a delegation of the Evangelical Protestant Church headed by Rev. Carl August Voss. Two years later the negotiations which had preceded the Springfield Council meeting were consummated at the Council at Washington in 1925. On recommendation by the Commission on Interchurch Relations the Evangelical Protestant Churches of North America were received as a conference on parity with state conferences and with the relationship to the National Council of state conference. The *Year Book* for that year lists the Evangelical Protestant Conference with twenty-three churches. These churches have continued their Congregational affiliation, many of them since uniting with the state conference in which they are located.

The history of the Evangelical Protestant churches is a dramatic chapter of American Protestantism. In the early years of the nineteenth century, great numbers of Germans and German Swiss came to America, many were from the Evangelical Lutheran Church and the Swiss Reformed Church. The oldest church of this group was the church now known as "the German Evangelical Protestant (Smithfield) Church, Congregational" at Pittsburgh, Pennsylvania. The formation of this church is typical of most of the Evangelical Protestant churches. It was founded by German settlers from the Lutheran and the Reformed churches uniting under the name "Evangelical Protestant."

There was no fixed organization of the more than one thousand German churches established between 1800 and 1850. Gradually they became grouped around certain centers. The Lutherans and the Reformed churches each drew some congregations into those denominations while the Evangelical Protestant remained outside these two major groups. As time went on they were handicapped by the lack of training schools for young ministers of religious literature and of fellowship. Eventually the churches in the Ohio Valley from Pittsburgh to St. Louis, including churches in Cincinnati and Southern Indiana, formed a General Association under the leadership of Dr. Carl August Voss.

The Evangelical Protestant churches have always been noted for their liberal views and theology and for their consciousness of need for social amelioration. Their teaching may be summed up in the words of Pastor Gustav Schmidt who served for forty-two years as pastor at McKeesport: "Dear children, love one another. The Christian teaching is love to God, love to neighbor, the duty of right living and charity—these are the simple tenets of faith in the Evangelical Protestant Church." They established and maintain such charitable institutions as the Pittsburgh Orphanage and the *Altenheim,* one of the finest institutions for elderly persons under church auspices in America.

XIII

THE GERMAN CONGREGATIONAL CHURCHES

In addition to the Evangelical Protestant Conference, there is also a General Association of German Congregational Churches. This was organized by the descendants of Germans who came to America by way of Russia as early as 1846. These Germans had migrated to Russia in the days of Catherine. Conditions became difficult and in 1870 they were ordered to become Russians. Desiring to maintain their traditional German life many of them escaped to America and found homes in Colorado, Nebraska, the Dakotas and the Pacific states.

They were free, independent church people and naturally adopted the Congregational polity. They have their own association, a publishing house, a theological school in connection with Yankton College and extensive foreign mission work among the Germans in South America. In the United States they now number 250 congregations with more than 23,000 members served by 110 pastors. In addition to their German Church Associations, they also have a close relationship with the Congregational churches in the states where they are located and form a large body of free Christians, loyal to Congregational ideals.[22]

XIV

THE UNIVERSALIST CHURCHES

Preceding the Council meeting at Washington, D. C. in 1925, the Universalist State Convention meeting at Bangor expressed a desire for union with the Congregationalists. Committees were appointed and held meetings during the next two years. A joint statement was drawn up which was considered by the Council in 1927. When the Universalist Convention met at Hartford on October 20, 1927, the statement was approved as providing closer fellowship with the Congregational churches, but it was stated "that nothing in this joint statement commits us to organic union." More meetings were held but as the Universalist members of the joint committee felt bound by the action of their Convention to work for closer relationships but not for organic union. The proposal was laid on the table, where it still remains.

XV

THE SECOND PROPOSAL FOR MERGER WITH THE CHRISTIANS

The negotiations with the Christian Churches begun in the 1890's had come to a close in 1898. In 1923 the matter was taken up *de novo*, with no reference to past negotiations in the correspondence between Dr.

[22] Eisenach, *A History of the German Congregational Churches in the United States.*

W. G. Sargent of Rhode Island and Dr. Burton of the Congregational National Council. Dr. Burton, secretary of the Council, at a meeting of the Congregational Commission on Interchurch Relations held in New York December 15, 1923, presented their correspondence saying, "This indicates that the Christian denomination is evidently quite ready for federation if not for merger."

At the same time Dr. Sargent, president of the New England Christian Convention, wrote an article for the *Herald of Gospel Liberty* indicating that the New England Christian churches were ready to unite with the Congregationalists. The matter having thus been reopened correspondence continued and joint meetings of official representation were held during the next two or three years. After an extended discussion, at a joint meeting of the two churches' representatives in Toledo in June, 1926, findings were drawn up for a complete merger of the two denominations. These findings were approved by the General Convention of the Christian Church meeting in Urbana, Illinois, in October, 1926 and by the National Council of the Congregational Churches meeting in Omaha, in May, 1927. The Toledo statement was printed in the reports of both conventions and the two committees were encouraged to explore the matter further.

There were many questions requiring careful analysis. Rev. Seldon B. Humphrey, member of the Christian fellowship sums up some of the problems that these committees faced:

The two denominations were strikingly different. in both their origin and the character of their constituencies. Congregationalism, although it first became definitely organized in this country, was formed from Puritan and Pilgrim groups from England. Its leaders were founders of the New England Colonies; its membership was from the educated, dominant groups at first in New England and later also in urban centers throughout the states; it was characterized by a trained ministry, substantial financial support, and a growing emphasis upon educational rather than revivalist methods of evangelism. The Christian Church, on the other hand, was indigenous to America and had its beginnings after the Revolutionary War. It was made up of three like-minded groups, one from the South, one from New England, and one from the newly opened Mid-West. Many of its early leaders were itinerant evangelists of slight education; its membership was largely rural and from the less favored economic groups; and revivals were widely used in forwarding the work of the church.

Nevertheless there were compelling likenesses in their polities and beliefs. Both believed in the principle of the local autonomy of churches; both emphasized the freedom of individuals in matters of belief; both expressed their desire for fellowship through regional and national organizations; and in both denominations there was a strong spirit favoring church union. It was this dominating spirit which led these two Churches to overcome obstacles implied in geographical distribution, property evaluation, size of churches, average annual expenditures of churches, and size of membership of the two denominations. It was this spirit which caused their leaders, in spite of a long series of unsuccessful negotiations in the 1890's to try again in the 1920's to solve many problems, and finally to bring about a successful union.[23]

Other items required attention before the merger could be consummated. For example, the National Council "amended the Committee's report to strike out all reference to the 'Kansas City Declaration' that there might not be even the suggestion of a creedal statement to stand in the way of union. The other gesture was the unanimous vote on article VI of the recommendations that the name 'Congregational' should be given up if that would further the cause of church union."[24]

The Christian representatives expressed appreciation of the "humble spirit" of the Congregational representatives who were willing to drop the historic name "Congregational" from the title of the merged national organization. The representatives of the Christian Church proposed that the basis of union

be conditioned upon the acceptance of Christianity as primarily a way of life, and not upon uniformity of theological opinion or any uniform practice of ordinances. The autonomy of the local congregation and the right of each individual member to follow Christ according to his own conscience should remain undisturbed. The name 'Congregational Christian' should be used for the time being, allowing each local church to continue to use its present name if it so desires."

When the Congregational Council met in 1929, the Commission on Interchurch Relations proposed an enabling act authorizing the Congregational representatives to join with representatives of the Christian churches in drawing up a constitution for the united churches. This authorization was voted. During the two years following, the representatives of the two churches were busy drafting a constitution and a plan for the mergers of the various boards and other denominational agencies. The National Council and the General Convention of the Christian Churches arranged to hold meetings at Seattle at the same time.

The Congregational National Council heard the reports of its committee on the merger. The proposed constitution was presented, and a full discussion followed. Some amendments were proposed by the Congregational National Council. These were accepted by the General Convention of the Christian Church, meeting in separate session. Then each body, acting separately, adopted the constitution. The doors of Plymouth Church, where the Congregational National Council was in session, were opened and the members of the General Convention en-

---

[23] Humphrey, *The Union of the Congregational and Christian Churches*, p. iii.
[24] *The Herald of Gospel Liberty* June 23, 1927. p. 579. Humphrey, *The Union of the Congregational and Christian Churches*, p. 235.

tered. In a united session, the new constitution was adopted and the merger was completed. All joined in singing "Blest Be the Tie That Binds." The President of the General Convention, Rev. Frank G. Coffin of Ohio, and the Moderator of the Congregational National Council, Rev. Carl S. Patton of Los Angeles, became joint moderators. Rev. Warren H. Denison, secretary of the General Convention of the Christian Churches became a secretary of the General Council of the Congregational and Christian Churches.

Following this merger of the two national bodies, the Christian Foreign Missionary Society merged with the American Board of Commissioners for Foreign Missions; the Home Boards were merged; and states where there were both Christian and Congregational churches merged into state Congregational Christian conferences. Some local churches have since merged as Congregational Christian churches.

CHAPTER XXI

The Ministry in Congregationalism

THE Pilgrims came to America without their pastor, Rev. John Robinson, and were under the spiritual direction of Elder Brewster whose duties were similar to those of a lay preacher. They continued under his leadership during the early years at Plymouth. When the Puritans came to Salem and organized a church, their problem was how to select and install a minister. The Salem Puritans did not belong to Separatists in England, but when they reached America they decided to organize their own independent church.

I

EARLY ORDINATIONS

There were two men in the Salem group who had been Anglican clergymen. The story of how they organized their church and inducted into office the minister and the teacher appears in practically every history of early New England. The plan they originated became the pattern followed by many colonial churches.

On that day, July 20, all places of business being closed, Messrs. Higginson and Skelton gave their views as to the church and answered questions as to the ministerial calling; and their statements being satisfactory, a ballot was taken, "every fit member voting," and Mr. Skelton was chosen pastor and Mr. Higginson, teacher. This is the first instance on record of the use of the printed ballot in America. These two men accepted the call thus extended, and at once were formally set apart for their work. First Mr. Higginson, with three or four of the gravest members, laid hands on Mr. Skelton with prayer. Then, in like manner, hands were laid on Mr. Higginson.[1]

There were variations in their method. For example, when the church was established at Taunton, the minister, a Mr. Hooker, was ordained by the schoolmaster and one other member. Another interesting example of their method was an ordination held in Woburn in 1642. A number of ministers were present at this event, but "the people were tenacious of their right to ordain, supposing that yielding it might lead to dependency and so to presbytery." And so the chosen members of the Congregation ordained the new minister while the visiting ministers were witnesses to the ceremony.

In his *Biographical Dictionary* Elliot tells of the ordination of Israel

[1]Dunning, *Congregationalists in America*, p. 104.

Chauncy in Stratford where "by forgetfulness (I rather think in contempt of habits and ceremonies) the elder imposed his hand with a leather mitten upon it." There are many records in the first years where the ordination was by members of the church. In later years, when the practice of ordination by ministers came into effect, Increase Mather wrote, "Where elders cannot be had, ordination may be performed by those not elders."

The doctrine back of this form of ordination by members of the church lay at the foundation of their polity. The local church was independent and complete within itself and could neither give authority to those outside the church nor receive by authority anything from outside. They rejected the idea that some other body or some other church could ordain a man whose ordination would be valid as pastor of a church which had not itself ordained him. Later on, when the practice grew to invite ministers from surrounding churches to the ordination for a new minister, it was clearly stated that these visiting ministers were performing this service by direct and specific invitation and authority of the church electing the new minister. These visiting ministers represented the members of the church in performing the simple act of ordination. One incident illustrates their attitude: When Benjamin Colman was ordained by a free church in London before coming to America in 1699 to be pastor of the Brattle Street Church, there was much opposition led by Increase Mather who applied a meaningful epithet to the church by calling it "a Presbyterian brat."[2]

The early churches did not license men for the ministry. This practice came into use after ministerial associations were formed. A young man of promise in a congregation would be encouraged to exercise his gifts in public speaking. If he proved acceptable and his life was in harmony with the calling, a church without a pastor desiring him to become its pastor, would first invite him to become a member of that church. This was the first and necessary step toward becoming a minister of a church, for no one but a member would be elected its minister.

The young aspirant to the ministry would be received as a new member into the pastorless church and having become a member of that church the way was then cleared, should the church so desire, to elect him minister. This insistence on membership in the church as a prerequisite to calling a person to be minister should be noted as one of the doctrines in early Congregationalism, which has changed with the years. The candidate having thus been called or elected, usually by ballot, he became minister immediately thereupon.

The controversy that split the First Church in Boston after the death of Rev. John Cotton was caused by the calling of Rev. John Davenport

[2] Elliot, *Biographical Dictionary*, p. 125.

of New Haven to be its new pastor when he was not a member of the First Church, nor would the church in New Haven grant him a letter of transfer of membership since it did not approve his going to Boston.

The story of the way Davenport became a member of the First Church by a forged letter is told in the historic documents in the *History of the Old South Church, Boston.* This church was formed by those who withdrew when a forgery was revealed and the First Church in Boston refused to dismiss Mr. Davenport. The First Church was determined to have Mr. Davenport and the New Haven church was just as determined not to give him a valid letter of transfer of church membership, therefore the advocates of Mr. Davenport resorted to a scheme by which Davenport could become a member of the church in Boston, a necessary prerequisite to his being called a pastor. The forgery created a scandal, dividing the church and causing a division in the town which lasted many years.

In the early years, as soon as the minister was elected the officers conferred upon him the office of minister by the laying on of hands and the saying of a prayer. This, in their practice, was all the ordination that was necessary. It was not long, however, before neighboring ministers were invited as guests and witnesses to the election and ordination, which was also an installation. The practice grew of requesting the visiting ministers to perform the ceremony of ordination in the name of the local church. During these early years it was everywhere asserted that election as minister of a church was the official act in the making of a minister and that the ordination and installation service was but a public recognition of what had been completed in the election.

The Cambridge Platform says, "This ordination we account as nothing else but the solemn putting a man into his place and office in the church."[3] This was not a new doctrine originating in the colonies, for in 1574 there had been published the Declaration of Discipline which asserted that ordination was a "solemn investing or installing into office" and Hall, the Puritan writer, had written even before that "to ordain elders means simply to establish them." Hooker in his *Survey* says, "Ordination is the installing of an officer into an office to which he was previously called." Installation, therefore, was but another name for ordination and this was true in actual practice for many years.

There were several corollaries to this relationship of the minister to his church. When a man was no longer minister of a local church, either by his own resignation or by discharge, he lost his standing as a minister and became a layman. Should he later be elected minister of another church his ordination and installation would proceed all over again exactly as if he had never been a minister. Furthermore, a visiting minister had no

[3] *Cambridge Platform,* chap. 9, sec. 2.

right to exercise the office of minister in any other church. He was not authorized to conduct a service or administer baptism. Rev. John Cotton refused to baptize his own child, born at sea and given the name of Seaborn, for it was his contention that a minister was only a minister when he officiated in the congregation which had elected him. The minister was by right of office usually the moderator of any church meeting, but his vote counted no more than that of any other member. He was in charge of the pulpit and his duties were briefly to "rule over" the church in these three things: "To declare to them the mysteries of the kingdom of God; so that, whether they exhort, teach, or admonish, they do it with authority; to call the church assemblies together, and to dismiss them, and *moderate* matters in the assembly"; and "they are the mouth and hands of the church, by which they execute the power of the censures."

During the two hundred years preceding the Council of 1865 the usage had developed which included permanent ordination, preceded at times by a period "under license," and there had arisen the ordaining council which also acted as an installation council if the church so desired. Ministerial standing by membership in a ministers' association or an association of churches and ministers had come into general use, as will be explained below.

Dr. Leonard Bacon, in speaking on church polity before the Council of 1865, said:

A man may be a minister of the gospel who has received the right hand of fellowship of the ministers. He may be employed in the work of the ministry in foreign missions. Eliot, the apostle to the Indians, was pastor of a church over here in Roxbury as long as he lived. The churches at that time had no idea that a man could really be an ordained missionary, a missionary having the powers of a minister of the church, unless he was an officer in the church. We have outgrown that, and it is an inevitable necessity for us to outgrow it. We have none of the fear which they had, that a ministry would be a hierarchy. Our churches have grown to age, and can take care of themselves. There is no danger of a hierarchy.[4]

The usage of ordaining a minister for general service was inaugurated when the need arose to send missionaries to the Indians. Then the churches were confronted with a very perplexing problem, for certainly the group of Indians whom the missionary would serve were in no sense a church. They solved this difficulty at first by providing that Eliot who was to be the first missionary to the Indians, was also to be minister of the church at Roxbury.

Soon it became necessary to commission men who would minister to the small, poverty-stricken groups in new settlements who had not yet established a church and could not afford a settled minister. The services

[4] *Minutes of the National Council, 1865,* p. 454.

of a visiting minister who could legally administer the sacrament and baptism were necessary. Nathaniel Mather in his *Disquisition* suggested that "if they are too poor to furnish themselves with pastors, the sister churches should give them pecuniary help, not officious." This did not solve the problem.

Another situation developed demanding a change in their practice. In the absence of the regular minister, was the church to invite a neighboring minister to serve? Samuel Mather in *Ratio Disciplinae* maintained that the only legal thing to do in this situation was by vote to confer the right to administer the sacrament or baptism on a lay member. The churches were reluctant to do this. Force of circumstance and new situations slowly changed their early practices.

First, they began to license young men to preach. As the learned ministers from England gave up their churches because of age or death, young men of the Colonies had to be trained for the ministry. It seemed right and proper that these men should be given credentials that would enable them to accept the invitations of the churches as lay speakers. It had always been the rule that any lay member could speak in the pulpit on religion by invitation of the church, but these men needed more official credentials for churches of which they were not members. They were given at first a recommendation signed by a minister with whom they had been studying, which was accepted rather as a letter of introduction than as an official license. The ministers had begun to meet informally and to discuss matters relating to the work of the church. They would sometimes include these young men in their discussions. So the young candidate would ask more than one man to give him a recommendation.

The next step came naturally and logically when the ministers' meeting became organized as an association. This body began issuing licenses to those qualified to speak in the churches. As the association had issued the credentials, it naturally assumed oversight and hence grew the practice which has become common—that licensees should continue their studies and work under care of the association granting the license. A hundred years later when churches began to form associations, many ministerial associations united with the church associations and carried into that body the right and duty of licensing. Today this is the function of the association in most parts of the country, although there are ministers' associations in New England separate from the Associations of Ministers and Churches in which licensed standing is held. In some situations the old ministers' association is continued as the Committee on Licensure by the Association of Churches and Ministers.

The granting of standing to ministers who had left the pastorate came about in this way: teaching of the Cambridge Platform that the single act of removal from the ministry made the minister a layman did not long prevail. It was not formally rejected until the Council of 1865 which declared that the ministry included all who had been ordained and who had not been deposed.[5] While ordination had come to be recognized as permanent the minister was not given any right in a church over which he was not settled as minister. He ranked in the church simply as a lay member. His standing, however, was no longer with the church that ordained him but in an association into whose fellowship he had been formally received by vote. This association, not a local church, had the right to depose from the ministry should charges be made and sustained against a minister.

II

INSTALLATION

Installation, which in the early years was synonymous with election and ordination, came to be a separate act having reference to a particular pastorate and was in effect only as long as that pastorate continued. When the practice grew of calling men previously ordained to the pastorate of a church they often entered upon their duties without a formal service. This informal method of beginning a pastorate has become the practice of many churches of our fellowship, greatly to the loss of the dignity and influence of the minister and often to the peace and prosperity of the church. Where the minister serves only by election of the local church without any public recognition of this relationship by the churches of the fellowship, he is often under the necessity of constant reelections for a year or a period of time and there is bound to be a feeling of instability and opportunity for friction. On the other hand, some churches became burdened by the obligations implied in installation. Installation is a relationship of indeterminate length and is protected by the dismissal council. Where the minister is installed it is required, unless the call for the installation council expressly states that dismission may be without a council's advice, that a dismissal council shall convene which examines into the facts and reasons for termination of the pastoral relationship; and if it finds that full justice has not been done it can create an embarrassing situation for the church or the pastor. For this reason many churches avoid installation.

III

RECOGNITION

As a method of stabilizing the relationship between pastor and church, a secondary plan known as recognition is widely used. This method was inaugurated in Michigan in 1882 by the following vote:

[5] *Minutes of the National Council, 1865*, pp. 55, 56.

a. Whenever a minister accepts a call to the pastoral charge of any church, whether for a definite or indefinite term, a council of neighboring churches of our order should be called by such church and pastor, at their earliest convenience, for his *recognition* as pastor of said church—it being understood that the action of said council shall have no bearing whatever upon the legal or ecclesiastical tenure, as to the fact, name, salary, or time of the pastorate thus recognized.

b. The duties of this Council shall be:

(1) The examination of the pastor's qualifications for his position, especially in ministerial standing, in doctrinal views, and in religious experience.

(2) The approval or disapproval of these by formal vote.

(3) The recognition, if the vote is one of approval, in public services, as sermon, prayer, and right hand of fellowship.[6]

The early books on Congregationalism (those of Cotton, Hooker, the Mathers and Wise) devote extended space to the discussion of the minister. The same is true of books published in more recent times. The statement in the Bacon-Quint report to the Council of 1865 has a section which reads:

The office of elder, or bishop, in the church is two-fold: to labor in word and doctrine, and to rule. As laboring in word and doctrine, elders are pastors and teachers, for the perfecting of the saints, for the work of the ministry, for the edifying of the body of Christ; and in order to do this, they are rightly to divide the word of truth, and to administer those sacramental ordinances in which the grace of the gospel is visibly set forth and sealed. Like all whom God has put into the ministry of his gospel, they are to preach the word, and are to be instant in season and out of season, reproving, rebuking, exhorting, with all long-suffering and patience, holding forth the faithful word, that they may be able by sound doctrine both to exhort and to convince the gainsayer. As ruling in the church, they are to be not lords over God's heritage; but being the servants of all, for Jesus' sake, they are to watch for souls as they that must give account. They are to open and shut the doors of God's house by the admission of members approved by the church, by ordination of officers approved by the church, by excommunication of obstinate offenders denounced by the church, and by restoring penitents forgiven by the church. They are to call the church together when there is occasion, and seasonably to dismiss them again. They are to prepare matters for the hearing of the church, that in public they may be carried to an end with less trouble and more speedy dispatch. They are to preside in the meetings of the church, whether for public worship or for the transaction of church business. They are to be guides and leaders in all matters pertaining to church administration and church actions; but they have no power to perform any church act save with the concurrence and by the vote of the brotherhood. They are to care for the spiritual health and growth of individual members, and to prevent and heal such offenses in life or doctrine as might corrupt the church; and they are to visit and pray over their brethren in sickness when sent for, and at such other times as opportunity shall serve.[7]

This report shows the progress the church has made since the early

[6] *Minutes of the General Association for 1882*, p. 45.
[7] *Minutes of the National Council, 1865*, p. 109.

days in New England, but the churches reserved the right, if need be, of lay ordination and insisted that in Councils "when convened there is no distinction between the pastor and other delegates."[8]

This was the first time in two hundred years that there had been an opportunity to define Congregational polity in a council. The rule in the early churches that the minister's ordination was in effect only as long as he was serving as pastor of that particular church had been long outgrown. From the first it had been generally accepted that a man who had served as minister acquired thereby "an odor of sanctity" which could not be dissipated should he be without ministerial employment. Gradually ordination had come to be considered a permanent status.

When the Bacon-Quint Committee faced the question of whether ordination was temporary or permanent it stated that "necessity for a recognized class of ministers not holding office in any church is manifold," and listed the employments of ordained ministers outside the pastorates. First, there were the missionaries; second, those who supplied an occasional or temporary ministry; third, those who taught and trained men for the ministry; fourth, accredited men who because of their natural endowments, learning, and study were called to general service; fifth, retired ministers who ought not to be deprived of their standing because of age, having "discharged with commendation as a good and faithful servant of Christ the duties of the ministry."

IV

THE NATURE OF THE PASTORAL OFFICE

When the report came before the Council, various questions were raised and since many of these questions are still unanswered, it is worth listing them as they indicate that the Bacon-Quint report, extensive as it was, failed to answer all the questions relating to the ministry. "Sundry questions concerning *ministers* and the *pastoral office* such as these: Should a minister be a member of the church of which he is pastor? What should be the office of the pastor in inaugurating and administering discipline in the church? Is a pastor, *ex officio,* the moderator of all the meetings of the church? Are the *rights* and *powers* of a pastor correctly stated? Should the pastor have entire control of the service of *teaching* or *preaching* in his own pulpit? Should a *church* ordain and depose from the ministry, or only a *council?*"

In commenting upon these questions and defending his committee for not giving a definite teaching, Dr. Quint said:

It is questioned whether a minister should be a member of his own church. That question should not be settled. There are things that we want to remain

[8] *Minutes of the National Council, 1865,* p. 119.

in doubt. We don't want to be tied down in reference to all these petty details. While I think a minister better be and ought to be a member of his own church, I am not going to complain of any man who thinks it is not best, and say he has got to be, or not be a minister. There is one thing that might offend somebody, and that is to say that a Congregationalist minister ought to be and must be a member of a Congregationalist church, not of some other church. Such a declaration, I can well imagine, might stir up some people. (Laughter) [9]

Professor Edwards Park called attention to the way in which Congregational usage in this particular as well as in others was most flexible:

Should a minister belong to his own church? There are some councils which will not ordain a minister unless he will promise to belong to the church over which he is pastor; and there are some councils which will not ordain a minister if he *does* belong to the church over which he is pastor. Now, this is an apparent difference of opinion! (Laughter) It appears to the committee, Mr. Moderator, that where such great diversities of usage exist, they should be stated, and the reasons for one usage and the reasons for another usage be stated, and preference be given to one over another, provided there be any such preference found in the minds of the able men who may be appointed to present this document to the world. They think, sir, that there are many instances in which there are the greatest diversities among the churches, and that those instances may very properly be specified in the document that this Council may issue.[10]

Dr. Leonard Bacon requested the Council not to go too far afield, saying, "For a long time we have been trying to tinker up Congregationalism by borrowing, and the process is not ended yet; borrowing a usage or a principle from Presbyterianism; borrowing some little bit of ritual, perhaps, from Episcopalianism; borrowing in this direction and borrowing in that, instead of developing our system from its original ideas, in which it has its whole being, as the chicken is in the egg and the oak in the acorn."[11]

Dr. Bacon called attention to the fact that English Congregational churches ordained ministers by their own officials without any reference to a consultation with neighboring churches. He contended "the church under American usage that ordains him is responsible to all the churches to give an account whom it is that they elect to that office, what he is, what qualifications he has, because now ordination gives a man standing in the churches at large. Although the ordination is by the authority of a local church the churches at large should have the opportunity of advising with that church whether or not the man they wish to ordain has the gifts and graces and the character worthy of ordination."

Every phase of the minister's relationship to the church was canvassed

[9] *Minutes of the National Council, 1865*, p. 442.
[10] *Minutes of the National Council, 1865*, pp. 444–445.
[11] *Minutes of the National Council, 1865*, p. 446.

in the debate and it was shown that "there is recognized among us a professional ministry consisting of men devoted and consecrated by ordination to the work of preaching the gospel. The fact that churches had feared to allow an ordained man to have some standing outside his own church was grounded in that deeper fear that if ministers became a class and began to organize it would not be long until the church would fall into the grip of the Presbyterian order, but by 1865 the democratic principle of the local church and association was so well grounded that this fear no longer dominated the thoughts and minds of men." To reaffirm the historic doctrine the Council thought well to vote that the ministry conferred a standing, but "with no powers, no prerogatives, no jurisdictions, no authority over the churches."

To trace the development of the practice and note the variations in usage since 1865, reference is made to the minutes of the National Council, especially to those of the Councils of 1886, 1889, 1892, 1895, 1904, 1915, 1929 and 1940. To each of these Councils came recommendations from a stated committee, sometimes known as the Committee on Polity. The Commission on Recruiting for the Ministry, and later on, the Commission on the Ministry have had the same purpose and purport. The Council of 1886 adopted a report on the status of the ministry including this summary: "Resolved: (1) That standing in the Congregational ministry is acquired by the fulfillment of these three conditions, namely: (1) membership in a Congregational church; (2) ordination to the Christian ministry; and (3) reception as an ordained minister into the fellowship of the Congregational churches in accordance with the usage of the state or territorial organization of churches in which the applicant may reside; and such standing is to be continued in accordance with these usages, it being understood that a *pro re nata* council is the resort in all cases in question."

In 1904, the Committee on Polity was authorized to prepare a minimum required course of study for men seeking ordination and at the next Council such a plan was proposed. But outside of a few states having a state reading course recommended to those seeking ordination, there has been, as far as the records go, no church or ordaining body that has conditioned ordination of a candidate on his having completed such a course of study. There are, however, a few associations which require the completion of a college and a seminary course as a prerequisite, notably the New York City Association and the Chicago Association.

At the Council meeting of 1938 at Beloit, the Commission on the Ministry presented a careful study of the various aspects of the ministry and concluded the report with two pages of important recommendations relating to improvement of quality. Advice was given to seminaries as to more careful methods of selecting students and the strengthening of their courses. Written and oral examination was recommended for ordination. It was urged that men now in the ministry be given some opportunity for a period of absence from their church for a seminary "refreshment course." The committee appointed by the 1938 Council took the list of recommendations adopted by the Council seriously and elected to the Commission a strong group of ministers and laymen. The Commission divided the recommendations into three groups, each assigned to a sub-committee, and set itself for a thoroughgoing and exhaustive study.

V

Changes Proposed at the Berkeley Council

The report of that Commission to the Berkeley Council in 1940 is worthy of consideration by all churches. The Commission advised that licensure should be available only to those who were planning for ordination in the immediate future. This would make the status of licensee open to students or others who had completed their course of training and were looking for a church, but who would not be ordained until a call was received. The Commission in recommending this provision realized that the practice had grown for Christian workers, both men and women, in various types of religious and administrative work, some as home missionaries and teachers, to secure licenses which had continued by renewal year after year. The recommendations also advised that those who desired to exercise a limited ministry, as supply preacher, teacher, etc., but who were not prepared or did not desire regular ordination, should be admitted to the status of "local minister," by being ordained by a local association for service within the bounds of that association only.

This Commission is continuing its study, in particular on such matters as current practice of recognition and installation and sources of the ministry. Its motive is that the denomination through its accustomed agencies has no greater responsibility than that of providing the churches with a reasonable and workable polity that will maintain an effective ministry under proper denominational safeguards.

The place of the minister in the church and of the church in the community is well stated by Dr. Perry Miller in these words:

The Congregational idea was undoubtedly inspired in part by a similar spirit; the surge of religious conviction carried the sober theologians and solid magistrates of New England to the very brink of frenzy, but their strong sense of social responsibility, their profound communal instinct, counterbalanced the intoxication of piety. They were eager to fashion the natural order upon the spiritual, but they were uncertain that it must be an order, a regulated, a disciplined and a steady commonwealth. New England piety was intense, but in the seventeenth century it did not often become delirious, and the ecclesiastical system expressed both the religious inspiration and the corporate solidarity. Except for some rather desultory efforts at converting a few Indians—to be cited in justifying the colonies at home—the New England brand of Christianity was not a missionary creed; it did not drive men into the trackless wilderness, but called them to their places within settled associations. Its first aim was sorting out the elect from the mass, and its second providing a method whereby both could live in stable concord under the rule of the elect. The church was the center of a communal system, and the process of conversion was always to take place within a rigid frame of public observance. Grace like love was to grow and be consummated within legal forms. Although men ought to be saints before being received as members, said Cotton, "yet we believe this Saintship and Regeneration is wrought ordinarily not without the Church, but within the Church; that is to say, wrought in such, as in the assembly of the Church doe attend upon the meanes of grace dispensed by the Ministry of the Church." If the New England system be considered by purely sociological criteria, it becomes a fascinating scheme for securing rectitude in a community without sacrificing cohesion. Within the church the fraternity was made one by their mutual and irrevocable pledge; the members entered "all of them together (as one man) into an holy covenant with himselfe, To take the Lord (as the head of his church) for their God, and to give up themselves to him, to be his Church and people"; by the power of their oath they must cleave one to another "as fellow-members of the same body in brotherly love and holy watchfulnesse unto mutuall edification in Christ Jesus." The children of the fraternity, growing up under the seal of baptism, by which they were taken into covenant with God at their birth, were also incorporated into the visible institution; when their baptism became, as was believed it always would become, the "means" of their regeneration, they automatically became active participants in the federation. And finally, those outside the church, the environing ring of inhabitants, were not left at loose ends, but were mobilized into an audience, bound to the church as the center both of their expectation and their township, whence alone they could hope to receive the vital current of regeneration. The theory of church covenant fused the saints into one conventicle, while the theory of the means tied the unregenerate to it no less firmly. The keys to the kingdom of heaven were the ordinances; the sermon and the Lord's Supper for the visible elect, the sermon and baptism for their children, and the sermon alone for the non-members. "By the opening and applying of these, both the gates of the Church here, and of heaven hereafter, are opened or shut to the sons of men." Whoever received grace obtained it through the agency of ordinances; those not yet converted should therefore attend upon them and not slight ordained ministers and public forms.[12]

VI

CONCERNING CONGREGATIONAL PREACHING AND PREACHERS

The nobly written passage on the interlocking religious essentials of the integrated Puritan-Congregational system in America, with which the last section closes, closes itself with an illuminating paragraph. There

[12] Miller, *The New England Mind*, p. 442. (Used by permission of The Macmillan Company, publishers.)

might be for the elect other keys to the Kingdom of Heaven than the sermon. But for the church folk as a whole the sermon was their key by which "the gates of the church and [possibly] of heaven hereafter were opened or shut." This therefore has made preaching an aspect of Congregational life and history which deserves at least some specialized attention. Preaching has always been crucial in Evangelical Protestantism. The spoken word is the first resource of any new cause and often—until it is forbidden—the last defense of any dying cause. Orders thus established must, during their first periods, maintain and extend themselves by the spoken word. Protestant history documents these generalities. As religious orders become assured and institutionalized the preaching tends to become only one aspect of an inclusive churchlife.

When worship becomes definitely liturgical, the sermon is no longer focal, though it continues to be important. The history of Protestantism also documents these generalities. All American denominational historians, therefore, summarizing the homiletic constants and variants in their own denominations would take rather parallel lines. They would note the changing attitudes of congregations from period to period toward preaching generally. They would point with pride to their own outstanding preachers and challenge the claims of other communions to consistent sermonic superiority. All this goes without saying, and yet the centrality of preaching in the Puritan-Congregational tradition is not easy to match. It has deep and long historical rootings. Puritanism was, amongst so many other things, a quest for good and right preaching— and a good and right clergy. The Puritan's quarrel (an ignoble word for a righteous contention) with the Establishment was occasioned in part by the now almost unbelievable ignorance, sloth and loose living of the Anglican clergy in the Elizabethan period. The Anglican authorities themselves acknowledged the situation and sought to correct it. The Puritans saw to it that they had a sufficiency of convincing and depressing data.[13] "A supplication of the cittie of London to the Parliament" describes half the churches "unfurnished with preaching ministers" "pestered with candlesticks not of gold but of claie" and "unworthie to have the Lorde's lights set in them," "clouds that have not water," and much else of a Biblically condemnatory sort. The gravamen of most of the charges is that the then Anglican could not preach. John Robinson later doubted their apostolic succession on much the same ground. The Puri-

13 For a bill of particulars running to over one hundred particularized pages see the second volume of a collection of documents edited by Dr. Albert Peel, called the *Seconde Parte of a Register,* Cambridge (England) University Press, 1915. These documents may be said to implement the Puritan indictment of the Established Church about 1593, and allowing for their ex parte character, their cumulative testimony is crushing.

tan was therefore under bond, when his turn came to prove that he was sermonically a candle of the Lord, to offer his own preaching as exhibits of what preaching ought to be, which he did at voluminous length. The religious leaders of the New England colonies brought this concern for a competent preaching ministry to Boston and New Haven and bequeathed it to their successors who have held it in trust across the centuries.

This insistence upon the importance of preaching gained rather than lost by the fusion of the Puritan and the Independent. For Separatism had to begin with no resource at all save the spoken word. It was, in a sentence of misleading brevity, preacher-made. The relative simplicity of Congregational worship, but slowly changed, made the sermon focal and has so continued it. The self-contained nature of any Congregational Church made it—and still makes it—usually dependent upon the force of its minister and in general the minister stands—or falls—by his preaching.[14] The centrality of preaching in Congregationalism has therefore been persistent.

The unusual and not altogether healthful authority possessed—and exercised—by the clergy in the Puritan Commonwealth has already been sufficiently noted. During the first period of New England Colonial history the ministers directed not only religion but politics, conduct, and social life through their sermons. When their undue authority was restrained, though their influence continued and the respect accorded them was but little diminished, they became increasingly dependent upon preaching power to maintain their stations. A tradition was thus created, which held in the older communities until the last quarter of the 19th Century. For their parishioners, of a Sunday, the sermon was the thing. They also inherited and continued a highly disciplined preaching technique. The Puritan contribution, which combined with Plymouth Independency, to make the "New England Way," magnified and sought to adorn the sermon as both a means of salvation and a work of art.[15]

The English public of the Seventeenth Century had an inexhaustible passion for listening to sermons. They crowded the churches and hung on the preachers' words. No sermon could be too long and published sermons had a market which would now delight any religious editor. Consequently, the art of preaching was exhaustively studied and a surprising number of books, variously named, came from the presses

[14] The late Dr. Carl Patton once said that though a minister must do many things beside preaching, he is not likely to get a chance to do them unless he can preach.

[15] For an exhaustive examination of the contribution of Puritanism to New England thinking and preaching, see *The New England Mind*, Perry Miller. The importance of this study in tracing the background sources of Seventeenth Century New England Puritanism cannot easily be over-stated.

in England, Holland and Germany. They seem to have said everything
that could be said about "Homiletics" before or since with a scholastic
superabundance of analysis, and a pedantic technique. The Puritan
preacher was, therefore, soundly trained in his art. He favored what
Miller calls the "plain style" as opposed to the ornate and highly rhetorical style which the Anglicans favored, of which John Donne is the
classic example.[16] At the same time he inherited the humanistic tradition
—a sermon should be right in all its literary qualities, but rhetoric should
be its servant and not its master. Preaching was to save sinful men and
not glorify the preacher. Rhetoric had its uses, but logic and grammar
came first. A bitter pill (and a deal of Puritan preaching was a bitter
pill) might be sugar coated, but the pill must not become entirely sugar.
So the protagonists of the two styles of preaching fought it out.

The plain style naturally went to Massachusetts Bay with Winthrop's
fleet and was there continued. Preaching was Biblical, textual, soundly
evangelical, and meant above all to set out and maintain a body of doctrine. This must be scripturally derived and scripturally defended, though
once it was proved from the Bible, other considerations might be urged
in its support. A preacher, therefore, must be a man well rounded in
physics and medicine and whatever else there was to know. Within this
control New England Congregational preaching lived and moved and
had its being, and in a general way, Congregational preaching has so
continued.

VII

Some "Commemorative Notices"

There is no specific history of American Congregational preaching,
nor indeed any adequate history of American preaching, though there is
an almost impossible abundance of material waiting to be digested. The
best biographical sources up to 1850 are in Sprague's *Annals of the
American Pulpit: or Commemorative Notices of Distinguished American
Clergymen of Various Denominations, from the Early Settlement of the
Country to the Close of the Year Eighteen Hundred and Fifty-five.* The
first and second volumes are devoted to Trinitarian Congregationalism.
This monumental work lives up to its awe-inspiring title. The Commemorative Notices were written by friends, associates, and sometimes members of the family. This naturally makes them more laudatory than
critical. It seems unlikely that so great a body of clergy through such a
long period could have been admirable in every faculty and so unspotted
from the world.

In 1855 there were (Sprague) 1,365 Congregational churches in New

---

[16] This has already been noted in an earlier chapter, but some repetition may be
pardoned.

England, and 1,154 in the rest of the United States—2,519 in all, served by 1,643 settled ministers. (Four hundred and seventy-nine ministers were without charges.) The *Annals* commemorate about 350 Congregational clergymen (all deceased) beginning with John Robinson in Leyden and ending with John King Lord, who died of cholera in Cincinnati in 1849. There is a fascinating and unexpected vitality in these Annals. They may not be pure, crude fact but they are

> "Secreted from man's life when hearts beat hard
> and brains, high-blooded, ticked . . ."

and, one might add, for 250 years. For they are woven through with all the organic filaments of American life for two and one-half centuries. Some of these men crossed and recrossed stormy seas; others shared the perils of embattled frontiers; a few were prisoners of war. The Annals reveal vanished truths and social orders, but certain dominants emerge.

The Congregational ministry have been soundly educated. The first generation were English born and university bred. Emmanuel College Cambridge trained most of them. The first immigrant ministers were Episcopally ordained, clergymen of the Church of England, and though there are instances of their reordination, that was rather a local recognition of office than the bestowal of sacerdotal authority. Increase Mather (1657–1723)[17] seems the first Congregational minister born in America. He was called Increase "from the circumstances of the great increase of every sort with which the country was found about the time of his birth." The native sons in due course were trained at Harvard and Yale.[18] They were sound scholars by all the standards of their times. Their Latinity was always competent for theological controversy with their peers. Thomas Parker (1643–1677) was quite blind toward the end of his life, but was still able to teach Latin, Greek and Hebrew with ease. Certain ministers dissatisfied with his opinions came to reason with him. They addressed him in English; he replied in Latin. They took to Latin; "he retired to Greek." They pursued him in Greek; he consolidated his position in Hebrew. They counterattacked in Hebrew; he entrenched himself in Arabic and held the terrain. He endured his blindness composedly. "My eyes," he said, "will be restored shortly, at the resurrection."

Thomas Thatcher (1643–1678) composed a Hebrew Lexicon. He was much celebrated for his beautiful hand-writing (he could write in Syrian) and was the author of the first medical tract ever published in Massachusetts, "A Brief Guide to the Common People in the Smallpox

---

[17] The dates in the *Annals* cover the periods of active ministry and do not connote birth and death.

[18] We have not checked all the 350 names but opening the volumes at random, there is again and again "entered Harvard" "entered Yale"—and usually at an early age. Later the Theological Schools and other colleges are cited.

and Measles" (1677). The Boston clergy were advocating inoculation for small-pox when the medical faculty was opposing it though they, the clergy, might believe in witchcraft at the same time. Dr. Mather Byles (1733–1788) corresponded with Pope and Watts. He was noted for his wit. Thomas Prince, then pastor of the Old South Church, Boston, had engaged to preach for him. They were to meet in the Hollis Street Church pulpit and Prince failed to come, whereupon Byles said he had no sermon but would for a little comment upon the third verse of the 146th Psalm; "Put not your trust in princes." He lost his charge through his Tory sympathies and his house was under guard because he prayed for the king. For all that he refused to preach politics—which was, perhaps, under the circumstances just as well. His daughters remembered that they had walked arm-in-arm with General Howe and Lord Percy on Boston Common, and refused to be reconstructed.

The clergy generally served rural and semi-rural churches, but they maintained a dignified estate upon most modest salaries, too often irregularly paid, which they supplemented by farming and tutoring. Moses Parsons (1744–1783) with $333.33 a year, and a good farm attached, educated three sons at Harvard University unassisted, lived liberally and entertained generously. They married well, their social station was good, and their wives bore them many children. This and the care of the temporal affairs of their unworldly husbands wore the wives down and they often died too soon. In due time the bereaved ministers were likely to seek another helpmate and sometimes a third. They were not accustomed to soft-pedal their prejudices. Samuel Eaton (1764–1822) shared the feeling of the Federalists toward President Madison. In the long prayer on one occasion he addressed the Lord; "Thou hast commanded us to pray for our enemies. We would, therefore, pray for the President and the Vice-President of these United States."

They were as forthright with their own congregation. Matthias Burnett (1744–1816) was a piously discreet Tory which fact saved his Long Island Church from destruction. For all that, his congregation ungratefully requested his resignation. He ended his farewell address by asking the congregation to sing a paraphrase of the 120th Psalm containing this verse:

> "O! Might I fly to change my place,
> How would I choose to dwell
> In some wild lonesome wilderness,
> And leave these gates of Hell."

They were men of marked individuality and unexpectedly various experiences, of masterful dispositions and engaging eccentricities.[19] The

[19] Samuel Moody, known as "Father" Moody, deserves a monograph.

Annals, incidentally, reveal the changing fortunes of the New England country districts. Josiah Stearns (1758–1788) was for thirty years minister at Epping, New Hampshire. He owned a slave, knew his Bible by heart, and wrote his sermon notes in so fine a hand "as to be nearly illegible without a microscope." From these he preached with "ease and fluency." His church was packed of a Sabbath; a hundred years later the meeting house was in ruins, the church nearly extinct, and fifty persons were a full congregation. Samuel Eaton (Harpswell, Maine, 1764–1822) was remembered for the variety of his pastoral services, his emotional earnestness, the fervor and eloquence of his prayers, and that his wig was almost the last in the ministry.

VIII

CONCERNING OLD SERMONS

Most of these men published occasionally, many of them copiously. The sermon titles are long and most various. For example and without specific citation: "A Sermon on the Means to be Used for the Conversion of Carnal Relations"; "Contemplations on Mortality"; "A Discourse of Secret and Preventing Mercies"; "The Triumph of Mercy"; "Jesus Christ, the Physician of Sin-Sick Souls Opened and Applied." There are ordination and funeral sermons beyond citing, "election" sermons and discourses delivered on a great variety of special occasions. Many of the sermons had controversial backgrounds, theological or otherwise. Quite generally these old pulpits, high or low, seem to have been entrenchments from which the clergy engaged each other with verbal bombardments over the heads of their congregations. Other controversial themes appear. Samuel Hopkins, as early as 1776, thought it "the duty and interest of the American States to emancipate all their African slaves."

The basis of all preaching in American Congregational and Presbyterian churches until well into the Nineteenth Century was theological and its motif was the salvation of sinners. It was somberly but earnestly evangelical. The current theologies were organized and mobilized to save the lost, if they were predestined to be saved. One notes changes through the changing years, but the motif does not change. Nathaniel Emmons' first volume of sermons was "On Some of the First Principles and Doctrines of True Religion." His titles are illuminating: "On The Being and Perfection of God"; "The Plenary Inspiration of the Scriptures"; "Love, the Essence of Obedience"; "The Primitive Rectitude of Adam"; "On Original Sin"; "The Divine Conduct in the Reprobation of Incorrigible Sinners, Both Illustrated and Justified"; "On the Unpardonable Sin," and so on and on to five hundred and ten yellow pages. The Sermon on Reprobation was intended, so the preacher said, to lead sinners to discover "the plague of their own hearts," though its peroration is depressing; "while the decree of reprobation [spelling modernized] is eternally executing on the vessels of wrath, the smoke of their torments will be eternally ascending in the view of the vessels of mercy, who, instead of taking the part of those miserable objects, will say, Amen Alleluia, Praise Ye the Lord." Homiletically these sermons are admirably organized, leavened with scripture quotations uncritically used, clear and nervous in style with the Eighteenth Century faculty for a good use of language; and solid as jade. They bear re-reading unexpectedly. These preachers had vigorous and disciplined minds.

Timothy Dwight's sermons (1828) were in more spacious regions since they were for the larger part Baccalaureate sermons (he was president of Yale), and bore titles such as these: "Secret Things Belong to God"; "On Revelation"; "The Sovereignty of God"; "Life and Immortality Brought to Light in the Gospel"; "The Danger of Opposing Religion"; "Life a Race"; "On the Parental Character of God"; "On Independence of Mind"; "On Doing Good." These sermons are well argued, elevated, occasionally noble in range, and monumental. For example, sermon XVI, "God Loves His Children Unto the End," has passages which match Newman. The sermon "On The Duties Connected with a Professional Life" might still be read with profit by any young minister, lawyer, or doctor. On the other hand the Baccalaureate sermon in 1810 must have had a solemnizing but certainly not a cheering effect upon those who heard it:

"The time is hastening when you will come to the bed of death . . . against some or other of your names the melancholy asterisk may make its appearance in the next triennial catalogue."

Samuel Worcester's sermons (1823) continue the evangelical appeal with a brighter note and kinder thoughts about God, who by this time seems to have "More pleasure in the conversion and salvation of sinners than in their condemnation" and has begun to escape the bonds of a hyper-Calvinism.[20]

The Unitarian "departure" diminished the prestige of the Trinitarian orthodox pulpit in New England, and the American pulpit generally lacked distinction toward the middle of the Nineteenth Century. So much of the country was still new, and while the always fluid frontier called for courage, missionary spirit, evangelistic zeal, and adaptability, it did not mature the qualities usually associated with outstanding preaching. The Methodists had had Francis Asbury, to whom American Methodism owes an almost immeasurable debt, and were nurturing Matthew Simpson, one of the greatest American preachers of any period.

[20] A little volume of sermons to young women by Dr. James Fordyce (Boston, 1796) is an exhibit of ideal feminine virtues up to date.

Peter Cartwright had been the typical circuit rider of the frontier states.[21] Finney had exercised his almost hypnotic power in Northern Ohio and New York; Henry Ward Beecher, clothed with his tongue of fire, had come to Brooklyn from Indiana; Albert Barnes of Philadelphia had adorned the Presbyterian pulpit; but in general the American could not compare with the British pulpit.

IX

NEW TIMES; NEW VOICES

The National Congregational Council of 1865, which is chronologically and for other reasons the point of departure for the second section of this history, was suggested to the churches by a series of resolutions adopted by the Congregational churches of the Northwest in convention assembled in 1864. The first "whereas" declared structural society and ecclesiastical organization to be either dissolved or greatly changed throughout a large section of the United States. The convention seemed to contemplate a new opportunity for free speech, free thought, and free missions in "vast regions heretofore sealed against them" (evidently the then "South"), and thought it likely that "ideas and emigration from the Free States [would] follow the triumph of the Union cause southward." Those general and fraternal hopes were rather premature, but a new epoch for Congregationalism dates from the 1865 Council.

For one thing there appeared a new galaxy of names, not always of the first magnitude. The Congregational Church had changed since John Lord (his is the last name in Sprague's *Annals*) had died of Cholera in Cincinnati in 1849, only sixteen years before. There is no room here for the lists of delegates, but they belong historically to a transition period. The Council sermon was preached by Dr. Julian M. Sturtevant, president of Illinois College. The occasion demanded a consideration of the policy, principle, and the historic mission of Congregationalism, but even so a great gulf is fixed between it and such sermons as we have been considering. Those delegates were no longer "colonists of Heaven"; they were citizens of a Republic which had come through a baptism of fire. Liberty for them was no academic speculation about the freedom of the will. It was the heritage and mandate of America. They naturally charged the Congregational churches with a unique responsibility for its preservation more than sufficient for its actual existence. The preacher himself could not conceive how free men "would ever have invented any other church policy than independency." The debates discussed new subjects in a new spirit. All this was seen profoundly to influence Congregational preaching.

[21] Hoyt, *The Pulpit and American Life*, p. 204.

The next forty years were a kind of golden age for Congregational preaching, though one must be careful here. American preaching generally was then of a higher quality, an aspect of American culture which secular historians have not often noted. The processes of the melting pot had begun—at least the then alien racial element which was later to become so significant had begun—under manifold stimulation to pour in through all the northern ports of entry. But the country was still outstandingly homogenous racially, save for the Negro, and predominantly Protestant. The period of urbanization had begun. Old cities were multiplying their populations, new cities growing magically. Consequently the rural pulpits became less attractive, the city pulpit offered the competent minister a most desirable station. The outstanding city churches were able to command the best preachers. The men who finally won them were products of a pretty competitive process of natural homiletic selection. They became recognized, were acclaimed and possibly envied. The ministry began to begin to be a career.

There were, naturally, regional and denominational distributions of available clerical talent. The war between the states had tragically divided the churches into North and South, and for an indefinite period there would be little Christian commerce between them. Northern Presbyterianism shared the stronger churches of the middle states with the Episcopalians and Methodists (the Baptists would ask to be included), but New England was still Protestant and Congregational, and the churches of New England cities were eminently desirable stations and thus able to command distinguished preaching. Boston and its suburbs were a preachers' paradise. Brooklyn was a second Congregational stronghold, with the largest churches, numerically, in the denomination. There was usually one strong Congregational church in most of the mid-western cities whose pulpit was nationally known. Chicago Congregationalism was strong, and so on and on.

X

A RENAISSANCE OF PUBLISHED SERMONS

The very individualism of Congregational churches magnified the clerical office and fostered a holy local pride in the distinction of their respective ministers, whom they rewarded generously. They did not confine themselves to purely Congregational sources of supply in their quest for the best. The allure of a free pulpit in historic churches with good salaries appealed to unusually capable men in other denominations. Transfer was facile, and a "call" to Boston, Brooklyn, Springfield or what you please was recognized as the call of the Lord. Preaching was cultivated as a fine art and the sermon began to be an end in itself. The result was preaching of a marked literary quality, almost a sermonic essay. (Theodore Munger excelled in this.) It was not difficult for preachers with this gift to contribute acceptably to the *Century* or *Atlantic Monthly,* or to publish volumes from time to time.

Beecher's sermons were always in demand, and, in time, Phillips Brooks'. Lesser luminaries began to get their sermons published through the "eighties" and "nineties." Ministers generally did not over-publish and what they did publish had a quality both of thoughtfulness and literary distinction which would later be lost in the multitude of books issuing from the religious presses. An examination of titles not possible here would place Congregational ministers from 1880 to 1900 in the top group in these fields. In addition, the presidents of the older New England colleges and strong colleges and state universities outside New England were Congregational ministers. Their writings and public addresses went in part to the intellectual credit of the denomination. After a long tradition, Congregational ministers are called to be "pastors and teachers" and have generally sought to honor both offices. This has given Congregational preaching a marked teaching quality. Its liberal leaders rendered a great service in the reconciliation of the critical interpretations of the Bible and the more tested conclusions of biology and geology with an entirely adequate Christian faith. Congregational teachers and preachers widened and precised the social leanings of the teachings of the prophets and the gospels. The result was a noble vitality of message.

Congregational preaching has also moved along a wide cultural front with insight and imagination. It can hardly be called characteristically emotional,[22] though it has never entirely lost a somewhat restrained evangelical fervour. It has, with exceptions of course, been more notable for its consistent elevation than for oratorical and dramatic peaks, and it has, in part, always had to create the mind which responded to it. In the International Councils which brought British and American Congregationalists to the same platforms, toward the turn of the century, there was usually a timbre to the English addresses which the Americans lacked. Possibly this was because the English Free churches maintained themselves only by the exercise of militant conviction; possibly because many of the English preachers had been mentally suppled by political activities outside the pulpit; and possibly it was because of their rich cultural inheritance. Too much shelter has never been good for preaching. One may conclude a section of this history which might easily become a volume in itself by saying that throughout its entire history Congregationalism has exerted its really far-reaching influence predominantly through the writing and preaching of its ministers.

[22] Hoyt, *The Pulpit and American Life.*

XI

A writer who would undertake to catalogue and classify the Congregational preachers of the last seventy-five years as major and minor prophets would be seeming "to discriminate between the Lord's annointed." At any rate the evaluation of preaching is an affair of subtle and subjective difficulties. There is a "rule of the thumb" test. Any denomination assigns its most distinguished clergymen to stellar roles in its stellar meetings. Here are the National Council preachers from 1865 to 1940: Julian M. Sturtevant, Leonard Bacon, Richard S. Storrs, Zachary Eddy, Samuel E. Herrick, Frederick A. Noble, Professor George P. Fisher, Israel E. Dwinell, Charles M. Lamson, F. W. Gunsaulus, Albert J. Lyman, William J. Tucker, Alexander McKenzie, George A. Gordon, President W. D. Mackenzie, Charles E. Jefferson, Ozora S. Davis, Charles S. Mills, Raymond Calkins, Gaius Glenn Atkins, S. Parkes Cadman, Carl S. Patton, Albert W. Palmer, Henry K. Booth, Harry P. Dewey, Ashley Day Leavitt, Ferdinand Q. Blanchard, Oscar E. Maurer, McIlyar H. Lichliter.

Congregationalism has also honored its outstanding clergymen with the office of Moderator, alternating with distinguished laymen. Omitting duplicated names (as preachers) the Clergymen moderators have been.[23] William I. Budington, Henry M. Dexter, Arthur Little, A. H. Quint, Amory H. Bradford, Washington Gladden, Nehemiah Boynton, Charles R. Brown, William Horace Day, Henry C. King, William E. Barton, Rockwell H. Potter, Dan F. Bradley, Fred B. Smith, Jay T. Stocking. Other names may be added with general agreement: Henry Ward Beecher, Newell Dwight Hillis, Frederick K. Shannon. The delegates and speakers in the National Council of 1865 would be representative for that period. Discrimination is difficult, but Noah Porter, Edward Beecher, Samuel Harris, Josiah T. Harris, Henry M. Dexter, Edward N. Kirk, Edwards A. Park, Ray Palmer, James P. Thompson, James H. Fairchild, Samuel Wolcott, and Leonard Swan may be taken as representative. American Congregationalists speaking on the Lyman Beecher Foundation supplies another check, as well as the preachers at the annual meetings of the American Board. There were no sermons at the first three annual meetings of the American Board, but since then (1813) more than 125 sermons have been delivered at the Annual Meetings, and the Board has always been able to command the most distinguished preachers. (During the Plan of Union period Presbyterians would be heard.) Timothy Dwight of Yale preached the first sermon, and though the entire list cannot be reproduced here notably among his successors are: Lyman Beecher, Edward Griffin, Albert Barnes, Joel Hanes, Richard S. Storrs, Leonard Bacon,

[23]For complete list of moderators, see table "Meetings of Councils," pp. 406–407.

Mark Hopkins, George W. Betheine, Julius Seelye, A. J. F. Behrends, George Leon Walker, Arthur Little, A. J. Lyman, George A. Gordon, Edward C. Moore, Willard L. Sperry, Reuen Thomas, Joseph H. Twichell, Jay T. Stocking, Albert W. Palmer, Ashley Day Leavitt, Russell H. Stafford.

There is naturally in the various program-makings of National and International Councils, American Boards and other honorific bodies, an inevitable duplication of names and a considerable repetition of the same names. Denominational stars are never of perpetual apparition, but once established in the forensic firmament, no meeting seems complete without them, and they keep on and on. For the main part, the names of American Congregational lecturers on the Lyman Beecher Foundation have already been noted. Nathaniel Judson Burton belongs, not only for the unusual quality of his own preaching, but for a series of lectures unmatched in the long series for beauty of style and the scintillating play of his mind.

An appraisal of Congregational preaching for the last decade is not here indicated, and besides time is the only final appraiser of anything. An earlier chapter recognized the confusion into which theology has fallen. Confused theological thinking and differences in social and ethical positions are sure to affect preaching. The preaching of our age of dissolutions will move along a wide front, but it will lack authority, and the trumpets will too often give forth an uncertain sound. The American Protestant pulpit has reflected such conditions since the first world war. Great preachers, moreover, like their fellow artists in literature, music and the fine arts, do not come by command. The concern for worship, noted in another section, has eased the burdens which, by inheritance, the sermon carried. Preaching may not now have the strategic significance it once had and this, too, may be affecting the American Protestant pulpit generally. One can only say in conclusion that the contemporaneous Congregational pulpit holds its own with other denominations.

CHAPTER XXII

An Adventure in Liberty

NEITHER Protestantism itself nor the majority of its communions is felicitously designated. Some of the names have been self-assumed; some perpetuate the names of historic leaders. One of the greatest of the Protestant denominations has given high distinction to a title bestowed half in derision upon a group of praying students. A fellowship which has demonstrated the way of Jesus in quiet heroisms was named for its apparent fears, and not its courage. Many of the names over-emphasize a particular polity; few of them are neat and compact. They all tend, under consideration, to become "isms": Methodism, Lutheranism, Presbyterianism, Congregationalism—even the Latin Catholic Church has not been able to escape that. The Baptists have been more fortunate; they have never been called Baptismists.

For all that, the issues thus christened have been vaster and more significant than their denominations. They represent in their entirety the prolific possibilities of Christianity under the impulse, historically, of the Renaissance and Reformation; that is, under the relatively free impulse of the exploring religious mind in Western Europe, then more specifically in England and Scotland, then finally and most specifically in America. We have noted already in these pages the crucial distinction between the "continuing" and the "gathered" churches in the theory and practice of the Reformation, but even in the "gathered" churches the break with the past was more apparent than real. The historic creeds still controlled the faith of the Protestant mind. The very language of Christianity continued unchanged; the old literatures maintained their authority. The central currents of inherited theology flowed on, though in changed channels. The pristine devotions of the Christian spirit continued in habits of prayer and praise and ordered worship, however much the forms were changed.

All this was inevitable and entirely consistent, for the power of Christianity always has been in its central steadfastness and its marginal elasticities. Its wide range of accommodation, its many-gated openness to ever-varying minds, temperaments, and situations has secured and maintained its sovereignty. It has never submitted to long-held and rigidly-enforced patterns without impulses to escape, as though otherwise it would lose its soul, as it has again and again been in peril of doing.

384

These creative escapes have not been schisms, as the pattern-makers and keepers have called them, any more than the branches of a tree are schismatic. They have been the lift and spread of Christian faith and the Christian way, the achievement of its native amplitude. The entire Christian order has thereby been enriched.

I

PROTESTANTISM—AN ADVENTURE IN LIBERTY

Protestantism, though it did get its name from a protesting document, was never negative nor merely a protest.[1] Its affirmatives have always been central; its negatives marginal and corollaries of its affirmatives. For example, if a believer is justified by faith he does not need a priestly justification, a sacerdotal church, or any of its hoarded and accumulated furnishings. But beyond all this, Protestantism was and continues to be an adventure in Christian liberty, though it has not always so recognized itself. Its Magna Charta was Luther's "liberty of a Christian man." Luther's Magna Charta was St. Paul's letter to the Galatians and St. Paul's Magna Charta was his vision on the Damascus road.

Luther did not, however, accept the issues of his own emancipation proclamation and see them through to the end. Neither, on the whole, has Protestantism ever been consistently true to its own genius, nor has it ever completely trusted its right and reason to be: that the Spirit-guided life could safely be left to itself as competent to manage its own affairs. The reasons are plain enough. Right liberty has always been hard to get, hard to keep, and harder still to demonstrate in order and splendor of soul and state. Self-government is the costly issue of being taught wisdom by many mistakes, the priceless survival of success after many failures. It needs selected material and very great courage, a rare faith in human nature and, where it has hitherto held its own against inner corrosion and outer challenge, the undergirding of an heroic Christian faith and a high sense that God himself is for it.

If one stands far enough away from the massive and entangled action of the Reformation, he sees throughout its course a growing quest for realization of the independence of the Spirit-guided Christian life, both in theory and practice. Protestantism was bound by the very genius of it, when the right time came, to try the experiment of the liberty of a Christian man with all its implications and issues, completely and at all costs. No historian of the Congregational way dares to say that there, at last, in Leyden or New England Plymouth or Massachusetts Bay was

---

[1] After all there is nothing to be ashamed of in protest. It has been over and over a splendor, a heroism, and a prophecy. For the most part the orders against which the great historic protests have been made are on the defensive.

the predestined issue of the Protestant Reformation, or the heirs "of all the ages, in the foremost files of time." He can say that an opportunity was there afforded for an experiment in the liberty of a Christian man in a very complete way. Any final appraisal of Congregationalism, therefore, must be an examination of how it administered its trust, what it made of its opportunity and what was thereby contributed to the religious, social, and political order in America. Such an appraisal has become, as this final chapter is written,[2] both difficult and timely, though headlines of world news would seem to make it no more than a footnote in an era of transition whose issues are being fought out along battle lines which girdle the globe. All the inherited liberties are in desperate peril and the idealisms and philosophies which have hitherto supported the free self-government of the church, state, and society are mortally challenged by opposing idealisms and philosophies which are as strongly drawn as the forces which seek to make them dominant are massively armed.

Protestantism itself has long been examining its own idealisms and situations, as though, with a half-unconscious premonition, it was mobilizing its forces for its own part and place in an epochal recasting of all its historic inheritances. There is a widely-shared persuasion that the processes of sectarian division, with their minor but significant emphases, have more than served their purpose, and that a working unity of many-branched Protestantisms is vital to its very survival and must be accomplished. This is being supported by a theory of the church to which Congregationalism with all its implications seems alien. In the current and somewhat heated criticism of Protestantism by those who owe to it everything they are and have, including their liberty to criticize it, Congregationalism is called "the *ne plus ultra* of sectarianism"[3]—the final and complete negative of catholicity. The only answer to all this is the record.

II

CONGREGATIONALISM—A HISTORIC DEVELOPMENT OF THIS
ADVENTURE IN LIBERTY

One may not accurately maintain that in America the case rests with the American Congregational churches so denominated. It is true that historically they have made the Congregational way of exercising the liberty of the Christian more consistently central than any other of the denominations whose polity is Congregational.[4] The polity itself, as one

[2] April, 1942.
[3] Morrison, *What is Christianity?*, pp. 240–41 ff. Morrison is here writing of Congregationalism as an ideology and not as a specific denomination.
[4] "If one adds up all the communions of a Congregational polity, almost half American Protestantism is thus administered." This confessedly *ex parte* claim certainly

sees it in its entirety, has always been a means to an end: the right and duty of the church member to administer his own church business with a direct control; a minimum of ecclesiastical machinery; willing obedience to majority discussions; a disciplined respect for the right of the minority. Congregationalism believes this to be necessary to the liberty of a Christian man, and whatever else is built must be upon this foundation.

This liberty may be surrendered, but only for the sake of a larger and more inclusive liberty, since freedom is always coöperative and must always extend its corporate frontiers to maintain its central sanctities. But in every aspect of this always widening process, it must trust itself and its agents. Fundamentally this involves the rights and acknowledges the sovereignty of the laity of the church. A vast deal of the Reformation continued a diminished clerical administration of the reformed churches from the top, the somewhat frayed remnants of a millennium and a half of ecclesiasticism. They did not trust the Christian folk of Christian churches. Congregationalism began and continued with a new conception of authority, the authority of the Christian fellowship, in essence a spiritual democracy, and beneath this the conviction that the sources of this authority are the enduements and directions of the Holy Spirit, and that thus God comes into action through human mediation. This is to establish the church upon foundations which no tumult can overthrow and whose august sovereignties make hierarchies only incidents in a vaster process. The significance of this cannot be over-stressed. Protestantism, as a whole, shifted in varying degrees the seat of authority. Congregationalism made the church-meeting a throne room.

The covenant came next; the instrument of Congregational communion—*"koinonia."* Here also was, and is, a conception of "communion" immediate, cooperative, vital, tenacious, and elastic. It is a direct sharing of undertakings and responsibilities, friendships and the fruits of the Spirit. Nothing in religious history is more moving than the covenants by which members of the early Congregational churches bound themselves together in the face of manifold perils, for the conduct of enterprises whose simplicity masked their splendor. The result, at its best, has been an immediacy of Christian fellowship whose tender beauty cannot be put into words.

needs qualification. The Baptists may meet it quite conclusively with Roger Williams' slogan of "Soul Liberty," when there was apparently very little "soul liberty" around Massachusetts Bay. They may also claim priority in advocating the separation of Church and State while the Congregational way was tax-supported and enforced by the magistrates. The Friends may also prove that there was complete toleration in William Penn's colony when there was none in New England. American religious liberty is the joint creation of many forces and influences, some of them entirely unecclesiastical. For all that, using the above word "central," the claim—in view of the whole history of Congregationalism in England and America—may be allowed to stand, at least in this history.

Necessity and a sound sense both for order and fellowship—and some Presbyterian influence—led the New England Colonial churches within thirty years to associate themselves together for mutual advice, support, and edification. In a precise way it was an extension of the covenant conception, the communion of members of one church, to all the churches. This history has traced the genesis and development of this association principle. It has been modified and improved, but it has held true to its primary inspiration. The compulsions of Congregationalism have always been rooted in free consent. They represent shared visions and shared undertakings. The result has been a fellowship of churches which, though they have never called themselves a Church, have secured a community woven together of strong and countless filaments—no more sectarian than truth, goodness, and Christian discipleship are sectarian, and never making any monopolistic claims. Here is a conception and accomplishment whose values may gain new recognition from what imperils them.[5]

Such a system needs a disciplined constituency and a capable, trained leadership. This also the founders of Congregationalism saw clearly and sought to secure. The result was a concern for education in all its forms and grades, whose creative impact upon American life cannot easily be over-estimated. Just as Congregationalism has trusted the free operation of the spirit in religion, it has to an unusual degree trusted the free operation of truth upon the mind. Its dogmatisms have never been rigid; it has held its convictions open to correction and sought so to inform the societies of which it has been a part. It has had, therefore, a faculty for adjustment to changing minds and times which has brought it through many crisis periods with no dissolution of the bonds which hold its fellowship together and no surrender of the central Christian beliefs.[6]

III

LIBERTY BECOMES SERVICE

The minimum of concern for ecclesiastical machinery which long characterized Congregationalism, to its own institutional loss, left it free to find for its relatively great force missionary, benevolent, and human-betterment channels which have made it tributary to something much greater than its own denominational life. Its first home-missionary societies were never sectarian; its foreign missionary society was the "American" Board. Its concern for the freedom of the slave had no sectarian bias, and its long and distinguished contribution to the second, and far

---

[5] The institutional limits and weaknesses of the Congregational way have been frankly acknowledged in this study. They are in a way incident to all self-government established on communal basis.

[6] The Unitarian "departure" apparently contradicts this rather spacious statement.

more difficult, emancipation of the Negro has been a contribution for which it asked and received no denominational returns. Once more the very genius of its relatively simple ecclesiastical machinery has made this possible. Its halo has flickered often enough and those who care for it must recognize its limitations, but it has sought and served, far beyond its own immediate and particular interests, the realization of the Christian way in strategic human enterprises.

The particular relation of Congregationalism to the society of which it was long the predominantly religious aspect has also been sufficiently noted in these pages. Here one must acknowledge its limitations as a system. It has been and probably still is unusually dependent upon its cultural environment. But it has in turn made its own environment germane to its needs. There has thus been between religious and political democracy a process of creative interaction in which each has supported the other; the result is one of the bright strands of the history of the Republic.

It is very significant that while American Protestantism is increasingly critical of its own liberties in theory, churches of all denominations are growing more independent in practice. Actually all this is implicit in the growth of a free society. Church polities cannot be kept in water-tight compartments. The voice of the layman is bound to make itself heard. Those who administer their own affairs in every other life region will carry a measure of that administration through any church door. Laymen and women increasingly control their own local church affairs. Even under the most episcopal of bishops they generally get rectors of their own choosing.

One may be cynically practical and say that those who pay the piper set the tune, but it goes deeper than that. There is a force in the fundamental affirmation of Congregationalism which will not be denied expression. Creed subscription has been diluted in the most strongly indoctrinated denominations. What remains of hierarchical authority is only the ghost of former authoritarianisms sitting vestured upon the grave thereof. Thought is as free as it wants to be. Ecclesiastical machineries may have no place for a "church meeting," but not even the most absolute can indefinitely run counter to the matured opinions of their communicants.

IV

The Vitality of the Principles Involved

One must not say that these aspects of present-day American Protestantism are due entirely to an acknowledged or unacknowledged diffusion of Congregational influence. They simply demonstrate that the Congregational way possessed a power and principle which will always be asserted and realized in a free society. They are of the nature of such a society, whether in church or state. Unless the possible ecumenical Church of the future recognizes them and provides for their exercise, it will carry within itself a force to undo it as long as there shall be free men in a free society.

Some early "Independent Puritans" had, as we have seen, the conception of an English church whose unit members could exercise local autonomy under national control. That was then impossible, though the Independent Puritan definitely influenced the early development of New England Congregationalism, but it was prophetic. The United Church of Canada, leaving the state out, has achieved just that.[7] There Congregationalism has already fulfilled what may be seen, in a future yet unknown, to have been its destiny in the United States. It has lost its name, but saved its soul in perpetuating the near-to-life and vital breath of the liberty of Christian men.

A single close-printed page in the *Year Book of the Congregational Christian Churches for 1940* summarizes their principles of Christian Fellowship, the form of their government, their historical sources, their religious and spiritual confidences, their practices and achievements—a luminous page written by at least four centuries of heroic quest and realization, and not uncolored by the martyr's blood.

There are two key words in the recital: "fellowship" and "free." "Fellowship" makes it Christian. "Free" makes it great, for it catalogues as its bequests to the well-being of all "the free state, the free school, the free society life of our Country." Against the dark denials of such freedoms or their imperiled existence in every inherited civilization, they take on a stellar brightness. They are more precious than life, for without them life has lost its meaning and Christianity its mandate.

This history in its entirety is no more than the telling of how one communion among the great fellowship of Christian communions has conceived and served these freedoms and helped to make them, after its power and fashion, a priceless part of our inheritance. They carry with them their own validations. Their forms may be modified; but their spirit, timeless and treasured in the Mayflower compact and the Gettysburg dedication, is its own prophecy of victorious continuance.

[7] There the local church is autonomous for its own local affairs, including its creedal bases.

Appendixes

APPENDIX I

Creeds and Covenants

THE FIRST CONGREGATIONAL COVENANT

By Richard Fitz

Adopted by the First Congregational Church in the Bridewell. 1567.

The Order of the Priuye Church in London, which by the malice of Satan is falsely slandered, and euill spoken of.

The myndes of them, that by the strengthe and workinge of the almight, our Lorde Iesus Christ, haue set their hands and hartes, to the pure, unmingled and sincere worshipinge of God, according to his blessed and glorious worde in al things, onely abolishinge and abhorringe all tradicions and inuentions of man, whatsoever in the same Religion and Seruice of oure Lord God, knowinge this alwayes, that the Christe, eyther hathe or else euer more continually under the crosse striueth for to have. Fyrste and formoste, the Glorious worde and Euangel preached, not in bondage and subjection, but freely, and purely, onleye and all together accordinge to the institution and good worde of the Lorde Iesus, without any tradicion of man. And laste of all to haue, not the filthye Cannon Lawe, but dissiplyne onelye, and all together to the heavenlye and allmighty worde of our good Lorde, Isus Chryste.

(Signed) Richard Fytz (Fitz), minister.

SELECTIONS FROM ROBERT BROWNE

"A Booke WHICH SHEWETH THE *life and manners of all true Christians,* and howe unlike they are unto Turkes and Papistes and Heathen folke. By me, ROBERT BROWNE, Middleburgh, Imprinted by Richarde Painter. 1582."

1. Wherefore are we called the people of God and Christians? Because that by a willing Couenaunt made with our God, we are under the gouernement of God and Christe, and thereby do leade a godly and christian life. Christians are a companie or number of beleeuers, which by a willing couenaunt made with their God, are under the gouernement of God and Christ, and keepe his Lawes in one holie communion: Because they are redeemed by Christe unto holines & happines for euer, from whiche they were fallen by the sinne of Adam.

36. Howe must the churche be first planted and gathered under one kinde of gouernement?

First by a couenant and condicion, made on Gods behalfe.

Secondlie by a couenant and condicion made on our behalfe.

Thirdlie by using the sacrament of Baptisme to seale those condicions, and couenantes.

393

The couenant on God's behalf is his agreement or partaking of condicions with us that if we keepe his lawes, not forsaking his gouernment, hee will take us for his people, & blesse us accordingly.

37. What is the couenant, or condicion on Gods behalfe? His promise to be our God and sauiour, if we forsake not his gouernement by disobedience.

Also his promise to be the God of our seede, while we are his people. Also the gifte of his spirit to his children as an inwarde calling and furtheraunce of godlines.

His promise to his church, is his sure couenant, remembred, taught, and held by the church, and the seede thereof: whereby it onely hath assurance of saluation in Christ.

38. What is the couenant or condicion on our behalfe?

We must offer and geue up our selues to be of the church and people of God.

We must likewise offer and geue up our children and others, being under age, if they be of our households and we haue full power ouer them. We must make profession, that we are his people, by submitting our selues to his lawes and gouernement.

The couenaunt on our behalfe, is our agreement and partaking of conditions with God, That he shal be our God so long as wee keepe under his gouernement, and obey his lawes, and no longer.

39. How must Baptisme be used as a seale of this couenaunt?

They must be duelie presented, and offered to God and the church, which are to be Baptised.

They must be duelie received unto grace and fellowship.

Baptisme is a Sacrament or marke of the outwarde church, sealing unto us by the washshing of our bodies in water, and the word accordingly preached, our suffering with Christ to die unto sinne by repentance, and our rising with him to liue unto righteousness, and also sealing our calling, profession, and happines gotten by our faith in our victorie of the same Iesus Christ.

Baptising into the bodie and gouernement of Christ, is when the parties Baptised are receyued unto grace and fellowshippe, by partaking with the church in one Christian communion.

THE SEVEN ARTICLES OF THE LEYDEN CHURCH, 1617, LEYDEN

THE LEYDEN PILGRIMS applied to the London-Virginia Company, in 1617, for permission to settle somewhere on the wide stretch of American coast then known by the name of Virginia, and the agents of the church, Deacon John Carver and Robert Cushman, carried with them to London the seven articles of belief which are here presented, designing them to serve as an assurance to the company or the king should doubt be cast upon their orthodoxy or loyalty.

THE SEVEN ARTICLES

Seven Artikes which ye Church of Leyden sent to ye Counsell of England to bee considered of in respeckt of their judgments occationed about theer going to Virginia Anno 1618.

1. To ye confession of fayth published in ye name of ye Church of England & to every artikell thereof wee do wth ye reformed churches wheer wee live & also els where assent wholy.

2. As wee do acknolidg ye docktryne of fayth theer tawght so do wee ye fruites and effeckts of ye same docktryne to ye begetting of saving fayth in thousands in ye land (conformistes & reformistes) as ye ar called wth whom also as wth our bretheren wee do desyer to keepe sperituall communion in peace and will pracktis in our parts all lawfull thinges.

3. The King's Majesty wee acknolidg for Supreame Governer in his Dominion in all causes and over all parsons, and ye none maye decklyne or apeale from his authority or judgment in any cause whatsoever, but y in all thinges obedience is dewe unto him, ether active, if ye thing commanded be not agaynst God's woord, or passive yf itt bee, except pardon can bee obtayned.

4. Wee judg itt lawfull for his Majesty to apoynt bishops, civill overseers, or officers in awthoryty onder hime, in ye severall provinces, dioses, congregations or parrishes to oversee ye Churches and governe them civilly according to ye Lawes of ye Land, untto whom ye ar in all thinges to geve an account & by them to bee ordered according to Godlynes.

5. The authoryty of ye present bishops in ye Land wee do acknolidg so far forth as ye same is indeed derived from his Majesty untto them and as ye proseed in his name, whom wee will also theerein honor in all things and hime in them.

6. Wee beleeve yt no sinod, classes, convocation or assembly of Ecclesiasticall Officers hath any power or awthoryty att all but as ye same by ye Majestraet geven unto them.

7. Lastly, wee desyer to geve untto all Superiors dew honnor to preserve ye unity of ye speritt wth all y feare God, to have peace wth all men what in us lyeth & wheerein wee err to bee instructed by any.

Subscribed by
John Robinson,
and
William Bruster (Brewster)

THE MAYFLOWER COMPACT

On Board "Mayflower," Cape Cod, Nov. 11, 1620

Before leaving the *Mayflower*, forty-one persons signed the following compact:—

In ye name of God Amen. We whofe names are underwriten, the loyall fubjects of our dread foveraigne lord King James, by ye grace of God, of great Britaine, Franc, & Ireland king, defender of ye faith, &c.

Haveing undertaken, for ye glorie of God, and advancemente of ye chriftian faith and honour of our king & countrie, a voyage to plant ye firft colonie in ye Northerne parts of Virginia. Doe by thefe prefents folemnly & mutualy in ye prefence of God, and one of another; covenant, & combine our felves togeather into a civill body politick; for our better ordering, & prefervation & furtherance of ye ends aforefaid; and by vertue hearof to enacte, conftitute, and frame fhuch juft & equall lawes, ordinances, Acts, conftitutions, & offices, from time to time, as fhall be thought moft meete & convenient for ye generall good of ye Colonie:

unto which we promife all due submiffion and obedience. In witness whereof we have hereunder fubfcribed our names at Cap-Codd yᵉ .11. of November, in yᵉ year of yᵉ raigne of our foveraigne lord king James of England, France, & Ireland yᵉ eighteenth and of Scotland yᵉ fiftie fourth. Anᵒ Dom. 1620.

John Carver	Degory Prieft
William Bradford	Thomas Williams
Edward Winflow	Gilbert Winflow
William Brewfter	Edmund Margefon
Ifaac Allerton	Peter Brown
Myles Standifh	Richard Britteridge
John Alden	George Soule
John Turner	Edward Tilley
Francis Eaton	John Tilley
James Chilton	Francis Cooke
John Crackfton	Thomas Rogers
John Billington	Thomas Tinker
Mofes Fletcher	John Ridgdale
John Goodman	Edward Fuller
Samuel Fuller	Richard Clark
Chriftopher Martin	Richard Gardiner
William Mullins	John Allerton
William White	Thomas Englifh
Richard Warren	Edward Doty
John Howland	Edward Leifter
Stephen Hopkins	

THE CAMBRIDGE SYNOD

THE CAMBRIDGE PLATFORM

Cambridge, Mass., Sept., 1646—14 days. June 8, 1647; adjourned. Oct. 27, 1647; adjourned. Aug. 15, 1648 to Aug. 25, 1648.

Ministers in England sent a Letter of Inquiry to New England, requesting the judgment of their brethren concerning "nine positions." At about the same time the Puritan churches in England sent a communication to the churches in New England, in which thirty-two questions were asked, covering the whole field of church government. The General Court of Massachusetts was petitioned in May, 1646, to convene the churches in a synod.

The text of the call is as follows:—

"That there be a public assembly of the Elders and other messengers of the several churches, within this jurisdiction, who may come together, and meet at Cambridge, upon the first day of September, now next ensuing, then to discuss, dispute, and clear up by the Word of God, such questions of church government and discipline, in the things aforementioned or any other, as they shall think needful and meet, and to continue so doing till they or the major part of them shall have agreed and consented upon one form of government and discipline, for the main and substantial parts thereof, as that which they judge agreeable to the Holy Scriptures."

The work of this synod dealt with subjects as follows:—

Chapters 1–4.   Church government.
Chapter 5.   Brethren elect Elders: Elders have power.
Chapter 6.   The two orders: Elders and Deacons.
Chapter 7.   Duties of Elders and Deacons.
Chapter 8.   How officers are chosen.
Chapter 9.   Manner and meaning of ordination.
Chapter 10.   Relation and powers of Elders and brethren.
Chapter 11.   Financial support of church officers.
Chapters 12–14. Reception, dismission, and discipline of members.
Chapter 15.   Fellowship of the churches.
Chapter 16.   Nature of synods: how to call synods.
Chapter 17.   Relation of church officers to civil government.

This platform obtained with the churches as the standard until 1780.

HOOKER'S SUMMARY OF CONGREGATIONAL PRINCIPLES, 1645

(From Preface of *A Survey of the Summe of Church Discipline*)

THE PRINCIPLES OF 1645

"*If the Reader* shall demand how far this way of Church-proceeding receives approbation by any common concurrence amongst us: *I shall plainly and punctually expresse my self in a word of truth, in these following points, viz.*

Visible Saints are the only true and meet matter, whereof a visible Church should be gathered, and confoederation is the form.

The Church as *Totum essentiale,* is, and may be, before Officers.

There is no Presbyteriall Church (i e. A Church made up of the Elders of many Congregations appointed Classickwise, to rule all those Congregations) in the N. T.

A Church Congregationall is the first subject of the keys.

Each Congregation compleatly constituted of all Officers, hath sufficient power in her self, to exercise the power of the keyes, and all Church discipline, in all the censures thereof.

Ordination is not before election.

There ought to be no ordination of a Minister at large, *Namely, such as should make him Pastour without a People.*

The election of the people hath an instrumentall causall vertue under Christ, to give an outward call unto an Officer.

Ordination is only a solemn installing of an Officer into the Office, unto which he was formerly called.

Children of such, who are members of Congregations, ought only to be baptized.

The consent of the people gives a causall vertue to the compleating of the sentence of excommunication.

Whilst the Church remains a true Church of Christ, it doth not loose this power, nor can it lawfully be taken away.

Consociation of Churches should be used, as occasion doth require.

Such consociations and Synods have allowance to counsell and admonish other Churches, as the case may require.

And if they grow obstinate in errour or sinfull miscarriages, they should renounce the right hand of fellowship with them.

But they have no power to excommunicate.

Nor do their constitutions binde formalitèr and juridicè.

In all these I have leave to professe the joint judgement of all the Elders upon the river: Of New-haven, Guilford, Milford, Stratford, Fairfield: *and of most* of the Elders of the Churches in the Bay, *to whom I did send in particular, and did receive approbation from them, under their hands: Of the rest (to whom I could not send) I cannot so affirm; but this I can say, That* at a common meeting, *I was desired by them all, to publish what now I do.*

THE HALF-WAY COVENANT

THE HALF-WAY COVENANT AS ADOPTED AT SALEM (After 1665)

I do heartily take and avouch this one God who is made known to us in the Scripture, by the Name of God the Father, and God the Son even Jesus Christ, and God the Holy Ghost to be my God, according to the tenour of the Covenant of Grace; wherein he hath promised to be a God to the Faithfull and their seed after them in their Generations, and taketh them to be his People, and therefore unfeignedly repenting of all my sins, I do give up myself wholly unto this God to believe in love, serve & Obey him sincerely and faithfully according to his written word, against all the temptations of the Devil, the World, and my own flesh and this unto the death.

I do also consent to be a Member of this particular Church, promising to continue steadfastly in fellowship with it, in the publick Worship of God, to submit to the Order, Discipline and Government of Christ in it, and to the Ministerial teaching, guidance and oversight of the Elders of it, and to the brotherly watch of Fellow Members: and all this according to God's Word, and by the grace of our Lord Jesus Christ enabling me thereunto. Amen.

THE HALF-WAY COVENANT AS ADOPTED AT HARTFORD (1696)

We do solemnly in ye presence of God and this Congregation avouch God in Jesus Christ to be our God one God in three persons ye Father ye Son & ye Holy Ghost and yt we are by nature childrn of wrath & yt our hope of Mercy with God is only thro' ye righteousnesse of Jesus Christ apprehnded by faith & we do freely give up ourselves to ye Lord to walke in communion with him in ye ordinances appointed in his holy word & to yield obedience to all his commands & submit to his governmt & whereas to ye great dishonr of God, Scandall of Religion & hazard of ye damnation of Souls, ye Sins of drunkenness & fornication are Prevailing amongst us we do Solemnly engage before God this day thro his grace faithfully and conscientiously to strive against those Evills and ye temptations that May lead thereto.

PLAN OF UNION AS ADOPTED IN 1801

"Regulations adopted by the General Assembly of the Presbyterian Church in America, and by the General Association of the State of Connecticut (provided said Association agree to them), with a view to prevent alienation, and to promote union and harmony in those new settlements which are composed of inhabitants from these bodies.

1. It is strictly enjoined on all their missionaries to the new settlements, to endeavour, by all proper means, to promote mutual forbearance, and a spirit of accommodation between those inhabitants of the new settlements who hold the Presbyterian, and those who hold the Congregational form of church government.

2. If in the new settlements any church of the Congregational order shall settle a minister of the Presbyterian order, that church may, if they choose, still conduct their discipline according to Congregational principles, settling their difficulties among themselves, or by a council mutually agreed upon for that purpose. But if any difficulty shall exist between the minister and the church, or any member of it, it shall be referred to the Presbytery to which the minister shall belong, provided both parties agree to it; if not, to a council consisting of an equal number of Presbyterians and Congregationalists, agreed upon by both parties.

3. If a Presbyterian church shall settle a minister of Congregational principles, that church may still conduct their discipline according to Presbyterian principles, excepting that if a difficulty arise between him and his church, or any member of it, the cause shall be tried by the Association to which the said minister shall belong, provided both parties agree to it; otherwise by a council, one-half Congregationalists and the other Presbyterians, mutually agreed upon by the parties.

4. If any congregation consist partly of those who hold the Congregational form of discipline, and partly of those who hold the Presbyterian form, we recommend to both parties that this be no obstruction to their uniting in one church and settling a minister; and that in this case the church choose a standing committee from the communicants of said church, whose business it shall be to call to account every member of the church who shall conduct himself inconsistently with the laws of Christianity, and to give judgment on such conduct. That if the person condemned by their judgment be a Presbyterian, he shall have liberty to appeal to the Presbytery; if he be a Congregationalist, he shall have liberty to appeal to the body of the male communicants of the church. In the former case, the determination of the Presbytery shall be final, unless the church shall consent to a farther appeal to the Synod, or to the General Assembly; and in the latter case, if the party condemned shall wish for a trial by a mutual council, the cause shall be referred to such a council. And provided the said standing committee of any church shall depute one of themselves to attend the Presbytery, he may have the same right to sit and act in the Presbytery as a ruling elder of the Presbyterian Church.

On motion,

Resolved, That an attested copy of the above plan be made by the Stated Clerk, and put into the hands of the delegates from this Assembly to the General Association, to be by them laid before that body, for their consideration; and that if it should be approved by them, it go into immediate operation."

THE END OF THE PLAN OF UNION, ALBANY CONVENTION, 1852

"*Whereas,* the Plan of Union formed in 1801, by the General Assembly of the Presbyterian Church and the General Association of Connecticut, is understood to have been repudiated by the said Assembly before the schism in that body of 1838, though this year acknowledged as still in force by the General Assembly which met last at Washington, D. C.; and

"*Whereas,* many of our Presbyterian brethren, though adhering to this Plan in some of its provisions, do not, it is believed, maintain it in its integrity; especially in virtually requiring Congregational Ministers settled over Presbyterian Churches and Congregational Churches having Presbyterian Ministers, to be connected with Presbyteries; and

"*Whereas,* whatever mutual advantage has formerly resulted from this Plan to the two denominations, and whatever might yet result from it if acted upon impartially, its operation is now unfavorable to the spread and permanence of the Congregational polity, and even to the real harmony of these Christian communities:—

"*Resolved,* 1st. That in the judgment of this Convention it is not deemed expedient that new Congregational Churches, or Churches heretofore independent, become connected with Presbyteries.

"2nd. That in the evident disuse of the said Plan, according to its original design, we deem it important, and for the purposes of union sufficient, that Congregationalists and Presbyterians exercise toward each other that spirit of love which the Gospel requires, and which their common faith is fitted to cherish; that they accord to each other the right of pre-occupancy, where but one Church can be maintained; and that, in the formation of such a Church, its ecclesiastical character and relations be determined by a majority of its members.

"3rd. That in respect to those Congregational Churches which are now connected with Presbyteries,—either on the above-mentioned Plan, or on those of 1808 and 1913, between Congregational and Presbyterian bodies in the State of New York,—while we would not have them violently sever their existing relations, we counsel them to maintain vigilantly the Congregational privileges which have been guaranteed them by the Plans above mentioned, and to see to it that while they remain connected with Presbyteries, the true intent of those original arrangements be impartially carried out."

BURIAL HILL DECLARATION

Adopted 1865

Standing by the rock where the Pilgrims set foot upon these shores, upon the spot where they worshiped God, and among the graves of the early generations, we, elders and messengers of the Congregational churches of the United States in National Council assembled—like them acknowledging no rule of faith but the Word of God—do now declare our adherence to the faith and order of the apostolic and primitive churches held by our fathers, and substantially as embodied in the confessions and platforms which our synods of 1648 and 1680 set forth or reaffirmed. We declare that the experience of the nearly two and a half centuries which have elapsed since the memorable day when our sires founded here a Christian commonwealth, with all the development of new forms of error since their times, has only deepened our confidence in the faith and polity of those fathers. We bless God for the inheritance of these doctrines. We invoke the help of the Divine Redeemer that, through the presence of the promised Comforter, he will enable us to transmit them in purity to our children.

In the times that are before us as a nation, times at once of duty and of danger, we rest all our hope in the gospel of the Son of God. It was the grand peculiarity of our Puritan fathers that they held this gospel, not merely as the ground of their personal salvation, but as declaring the worth of man by the incarnation and sacrifice of the Son of God; and therefore applied its principles to elevate society, to regulate education, to civilize humanity, to purify law, to reform the church and the state, and to assert and defend liberty; in short, to mold and redeem, by its all-transforming energy, everything that belongs to man in his individual and social relations.

It was the faith of our fathers that gave us this free land in which we dwell. It is by this faith only that we can transmit to our children a free and happy, because a Christian, commonwealth.

We hold it to be a distinctive excellence of our Congregational system that it exalts that which is more above that which is less important, and, by the simplicity of its organization, facilitates, in communities where the population is limited, the union of all true believers in one Christian church; and that the division of such communities into several weak and jealous societies, holding the same common faith, is a sin against the unity of the body of Christ, and at once the shame and scandal of Christendom.

We rejoice that, through the influence of our free system of apostolic order, we can hold fellowship with all who acknowledge Christ, and act efficiently in the work of restoring unity to the divided church, and of bringing back harmony and peace among all "who love our Lord Jesus Christ in sincerity."

Thus recognizing the unity of the church of Christ in all the world, and knowing that we are but one branch of Christ's people, while adhering to our peculiar faith and order, we extend to all believers the hand of Christian fellowship upon the basis of those great fundamental truths in which all Christians should agree. With them we confess our faith in God, the Father, the Son and the Holy Ghost, the only living and true God; in Jesus Christ, the incarnate Word, who is exalted to be our Redeemer and King; and in the Holy Comforter, who is present in the church to regenerate and sanctify the soul.

With the whole church we confess the common sinfulness and ruin of our race, and acknowledge that it is only through the work accomplished by the life and expiatory death of Christ that believers in Him are justified before God, receive the remission of sins, and through the presence and grace of the Holy Comforter are delivered from the power of sin and perfected in holiness.

We believe also in the organized and visible church, in the ministry of the Word, in the sacraments of Baptism and the Lord's Supper, in the resurrection of the body and in the final judgment, the issues of which are eternal life and everlasting punishment.

We receive these truths on the testimony of God, given through prophets and apostles, and in the life, the miracles, the death, the resurrection, of His Son, our Divine Redeemer—a testimony preserved for the church in the Scriptures of the Old and New Testaments.

Affirming now our belief that those who thus hold "one faith, one Lord, one baptism," together constitute the one catholic church, the several households of which, though called by different names, are the one body of Christ, and that these members of His body are sacredly bound to keep "the unity of the spirit in the bond of peace," we declare that we will co-operate with all who hold these truths. With them we will carry the gospel into every part of this land, and with them we will go into all the world and "preach the gospel to every creature." May He to whom "all power is given in heaven and earth" fulfill the promise which is all our hope: "Lo, I am with you alway, even to the end of the world. Amen."

DECLARATION ON THE UNITY OF THE CHURCH
Adopted 1871

The members of the National Council, representing the Congregational churches of the United States, avail themselves of this opportunity to renew their previous declarations of faith in the unity of the church of God.

While affirming the liberty of our churches, as taught in the New Testament, and inherited by us from our fathers and from martyrs and confessors of foregoing ages, we adhere to this liberty all the more as affording the ground and hope of a more visible unity in time to come. We desire and purpose to co-operate with all the churches of our Lord Jesus Christ.

In the expression of the same catholic sentiments solemnly avowed by the Council of 1865, on the Burial Hill at Plymouth, we wish, at this new epoch of our history, to remove, so far as in us lies, all causes of suspicion and alienation, and to promote the growing unity of counsel and of effort among the followers of Christ. To us, as to our brethren, "there is one body and one spirit, even as we are called in one hope of our calling."

As little as did our fathers in their day, do we in ours make a pretension to be the only churches of Christ. We find ourselves consulting and acting together under the distinctive name of Congregationalists, because, in the present condition of our common Christianity, we have felt ourselves called to ascertain and do our own appropriate part of the work of Christ's church among men.

We especially desire, in prosecuting the common work of evangelizing our own land and the world, to observe the common and sacred law, that in the wide field of the world's evangelization we do our work in friendly co-operation with all those who love and serve our common Lord.

We believe in "the holy catholic church." It is our prayer and endeavor that the unity of the church may be more and more apparent, and that the prayer of our Lord for his disciples may be speedily and completely answered, and all be one; that by consequence of this Christian unity in love the world may believe in Christ as sent of the Father to save the world.

THE CREED OF 1883

I. We believe in one God, the Father Almighty, Maker of heaven and earth, and of all things visible and invisible;

And in Jesus Christ, His only Son, our Lord, who is of one substance with the Father; by whom all things were made;

And in the Holy Spirit, the Lord and Giver of life, who is sent from the Father and Son, and who together with the Father and Son is worshiped and glorified.

II. We believe that the providence of God, by which he executes his eternal purposes in the government of the world, is in and over all events; yet so that the freedom and responsibility of man are not impaired, and sin in the act of the creature alone.

III. We believe that man was made in the image of God, that he might know love, and obey God, and enjoy him forever; that our first parents by disobedience fell under the righteous condemnation of God; and that all men are so alienated from God that there is no salvation from the guilt and power of sin except through God's redeeming grace.

IV. We believe that God would have all men return to him; that to this end he has made himself known, not only through the works of nature, the course of his providence, and the consciences of men, but also through supernatural revelations made especially to a chosen people, and above all, when the fullness of time was come, through Jesus Christ his Son.

V. We believe that the Scriptures of the Old and New Testaments are the record of God's revelation of himself in the work of redemption; that they were written by men under the special guidance of the Holy Spirit; that they are able to make wise unto salvation; and that they constitute the authoritative standard by which religious teaching and human conduct are to be regulated and judged.

VI. We believe that the love of God to sinful men has found its highest expression in the redemptive work of his Son; who became man, uniting his divine nature with our human nature in one person; who was tempted like other men, yet without sin; who by his humiliation, his holy obedience, his sufferings, his death on the cross, and his resurrection, became a perfect Redeemer; whose sacrifice of himself for the sins of the world declares the righteousness of God, and is the sole and sufficient ground of forgiveness and of reconciliation with him.

VII. We believe that Jesus Christ, after he had risen from the dead, ascended into heaven, where, as the one mediator between God and man, he carries forward his work of saving men; that he sends the Holy Spirit to convict them of sin, and to lead them to repentance and faith, and that those who through renewing grace turn to righteousness, and trust in Jesus Christ as their Redeemer, receive for his sake the forgiveness of their sins, and are made the children of God.

VIII. We believe that those who are thus regenerated and justified, grow in sanctified character through fellowship with Christ, the indwelling of the Holy Spirit, and obedience to the truth; that a holy life is the fruit and evidence of saving faith; and that the believer's hope of continuance in such a life is in the preserving grace of God.

IX. We believe that Jesus Christ came to establish among men the kingdom of God, the reign of truth and love, righteousness and peace; that to Jesus Christ, the head of this kingdom, Christians are directly responsible in faith and conduct; and that to him all have immediate access without mediatorial or priestly intervention.

X. We believe that the Church of Christ, invisible and spiritual, comprises all true believers, whose duty it is to associate themselves in churches for the maintenance of worship, for the promotion of spiritual growth and fellowship, and for the conversion of men; that these churches, under the guidance of the Holy Scriptures and in fellowship with one another, may determine—each for itself—their organization, statements of belief, and forms of worship, may appoint and set apart their own ministers, and should coöperate in the work which Christ has committed to them for the furtherance of the Gospel throughout the world.

XI. We believe in the observance of the Lord's Day, as a day of holy rest and worship; in the ministry of the word; and in the two sacraments, which Christ has appointed for his church: Baptism, to be administered to believers and their children, as the sign of clearness from sin, of union to Christ, and of the impartation of the Holy Spirit; and the Lord's Supper, as a symbol of his atoning death, a seal of its efficacy, and a means whereby he confirms and strengthens the spiritual union and communion of believers with himself.

XII. We believe in the ultimate prevalence of the kingdom of Christ over all the earth; in the glorious appearing of the great God and our Savior Jesus Christ; in the resurrection of the dead; and in a final judgment the issues of which are everlasting punishment and everlasting life.

THE KANSAS CITY STATEMENT

Adopted 1913

The Congregational Churches of the United States, by delegates in National Council assembled, reserving all the rights and cherished memories belonging to this organization under its former constitution, and declaring the steadfast allegiance of the churches composing the Council to the faith which our fathers confessed, which from age to age has found its expression in the historic creeds of the Church universal and of this communion, and affirming our loyalty to the basic principles of our representative democracy, hereby set forth the things most surely believed among us concerning faith, polity, and fellowship:

FAITH

We believe in God the Father, infinite in wisdom, goodness and love; and in Jesus Christ, his Son, our Lord and Saviour, who for us and our salvation lived and died and rose again and liveth evermore; and in the Holy Spirit, who taketh of the things of Christ and revealeth them to us, renewing, comforting, and inspiring the souls of men. We are united in striving to know the will of God as taught in the Holy Scriptures, and to our purpose to walk in the ways of the Lord, made known or to be made known to us. We hold it to be the mission of the Church of Christ to proclaim the gospel to all mankind, exalting the worship of the one true God and laboring for the progress of knowledge, the promotion of justice, the reign of peace, and the realization of human brotherhood. Depending, as did our fathers, upon the continued guidance of the Holy Spirit to lead us into all truth, we work and pray for the transformation of the world into the kingdom of God; and we look with faith for the triumph of righteousness and the life everlasting.

POLITY

We believe in the freedom and responsibility of the individual soul, and the right of private judgment. We hold to the autonomy of the local church and its independence of all ecclesiastical control. We cherish the fellowship of the churches, united in district, state, and national bodies, for council and co-operation in matters of common concern.

THE WIDER FELLOWSHIP

While affirming the liberty of our churches, and the validity of our ministry, we hold to the unity and catholicity of the Church of Christ, and will unite with all its branches in hearty co-operation, and will earnestly seek, so far as in us lies, that the prayer of our Lord for his disciples may be answered, that they all may be one.

APPENDIX II

Meetings of Councils 1637–1942

YEAR	PLACE	MODERATOR	FIRST ASSISTANT	SECOND ASSISTANT	PREACHER
1637	Newtowne, Mass.	Rev. Peter Bulkeley			Rev. Ezekiel Rogers
		Rev. Thomas Hooker			
1646-8	Cambridge, Mass.	Rev. Thomas Hooker			
		Rev. John Cotton			
1852	Albany, N. Y.	Rev. T. W. Dwight	Rev. Noah Porter	Rev. Asa Turner	Rev. Julian M. Sturtevant
1865	Boston, Mass.	Hon. W. A. Buckingham	Hon. C. G. Hammond	Rev. J. P. Thompson	Rev. Leonard Bacon
1871	Oberlin, Ohio	Rev. W. I. Budington	Gen. O. O. Howard	Rev. George H. Atkinson	Rev. Richard S. Storrs
1874	New Haven, Conn.	Hon. L. S. Foster	Rev. G. F. Magoun	Rev. I. E. Dwinell	Rev. Zachary Eddy
1877	Detroit, Mich.	Hon. W. B. Washburn	Rev. A. L. Chapin	Hon. C. G. Hammond	Rev. Samuel E. Herrick
1880	St. Louis, Mo.	Rev. Henry M. Dexter	Rev. J.M.Sturtevant,Jr.	Rev. John D. Smith	Rev. Frederick A. Noble
1883	Concord, N. H.	Rev. Arthur Little	Frederick Billings	Rev. Cushing Eells	Prof. George P. Fisher
1886	Chicago, Ill.	Hon. Lorrin A. Cooke	Rev. John K. McLean	Rev. Benjamin A. Imes	Rev. Israel E. Dwinell
1889	Worcester, Mass.	Pres. Cyrus Northrop	Ira H. Evans	Rev. Franklin S. Fitch	Rev. Charles M. Lamson
1892	Minneapolis, Minn.	Rev. A. H. Quint	Hon. B. M. Cutcheon	Rev. George C. Rowe	Rev. F. W. Gunsaulus
1895	Syracuse, N. Y.	Hon. Nelson Dingley	Rev. Charles O. Brown	Rev. G. W. Henderson	Rev. Albert J. Lyman
1898	Portland, Ore.	Rev. Frederick A. Noble	Rev. George C. Adams	O. Vincent Coffin	Rev. William J. Tucker
1901	Portland, Me.	Rev. A. H. Bradford	William H. Strong	Rev. S. B. L. Penrose	Rev. Alexander McKenzie
1904	Des Moines, Ia.	Rev. Washington Gladden	Hon. J. H. Perry	Rev. H. H. Proctor	Rev. George A. Gordon
1907	Cleveland, Ohio	Hon. T. C. MacMillan	Pres. J. G. Merrill	Rev. F. L. Goodspeed	Pres. W. D. Mackenzie
1910	Boston, Mass.	Rev. Nehemiah Boynton	Rev. Arthur H. Smith	Pres. Charles S. Nash	Rev. C. E. Jefferson
1913	Kansas City, Mo.	Rev. Charles R. Brown	Hon. H. M. Beardsley	Rev. A. C. Garner	Rev. Ozora S. Davis
1915	New Haven, Conn.	Hon. H. M. Beardsley	Rev. William Horace Day	Rev. Alfred Lawless	
1917	Columbus, Ohio	Rev. William Horace Day	Rev. William E. Barton	Rev. H. M. Kingsley	Rev. Charles S. Mills
1919	Grand Rapids, Mich.	Pres. Henry C. King	Rev. R. A. Hume	Rev. W. N. DeBerry	Rev. Raymond Calkins

Year	Place				
1921	Los Angeles, Calif.	Rev. William E. Barton	Rev. R. H. Potter	Rev. E. G. Harris	Rev. Gaius Glenn Atkins
1923	Springfield, Mass.	Rev. Rockwell H. Potter	Rev. Hilton Pedley	Rev. C. W. Burton	Rev. S. Parkes Cadman
1925	Washington, D. C.	Frank J. Harwood	Mrs. E. A. Osbornson	Rev. William L. Cash	Rev. Carl S. Patton
1927	Omaha, Neb.	Rev. Ozora S. Davis	Rev. Rockwell H. Potter	Rev. William Horace Day	Rev. Albert W. Palmer
1929	Detroit, Mich.	Fred B. Smith	Rev. Rockwell H. Potter	Rev. William Horace Day	Rev. Henry K. Booth
1931	Seattle, Wash.	Rev. Carl S. Patton; Rev. Frank G. Coffin	Rev. Rockwell H. Potter	Rev. William Horace Day	Rev. Harry P. Dewey
1934	Oberlin, Ohio	Rev. Carl S. Patton; Rev. Frank G. Coffin	Rev. Rockwell H. Potter	Rev. William Horace Day	Rev. Ashley Day Leavitt
1936	South Hadley, Mass.	Rev. S. Parkes Cadman, Hon.; Rev. Jay T. Stocking	Hon. John V. Sees	Hon. John V. Sees	Rev. Ferdinand Q. Blanchard
1938	Beloit, Wis.	Pres. Mary E. Woolley, Hon.; Roger Babson	Hon. John V. Sees	Hon. John V. Sees	Rev. Oscar E. Maurer
1940	Berkeley, Calif.	Rev. Oscar E. Maurer	Hon. John V. Sees		Rev. McIlyar H. Lichliter
1942	Durham, N. H.	Hon. William E. Sweet	Hon. John V. Sees; Rev. Henry K. Booth; Pres. Mary E. Branch		Rev. Miles H. Krumbine

SECRETARIES: John Higginson (Scribe) 1637; Rev. R. S. Storrs (Scribe) 1852; Rev. Henry M. Dexter (Scribe) 1865; Rev. Alonzo H. Quint, 1871–83; Rev. Henry A. Hazen, 1883–1900; Rev. Asher Anderson, 1900–13; Rev. Hubert C. Herring, 1913–20; Rev. Edward D. Eaton, ad interim, 1920–1921; Rev. Charles E. Burton, 1921–1938; Rev. Frederick L. Fagley, Associate Secretary, 1922–; Rev. Warren H. Denison, Assistant Secretary, 1931–1938; Rev. Douglas Horton, Minister and Secretary, 1938–;

TREASURERS: Charles G. Hammond, 1871–74; Charles Demond, 1874–78; Rev. Henry M. Dexter, 1878–80; Rev. Lavelette Perrin, 1880–89; Rev. Samuel B. Forbes, 1889–1907; Rev. Joel S. Ives, 1907–15; Rev. John J. Walker, 1915–19; Frank F. Moore, 1919–23; Franklin H. Warner, 1923–27; Edwin G. Warner, 1927–30; William T. Boult, 1930–1938; Arthur Y. Meeker, 1938–40; L. Nelson Nichols, 1940–

Meetings of the International Council 1891–1930

Date	Place	President	Secretaries	Preacher
1891	London	Rev. R. W. Dale	Rev. Alexander Mackennal	Rev. E. P. Goodwin
1899	Boston	James B. Angell	Rev. Henry A. Hazen	Rev. Andrew M. Fairbairn
1908	Edinburgh	Sir Albert Spicer, Bart.	Rev. Henry A. Hazen Rev. William J. Woods	Rev. George A. Gordon
1920	Boston	Rev. James L. Barton	Rev. Richard J. Wells Rev. Asher Anderson	Rev. J. D. Jones
1930*	Bournemouth	Rev. J. D. Jones (Moderator)	Rev. Richard J. Wells Rev. Sidney M. Berry Rev. Charles E. Burton	Rev. Jay T. Stocking

*The official delegation to this Council was accompanied by over five hundred members of American churches who made a Goodwill Pilgrimage to the English churches. Dr. Fred B. Smith was Chairman of the Pilgrimage and Rev. Frederick L. Fagley was Manager. The members of the Pilgrimage visited Congregational shrines and churches, attended the sessions of the Council and were given a civic banquet at the Guildhall, London. This visit of Americans to England was a return visit of more than twelve hundred English Congregationalists who had visited America two years earlier. Of the English group, Rev. Sidney M. Berry was Chairman and Rev. A. G. Sleep was Manager.

Bibliography

Bibliography

BOOKS

Adams, Brooks, *The Emancipation of Massachusetts,* Houghton Mifflin Company, Boston, 1887.

Adams, Charles Francis, *Three Episodes of Massachusetts History, etc.,* Houghton Mifflin Company, Boston, 1892.

Adams, James Truslow (editor), *Dictionary of American History,* 5 vols., Charles Scribner's Sons, New York, 1940.

Allen, Alexander Viets Griswold, *Jonathan Edwards,* Houghton Mifflin Company, Boston, 1889.

The Ancient Platforms of the Congregational Churches of New England, with a Digest of Rules and Usages in Connecticut, etc., published by direction of the General Association of Connecticut, Edwin Hunt, Middletown, 1843.

Anderson, Asher (editor), *The National Council Digest,* The National Council of Congregational Churches in the United States, Boston, 1905.

Anderson, Joshua, *Memorial Volume of the First Fifty Years of the American Board of Commissioners for Foreign Missions,* A.B.C.F.M., Boston, 1861.

Arber, Edward (editor), *The Story of the Pilgrim Fathers, 1606–1623 A.D., etc.,* Houghton Mifflin Company, Boston, 1897.

Archer, Gleason L., *With Axe and Musket at Plymouth,* The American Historical Society, Inc., New York, 1936.

Bacon, Leonard, *The Genesis of the New England Churches,* Harper and Brothers, New York, 1874.

Thirteen Historical Discourses on the Completion of Two Hundred Years from the Beginning of the First Church in New Haven, Durrie and Peck, New Haven, 1839.

Baldwin, Alice Mary, *The New England Clergy and the American Revolution,* Duke University Press, Durham, N. C., 1928.

Barton, William E., *The Law of Congregational Usage,* Advance Publishing Company, Chicago, 1916.

Bates, Ernest Sutherland, *American Faith,* W. W. Norton and Company, New York, 1940.

Boardman, George Nye, *Congregationalism,* Advance Publishing Company, Chicago, [1889].

A History of New England Theology, A. D. F. Randolph Company, New York, 1899.

Boynton, George M., *The Congregational Way,* The Pilgrim Press, Boston, 1903.

Bradford, William, *History of Plymouth Plantation,* Little, Brown and Company, Boston, 1856.

Brown, John, *The Pilgrim Fathers of New England and their Puritan Successors,* Fleming H. Revell Company, New York, 1896.

Burgess, Walter H., *The Pastor of the Pilgrim Fathers, a Biography of John Robinson,* Harcourt, Brace and Howe, New York, 1920.

Burrage, Champlin, *The Early English Dissenters in the Light of Recent Research (1550–1641),* 2 vols., Cambridge University Press, Cambridge, England, 1912.

Burton, Charles Emerson (editor), *The National Council Digest, 1930,* The Pilgrim Press, Boston, 1930.

The Cambridge Platform: *A Platform of Church-Discipline, Gathered out of the Word of God; and Agreed upon by the Elders and Messengers of the Churches Assembled in the Synod at Cambridge in New England, 1649,* printed by Marmaduke Johnson, Cambridge, 1671.

Campbell, Douglas, *The Puritan in Holland, England and America,* Harper and Brothers, New York, 1892.

Clark, Calvin Montague, *History of the Congregational Churches in Maine,* 2 vols., The Congregational Christian Conference of Maine, Portland, 1935.

Clark, Joseph Bourne, *Leavening the Nation; the Story of American Home Missions,* The Baker and Taylor Company, New York, 1903.

Clark, Joseph Sylvester, *A Historical Sketch of the Congregational Churches in Massachusetts, from 1620 to 1838,* Congregational Board of Publication, Boston, 1858.

Comstock, John M., *The Congregational Churches of Vermont and Their Ministry,* The Caledonian Company, St. Johnsbury, 1915.

Cooke, George Willis, *Unitarianism in America,* American Unitarian Association, Boston, 1902.

Cotton, John, *The Keyes of the Kingdom of Heaven, and Power thereof, according to the Word of God,* Thomas Goodwin and Philip Nye, London, 1644; reprinted by Tappan and Dennet, Boston, 1843.
   The Way of the Churches in New-England, or the Way of Churches Walking in Brotherly Equalitie, etc., printed by Matthew Simmons, London, 1645.
   The Way of Congregational Churches Cleared: in Two Treatises, printed by Matthew Simmons for John Bellamie, London, 1648.

Cummings, Preston, *A Dictionary of Congregational Usages and Principles, according to Ancient and Modern Authors, etc.,* S. K. Whipple and Company, Boston, 1852.

Dale, Robert William, *History of English Congregationalism,* Hodder and Stoughton, London, 1907.

Davis, Ozora Stearns, *The Pilgrim Faith,* The Pilgrim Press, Boston, 1913.

Debates and Proceedings of the National Council of Congregational Churches, Held at Boston, Mass., June 14–24, 1865, American Congregational Association, Boston, 1866. (Minutes of the National Council, 1865.)

Dexter, Frank N. (editor), *A Hundred Years of Congregational History in Wisconsin,* Wisconsin Congregational Conference, Madison, 1933.

Dexter, Henry Martyn, *The Congregationalism of the Last Three Hundred Years, as Seen in Its Literature,* Harper and Brothers, New York, 1880.
   Congregationalism: What it is; Whence it is; How it Works, etc., Nichols and Noyes, Boston, 1865.
   A Hand-book of Congregationalism, Congregational Publishing Society, Boston, 1880.

Douglass, Truman Orville, *The Pilgrims of Iowa,* The Pilgrim Press, 1911.

Dunning, Albert Elijah, *Congregationalists in America,* J. A. Hill and Company, New York, 1894.

Earle, Alice Morse, *The Sabbath in Puritan New England,* Charles Scribner's Sons, New York, 1891.

Eisenach, George John, *A History of the German Congregational Churches in the United States,* The Pioneer Press, Yankton, S. D., 1938.

Elsbree, Oliver Wendell, *The Rise of the Missionary Spirit in America,* published by the author, Lewisburg, Pa., 1928.

Fagley, Frederick Louis, *The Congregational Churches,* The Pilgrim Press, Boston, 1925.

   (editor), *The Gospel, the Church and Society: Congregationalism Today,* The General Council of the Congregational and Christian Churches, New York, 1938.

Felt, Joseph Barlow, *The Ecclesiastical History of New England,* 2 vols., Congregational Library Association, Boston, 1855–62.

Fiske, John, *The Beginnings of New England,* Houghton Mifflin Company, Boston, 1889.

Fleming, A., *Church Polity: its Spiritual Grounds and Congregational Superstructure,* Congregational Sabbath School and Publishing Society, Boston, 1869.

Foster, Frank Hugh, *A Genetic History of the New England Theology,* The University of Chicago Press, Chicago, 1907.

Gladden, Washington, *Recollections,* Houghton Mifflin Company, Boston, 1909.
   Working People and Their Employers, Funk and Wagnalls, New York, 1885.

Goodwin, John Abbott, *The Pilgrim Republic,* Houghton Mifflin Company, Boston, 1920.

Gordon, George A., "The Theological Problem for To-day," chap. 4 in *The New Puritanism—Papers by Lyman Abbott, etc.,* Fords, Howard and Hulbert, New York, 1897.

Haller, William, *The Rise of Puritanism,* Columbia University Press, 1938.

Hart, Albert Bushnell (editor), *Commonwealth History of Massachusetts,* 5 vols., The States History Company, New York, 1927–30.

Hood, Edmund Lyman, *The National Council of Congregational Churches of the United States,* The Pilgrim Press, Boston, 1901.

Hooker, Thomas, *A Survey of the Summe of Church-Discipline,* etc., printed by A. M. for John Bellamy, London, 1648.

Hoyt, Arthur Stephen, *The Pulpit and American Life,* The Macmillan Company, New York, 1921.

Humphrey, Seldon B., *The Union of the Congregational and Christian Churches,* a dissertation presented to the Faculty of the Graduate School of Yale University, in candidacy for the degree of Doctor of Philosophy, 1933.

Huntington, George, *Outlines of Congregational History,* Congregational Sunday-School and Publishing Society, Boston, 1885.

Hutchinson, Thomas, *History of the Colony and Province of Massachusetts-Bay,* edited by Lawrence Shaw Mayo, 3 vols., Harvard University Press, Cambridge, 1936.

Inge, William Ralph, *The Platonic Tradition in English Religious Thought,* Longmans Green Company, New York, 1926.

Jones, David, *Memorial Volume of Welsh Congregationalists in Pennsylvania,* U. S. A., 1934.

Knappen, Marshall Mason, *Tudor Puritanism; a Chapter in the History of Idealism,* The University of Chicago Press, Chicago, 1939.

Lawrence, Robert F., *The New Hampshire Churches,* published by the author, Claremont, N. H., 1856.

Lewis, H. Elvet, *Homes and Haunts of the Pilgrim Fathers,* George W. Jacobs and Company, Philadelphia, 1920.

Lindsay, Thomas Martin, *History of the Reformation*, 2 vols., Charles Scribner's Sons, New York, 1906.

McGiffert, Arthur Cushman, *The Rise of Modern Religious Ideas*, The Macmillan Company, New York, 1915.

Mather, Cotton, *Magnalia Christi Americana: or, The Ecclesiastical History of New England, etc.*, London, 1702; also, 2 vols., Silas Andrus, Hartford, 1820. *Ratio Disciplinae Fratrum Nov-Anglorum; A Faithful Account of the Discipline Professed and Practiced in the Churches of New England*, S. Gerrish, Boston, 1726.

Mather, Richard, *Church-Government and Church-Covenant Discussed, in an Answer to the Elders of the severall Churches in New-England to two and thirty Questions*, printed by R. O. and G. D. for Benjamin Allen, London, 1643.

Mather, Samuel, *An Apology for the Liberties of the Churches in New England: to which is Prefix'd a Discourse concerning Congregational Churches*, printed by T. Fleet for Daniel Henchman, Boston, 1738.

Micklem, Nathaniel (editor), *Christian Worship; Studies in its History and Meaning by Members of Mansfield College*, Oxford Press, London, 1936.

Miller, Perry Gilbert Eddy, *The New England Mind; the Seventeenth Century*, The Macmillan Company, New York, 1939. *Orthodoxy in Massachusetts*, Harvard University Press, Cambridge, 1933.

Minutes of the General Association of Congregational Churches of Connecticut for 1882.

Minutes of the General Council of Congregational and Christian Churches, 1931–1940.

Minutes of the National Council of Congregational Churches, 1865–1929.

Mitchell, John, *A Guide to the Principles and Practice of the Congregational Churches of New England: with a Brief History of the Denomination*, J. H. Butler, Northampton, 1838.

Morison, Samuel Eliot, *Builders of the Bay Colony*, Houghton Mifflin Company, Boston, 1930.

Morrill, Milo True, *A History of the Christian Denomination in America*, The Christian Publishing Association, Dayton, Ohio, 1912.

Morrison, Charles Clayton, *What Is Christianity?*, Willett, Clark and Company, Chicago, 1940.

Morton, Nathaniel, *The New-England's Memorial: or, a Brief Relation of the Most Memorable and Remarkable Passages of the Providence of God, Manifested to the Planters of New-England, etc.*, printed by Allen Danforth, Plymouth, Mass., 1826.

Munger, Theodore Thornton, *The Freedom of Faith*, Houghton Mifflin Company, Boston, 1883.

Neal, Daniel, *The History of New England*, Vol. I, John Clark, London, 1720. *History of the Puritans*, Longman, Hurst, London, 1811.

Oviatt, Edwin, *The Beginnings of Yale (1701–1726)*, Yale University Press, New Haven, 1916.

Palfrey, John Gorham, *History of New England*, 5 vols., Little, Brown and Company, Boston, 1859–90.

Parker, Edwin Pond, *History of the Second Church of Christ in Hartford, 1670–1892*, Connecticut Historical Society, 1892.

Peel, Albert, *Essays Congregational and Catholic,* Independent Press, London, 1931.
The First Congregational Churches—New Light on Separatist Congregations in London 1567–81, Cambridge University Press, England, 1920.
Plain Dealing and its Vindication Defended, etc., 1716. (Copy in Congregational Library.)
Proceedings of the International Congregational Council, 1891, 1899, 1909, 1920, 1930.
Punchard, George, *History of Congregationalism,* 5 vols., revised edition, Congregational Publishing Society, Boston, 1865–81.
A View of Congregationalism, John P. Jewett, Salem, 1840.
Quincy, Josiah, *The History of Harvard University,* 2 vols., John Owen, Cambridge, 1840.
The Records of the General Association of the Colony of Connecticut, Begun June 20th, 1738, Ending June 19th, 1799, The Case, Lockwood and Brainerd Company, Hartford, 1888.
Richards, Thomas C., *Samuel J. Mills, Missionary, Pathfinder and Promoter,* The Pilgrim Press, Boston, 1906.
Robbins, Chandler, *History of the Second Church, or Old North, in Boston,* John Wilson and Son, Boston, 1852.
Ross, A[bel] Hastings, *A Pocket Manual of Congregationalism,* E. J. Alden, Chicago, 1883.
Roy, Joseph Edwin, *A Manual of the Principles, Doctrines and Usages of the Congregational Churches,* revised edition, Congregational Publishing Society, Boston, 1865.
Smyth, Newman, *Christian Ethics,* Charles Scribner's Sons, New York, 1896.
Sprague, William Buell, *Annals of the American Pulpit: or Commemorative Notices of Distinguished American Clergymen of Various Denominations, from the Early Settlement of the Country to the Close of the Year Eighteen Hundred and Fifty-five.* Vols. I and II, Robert Carter and Brothers, New York, 1857.
Stephen, Sir Leslie, *History of English Thought in the Eighteenth Century,* 2 vols., G. P. Putnam's Sons, New York, 1876.
Stoddard, Solomon, *A Guide to Christ; or, the Way of Directing Souls that are under the Work of Conversion; Compiled for the Help of Young Ministers, etc.,* printed by B. Green for D. Henchman, Boston, 1714.
Storrs, Richard Salter, *The Divine Origin of Christianity, Indicated by its Historical Effects,* The Pilgrim Press, Boston, 1884.
Strong, William E., *The Story of the American Board,* The Pilgrim Press, Boston, 1910.
Summerbell, Nicholas, *History of the Christian Church from its Establishment by Christ to A.D. 1871,* second edition, The Christian Pulpit, Cincinnati, 1871.
Sweet, William Warren, *The Congregationalists,* Vol. III of *Religion on the American Frontier, 1783–1850,* The University of Chicago Press, Chicago, 1939.
The Presbyterians, 1783–1840, Vol. II of *Religion on the American Frontier, 1783–1850,* Harper and Brothers, New York, 1936.
Taylor, Henry Osborn, *Thought and Expression in the Sixteenth Century,* 2 vols., The Macmillan Company, New York, 1920.

Trumbull, Benjamin, *A Complete History of Connecticut, Civil and Ecclesiastical, etc.,* Maltby, Goldsmith and Company, New Haven, 1818.

Uhden, H. F., *The New England Theocracy; a History of the Congregationalists in New England to the Revivals of 1740,* Gould and Lincoln, Boston, 1858.

Upham, Thomas Cogswell, *Ratio Disciplinae; or, The Constitution of the Congregational Churches,* Shirley and Hyde, Portland, Me., 1829.

Upham, Warren (editor), *Congregational Work of Minnesota 1832–1920,* Congregational Conference of Minnesota, Minneapolis, 1921.

Waddington, John, *Congregational History, 1200–1567,* John Snow and Company, London, 1869.

Walker, Williston, *The Creeds and Platforms of Congregationalism,* Charles Scribner's Sons, New York, 1893. Contains, among others: The Burial Hill Declaration, The Cambridge Platform, The Confession of 1860, The Half-Way Covenant, The Plan of Union, The Saybrook Platform.

A History of the Congregational Churches in America, Vol. III of *American Church History,* Charles Scribner's Sons, New York, 1916.

Ten New England Leaders, Silver, Burdett and Company, Boston, 1901.

Watson, E. O. (editor), *Year Book of the Churches, 1921–22,* The Federal Council of the Churches of Christ in America, New York, 1922.

Weigle, Luther Allan, *American Idealism,* Vol. X in *The Pageant of America,* Yale University Press, New Haven, 1928.

White, Daniel Appleton, *New England Congregationalism,* Essex Institute, Salem, 1861.

Williams, Charles, *The Descent of the Dove; a Short History of the Holy Spirit in the Church,* The Religious Book Club, London, 1939.

Winslow, Ola Elizabeth, *Jonathan Edwards, 1703–1758,* The Macmillan Company, New York, 1940.

Winthrop, John, *History of New England from 1630 to 1649,* 2 vols., edited by James Savage, first edition, printed by Phelps and Farnham, Boston, 1825.

(supposed author), *A Short History of the Rise, Reign and Ruin of the Antinomians, Familists and Libertines that Infected the Churches of New-England; etc.,* printed for Ralph Smith, London, 1644. (Preface signed T. Welde, to whom the work was formerly ascribed.)

Wise, John, *A Vindication of the Government of New England Churches; and The Churches' Quarrel Espoused, or A Reply to Certain Proposals,* fourth edition, Congregational Board of Publication, Boston, 1860.

PERIODICALS

Advance

The Arena

Boston Review (also called *Congregational Review*)

The Christian Annual

The Christian Union

The Congregational Quarterly

The Congregationalist

The Herald of Gospel Liberty

Index

Index

Abbott, Lyman, 244, 251
Act of Union with Methodist Protestants and United Brethren, 353–354
Adams, Brooks, quoted, 79
Adams, Charles Francis, quoted, 140
Adams, George C., 406
Adams, George E., 200
Adams, John Quincy, 303
Advance, 244–45
Advent Season, 275–76
Advisory Committee, 311–15
Ainsworth, Henry, 45; version of the Psalms, 280
Albany Convention, 196–98, 207, 300–01, 400
Allen, Alexander Viets Griswold, quoted, 111
Allen, Ernest Bourner, 273
Allen, Ethan, 136
Allen, George, 204
American Anti-Slavery Society, 249
American Bible Society, 304
American Board of Commissioners for Foreign Missions, 192, 245, 300, 307, 309, 310, 318, 337; becomes interdenominational, 162; incorporated, 160–61, 302; meets with Council of 1907, 312; organized, 158–62, 194–95, 301–02; Prudential Committee, 300, 339; and social welfare, 255; work with American Indians, 156–57, 308
American College and Education Society, 233, 234
American Congregational Association, 200, 304, 307
American Congregational Union, 200, 222–23
American Congregationalism, *see* Congregationalism
American Education Society, 192, 233
American and Foreign Christian Union, 308
American Home Missionary Society, 197; organized, 150–51
American Missionary Association, 198, 245, 249, 300, 303–04, 307; foreign missions of, 308; and social welfare, 255
American Seamen's Friend Society, 304
American Society for the Education of Pious Youths for the Gospel Ministry, 233, 302
American Unitarian Association, 132
Amherst College, 236
Amistad, 303–04
Anabaptist movement, 21–3
Ancient Church in Amsterdam, 45–6

Anderson, Asher, 222, 227, 407, 408
Anderson, Joshua, quoted, 160
Anderson, Rufus, 207
Andover Seminary, 159, 242, 254; Controversy, 179–80; Creed, 130; founded, 130, 173; students to Iowa as missionaries, 155–56; students ordained in Denmark, Iowa, 156
Andrews, Israel W., 211 *n.*
Angell, James B., 408
Anglican Church, 12 *ff.*, 340, 372; in America, 104; Bishops, 12; in New England, 96; objects to taxation for Congregational worship, 126; place of preacher, 69; Reformation, "Middle Way," 42; Thirty-nine Articles, 13; treatment of independency, 43
Annuity Fund, 228, 323–24
Anti-slavery movement, 198, 249
Apportionment Committee, 326
Apportionment Plan, 312–14, 318
Appraisal Committee, 335
Arber, Edward, quoted, 41, 49 *n.*, 52 *n.*, 60 *n.*
Asbury, Francis, 378
Association and Agreement of Pilgrims, *see* Mayflower Compact
Association, ministers', 102, 186–87, 292
Atkins, Gaius Glenn, 382, 407
Atkinson, George H., 213, 406
Atkinson, Henry A., 257–59
Atkinson, T., 223
Atlanta Theological Seminary, 243
Autonomy of local church, 319, 341; safeguarded, 201

Babson, Roger, 407
Bacon, David, 153
Bacon, Leonard, 153, 197, 200, 203, 204, 209, 211 *n.*, 212, 249, 283, 288–90, 293, 295–97, 368, 382, 406; on church polity, 363
Bacon-Quint Report, 366–67
Baldwin, Alice Mary, 115 *n.*
Baldwin Committee, 228
Baldwin, Simeon E., 227, 319
Ballantine, William G., 283
Bangor Theological Seminary, 242
Baptism, 93; of infants, 100
Baptists, churches in America, 104; churches in Mass., 96; object to taxation for Congregational worship, 126; persecuted in Va., 90 *n.*; position on baptism, 93; Puritan treatment of, 86–8

419

ERRATA

Sally Kirkland, in text, page 104 and index should be Sophia Hopkey.